chanting as the theatre itself. Whether he is describing Mary Martin's "astonishingly full low voice that seems to be singing to you alone," or the way Katharine Hepburn communicates both the "brightness of sophistication and the feel of its emptiness," Howard Taubman finds precisely the right phrase to capture his subject and invoke in the reader a rush of nostalgic remembrance. It is a volume to be treasured by every theatregoer as well as all readers interested in American society and culture as reflected upon our stage.

Howard Taubman

Howard Taubman has been with *The New York Times* for more than 30 years, as music editor, music critic and, since 1960, as drama critic. His numerous books include *Music on My Beat, Opera Front and Back,* and *The Maestro: The Life of Arturo Toscanini.*

THE MAKING OF THE
AMERICAN THEATRE

THE MAKING OF

THE AMERICAN
THEATRE

By HOWARD TAUBMAN

COWARD McCANN, INC. CMC NEW YORK

Second Impression

Library of Congress Catalog Card Number: 65-20410

MANUFACTURED IN THE UNITED STATES OF AMERICA

CONTENTS

[7]

CONTENTS [9]

ILLUSTRATIONS FOLLOW PAGES
98, 194 and 290

PREFACE

The history of the American theatre is properly everything that has happened in it for more than two centuries. To account for every production, playwright, composer, player, director, designer and producer would require scores, if not hundreds, of volumes. There are literally thousands in the shape of histories, biographies, autobiographies, memoirs, diaries, letters, criticism, texts and song-books, and what is available between covers can be supplemented by resort to the files of newspapers, periodicals and the archives of playbills and sheet music.

I have read or glanced through much of this material, though I cannot pretend to have perused it all. I have read hundreds of old plays not likely to see the lights of a stage again, and I have reread many that once provided me with enchantment and excitement in the theatre.

I have naturally not described everything I have seen or read. I have been a theatre buff almost as long as I can remember. I recall the thrill of sentiment that deliciously pulsed through me when I saw the long, thin shadow on the stairs in *Daddy Long Legs,* the first play that clings to memory. As a young man I stood through every note of more than four hours of *Parsifal,* not once but twice in the same week, and left each time exhilarated rather than exhausted. In the 1920's, thanks to the Leblang cut-rate ticket agency under Gray's Drug Store on Times Square, I could see two plays for the price of one, and many Saturdays I would sit through a matinee, then an evening performance, at a total cost of $1. It was not considered infra dig in my set to perch in the rear rows of the second balcony. To be anywhere in a theatre was a privilege. One's standards rose as one moved from the middle to the late teens and into the proud maturity of college years, but even a disappointing play was preferable to the movies and certainly to no play at all.

In compressing the history of the American theatre I have necessarily omitted vastly more than I have included. If you are annoyed by the absence of plays and players that glow fondly in your memory, I don't blame you. I have been a rank traitor to some of my dearest recollections by excluding them. But there was no alternative if this book was not to become as ponderous as an encyclopedia. I feel confident, however, that I have covered most of the high points and, I hope, a good many of the low in the making of the American theatre.

I am especially grateful to my wife who helped with research, spending hours at the New York Historical Society, the New York Public Library's Theatre Collection and the library of the Players Club, all of whom gave gracious cooperation. I am also grateful to Ellis Amburn, editor at Coward-McCann, who, a theatre buff like myself, ruthlessly plied a blue pencil and persuaded me to eliminate plays, players, performances and memories over which both of us would gladly have lingered. *Eheu, fugaces!*

THE MAKING OF THE
AMERICAN THEATRE

CHAPTER I

CHANGING AND UNCHANGING

ALTHOUGH OUR THEATRE began humbly and appeared sporadically long before we were a nation and long, long before we had anything like a national theatrical profile, our stage always has had something in common with every stage that ever was. Even if our first plays were London imitations presented largely by amateurs or professionals of English origin, our urge for theatre grew out of instincts and impulses that helped to shape the drama in epochs hundreds of years apart and in lands separated by seas and mountains.

The theatre appeals to man as an individual and as a social animal. It satisfies his need to think and feel privately and yet to be part of a group. He responds to theatre of all sorts because his eagerness for magic and fantasy is never sated, because he yearns to have his homely concerns, irritations and observations transformed into laughter, because he cannot go on without myths that illuminate and transfigure his fears and aspirations.

He is pulled in opposite directions; he wants to be led down the path of reality where he must look himself, his family, his neighbors and his world in the face, and he wants to be wafted into escape on the winds of enchantment. He wants from the theatre many things that are either lacking or not comprehended in his own life; he wants gaps filled and perceptions clarified and intensified. He goes to the theatre to laugh and weep at others, to comfort himself by feeling superior to other men, and, in deeper truth, to laugh at his own follies, weep at his own sorrows, and, if possible, to be exalted and inspired by the potentialities of his nature.

With an elasticity as remarkable as man's own gift for survival and adaptation, the theatre has been molded into a multiplicity of forms and styles to suit the requirements of particular races, climates, and civilizations. It has been as many things as man's institutions, emotions and thoughts wished it to be: untrammeled or formalized, spontaneous or rigid, shy or bold, plain or subtle, robust or refined, austerely spare or magnificently caparisoned. It has been reduced to the barest minimum of word and motion, and it has been an amalgam of gorgeous sight and resplendent sound.

Its possibilities are beyond conceiving. Despite recurrent attempts to limit it in every land and period, the theatre blithely or defiantly refuses to submit. Theorists earnestly propose theories as if they were immutable laws. Then a bold creator flouts the theories, and the deep thinkers retreat to their cells and formulate new principles, only to have them violated by artists big enough to make their own laws. So it goes and so hopefully it shall always be: codification follows practice, and the creative spirit remains triumphantly free to have the last word.

The theatre, like the other arts, cannot be pinned down and schematized for all time. It has a curious way of shifting in different civilizations, assuming different shapes and significances under different cultures, religions and social structures. It remains as diverse as the perception of the senses, as uninhibited as the imagination and as fertile in permutations as the vision and the ingenuity of man can make it. This is not the place for a history of the world's theatre. But it must never be forgotten that the theatre experience reflects the incomparable diversity of man's experience on earth, his terror of hell and his hope of salvation.

We in the West may find Chinese opera, which is not opera as we know it, Japan's Nō and Kabuki, classic Hindu theatre and the Javanese dance-theatre with its gamelan accompaniment difficult to assimilate, if not utterly meaningless. Yet these Asian celebrations have endured because for centuries they have been a satisfying communication between artist and public.

No doubt millions of Chinese, Japanese, Indians and Javanese would find our theatre forms puzzling, if not obvious and coarse. Indeed, some Westerners cannot abide some of their own forms. How often does one encounter a knowledgeable theatregoer who ridicules the classic ballet of the West as artificial and vapid? How often does one meet a votary of the spoken drama who scorns as oppressive and boring the greatest operas by Mozart and Verdi?

Rank arrogance? Of course. It is a common and frequent failing to blame one's own narrow range of response and sympathy on supposed flaws in the work or style being examined and, alas, not perceived.

No individual can expect that every form of theatre, ancient or contemporary, will divert, stimulate or uplift him. Indeed, it is madness to demand catholicity of interest in anyone. In our expanding democratic society, which earnestly propagates the philosophy that the good life must be placed within the reach of all, there is an understandable urgency to make the arts the joy of every man, woman and child's desiring. The aim is commendable but full of danger. People are constantly being intimidated into professing respect for what they do not grasp and into exclaiming in admiration over what they do not like.

Both are perilous: too much satisfaction with one's own tastes and standards, and too little. To avoid both pitfalls it is useful to reexamine one's values in the perspective of the past. Today's revolutionary form may look like a violent upheaval, but only when compared with today's conventions. Compared with yesterday's revolutions, today's are evolutions. Compared with forms and techniques practiced centuries and millennia ago, today's drastic departures, mirabile dictu, are returns to the past.

Improvisation has been in recently, and its supporters murmur Pirandello or mention the early stirrings of jazz in New Orleans as the spirit they seek to recapture. But improvisation was a vital way station more than three or four thousand years ago on the journey to the classic Greek drama, which began in the mists of history as an impulse to pay homage to Dionysus and which evolved from dance, song and the ecstatic strains of dithyramb into the golden age of Aeschylus, Sophocles, Euripides, Aristophanes and the lost Menander.

Did Caligula put a comedian publicly to death for uttering outrageously pertinent remarks in a farce, and did the comedian daringly and mischievously, if imprudently, insert the offending lines on the spot? In medieval and Renaissance Italy the commedia dell'arte with its spontaneous invention and its exuberant earthiness practiced techniques of improvisation that evolved from the rough and ready to the mannered and elegant. Were its practitioners aware that they owed something to the entertainments of imperial Rome as some of our entertainers are indebted to commedia dell'arte?

Consider the infinite variety of stylization in theatrical history. Haven't mannerisms, costumes or attributes of stage figures often served as a shorthand of characterization? In the Chinese theatre of long ago only the good guys wore mustaches. How naïve, we murmur, but in the melodramas that overflowed our stage in our age of innocence and in the stuff that perpetuates it on movie and television screens, you can usually tell a devious city slicker, a villainous farmhand or a vicious hombre out on the range by his moustache.

Is there something tricky or darkly magical in the very fact of actors—or mimes, as Max Beerbohm was fond of calling them—impersonating gods and demons and heroes? Solon, lawgiver in Athens, objected to impersonations because he regarded them as deceptions. Centuries later the Church also had strong doubts. Both were on the right track—for the wrong reasons. Impersonations in a theatre are simulations, no doubt of that. But deceptions? On the contrary. Brilliantly and probingly encompassed by great performers, they have a shattering reality that transcends what we imagine of reality. Impersonations on the stage, at their best, can be devastating revelations of truth.

If you recall how recent dictators have sought ruthlessly to root out any intimations on their stages that a freer world was possible, you will realize how disturbing the theatre's impersonations can be. Look at the history of our tortured century, look about you today, and you will find dictatorships policing stages to make sure that their "deceptions" are not too close to the bone. Listen to the self-appointed guardians of morals and manners in the free countries and you will hear outraged protests whenever the theatre indulges in impersonations that tear the masks off polite society and disclose the brutal or frightened savage who lurks under the skin of so many men, women and children. Solon was wise, and he knew that the stage could be the enemy of decorum and unquestioning submission.

Does our stage wallow in an excess of plain speaking? Read Aristophanes and the Roman comedies, savor the robust earthiness of Italy's Renaissance stage, note the unbuttoned bluntness of Shakespeare and listen to the ribald tone of Restoration comedy. A good deal of the time our occasionally gamy theatre is less outspoken than its precursors of old. We may, like impudent children, blurt out four-letter words not normally used in genteel society, but in themselves their capacity to shock is soon dulled by overuse.

In one way we seem to have advanced, for haven't we tamed the theatre to demand no more of us than the two and a half hours between 8:30 to 11 P.M.? We are much too preoccupied by our daily chores, our jobs, our travels, our civic obligations, to manage otherwise; our vaunted leisure has been filled with a bustle of small duties. We are not like the Athenians, are we?, who thought nothing of attending day-long dramatic festivities, sitting on the backless stone seats of the amphitheatre of Dionysus, under the brow of the Acropolis, with no cover to shield them from the Mediterranean sun. Nor are we like Londoners 150 years ago who sat uncomplainingly on unupholstered seats from 6 P.M. to 1 A.M. through a farce, a complete Shakespeare play *and* a light opera? Well, why should they complain? They were getting a generous run for their money, and the theatre was probably just as comfortable as their cold, damp homes.

Our theatres—and our homes—are more comfortable, but we are not all that different from the Athenians and Londoners. Does O'Neill compose *Strange Interlude* or *Mourning Becomes Electra* and expect us to devote part of the afternoon as well as the evening to the theatre? We rise to his challenge. Ah, but that's art. Well, what about the people who gladly sit through a baseball double-header on a hot Sunday from shortly after noon until nightfall? And what about those seekers after entertainment who devote endless hours of a winter weekend facing their television sets?

Turn to the theatre's technical side—its layout of playing space and its techniques of furniture, paint and light. Having new electronic marvels at fingertip control, we can conjure up undreamed-of wonders in a flash and we can dissolve them in a split instant into new miracles of fantasy. Surely no age has had so much technical resource to free the imagination, enabling it to command and dispose more swiftly than the breath of a djinn.

But even as our resources exceed the sorcerer's, we back away from the intricacies of machinery, the fussiness of authentic detail in dress and the opulence of grand furnishings, and seek to recapture uncluttered simplicity. We turn to the small arena stage to avoid the expense of modern staging. We embrace simplicity as a matter of principle—new theatres like the one in Lincoln Center, the unadorned square playing space of Washington's Arena Stage and the outthrust stage in the open arena of the Tyrone Guthrie Theatre in Minneapolis. These theatres are not merely a retreat to Shakespeare's Globe or the Elizabethan style; they are meant for new plays as well.

Past, present and future intermingle as attitudes and style shift. On our new stages, whether open or picture-frame, we play with platforms, elevators and lights as on an organ keyboard—and an electrically powered instrument at that. Our ingenious technicians will not be driven out of town as Jacques Torelli was hounded out of Venice in the seventeenth century because his stage effects were so fantastic that he was accused of being in league with the devil. But it may well be that some of our proud effects are no marked advance on Torelli's. We derive innocent pleasure from the magic of the revolving stages that have become familiar in the West in recent decades, but the device was employed in Japan, first in the doll theatres and then Kabuki, several hundred years ago. We still applaud when we watch a rapid and remarkable scene change as cloths drop from overhead grids and flats slide swiftly from the

sides. As we smile complacently at our own cleverness, it might be
well to remember that in seventeenth-century England an architect
named Inigo Jones devised a series of grooves on the stage for the
quick shifting flats, conceived the proscenium arch, introduced perspective in scene painting and thought of the front curtain.

What about footlights? The very word is synonymous with the
theatre. Yet where are they now? In the eighteenth century Garrick,
learning from Italy and France, brought them in to replace lighting
by overhead chandeliers, and for a century or more, until Edison
showed us how to imprison light in a vacuum tube, we could not
imagine a theatre without candle or gaslights at the foot of the
stage. But lighting is more sophisticated today. It throws its beams
from the ceiling, the sides and from sources that themselves seem
invisible. But would it surprise you if one of these days someone
attempted a fresh application of the old footlight techniques?

Adventurous impresarios of our day, in their enthusiasm to bring
live theatre to a public too long accustomed to one-dimensional
images on screens, have taken to the road with trucks and wagons.
They have a precedent going back to the Middle Ages when scenes
from the Mystery Plays were peripatetic, with players and meager
props carried on blunt-wheeled carts to the town squares and with
the carts turned into stages as the crowds of ordinary people, ever
mindful of pickpockets, formed a tight knot around the wagon and
watched a brief moment of theatre. If you should ever visit York,
city of the white medieval walls, during the triennial revival of its
famous Mystery Play, you would see a faithful renewal of the traveling carts carrying their players. Joseph Papp, determined bringer
of free theatre to a disfranchised public, has carried Shakespeare to
teeming sections of New York by truck and trailer, thus converting
history's strolling players into today's rolling players.

With our instantaneous communications, word of a new writing,
acting, directing or designing talent spreads across continents in
minutes and days. If the theatre of the absurd takes hold in Paris,
it will not be many months before it will spread to other countries,
save those closed societies where governments dominate the stage.
But the absence of telephones, cables and wireless devices did not
prevent the interchange of new ideas and the impact of new influ-

ences across borders. Several years ago I saw in Warsaw a revival of an old miracle play, written long ago by a Polish monk, and it made me think immediately of York's Mystery Play. The details of the Sacred Story had a similar elemental simplicity, and the rustic interludes were homely and comic like passages in the old English work. In both one felt the hand of the calculating showman who was bound to amuse the plain folks even as he instructed and moralized.

The showman's shrewd instinct is universal and unchanging. He never refrains from attempting to entice with a shapely leg or a delectable body. In eighteenth-century England pretty actresses were garbed as boys in tight breeches the better to disclose a tantalizing ankle, calf and thigh. And almost by accident, our musicals were born because someone combined a conventional melodrama with the girls in a ballet troupe that happened to be at liberty.

Are actors worshiped today as the embodiment of romantic, comic and noble dreams? In every age and land they have been treasured symbols. Richard Burbage for whom Shakespeare wrote imperishable roles was more venerated for the parts he played than for himself. In Italy, not long after, an actress named Isabella Andreine became so adored that the French King insisted on paying her personal homage and Tasso sang her praises in his sonnets.

Yet much as he is admired, the actor still occupies a precarious position. In eighteenth-century France Voltaire had to fight to remove the social stigma from the actor and his profession, even though the theatre had been the delight of Louis XIV. Ah, but we are different. What if in 1870 an actor could not get a Christian funeral service in New York's churches until the pastor of the Church of the Transfiguration, which became known affectionately as the Little Church Around the Corner, agreed that his remains could be accorded this respect? Today actors are welcomed in the White House like premiers and princes. Actresses are accepted as people, too, and not regarded sniggeringly as girls in an ambiguous, if not depraved, occupation. It is a long time since women were forbidden on the frank Elizabethan stage. But how many actors and actresses, for all their vaunted improvement in status, for all their celebrity as personalities, can count on a dependable income from year to year like other laborers worthy of their hire?

And what about the restrictive forces, always there to be opposed? Puritanism in England and the new colonies, clericalism in Spain, self-perpetuating juntas, proletarian dictatorships, tyrannies of the right, the apostolic Church, kings by divine right—at one time or another all fought the theatre as unclean, untrustworthy, disobedient or demoralizing.

In London long ago the stage retreated to the wrong side of the Thames close to the bear pits and the other entertainments of the unwashed and uncouth. In colonial America the theatre in some places was tolerated only outside city limits. Respectable women stayed away from old English and Spanish theatres or, if determined to enjoy the pleasures of the stage, came masked. The theatre has been the playground of the nobles and their mistresses and courtesans, the gathering place of bullyboys and roisterers and frequently turned into a cockpit of turmoil and rowdyism.

Industrialism and affluence have been great levelers, and anyone who can afford the theatre at all today is likely to come to it as neatly groomed as a millionaire. We are all respectable now, aren't we? We are polite, especially we Americans, applauding everything. It is inconceivable that we would hoot a distasteful actor off the stage. And if we don't approve of the price scale, we stay home, pull off our shoes and stare, as if drugged, at television. A contemporary public would not carry on like the habitués of London's Covent Garden Theatre in the early nineteenth century when John Philip Kemble raised his prices. They came to the playhouse and made a hash of the performance, roaring throughout, "Old prices! Old prices!" Although the riot act was read, the old prices had to be restored. But we are not always supine. Not too long ago audiences in our vaudeville houses howled for blood until a distraught manager applied the hook. At ball games or prizefights, you will hear the customer baying for the heads of the inept.

The pendulum never stops swinging. In one period a fashion in staging or acting becomes the rage; in the next it is replaced by its opposite; in the third we are back to the first fashion or some slight variant. The warm, flexible approach of a Garrick is succeeded by the reserve and stiffness of a Kemble, which is followed by the romantic panache of a Kean, which in turn is succeeded by the restraint and delicacy of a Booth, who probably has some artistic kinship to Garrick. Fantasy is followed by realism, and realism is banished by fantasy. Shakespeare is trimmed and tailored to suit an actor's notions, and a later generation, returning to the original, castigates the vandals it has replaced. But a new crop of producers sees fit to bring Shakespeare up to date, and in its modernizations manages to wreak fresh violence on him.

Nothing, not even milady's gowns and bonnets, changes more drastically than taste in the theatre. But even as we recognize the constancy of change, we must bear in mind that there is no single, all-embracing concept of taste that can, like an unimaginably comprehensive blanket, tuck in the planet. In any time and place a multitude of tastes contend with and complement one another.

Audiences are of all sorts, and each gathering is a heterogeneous commingling of unexplored combinations of personality and background. Here is a man who cannot abide slapstick, and there another who cares for little else. Here is a man whose cup floweth over when he beholds a shapely, scantily clad female, and there another who wants his undraped vision to be male. Here is one attuned to poetic fantasy, and there another who abominates soaring language. Here is a man who regards it as natural to hear a lover serenading his beloved in a conventional sixteen-bar chorus while rejecting as fatuous and incredible a lover's apostrophe in a rapturous Mozart melody. Here is one who wants his stage furnishings as tangible as his bacon and eggs, and there one who wants liberation from recognizable, earthly objects. Here is one who wants a slice of life, and there one who wants only symbols and parables. I have seen people sleep through conventional plays, and I have watched others stalk out of avant-garde dramas. I am fond of the reaction of a patient theatregoer who remarked after the first half of a fancy, symbolic opus, "It's confusing, but I like it," and after the second, "It's clearer, and I don't like it."

What endures in the theatre reflects the cultivated taste of generations of intelligent theatregoers. But what has its day—and even a precedent-shattering run for a popular success is only a day in the perspective of the theatre's history—has reasons for being. Successes are made not only by promotion but by the collective whim, temperature, tempo, spirit, call it what you will, of the moment. The value of such success *sub specie aeternitatis* is relative, but like them or not, they must also be understood and judged in the context of their time.

The events and forces that have gone into the making of America's theatre must be viewed from two different points of view: in the light of what they meant, said and did for their contemporaries, and in the perspective of centuries of world theatre history.

Obviously what was amusing, stirring and credible a century ago might be flat, boring and incredible to us, just as what diverts and excites us may well be ponderous and dull to another generation. We learn from the mistakes, excesses and successes of our ancestors as our descendants will from ours. If there is occasional growth in style, characterization, imagination, subtlety and quality, it is because tastes are constantly being cultivated and raised.

There are many ways of approaching the theatre—ranging from the furious rigor of those who will settle for nothing less than masterpieces to flabby indulgence that imposes no standards at all. It is wise, it seems to me, to think of the theatre as a mansion of many chambers, some homely and a few resplendent. We would cheat ourselves if we failed to recognize and admire the grandest chambers dedicated to the deepest meditation, the highest fancy and the noblest searching. Since we never cease from comparisons, we need an intelligent hierarchy of values. Shakespeare is Shakespeare, and boulevard comedy is boulevard comedy. It would be comforting if the twain never met, but you are likely to find them side by side in adjoining theatres or cheek by jowl in the programs of quite honorable repertory companies.

Choose one or the other, according to your taste and temperament. Enjoy both if you have different desires and moods at different times. Shakespeare is a sovereign enthroned in a regal chamber all his own, but the theatre's mansion has an abundance of modest chambers for creatures fond of undemanding stage pleasures. Each facet of theatre should be measured by standards that fit its category. A farce, a musical comedy or a circus is a far cry from a great, purging tragedy, but it has its place and public. The only standard that can and must be applied to all categories is the inescapable one of excellent, good, indifferent and poor, for each has it own gauge of value.

Genius and masterpieces are rare and unpredictable. If towering creative achievement were the only test, there would not be a great deal to say about the making of the American theatre. Compared with the greatest theatre works created in other places and at other times, our record is meager. But if we look back honestly at where we began and how we traveled, we can see that some time ago we learned to walk and even to soar, that we have managed some memorable voyages and that we have, indeed, come a long way.

It must never be forgotten that taste grows on what it feeds, and that it must grow on both sides of the stage. The public must constantly demand finer things of writers, performers, designers and producers, but it will be increasingly exacting only as the writers, performers, designers and producers provide finer things. It may be argued that the theatre cannot afford to elevate taste without public support, but a proud nation should declare boldly, "Damn the cost." The stage itself is the most effective means of educating and enlarging the public's theatrical taste. The theatre is the mirror of America, seeking to be gay and profitable and idealistic, chasing capriciously after new thrills and fashions and pausing occasionally to probe and hurt, purge and heal and laugh and sing. It is one of the few places left in a world of mass entertainment and blatant, intimidating promotion where small, silent or brave, thunderous voices can speak truths we desperately need to hear.

CHAPTER II

DECORUM AND MORALITY

FOR AN INSTITUTION whose business is the dissemination of pleasure, the theatre has had trouble, despair and disaster as its frequent companions. The triumphs and joys always are outnumbered by the fiascos and miseries, and as it is now in these United States, so it was in the beginning in the Colonies—only worse.

To have any theatre at the outset meant a struggle against religious and moral scruples. The Puritans and the Quakers in the northern colonies abhorred the stage on principle. They believed it was sinfully ostentatious. They charged that it dealt in symbols and was therefore an offense against the Biblical injunction not to worship false idols. They suspected that it was fun, in itself an affront to a pious, austere way of life.

In 1758, upon getting a brief season going in New York against official hostility, the company felt the need to placate the opposition, and one of the performers addressed the audience in propitiatory lines that began:

> Much has been said at this unlucky time
> To prove the treading of the stage a crime.
> Mistaken zeal, in terms oft not so civil,
> Consigns both play and players to the devil.
> Yet wise men own, a play well chose may teach

Such useful morals as the parsons preach;
May teach the heart another's grief to know,
And melt the soul in tears of generous woe.

When public officials frowned on stage spectacles, resourceful players invented subterfuges. In 1761 *Othello* was offered in New England as a "moral dialogue." Arthur Hobson Quinn in his *History of the American Drama* cites an example of cautious description of the roles:

> Mrs. Morris will represent a young and virtuous wife, who being wrongfully suspected, gets smothered (in an adjoining room) by her husband.

> Reader, attend: and ere thou goest hence
> Let fall a tear to hapless innocence.

In the early 1760's a theatre was built in Providence and, to avert opposition from the guardians of morality, it was actually called a "school house."

Another way of circumventing antagonism was the lecture. It was not until the second half of the nineteenth century that the idea of Chautauqua was founded on elevating lectures and became an immense circuit. But the notion that entertainment is best legitimatized if it is dubbed educational runs through American history. And it may be laid down as an axiom: the more instruction and the duller the performance the more suitable the entertainment because of the less peril of defilement.

The Lecture of the Heads, introduced to the New World in the 1770's as an import from England and persisting into the nineteenth century, was, if anything, a virtuoso performance by an actor as a one-man show. As summarized by George C. D. Odell in his multivolume *Annals of the New York Stage,* it was presented in three extensive parts. It dispensed homely and learned wisdom; it quoted the philosophers; with changes of costume and the help of visual aids in the form of props, the lecturer did character bits like Riding Hood, Young Wife and Old Maid, Old Bachelor, Englishman and Frenchman, Quaker Man and Woman, Virtuoso and Learn'd Critic. He told an anecdote of Landlord and Soldier. He descanted on the Origin of Ladies' Bonnets and Pompoons, offered a dissertation of Sneezing and Snuff Taking, commented on manners at the tea table and in the marketplace. Some of the material evidently was fixed, and some depended on the ingenuity of the actor-lecturer. One can almost imagine an eighteen-century Bob Hope, with his shrewd sense of timing and his gift for making the well-rehearsed line sound like an impromptu, doing the Lecture of the Heads.

Where moral obloquy did not stand in the way of the first theatres, parsimoniousness did. The Dutch were notably frugal and begrudged the expense of theatre tickets.

In the southern colonies, however, the Cavalier attitude prevailed. In 1665 three men in a court in Virginia's Accomac County defended themselves against the charge of acting a play, and were held free of crime. In Charles Town, a gay, walled city on the South Carolina coast, there were no restrictions against gaming, fox hunting and other pleasures, and in 1735 Otway's *The Orphan* was performed in the courtroom. Since the admission price was an astronomical 40 shillings, the event no doubt was an occasion designed for the "best people." Whether the players were experienced or amateurs is not recorded, but their modest little season apparently went well. *The Orphan* was repeated several times and was followed by *Flora, or Hob in the Well,* described as an opera and probably the first musical work presented in the New World, and by Dryden's *The Spanish Friar.*

The next year there was a flurry of theatre in Virginia's colonial capital. Students at William and Mary College played Addison's *Cato,* and the Virginia *Gazette* announced that "the company," consisting of "the gentlemen and ladies of this Country" would perform a trio of comedies, *The Busybody, The Recruiting Officer* and *The Beaux' Stratagem.* Probably like amateurs everywhere, they dug into their purses to meet the expenses of sets and costumes.

New York had a performance of Farquhar's *The Recruiting Officer* even earlier. In 1732 the comedy was performed in what was described as "the New Theatre in a building owned by the Hon. Rip Van Dam, Esq.," and a barber played a leading role. Odell believes that the theatre was on Broadway, just above Beaver Street. Although he could find no evidence, Odell was convinced that performances continued in the next few years.

It is certain, however, that professional actors persisted in offering dramatic productions in the Colonies. It was professionals who attempted to present such entertainments as animal acts and acrobats and puppet shows. As early as 1723 professional strolling comedians sought to ply their trade on Philadelphia's outskirts, not in the town where they were likely to be harassed.

These professionals were almost all from England. By the eighteenth century's end a native-born actor might turn professional and join a company. In a French city like New Orleans there were French drama and opera by French performers. Later there came to other American cities Germans, Frenchmen and performers from other lands. But the influence that dominated our stage for more than two centuries was that of the English commercial theatre. As against the Continental tradition of theatres founded and maintained by kings and princes and later by states and municipalities, the United States has followed the English way of the theatre of individual risk. The embattled professionals had little time or opportunity to argue for another method of supporting the stage. But they probably had their thoughts, and William Dunlap, an enthusiastic, gallant and engaging writer and manager, articulated them in the early nineteenth century.

Like a good democrat, he was contemptuous of "the bounty of the patron." In his *History of the Arts of Design*, he wrote of the Earl of Oxford's protection of a painter:

How did he protect him and from whom or what? The artist painted and engraved his picture. He gratified the earl's wishes, perhaps his vanity, and rescued his effigies from oblivion. Thus the artist conferred the favor, but the lord is called and acknowledged as the protector of the man whose knowledge and skill he sought for his own gratification and improvement. He (the artist) is represented as humble before his superiors. Who were they? The men who possessed castles and palaces and looked to him for an explanation of the treasures their libraries, cabinets and galleries contained.

In our country, Dunlap went on proudly, "the laws are our only protectors. Industry, virtue and talent the only patrons. The artist —the man who possesses the genius, skill and knowledge which entitles him to that name, will be honored and esteemed by his fellow-citizens; not seeking protection from them, or acknowledging superiority, except in superior worth."

Despite his patriotic fervor, Dunlap ended with little personal security to show for his years of dedication to the theatre. He came to recognize that the system of individual risk was chancy indeed. And he called for another way. In his *History of the American Theatre,* he stated his case:

If the fine arts . . . are effective instruments for promoting the best interests of man . . . it is the duty of every good citizen to encourage their cultivation in the country of his birth or residence, and to cherish the memories of those, whatever their motive, who introduce them.

That there are evils and perversions and abuses attendant upon theatrical exhibitions . . . no one is more ready to admit than the writer, and it shall be his aim to point them out as it is his wish to remedy them; but he firmly believes that the theatre is . . . a powerful engine well adapted to the improvement of man, and that it only wants the directing hand of an enlightened society to make it the pure source of civilization and virtue.

If we look back upon the history of nations, we shall find that their amusements mark the progress or degree of civilization they had attained at any one period. . . .

If the theatre is abandoned to the uneducated, the idle and the profligate, mercenary managers will please their visitors by such ribaldry or folly or worse, as is attractive to such patrons, and productive of profit to themselves. But the question arises—How are the evils flowing from theatrical representations to be banished and the good preserved? The answer is to make the theatre an object of governmental patronage.

The theatre, he cried out ringingly, must "be wrested from the hands of any person whose sole aim is profit." He came out, despite cautionary remarks about Germany and France, for government support after the usage in these countries. But aware that decorum and morality were powerful appeals to his countrymen, he gave these *desiderata* as vital goals. He pointed out that in America, as in England, certain sections of the theatre were set aside "to these unfortunate females who have been victims of seduction," his polite phrase for the professional prostitutes who displayed themselves in theatres. "No separate place should be set apart to present to the matron and the virgin the unabashed votaries of vice," he wrote, and argued that government support would insure the theatre's decency.

Dunlap's appeal for government support was in effect a cry from the heart. As a man of the theatre whose idealism was not impaired by hard, painful facts, he wanted something larger than decency; he wanted the theatre in America to be an art and an intellectual adventure.

From time to time these aspirations have been echoed by others in our theatre. Late in the nineteenth century James A. Herne, a playwright who earnestly sought to capture something of the truth of life, spoke up for a theatre purged of rank commercialism. He issued a call for an independent theatre, with the support of a distinguished group of American, including Thomas Bailey Aldrich, Hamlin Garland, Ralph E. Cram and others. In May of that year, as Herne's controversial *Margaret Fleming* fought to establish itself, a meeting was called in Boston "to consider plans for the establishment of a distinctively American theatre."

The call put it this way:

In general it is designed to forward the building of a theatre on a cooperative plan, and to open a Stage whereon the Drama shall be considered a Work of Art, and produced as such—independent of cheap popularity, and where Americanism and modernity shall be the prime requisites.

Nothing happened, but that such a demand could be articulated was a modest sign of progress.

The problems, in addition to moral and social prejudice, were many. Theatres at first were makeshift, and for a long time dangerous firetraps. One playhouse after another went up in smoke. Some were hastily rebuilt, only to be razed by another conflagration. The worst of the early disasters occurred in Richmond, Virginia, in 1811 the night after Christmas. The scenery caught fire and in a flash the house was a furnace. At least 70 persons were trampled to death or incinerated.

"The house was fuller than any other night of the season," according to Dunlap's history. "On the stage a shower of sparks from above. Some players began tearing down the scenery. Someone cried from the stage that there was no danger. Then someone yelled, 'The house is on fire.' In a moment all was appalling horror and distress. The general rush was to the lobbies and this was the cause of great loss of life because the general entrance to the pit and boxes was through a door that could admit only three persons abreast. To get to the boxes from the street there was a long passage and an angular staircase.

"Those who fell from the boxes into the pit fared better than those who jammed the exits. One man became unconscious in the crush as others climbed on top of the people ahead of them. But the unconscious man was moved on and out by the crush and awoke to consciousness in a bed."

Fire repeatedly took its toll of substance and human lives. It was not surprising if the fire companies felt that they had a claim on theatres. One company in Philadelphia played about 25 benefits for various volunteer units in one season. The Chestnut Street Theatre in Philadelphia went up in flames in 1820 so completely that only a mirror, a ship model and prompter's clock were saved, and the worst of this disaster was that the fire insurance had not been renewed. In the holocaust that swept the Iroquois Theatre in Chicago in 1903 well over 500 lives were sacrificed. And not too many years ago a raging blaze made an inferno of a circus under canvas in Hartford, causing hundreds of casualties. One of the rare exceptions was the theatre created out of William Plumsted's warehouse in Philadelphia in the middle of the eighteenth century. A brick building, it was that rarity—an early American theatre that stood for more than a century.

If theatres were uncomfortable and subject to perils like fire, they could be thrown up in a few weeks. In 1839 the Walnut Theatre in Philadelphia was completely redone in a weekend without the loss of a performance.

In Plumsted's Warehouse a company headed by Walter Murray and Thomas Kean played in Philadelphia in 1749. The city's Recorder objected before the Common Council against these performances but they went on for a time. Although this community dominated by the Quakers legislated against the stage, the Crown in England overruled the legislators, and there was a large enough representation of Church of England followers with a taste for the theatre to counteract the Quakers.

From Philadelphia the Murray-Kean company went to New York, having added to its ranks a young actress named Nancy George, whose defection to the stage shocked her rigorous Quaker City circles and merely proved that the theatre was a diabolical tempter. In a Nassau Street room these players undertook performances with some regularity, working in quarters that now would be below standard off Broadway. Their auditorium seated fewer than 300. Their stage had primitive equipment. Unaware of what New York could be like in July, they valiantly planned shows in that month and, of course, encountered weather so searing that at least one performance had to be postponed until there was a promise of "the Appearance of moderate Weather." In Philadelphia some 30 years later a novel, if primitive, form of air conditioning was hit upon. The fire engines were commandeered to to play their hoses on the roof in scorching, sticky weather. One would guess that the competition of the artificial waterfall must have been difficult for the actors.

The New York program was amazingly ambitious, including Shakespeare (*Richard III*), Congreve (*Love for Love*), Dryden (*The Spanish Friar*), Gay (*The Beggar's Opera*), Otway (*The Orphan*), Addison (*Cato*), Lillo (*George Barnwell*) and Farquhar (four of his pieces). Evidently there was not much audience for repeat performances; otherwise it would have been possible to carry on a season with fewer plays. But the company was eager to oblige. All it asked, according to a contemporary account, was "suitable encouragement."

From New York these players moved to Virginia where they built a theatre in Williamsburg in 1751. For several years they operated in the South, which apparently was prepared to offer suitable encouragement.

Their importance to the early American theatre, however, is small. "It is really with the coming of Lewis Hallam's company in 1752," says Quinn, "that our theatrical history begins."

The movement of the Hallams from England to the New World is material for a more colorful drama than many that reach our boards. Lewis Hallam was a member of a London theatrical family. He and his brother, who probably managed a London theatre, hoped to establish a remunerative foothold in the Colonies. Lewis, his wife; his three children, Lewis Jr., Adam and a daughter; and ten adult members of the company sailed from England in May on the *Charming Sally*. The voyage by sail required six weeks, and the company rehearsed on deck when not plagued by seasickness. They were, with the possible exception of young Adam and his sister, troupers all.

Arriving in Yorktown, Virginia, the company set up shop in the Williamsburg theatre that the Murray-Kean company had built. The playhouse had been altered and "finished in the highest Taste" so that it would be "fit for the Reception of Ladies and Gentlemen." You may take the word of Dunlap, who knew and talked to Lewis Hallam Jr. in the latter's old age, that the playhouse was in a rustic setting and that a member of the company could stand in a doorway, aim at wild pigeons in the woods and, if a good shot, have fresh meat on his table that day.

The Merchant of Venice was the Hallam company's maiden offering in America. George Washington, twenty-two and a military adjutant of the colony, may have attended the opening as well as other performances; all his life he was attached to the theatre. Mrs. Hallam was Portia; her husband played Launcelot Gobbo, and young Lewis, a trembling child, went on as Portia's servant. He soon learned to be at home on the stage. In 1759 at nineteen he played Romeo to his mother's Juliet, and by November 26, 1761, at twenty-one, he bestrode the stage as Hamlet. It is a pity that there is no detailed contemporary account of America's first Hamlet.

It required unremitting hardihood to be a manager or an actor in those days. Merely getting permission to perform was a constant

problem. Hallam and his company braved New York, only to find
that it was not easy to receive official sanction to appear in public,
that no proper theatre was available and, worst of all, that the community was scarcely waiting for them with bated breath. Hallam's
troubles were encountered by his successors. After his death, another actor-manager, David Douglass, married his widow, and they
brought the American company—a merger of Hallam's and Douglass's companies—to the Colonies from the West Indies, and they,
too, had to cope constantly with recalcitrant governors and councils.

In 1752, Hallam argued his case in print and in person, flattering
New York on its reputation for gentility and promising plays that
would confer instruction on the city. He rebuilt the theatre on
Nassau Street, and the season began with Steele's *The Conscious
Lovers,* a screed of unimpeachable moral character. For six months,
in performances on Monday, Wednesday and Friday evenings at 6,
the company diverted and, it is to be hoped, instructed New York.
Then, after overcoming the inevitable resistance, it served Philadelphia similarly.

It is easy to assume that New York saw *mise-en-scène* and acting
that would seem rudimentary, if not ludicrous, to us. The company
played Shakespeare—*Richard III, King Lear* and *Romeo and Juliet,*
all for the first time in New York—in the scandalously edited and
improved versions so popular before scholarship forced restoration
of the original text. What is impressive—and would be so even in
the light of our extensive theatre, and in the growth of our sophistication and culture—is the scope and variety of the repertory the
Hallam troupe was prepared to offer. A generous helping of Elizabethan drama, Restoration comedy and early eighteenth-century
tragedy and farce were on the overflowing bill of fare. Succeeding
companies were equally alert. In August 1773, for example, Lewis
Hallam Jr. offered his Tony Lumpkin for the delectation of New
York only a few months after London had its first glimpse of Goldsmith's *She Stoops to Conquer.*

In 1754 the Hallam troupe left the Colonies for Jamaica—the
plague may have been the cause. Its successor, the company led by
Douglass, returned in 1758, built a new theatre on Cruger's Wharf
in New York, then found it had no license to play. When it got per-

mission, it was only for a brief season. Moving to Philadelphia, it encountered similar obstacles. To avert antagonism, a theatre was built on Society Hill in Southwark outside the city limits. After opening with Marlowe's *Tamburlaine* the company found itself in further difficulties. Not only the Quakers but the representatives of the other sects demanded that the Assembly put a legal end to this theatrical invasion, and the legislators, ever sensitive to the clamor of their constituents, obliged by enacting a law. Being an artful politician as well as a man who liked the theatre, the Governor ruled that the new law, passed in June, would take effect in January. A Solomon-like judgment, it enabled the show to go on legitimately for the next six months. Then the King, whose writ was a nuisance in other ways but who did not frown on pleasure, threw out the law.

After a season with a formidable total of 80 plays, Douglass and his colleagues had a right to be satisfied, and they sought to conquer fresh territory. They moved south and then north into New England. Then back to New York where in several weeks a new theatre was thrown up at Nassau and what is now Beekman Street. These buildings were just elementary enough to be functional. Amenities backstage and out front were sparse or nonexistent. Heat was supplied by stoves in the lobby—and in the auditorium by the bodies of the customers packed into the seats. Plumbing, if any, was rudimentary; electricity did not exist.

The manners of the audience could be deplorable. In the Mercury of May 3, 1762, David Douglass published a notice offering "A Pistole Reward" to "whoever can discover the Person who was so very rude to throw Eggs from the Gallery, upon the Stage last Monday, by which the Cloaths of some Ladies and Gentlemen in the Boxes were spoiled, and the Performance in some measure interrupted."

Earnings were meager or nil. Actors who were often in need were expected to play constant benefits for the destitute. A performance of *Othello* in 1762, according to a notice in the *Mercury,* raised 114 pounds and 10 shillings "to relieve such poor families as are not provided for by the public." For an entire season of hard work, a company had earnings of 620 pounds. Nor was this sum net profit, for it had to cover living costs of the troupe. Then, and only then, could there be a division, according to the shares held by each member. Theatre companies began as cooperatives in America; the system of salaries and a management responsible for operation and finances did not come for a number of decades. The envious public tended to think that the actor was growing fat on his gains. The irony in 1762 was that Douglass's company, which was lucky enough to earn 620 pounds in a season, was charged with amassing a fantastic sum and preparing to carry away a substantial portion of the city's treasure.

Actors were expendable. In 1767 a stage wagon on a ferry crossing from Kill van Kull to Manhattan overturned and an actress and her servant were dumped overboard and drowned. The tragedy made only a mild stir. The bereaved husband of the actress got one night off to lament his loss.

Since the hazards were incalculable and the gains limited, there had to be a few compensations beyond money. One of these—and what could be dearer to an actor's heart—was a firm assurance of roles. The reward offered to Malone, one of Hallam's company, for the "long journey" from New York to Philadelphia and for the nasty task to "thrust himself face to face with those broad-brimmed, brown-wigged Quakers in their own stronghold" was the role of Falstaff. Clinching a fat part was not merely a source of gratification; it was a lock on a career. As Dunlap wryly explained, "At that period . . . the parts in which an actor was cast, if the manager's decree was confirmed by the public, became his inalienable property while in the company, and ofttimes the proprietor continued to figure as a youthful hero or lover long after all nature's qualifications for the part had become the prey of time the despoiler."

Douglass was evidently a resourceful manager. He knew when to stay and when to move on; when to go along with familiar faces and when to find new ones. He wandered in and out of the Colonies, and in 1766 tackled Philadelphia anew. He returned with additions to his company, notably a young Irishman named John Henry, whose romantic life was so varied and complicated that the gossips and the guardians of respectability had another shaft to aim at the American company, yet whose personal magnetism was so great that he became our first theatrical glamour boy. He knew how to carry it off. He had the temerity, in a community that looked down on actors, to have his own coach, a small one, it is true, with only one horse, but driven stylishly by a black boy and emblazoned with a coat of arms.

For this stand in Philadelphia, Douglass, according to Quinn, built "the first permanent theatre in America in South Street, above Fourth Street. It was called the Southwark Theatre, and was a rough brick and wood structure, painted red. The stage was lighted by oil lamps without glasses, and the view was interrupted by pillars that supported the upper tier and the roof. Yet it was an improvement on the temporary structures that had previously been erected, and it remained in use for theatrical purposes until the beginning of the nineteenth century."

Here Douglass presented the first drama by an American to be played by professionals. The author, Thomas Godfrey, had been dead four years when in April 1767 his *Prince of Parthia* had its one and only performance of the season, not to be attempted again until the University of Pennsylvania's Zelosophic Society revived it with an all-male cast in 1915. Despite a benevolent judgment that "it proved to be a very actable play," a reading of the published text makes one think of a parody of classic tragedy. It is easy to be condescending, particularly when one has the advantage of two centuries of hindsight. But even if the audience in 1766 saw a work like *The Prince of Parthia* in the light of what it knew of theatre, it could not fail to note the stilted diction and the stereotyped figures of Godfrey's work. The opening lines, spoken by the brother of the hero, suggest the flavor:

> He comes, Arsaces comes, my gallant Brother
> (Like shining Mars in all the pomp of conquest)
> Triumphant enters now our joyful gates;
> Bright victory waits on his glittering ear,
> And shows her favorite to the wond'ring crowd . . .

What a hero, Arsaces. Gotarzes tells us of a dread danger from which he saved him:

A monst'rous Leopart from a bosky fen
Rush'd forth, and foaming lash'd the ground,
And fiercely ey'd me as his destin'd quarry . . .

Then there is the passionate musing of Evanthe, the heroine:

Once I was free, then my exulting heart
Was like a bird that hops from spray to spray,
And all was innocence and mirth; but, lo!
The Fowler came, and by his arts decoy'd
And soon the Wanton cag'd.

It is Evanthe who complains, "Ah—what a cruel torment is suspense!" and who with a stunning premonition of the future uttered, if not coined, a cliché that was to ring through decades of American theatre, "Ha! villain, off—unhand me—hence—" It will not surprise you to hear that near the end the heroic Arsaces exclaims, "Break, break tough heart!" and that the tragedy, which did not forget to incorporate a ghost, ends with a plenitude of murder and suicide. As if to mitigate the general woe, the program proceeded to the afterpiece, a ballad opera called *The Contrivances*. One can only repeat the final words of the printed announcement, "Vivant Rex and Regina."

Criticism, however, was beginning to rear its insidious head. The *Pennsylvania Gazette* in 1767 carried a notice written by a "gentleman" who adjured Lewis Hallam Jr. to take "the inimitable Garrick" as a model and learn "to speak plain English," warning that "there is no necessity of destroying the least articulate Beauty of Language, thro' Fury, Eagerness, or Passion," and pointing to Miss Cheer, a favorite actress, who "never loses the sweetest Accent, or faulters in the Clearness of Expression" though "she is equally delicate and capable of feeling the Force of Passion."

In the autumn of 1767 Douglass once again turned his ambitions to New York, where he launched the construction of a theatre on John Street. Meant for permanence, the stage was more spacious than the makeshift quarters visiting companies had used. The wooden building, painted red, was 60 feet from the street and the path to the entrance was paved with wood. With capacity the house could take in $800 a night.

The John Street Theatre became the focus of New York's early theatre history. In it the Douglass company played an inaugural season of more than six months, offering 38 plays plus 31 afterpieces. Luck was variable; the enemies of the stage hammered away; business was often indifferent. Although life was hard, the company tried again and again. It also traveled to Philadelphia, Annapolis, Williamsburg and Charleston, hoping for better things in each port of call.

In Charleston, Douglass and his associates had their happiest season. In a new theatre, "the most commodious on the continent," according to a proud contemporary report, more than 100 performances were played from December 1773 to May 1774. The repertory was princely in its abundance with a grand total of 77 works, dramatic and musical, 14 by Shakespeare. There was even a native play called *Young America in London,* but no record of it remains. In Charleston, unlike the frosty north, the best people thronged the theatre. Even the ladies, as many as 250 in a single audience, attended without impeachment of their good names.

Charleston must have seemed to Douglass an ideal place for further cultivation. He made ambitious plans to improve his company and enlarge his repertory. But with the imminence of war, the future of the theatre turned bleak. In October 1774, the Continental Congress resolved that "we will, in our several stations, encourage frugality, economy, and industry, and promote agriculture, arts, and the manufacture of this country, especially that of wool; and will discountenance and discourage every species of extravagance and dissipation, especially all horse-racing, and all kinds of gaming, cock-fighting, exhibitions of shews, plays, and other expensive diversions and entertainments."

Charleston need not have heeded this request for uniform sobriety. But the fact of the crisis was incontrovertible. The Puritans and their kindred spirits prevailed. The colonial stages went dark.

CHAPTER III

PATRIOTISM AND AN
AMERICAN FLAVOR

ALTHOUGH HE ENDORSED the resolution demanding austerity of his countrymen and felt bound by it, George Washington at Valley Forge in 1778 let his forces present several plays and attended a performance of *Cato*. The hero of Addison's tragedy stood for liberty, and surely a play on this theme could be justified as instructive and inspirational as well as pleasurable. Whether its stuffy, pretentious periods pleased all the members of its Valley Forge audience is another question. It may have interested a few of the literate officers and men, and for the others, like men immemorially lodged in an encampment when they would have preferred to be at hearth or plow, it was a way to kill a few dragging hours.

When the American troops marched into Philadelphia later in 1778, they saw to it that the Southwark Theatre had plays on its stage by autumn. But the Congress would not tolerate such frivolity. It resolved that plays and playgoing would remain forbidden, and it expressly ruled that "any person holding an office under the United States" must not encourage, patronize or participate in a play. In his history of the American theatre, Glenn Hughes quotes a newspaper of the time as authority for a charming little story. On the very day this fresh resolution was passed, Lafayette invited Washington to be his guest at the Southwark Theatre. The Commander in Chief was obliged to decline. When Lafayette heard the explanation, he gallantly gave up his visit to the theatre. Under the circumstances there was no immediate future for plays at the Southwark and they were halted.

In happier times Washington did not hesitate to bestow the blessing of his presence on the theatre. In the spring of 1789, the festivities surrounding his inauguration as President gave New York a burst of gaiety and the theatre a spurt of hearty support. The new President himself attended performances at the John Street Theatre in May and June. On May 6 two of his favorites, *The School for Scandal* and *The Poor Soldier,* a farcical afterpiece by O'Keefe, made up the bill. In November, when the President paid another visit to the John Street Theatre, the company had a special interlude ready for him—a comic sketch by Dunlap called *Darby's Return,* which took pains to comment on contemporary matters and which paid compliments to the distinguished guest.

Among the lines Dunlap wrote to describe Washington and had spoken in his presence, according to Quinn, were:

> A man who'd fought to free the land from woe,
> Like me had left his farm a-soldiering to go;
> But having gain'd his point, he had, like me,
> Return'd his own potatoe ground to see,
> But there he couldn't rest; with one accord
> He's called to be a kind of—not a lord;
> I don't know what; he's not a great man, sure,
> For poor men love him, just as he was poor!
> They love him like a father or a brother.

Dunlap reports that the General's demeanor was grave as these lines were spoken. But he laughed heartily when the reminiscer was asked, "How look'd he, Darby? Was he short or tall?" and replied:

> Why sure I didn't see him. To be sure,
> As I was looking hard from out the door,
> I saw a man in regimentals fine,

All lace and glitter, botherum and shine,
And so I look'd at him till all was gone,
And then I found that he was not the one.

If the Continental Congress frowned on plays during the years of the fighting, the British did not. Their troops, often led by their officers, were eager to find amusement and mounted their own productions. In Boston, which had been adamant in its opposition to professional thespians, Faneuil Hall was used as a theatre. Gentleman Johnny Burgoyne, more than a century later to be turned into a mercurial and ironic figure by Bernard Shaw in *The Devil's Disciple,* joined in the performances and had his own piece, *The Blockade of Boston,* which mocked the Americans, in rehearsal. The Americans had the last laugh. Word of their attack on Bunker Hill arrived during a rehearsal, and the performers in uniform, without a thought for the actor's or soldier's pride, fled.

In New York, after Howe's troops took the city, the John Street Theatre was reopened. Between January and May there were 18 performances of six plays and nine afterpieces. British officers were among the actors, and at least one conveniently had his English mistress on hand to play female leads. When the British captured Philadelphia, "Howe's strolling players" took over the Southwark Theatre, which had been converted into a hospital, restored it to its original use and performed in it. Major André, the spy, was one of the officers who acted as well as painted scenery.

But the theatre is a phoenix that invariably rises from the ashes of severe restrictions. Draconian measures cannot long suppress it. Even while the fighting went on, the theatre showed its head here and there—for a spell in Baltimore, then in another flash in New York or Philadelphia. If the usual repertory did not suffice to circumvent official restraints, a patriotic piece might overcome resistance. Having failed to get the Pennsylvania Assembly to repeal its act of 1778, Hallam nevertheless managed to take over the Southwark Theatre again in 1784 for the presentation of a *Monody to the Memory of the Chiefs who have fallen in the Cause of American Liberty.*

Even before the shooting began, there were attempts to turn the grievances of the colonists into dramatic material, apart from crude, unplayable pieces like a tragedy about Pontiac, the Indian chief, and the relations between Indians and whites and another on the conquest of Canada. Mrs. Mercy Otis Warren, sister of the Massachusetts patriot, James Otis, and a lively, intelligent woman who knew the Adamses, John and Samuel, as well as many other leading Revolutionary figures, wrote at least two dramatic satires on patriotic themes. They were published, if not performed—*The Adulateur* in 1773, which had Thomas Hutchinson, governor of the colony, as its chief target, and *The Group,* written and printed in 1775, which savagely attacked the loyalist group willing to do the King's bidding after his abrogation of Massachusetts' charter.

Since many remained loyal to the British Crown, there were also satires from the Tory viewpoint. Other efforts, largely literary in pretension rather than dramatic in achievement, dealt with the burning issues of the day, for the Revolution and against.

Since their very craft was under constant moral suspicion, the actors of our Revolutionary time had every reason to display their patriotism. The American Company of Hallam and Henry made a brave show of celebrating July 4 in 1785. The *pièce de résistance* was the unveiling of a grand painting with a spread eagle gripping the sword in one claw and thirteen arrows in the other and, somewhat in the fashion of the balloons that in our day carry the dialogue of comic strips, an inscription issuing from the emblematic bird's mouth that bore the names of Washington and other American heroes.

Where patriotism and flag-waving did not soften the hearts of obdurate officials, subterfuges were resumed. Plays were again smuggled into theatres under the guise of lectures and concerts, and diversions took on the color of instruction. In Philadelphia a performance described as "A Lecture on the Vice of Gambling" turned out to be Moore's play, *The Gamester; The Pernicious Vice of Scandal* masked *The School for Scandal,* and the grandiloquent title, *A Lecture on the Disadvantages of Improper Education, Exemplified in the History of Tony Lumpkin* proved to be the elaborately transparent disguise for *She Stoops to Conquer.*

The American Company, moving to the John Street Theatre again in February 1787, had its meed of troubles. The press was beginning to be pointed in its comment; the *Advertiser* spoke out against sloppy staging and disappointing scenery and complained particularly of "a dirty piece of canvas" where "the author intended a handsome street or a beautiful landscape." There was also a blast at the musicians who "instead of performing between the play and the farce are suffered to leave the orchestra to pay a visit to the tippling houses, and the ladies in the meantime must amuse themselves by looking at the candles and the empty benches." The gentlemen, one must suppose, did not have to contemplate candles and empty benches, since it was all right for them to repair to the tippling houses.

Despite the company's shortcomings in 1787, it made a notable contribution. On April 16 it produced *The Contrast*, by Royall Tyler, the first comedy in our history by an American played by professionals. Unlike the hopelessly imitative *Prince of Parthia*, *The Contrast* had an American flavor. Its models might be Sheridan and Goldsmith and the other shrewd and boisterous English comedies of manners, but its setting was New York and some of its characters were every inch native citizens of the new country.

Tyler, a Bostonian by birth who was educated at Harvard and Yale, served as an officer in the Revolutionary army, where as an aide to General Benjamin Lincoln he took part in the pursuit of the British in Vermont. He reached New York in March 1787, when he was almost thirty. With his lively interest in the arts and especially the theatre, he began to frequent the John Street playhouse.

The actor who caught his eye and warmed his heart was Thomas Wignell, a cousin of Hallam, who had come to the colonies in 1774 after being in Garrick's company, and who, like the other actors largely barred from their trade in the years of fighting and austerity, managed somehow to survive and wait for the chance to return to the stage. He was evidently a resourceful comedian. Dunlap paid him the compliment of declaring that he was always faithful to the author, and Tyler paid a higher one of giving him the copyright to *The Contrast*, which Wignell published in 1790 for a subscription list led by Washington and four of his Cabinet.

The Contrast, which Tyler probably wrote in three weeks, poked

fun at the social pretensions of the best people, and it introduced
a staple of the American stage. In Jonathan, a comic rustic from
New England whose acuteness was masked by his good-natured
simplicity, the American stage saw for the first time the figure of
the half-educated, shrewd Yankee who delighted generations of
theatregoers. The character in later years underwent a variety of
transformations. He became the bumbling city worker, the dull-
witted sailor, the eternal hick, whose unsophisticated common sense
solved crises. He was the prototype that became stereotype, which
is with us yet. Take a look at television's situation comedy almost
any day.

The title page of the 1790 edition proudly proclaims *The Contrast* as "written by a Citizen of the United States" and records that
it was "performed with applause at the Theatres in New York,
Philadelphia, and Maryland." The play also met with success in
Richmond and Charleston as well as in Boston, where, with theatres still struggling for respectable acceptance, it was offered in
1792 as "A Moral Lecture in five parts . . . called the Contrast, delivered by Messrs. Harper, Morris, Mrs. Murry, Miss Smith, and
Mrs. Morris."

To underline the company's pride in the native authorship of
The Contrast and perhaps to drum up patriotic trade as well,
Wignell spoke a prologue, "written by a Young Gentleman of New
York":

> Exult each patriot heart—this night is shewn
> A piece, which we may fairly call our own;
> Where the proud titles of "My Lord! Your Grace!"
> To humble Mr. and plain Sir give place.
> Our author pictures not from foreign climes
> The fashions, or the follies of the times;
> But has confin'd the subject of his work
> To the gay scenes—the circles of New York.

Tyler had a good ear and a relish for the mockery of polite society. Of Maria, whose betrothal to Billy Dimple her father has
arranged, a friend remarks sharply and brightly, "As her taste improved, her love declined." Elsewhere Charlotte, a vivacious and
outspoken young woman, speaks of a girl not yet in her teens who,

the gossips say, is about to be married, "Why I think it is probable she cried for a plaything, and they have given her a husband."

If Tyler poked fun at the extravagances of fashion, he was also sharp with the hardheaded practicality of Van Rough, Maria's father, who advises his daughter that "it is money that makes the mare go; keep your eye on the main chance." With Jonathan he obviously could not miss. Shrewd enough to know that Jonathan, his yokel from a New England farm, would be funnier if set off against the airs of New York, Tyler pitted him against Jessamy, a servant as pretentious and mannered as Jonathan is plain and direct.

Through Jonathan *The Contrast* describes the sights and sounds of New York and comments on them. There is an affectionate and amusing scene in which Jonathan recounts his open-eyed visit to the theatre. There is another in which Jonathan tells of a surprising adventure to "a place they call Holy Ground":

Now I counted this was a place where folks go to meeting, so I put my hymn-book in my pocket, and walked softly and grave as a minister; and when I came there, the dogs a bit of a meeting-house could I see. At last I spied a young gentlewoman standing by one of the seats, which I have here at the doors—I took her to be a deacon's daughter, and she looked so kind and obliging, that I thought I would go and ask her the way to lecture, and would you think it—she called me dear and sweeting, and honey, just as if we were married; by the living jingo, I had a month's mind to buss her.

If it takes some time and help for Jonathan to realize the nature of the obliging girl's trade, it is not because he is bent on deviltry. On the contrary, he's a lad with a girl, Tabitha Wyman, the deacon's daughter, back home. Her father is prepared to give him "20 acres of land—somewhat rocky though—a Bible and a cow," and Jonathan feels that he's "as good as married."

"She and I have been courting a great while," he explains, "and folks say as how we are to be married; and so I broke a piece of money with her when we parted, and she promised not to spark with Solomon Dyer while I am gone. You wouldn't have me false to my true love, would you?" Nevertheless he lets Jessamy talk him into testing his charms on Jenny, the kitchen wench, and is slapped for his forwardness. "If this is the way with your city ladies," he says, "give me the 20 acres of rock, the Bible, the cow and Tabitha, and a little peaceable bundling."

The contrast between Jonathan and Jessamy is emphasized on a higher social level between Dimple, "a gentleman who has read Chesterfield and received the polish of Europe," and Manly, an unpolished, untraveled, sturdy American.

It seems hard to believe that Tyler or his audience could take Manly's pompous nobility seriously, but more than another hundred years passed before the theatre gave up the stereotype, if indeed it has been totally abandoned.

Though a solemn, principled chap, Manly is no fool. Early on he trots out his war record for the benefit of the 1787 public, "I have humbly imitated our illustrious Washington, in having exposed my health and life in the service of my country, without reaping any other reward than the glory of conquering in so arduous a contest."

At the end of the fourth act, when it appears that Manly's admiration for Maria and hers for him have gone awry, he is capable of a true gentleman's self-restraint as well as the dignity not to deny his ardor.

"We are both unhappy," says Manly, "but it is your duty to obey your parent,—mine to obey my honour. Let us, therefore, both follow the path of rectitude; and of this we may be assured, that if we are not happy, we shall, at least, deserve to be so. Adieu! I dare not trust myself longer with you."

All is resolved happily in the fifth act. Trust Tyler to end with a flourish that must have sent his audience home content. It is Manly who has the concluding speech:

And I have learned that probity, virtue, honour, though they should not have received the polish of Europe, will secure to an honest American the good graces of his fair countrywoman, and, I hope, the applause of THE PUBLIC.

How would *The Contrast* look today? Hopelessly dated, of course. But to its contemporaries? We know that *The Contrast* pleased its public. The *Daily Advertiser* carried a long critique by one who signed himself Candour.

I was present last evening at the representation of the *Contrast* and was very much entertained with it. It is certainly the production of a man of genius and nothing can be more praiseworthy than the sentiments of the play through out. They are the effusions of an honest patriot heart expressed with energy, eloquence. The characters are drawn with spirit, particularly Charlotte's; the dialogue is easy, sprightly and often witty, but wants the pruning knife very much. The author has made frequent use of soliloquies, but I must own, I think injudiciously; Maria's song and her reflections after it are pretty, but certainly misplaced. Soliloquies are seldom so conducted as not to wound probability. . . .

CHAPTER IV

A PROBLEM CHILD

As the old century, which came to stand for the age of enlightenment, was drawing to a close, an increasingly tolerant and enlightened attitude toward the theatre became manifest in the new nation. Dunlap recalled that a Judge Allan, rejecting a periodic demand in Philadelphia that the theatre be banned, remarked, "I have learned more moral virtue from plays than from sermons."

In 1792 even Boston, where a law since mid-century had effectively barred theatre, relented long enough to permit performances in a makeshift setting called cautiously the New Exhibition Room. A company of players from England and former members of the Old American Company presented plays for a time until the authorities closed the theatre and arrested one of the managers, but the public no longer remained silent. By the next year the law was thrown out, and Boston could openly commit itself to a new and proper playhouse and a season of drama. In Rhode Island a law against theatre was also abolished, and a brick building in Newport that had once been a market was turned into a playhouse. It was Dunlap who, recalling earlier barriers in this city, observed bitterly, "It appears the Thespians found foes among the slave dealers of Newport, who probably thought a stage player a greater abomination than the kidnapper or receiver and abettor of the kidnapper of the miserable Negro."

The theatre was becoming respectable. There was never a time —and there is none yet—when the stage offered its children, *les enfants du paradis,* as the mimes in Jean-Louis Barrault's lovely film were called, a reliable way of life. But having survived war and disease—in 1795 an epidemic of yellow fever shook New York and late in 1798 another wave of this plague took 2,000 of the town's 50,000 lives—the optimistic, expanding young country paid less heed to the self-appointed guardians of morals and more to its own instincts. It was actually becoming possible for a native citizen to elect a stage career, let alone attend a play. In 1767 a Mr. Greville, who had been a student at Princeton, had the temerity to join the Douglass Company. In 1792, John Martin, a native, entered on a professional life as an actor in Philadelphia. Thereafter the stream of American stage recruits widened and deepened.

Not that theatre folk sought to be indistinguishable from their contemporaries. Some, indeed, went out of their way to remind the world that they were different. There was John Hodgkinson, who arrived in the United States in 1792 at the age of twenty-six and was probably the ablest actor America had yet seen. He became celebrated; he also took pains to cut a noticeable figure.

Dunlap noted that "long after others wore their hair short and of nature's color, Hodgkinson had powdered curls at each side, and long braided hair twisted into a club or knot behind! Instead of pantaloons and boots, breeches and stockings and shoes. This costume, with his hat on one side, and an air and manner then known by the appellation of theatrical, marked him among thousands."

Better times for the drama were indicated by new, more commodious homes in various parts of the country. In New York the Park Theatre opened early in 1798, taking the place of the inadequate John Street house, and for the next two decades and more it filled a central role in the history of the American stage.

The Park on Park Row near Ann Street was built of stone and was three stories high. There were six steps up to the box entrance, and three green baize doors opened from the lobby. In a niche in the lobby's center a statue of Shakespeare eventually occupied a place of honor. The lobby, wide and carpeted, accommodated a stove at each end with blazing fires to warm patrons on cold nights.

A keeper of the boxes presided on the first tier and escorted holders into the honored places of vantage. There were two additional tiers of boxes as well as a gallery and a pit, and no lady was admitted to the first and second tiers unless accompanied by a gentleman. As if to leave no doubt about the meaning of the status of a lady, there were several private boxes off the proscenium where Dunlap's "unfortunate victims of seduction" made a public show of their wares and availability. In the boxes and pit there were cushioned seats instead of chairs. The interior was ornamented in light pink and gold, and the stage could accommodate more elaborate scenic equipment and effects than had the John Street Theatre.

The Park was a large house, and it raised the problem of traffic. Patrons coming to the grand opening were told in a newspaper advertisement: "Ladies and Gentlemen will please direct their servants to sit down with their horses' heads towards the New Brick Meeting, and take up with their horses' heads towards Broadway."

The cost of the new building outstripped estimates, as it always had and always will, time without end. A budget of $42,000 swelled to $130,000 (some sources suggested that the cost soared to $179,-000) and the money came from 113 persons. At opening-night prices of $1 and $2, the take, according to Dunlap, was $1,232 when it should have been a good deal more. But gate crashers were abundant, and the 113 owners insisted on free admission—not only at the inaugural but at every performance. Poor Dunlap, who had assiduously promoted the new theatre, and who with Hodgkinson was its lessee, endured no end of financial headaches that season. On the terms arranged with the owners of the theatre and with business falling below $500 some nights, he had no chance of turning the season into a profitable venture.

The performers were no longer willing to work on a cooperative basis. Their salaries, if not munificent, represented fixed costs. Hallam and his wife each received $25 a week. Thomas Abthorpe Cooper, a young actor of tragic roles newly imported from England by Wignell for his Philadelphia Company, insisted on staying in New York. Threats of a suit for breach of contract could not move him from his determination to be part of the more glamorous situation. The Park presented him as Hamlet in a performance whose proceeds were used to pay damages to Wignell. Cooper's weekly salary was $32, and others in the company got as little as $4 a week. The bill for an instrumental ensemble of ten ran to $140.

Dunlap was uneasy with his lease. He sought vainly to induce Hallam to buy into the management after Hodgkinson withdrew. He negotiated with the owners for better terms and arranged a new salary scale. He saw to it that the unfinished portions of the building were completed and he had the interior redecorated. He reopened the theatre in December after the yellow fever epidemic abated and seemed to be headed for further troubles, because business was poor to start with. Then he struck gold with his own adaptation of *The Stranger*, a melodrama by Kotzebue, a German playwright.

Dunlap stumbled on this lifesaver in "a wretched publication in which the plot and part of the dialogue of Kotzebue's play were given in language neither German nor English." The theme is enough to give one today the emotional shakes. In Quinn's words, "the motive of *The Stranger* is the return and repentance of an erring wife, who had deserted her husband and children years before with her lover. Her agony when she finds that her children have naturally forgotten her and she is unable to declare herself to them is a motive that has appealed to thousands of auditors and has been reproduced in plays and stories, of which *East Lynne* is one of the many examples."

The Stranger struck a chord with the New York public and was performed twelve times, an impressive run in those days. Dunlap got the message, and hastily turned to Kotzebue to shore up his shaky enterprise. The German as the American adapted him satisfied the tastes of the moment and became, despite a total lack of quality, a raging fashion. Reflecting the new democratic trends, Kotzebue, no doubt with considerable underlining by Dunlap, painted the patrician and the highly placed as evil and dangerous and the ordinary citizen as admirable. He had a flair for wildly romantic subjects, flamboyant characters and splashy situations, and he saturated everything in layers of sentimentality.

Dunlap, struggling to keep afloat, turned restlessly to whatever themes seemed to have promise, although his tastes were better than the thrills and tears he fed his public. He offered a glimpse of the noble savage, so beloved of our early theatre. He recalled historical figures like Peter the Great. He unleashed the swashbuckling bandit who for patriotic reasons conceals his noble birth. He sought out melodrama from French sources. He tried comedy, farce and opera. But his efforts availed him not. By February 1805, he was bankrupt, and he closed the theatre.

"After a struggle of years," he recalled later, "against the effects of yellow fever, and all those curses belonging to the interior of an establishment, badly organized when he found it, the manager's health yielded to disappointment and incessant exertion."

Although other men took on the management of the Park, Dunlap did not abandon the theatre. For a time he served as assistant manager to Thomas Abthorpe Cooper, the actor, who took over the lease. Later he assumed the hopeless task of watching over George Frederick Cooke, an English actor who enjoyed a distinguished reputation in tragedy and a fatal attraction for the bottle.

Cooke was hired by Cooper for 25 guineas, then $116, per week, for the 1808–09 season at the Park. Stephen Price, who had become Cooper's co-manager, exulted, according to Dunlap, "Now is the winter of our discontent made glorious summer by this son of York." Cooke was the most glamorous figure yet imported from England, and the public could hardly believe the promise of his coming. The Cooper-Price combine was shrewd enough to make the most of the excitement. The publicity campaign was, Odell observes, "almost the beginning of advance agenting in America. It was whispered and printed that Cooke had been guaranteed $14,000 for the season in addition to a series of benefits for his account." For his debut in America he was scheduled to play Richard III.

In his diary Dunlap communicates the stir Cooke created—and the difficulties. Price "hired a pilot boat and went down to the Hook to wait for his arrival, but came back disappointed." Cooke looked sixty but was probably fifty-five. He was, Dunlap continued, "mild and polite in the manner of the old school, his sober suit of grey, his grey hairs and the suavity of his manners gave no indication of the eccentric being":

He dined the next day with Price, sate late & got drunk. . . . On Wed. the 21st Nov. he made his first appearance on the American stage & play'd Richard with the enthusiastic applause of the Audience. His entré was truly dignified. I saw no vestige of the old man. His posture erect, his step firm, his eagle eye beaming fire. He return'd the salutes of the audience not as a player to the public on whom he depended but as a King acknowledging the acclamations of his subjects and yet before he went on he trembled like an aspen leaf.

So well, so good. Now the troubles began. Listen to Dunlap, his den father:

After playing he sup'd & drank freely; the consequence was that the next day he had no voice, but he thought that he could force it at night when he was to repeat Richard. . . . He whisper'd Richard thro' and was at the end of it pretty nearly drunk. . . .

To share in the guardianship of the Park's problem child Price invited Cooke to stay at his house "where every attention was paid him, and every endeavor made to keep him straight." But after his twelfth performance, Dunlap reported, "he sup'd as usual but got unusually drunk, abused Price in the grossest terms and finally caught up a Decanter to throw at him. P. seiz'd him and threw him down violently. Cooke exclaimed, 'Remember I am in your own house. Don't strike me.' Price insisted upon his going to his room. He went sullenly and as he had frequently done, sat up by the fire all night, going to bed in the morning. The next day he left an excuse with the serv. for not dining at home & went out. He rambled about the streets of the City, dined at Brydens [a coffee shop, where no doubt a man could get a comforting glass of something], got drunk and did not return to P's that night. He peep'd into the Theatre at rehearsal, ask'd the prompter if all was well. . . . He was so wild from the previous excess that his Cato, to which and for his benefit, an immense audience of the first of our people had assembled, was the most shamefull exhibition ever witness'd in N. Y."

"I was very much bewilder'd," Cooke told Dunlap. "Do you know that I could not remember one line after having recited the other. I caught myself once or twice giving Shakespeare for Addison."

Dunlap was accustomed to the peculiarities of actors. He could recall that in 1797 the smoldering rivalries between actors flamed into such a blaze on the stage of the John Street Theatre that a riot was almost set off. Mrs. Hallam, whose husband was still a member of the managerial group, was furious that she had not had sufficient chance to act. She walked out on the stage one night while Hodgkinson was playing a scene in *The Fashionable Lover*. "She looked beauty in distress," said Dunlap, "as she entered from the right, dressed in black silk, her hair parted on top of her head, combed down on each side of her face, and powdered." She clutched a written statement in her hand, and her entrance brought a burst of applause which, not unexpectedly, surprised Hodgkinson. Next Hallam himself appeared, decorously dressed, "stalking down the center of the stage, and advancing with many bows to the audience." He demanded that his wife be allowed to speak. Against an accompaniment of comment and plaudits from the public, she spoke and so did Hallam and Hodgkinson. Finally the play was resumed. But the bitter feelings lingered on. There were disputations, suits, the breakup of friendships; and, of course, the public joyously and passionately took sides and declared itself in the theatre with hissing and applause.

Of all the figures involved in the early history of the American theatre Dunlap was the most engaging. He was born in Perth Amboy, N. J., in 1766 and grew up there. An accident that caused the loss of the sight in his right eye when he was twelve ended his formal schooling. He recalled his debt to a remarkable old man, Thomas Bartow, his mentor in Perth Amboy. The lad would go to Bartow's home and wander through his garden as the old gentleman read Homer to him. Bartow, the only man of substance in town who owned no slaves, not only remembered Dunlap in his will but left him a legacy of character that shaped his own.

For a time young Dunlap turned to painting. In 1783 he had an opportunity to paint Washington, and in 1806, after he had been reduced from managing his own theatre to serving other managers, he returned occasionally to his palette. In a letter from Philadelphia in January 1806 to his wife, "my dear Bess," he tells of sitting down "to put a finishing hand to my Washington when behold, his black velvet coat was pealing off from the ivory and all in holes and patches" and that it came on "snow and frost so intense" that "several times when I attempted to put colour in the ivory it was mingled with icy christals."

In 1784 Dunlap went to England where he studied with Benjamin West and saw Shakespeare as well as contemporary plays and watched the acting of Charles Kemble and Mrs. Siddons. Back in America in 1787, he designed a frontispiece for *The Contrast.* He took to playwriting. He brought *The Modest Soldier,* which used *The Contrast* as a model, to Lewis Hallam and John Henry, who complimented him but did not produce his play. Eventually Dunlap learned why. He had failed to provide Henry and his wife with suitable roles. When he amended this oversight in his next play, *The Father, or American Shandyism,* the comedy was produced. Quinn thinks that this play "merits attention, both from the historical and absolute points of view," but it is impossible to agree with him. Even in his most ambitious work, *André,* couched in the poetic style that seemed then mandatory for tragedy, Dunlap resorted to elementary characterization—every person was nature's nobleman—and transparent dramatic development. The one impressive thing is Dunlap's refusal to turn André into a villain to gratify a chauvinistic public's desire to hate and hiss. The British spy is represented as a young man of character.

Washington appears as a commander of dignity who knows how to do his duty thoughtfully and without flinching. The young country's destiny is proudly proclaimed. Its spirit is summed up in these words,

> Now I see in this new world
> A resting spot for man, if he can stand
> Firm in his place, while Europe howls around him.

and again in these proud lines at the end:

> And may, in time to come, no foreign force,
> No European influence, tempt to misstate,
> Or awe the tongue of eloquence to silence.

CHAPTER V

ACTORS AND
"SHARP-SHOOTERS"

For several weeks in 1797 two companies played simultaneously in New York—a capable one headed by Wignell and Alexander Reinagle from Philadelphia, which took over an amphitheatre on Greenwich Street that had been devoted to horses, clowns, dancers, music and dramatic readings, and one led by Joseph Leger Solee, who had started a French theatre in Charleston and now attempted to organize a season in the John Street Theatre. Despite their rivalry these troupes were prudent enough to split the week, each company performing three times. The result was that New York for the first time had a play by professionals every night but Sunday.

Although it was a richer schedule than the small city could or would support, it was an earnest of what was to come. It was not many years before New York became the principal theatrical city in America. For a time Philadelphia could dispute its primacy, thanks to strongly entrenched dramatic forces, which also played Baltimore and Washington. The Boston theatre fared well in the early years of the nineteenth century, and in Charleston, which for some years reflected a lively independence of taste, the theatre prospered.

The theatre had almost no competition for the interest of thoughtful and lively New Yorkers, and there soon developed a vocal and literate reaction to its excesses. As early as 1796 a number of men who included Peter Irving, Washington Irving's older brother, Charles Adams, the son of the man who was to become the second President, John Wells, Elias Hicks, Samuel Jones and William Cutting formed the agreeable habit of jotting down their reactions after the play and meeting the next evening, probably at a friendly tavern, to examine each other's critiques. Signed with initials, these criticisms were then published in the press. The object, according to Dunlap, was "to correct the abuses existing in costumes, demeanor and general conduct of the actors of the stage." Since the comments were sharp, they aroused discussion. People speculated on the identity of the writers, and when it was discovered that the last initial identified the writer, deceptive tactics were adopted. Occasionally a D was used, presumably to imply Dunlap, though he did not belong to the Group.

The "sharp-shooters," as Dunlap called them, infuriated the actors. Giving what Dunlap called "good advice" to an actor named William King, they enraged him so that "he challenged them to mortal combat, severally and individually—but strange to say they took no notice of Mr. King."

Of an actor named Prigmore and his playing in *The Tempest* one of the Group wrote: "We have desisted from remarking on our old acquaintance, Prigmore, in the hope that he might (at least by accident) afford us something to applaud. But the same uniformity of acting which has ever characterized him, still continues. . . ."

Of a performance of *The School for Scandal,* there was this delicately phrased criticism: "Though Mrs. Hallam in Lady Teazle and Mr. Hallam as Sir Peter equalled our expectations, we could not forget that Mr. and Mrs. Henry formerly appeared in those characters; we could not but remember that such things were and were precious to us."

There is a contemptuous comment on applause by knocking or clapping "whenever the manager has delivered any thing extremely witty or sentimental, whether it is by direction of him 'whose sole ambition is the lust of praise,' or proceeds from the officiousness of some candidate for managerial favour, we shall not pretend to determine."

Hodgkinson's casts and productions were frequently on the Group's griddle. He was berated for casting of "the part of Widow Chesire to a man of the name of Lee—a heavy, stupid, vulgar fellow with no requisite for the stage but a bass voice and some knowledge of music."

Stung by these attacks Hodgkinson was driven to reply, using the pen name of Verax for his retorts.

One may imagine that the performances in those years were rarely brilliant, and that the players were a mixed crew. The Matthew Sully family which arrived in Charleston from England in 1792 was bound to make an impression on a relatively small, close-knit community merely by its size, for they were eleven, count 'em, eleven, with mother, father and nine children. Mr. Sully's sister happened to be the wife of Charleston's theatre manager, who knew the value of acquiring virtually an entire troupe at one swoop. Nearly all the Sullys had a whirl as actors. Whether they were capable actors or not it is hard to tell, but the father gained fame for his Harlequin.

The first of the three Joseph Jeffersons in America's stage history evidently was an actor of some quality. The son of a man in Garrick's London company and eventually the grandfather of the Joseph Jefferson who made a career out of Rip Van Winkle in the second half of the nineteenth century, he came to America in 1794 and began a long and successful career in comedy. He was one of those comedians who found profit in a Yankee character patterned after Jonathan in *The Contrast*. When *Tears and Smiles*, by James Nelson Barker, one of our early native playwrights, won a success in 1807, it owed its acceptance in large part to the Yankee the author wrote for Jefferson at the actor's request. In Philadelphia's Chestnut Street Theatre where *Tears and Smiles* first played, the dialogue was not always confined to the stage. On the second night certain gentlemen, whom Barker considered political enemies, fired a barrage of remarks from their seats in a stage box, and he hurried to the box to make a personal protest, apparently shaming the hecklers into silence.

Jefferson made his first appearance in New York in 1796, which also marked the debut of an actress whom New York took to its heart. She was Mrs. Elizabeth Johnson, and Dunlap described her as "a tall, elegant, beautiful young woman." In the manner of glamorous actresses, she became "a model for the belles of the city." Her "taste in dress" and her "manners were as fascinating off as on the stage."

I wish we knew more about the style and quality of the performances of the Miss Arnold who made her debut in Boston's new Federal Theatre on April 15, 1796. She received nowhere the attention of a fellow debutant, the English tragedian, John Brown Williamson, who came from London's Haymarket Theatre and impressed Boston with his Othello. Miss Arnold got her first chance as an entr'acte singer. Later one finds her doing boys' parts in Charleston, where her mother, Mrs. Tubbs, and the mother's husband, an actor who magnificently called himself Franciscus Decimus Coriolanus William Tubbs, were in Solee's company and became embroiled in a public controversy over back pay. Miss Arnold apparently became an able comedienne, and Dunlap told of her appearance with her husband, David Poe, in a play called *Castle Spectre,* in September 1809. That was after the birth in January in Boston of a son, Edgar Allan.

Of all the theatrical characters who bestrode the American stage in that era I have a special fondness for one named James Fennell, who had achieved fame in England in the great tragic roles. He was evidently a man of some talent, but his temper was fiery and his nature unquiet. When he joined the company in Philadelphia, Thomas Abthorpe Cooper in a fit of pique left it to go to New York. Fennell made so many difficulties for the management in Philadelphia that it had to close down the theatre for a week. He knew how to apologize but could not stay reformed. He joined the Park Theatre company in New York, refused to be contained by it, and presently took off to deliver discourses on the Bible and to refute "the Doctrines of Thomas Paine and others, comprehending historical proofs of the fulfillment of the Prophecies, and Dissertations on the Miracles." Then he began dramatic readings, returned from time to time to a stage that seemed always to have a place for him, devoted himself to odd sidelines like the invention of a salt-making gadget and its promotion, and died years later besotted and neglected.

To see the American theatre of this epoch as it looked to those who attended it we must turn to the testimony of eyewitnesses. Dunlap's history and diary are useful, for he was knowledgeable and honest, but being of the theatre, he was bound to be too lenient toward its peccadilloes. Fortunately, professional criticism was beginning to observe clearly and comment sharply. William Coleman in the *Evening Post* wrote boldly and bluntly, and in the *Morning Chronicle,* Washington Irving, young brother of Peter, the editor, contributed a series of letters in 1802 and 1803 under the nom de plume of Jonathan Oldstyle. Though not yet twenty when he began, Washington Irving had a bright, intelligent eye and a witty, caustic style. From a sampling of his letters we can derive a fair notion of the stage of his time.

"I wish," he once observed, "the manager would use a drop scene at the close of the acts; we might then always ascertain the termination of the piece by the Green Curtain. On this occasion I was indebted to the polite bows of the actors for this pleasing information."

He was galled—aren't we all?—by the chattering of the audience during a performance, no matter in what part of the house it occurred. But listen to him on the behavior of the gallery:

"The noise in this part of the house is somewhat similar to that which prevailed in Noah's Ark; for we have an imitation of the whistles and yells of every kind of animals. . . . And they commenced a discharge of apples, nuts and gingerbread on the heads of the honest folks in the pit." As if, he remarked, the dripping of the candle grease from the chandeliers were not enough of a trial for the gathering in the pit.

"At last the bell again rung," he continued, "and the cry of *down, down, hats off* was the signal for the commencement of the play."

He was impatient with other shortcomings. He complained that characters listed on the bill never appeared on the stage. He was annoyed when performers in the same piece dressed "in the fashions of different ages and countries, so that while one actor is strutting about the stage in the cuirass and helmet of Alexander, another dressed up in a gold lace coat and bag wig . . . is taking snuff in the fashion of one or two centuries back."

He advised actors to employ "less etiquette, less fustian, less buckram." The buckram in some costumes, he remarked, was so stiff that the actors in them could not move. He appealed to the musicians for new music and more of it. He bespoke patience, clean benches and umbrellas for the pit. To the boxes he recommended less affectation, less noise and fewer coxcombs. He pleaded for air and light, crying out against a theatre that was dark and "undergroundish" with a dungeonlike look, and he was not happy to grope through the dismal subterranean passage that leads from the pit to the "purer air of the park." For the whole, inside and out, he demanded drastic reform.

In a letter from an imaginary Andrew Quoz to his pseudonymous Jonathan Oldstyle, Irving, writing with elaborate sarcasm, summed up the stage, the patrons, the players and the futility of the critic:

The theatre, you observe, begins to answer all the purposes of a coffee-house. Here you are right; it is the polite lounge, where the idle and curious resort, to pick up the news of the fashionable world, to meet their acquaintances, and to show themselves off to advantage. As to the dull souls who go for the sake of the play, why, if their attention is interrupted by the conversation of their neighbours, they must bear it with patience; it is a custom authorized by fashion. Persons who go for the purpose of chatting with friends are not to be deprived of their amusement; *they have paid their dollar* and have a right to entertain themselves as well as they can. As to those who are annoyed by their talking, why they need not listen to it; LET THEM MIND THEIR OWN BUSINESS. . . .

In your remarks on the actors, my dear friend, let me beg of you to be cautious. I would not for the world that you should degenerate into a critic. The critics, my dear Jonathan, are the very pests of society; they rob the actor of his reputation—the public of their amusement; they open the eyes of their readers to a full perception of the faults of our performers, they reduce our feelings to a state of miserable refinement, and destroy entirely all the enjoyments in which our coarser sensations delighted. . . . Now, though I confess these critics have reformed the manners of the actors, as well as the tastes of the audience, so that these absurdities are almost banished from the New York stage, yet do I think they have employed a most unwarrantable liberty.

A critic, my dear sir, has no more right to expose the faults of an actor, than he has to detect the deceptions of a juggler, or the impositions of a quack. . . . Hath not an actor eyes, and shall he not WINK? If you censure his follies, does he not complain? If you take away his bread, will he not starve? If you starve him, will he not die? And if you kill him, will not his wife and seven small infants, six at her back and one at her breast, rise up and cry vengeance against you? . . . You will agree with me that, as the actor is the most meritorious and faultless, so is the critic the most cruel and sanguinary character in the world.

CHAPTER VI

"HURRAH FOR REPUBLICAN SIMPLICITY"

W ASHINGTON IRVING disregarded his early writings on the theatre when he sanctioned the publication of his collected works, and he refrained from taking public credit for his share in the composition of some plays by John Howard Payne. There is no doubt about their joint authorship of *Charles the Second, or the Merry Monarch,* which, like some popular successes today, had its initial performance in London, in May 1824, and reached New York in October.

An adaptation of a French play based on another French piece, which may have had an English ancestor, *Charles the Second,* was a comic success. It was regarded as a comedy of manners, but it reads like a romantic costume farce. It reminds me of a libretto for a Donizetti opera buffa. It was the first of Payne's plays in which Irving was aide or partner. Without any sure knowledge of which collaborator suggested what idea or line, students have made the natural assumptions: that Payne, a man of the theatre, contributed the craftsman's skill at construction and Irving, writer of fancy, added freshness and gaiety.

In this story of the playboy king and his night on the town with the roistering Earl of Rochester, it is tempting to be a detective. I would guess that Irving's hand is in a speech like Rochester's advice to the page, Edward, on the proper uses of the heart:

Yes; but I told thee to skim over the surface of beauty, just dipping down your wings, like a swallow, not plumping like a goose—I told you to hover from flower to flower like a butterfly, not to bury yourself in one like a bee. An honest attachment!—What a plebeian phrase!— There's a wife and children in the very sound of it.

I would think that both men relished inventing some of the expletives that issue from the lips of the innkeeper, Captain Copp, erstwhile seafarer, to whose place of refreshment Charles and Rochester come for their fun. Copp is full of phrases like "smite my timbers," "thunder and lightning," "fire and furies," "guns and blunderbusses," "come, come, messmate—I am too old a cruiser to be taken in by so shallow a maneuver." Speaking nostalgically of the habits of sailors, he declares merrily and tolerantly, "I recollect too well what it was to get on shore after a long voyage. The first glimpse of a petticoat—whew! up boarding pikes and grappling irons;" As he realizes that he is in the presence of his daughter, Mary, he pulls up short, "Ahem—no, no, child, mustn't venture in these latitudes."

There is evidence that Irving suggested the comic notion of having Copp often on the verge of a song and never getting it out. Payne reported that "Charles Lamb tells me he can't get Copp's song out of his head, and is very anxious for the rest of it. He says the hiatus keeps him awake o'nights."

Pierre M. Irving, his uncle's biographer, says that Mr. Irving "assisted in pruning the piece," but Payne himself was surely responsible for the scene in which Charles, deserted by Rochester, is left without funds to settle accounts with an angry and threatening Copp. The hand of the shrewd man of the theatre is in the farcical second-act curtain wherein Charles finally escapes through a window but not before stealing a kiss from the beauteous Mary.

Payne, like Dunlap, became a versatile man of the theatre. He fashioned an impressive career in England as well as America. By nature, I would guess, he was nimbler and more worldly than Dunlap, but could also strike a popular note. With a gift for finding material useful for adaptation in a variety of foreign sources, he turned out comedy, romantic tragedy, melodrama, historical drama, farce and opera librettos. He worked assiduously and prolifically, fashioning something like sixty stage works. Yet today he is remembered principally for a song in *Cleri* first sung in 1823 by Maria Tree to a tune by Henry Bishop based on a Sicilian air—"Home, Sweet Home."

Born in New York in 1791 and raised in Boston, Payne was precocious, with a special affinity for the stage. He took part in school theatricals, attended performances at the Federal Theatre, tried his hand at criticism at an incredibly early age and joined another incipient playwright, Samuel Woodworth, six years his senior, in publishing a little journal, called *The Fly*. Like Payne, Woodworth is best known today for a song—"The Old Oaken Bucket."

Payne's father, the headmaster of a Boston school, shared the Puritan distrust of the stage and sent the boy of fourteen to New York to serve an apprenticeship in commerce. Although the lad's activities were policed by a watchful guardian, he found a way to express his passion for the theatre. For some months he wrote and published every Saturday the *Thespian Mirror,* whose high-minded platform was "to promote the interests of the American Drama; and to eradicate false impressions respecting the nature, objects, design, and tendency of theatrical amusements." While still in his teens he moved in the best artistic circles of New York, counting Irving as a friend, and his first play, *Julia, or the Wanderer,* was written and produced at the Park Theatre before his fifteenth birthday. Before his eighteenth birthday he left Union College and became an actor to acclaim in New York, Boston and other towns. The established actors grew envious and intrigued against him. His friends and admirers, however, raised a fund of $2,000 and sent him abroad, where he acted in London and studied the theatre in Paris.

In December 1818, when he was only twenty-one, his *Brutus, or the Fall of Tarquin* was produced. This tragedy was the first by an American to win international success. Edmund Kean as Brutus helped to make a deep impression and in London the play had more than 50 performances in one season. It reached the Park in New York the following March. For more than half a century it served the principal players of the English and American stage: after Kean the Brutuses were Junius Brutus Booth and his son, Edwin, Edwin Forrest and the first of the Wallacks in America, James William.

Brutus is impossibly long, flamboyant and pretentious for our tastes, but for its time it was the shrewd concoction of a man with a flair for the theatre. Payne made no secret of his use of seven older dramas on the subject, taking a scene from this playwright and lines from that, including Voltaire. His trick was that he knew how to transpose, condense and unify.

As a stage craftsman, he did not delude himself about his journeyman work. In a preface to *Therese*, a tear-soaked melodrama from the French, he addressed himself to "my friends the critics" to declare that the piece was "planned for stage effects exclusively, and printed for managers and actors only." Because "the peculiarities of leading performers" and "the restive spirit" of the public had to be considered, he laid it down that it was "almost hopeless to look to the stage of the present day for a permanent literary distinction. An actable play seems to derive its value from what is done more than from what is said, but the great power of literary work consists in what is said, and the manner of saying it. He, therefore, who best knows the stage, can best tell why, in the present temper of the audience, good poets should so often make bad dramatists."

Although his plays are forgotten, Payne has a claim to remembrance as an early spokesman for the dignity and economic justice due the American playwright. In his time, writers for the stage had no national or international protection, and it was to be many decades before they acquired the sanction of copyrights. Payne sold the rights to *Charles the Second* in England for 50 guineas, not bad compensation compared with the pittance he received for some of his plays at home. The largest single sum he derived from the theatre came from a testimonial in his honor late in 1832. Before a gala gathering at the Park, Charles Kemble appeared as Petruchio to his daughter's Katherine; Edwin Forrest played Brutus, and Wallack disported himself as Copp. There were speeches, a full house and proceeds of $7,000 for Payne. In response to other public tributes he reminded his fellow citizens that an American could not earn a living from his stage writings, even if they were successfully performed in his own country.

To understand the miserable position of the playwright it is useful to look at the financial transactions between Edwin Forrest and Robert Montgomery Bird, a writer formed by respected literary models and personal sensitivity, who turned out such works as *The Gladiators,* a play about Spartacus and the struggle against tyranny; *The Broker of Bogota,* an attempt at heroic tragedy on a domestic theme; and *Metamora,* an extensive rewrite of an Indian play by John A. Stone.

Remember that Bird and Forrest were once close friends. Yet Forrest shamelessly shortchanged Bird. It appears that Forrest, who played *The Gladiators* more than 1,000 times, paid Bird $1,000, and compensated the author with a similarly paltry sum for *The Broker of Bogota.*

It was mean-spirited of Forrest not to reward the playwright better than he did for plays that served him long and well. He was even more reprehensible when he prevented their publication. He was not alone in his disregard of the man who provided the basic material. It was the way things were done. Once a playwright sold his play to a manager or an actor, he ceased to have any rights in it. There is on record the experience of James Nelson Barker with a play called *The Embargo, or What News?* He turned the manuscript over to a comedian named Blissett, who performed it in Philadelphia, took it to Baltimore and then sent it to another manager in Boston. Barker not only was ignored but could not even get his manuscript back for printing.

Forrest's obduracy is emphasized by an 1869 exchange of letters, recorded by Quinn, between him and Bird's son. In a desire to publish his late father's plays, Frederick M. Bird wrote tactfully to Forrest, "not at all to discuss the question of ownership, on which we probably might not agree, but simply to inquire your views and intentions in the matter."

Forrest made his "views and intentions" ruthlessly plain, telling the son that "the heirs of the late Dr. R. M. Bird have neither right, title, nor any legal interest whatever in the plays written by him for me." And that was that, until the laws were amended and the Dramatists Guild came into being.

A word about *Metamora*. Although Forrest commissioned Bird to rewrite it and failed to compensate him properly, he probably used John Augustus Stone's original. The author, an actor, had submitted his manuscript for a $500 prize offered by the actor in 1828, and he made much of the role of the noble savage. The play helped to secure his fame, and he played it throughout his long career. Stone, to quote Quinn, "shared in no way in this prosperity." He could not make his way in the theatre and "in despaire threw himself into the Schuylkill River" in 1834. "Forrest," remarks Quinn, "erected a handsome tombstone in his memory."

Despite the Paynes, Barkers, Birds and other writers of varying gifts, the playwright occupied a distinctly secondary role. In intelligent, literate circles it was understood that he was the foundation on which an American theatre must be based. Indeed, no one stated the future of the American playwright better than a woman who was born in Scotland and who lived for a time in America. Frances Wright, whose *Altorf,* based on Swiss history, was played at the Park in 1819, was obviously a remarkable woman. She spoke up for the right of her sex to vote, and she ran a center for freed slaves in Tennessee. She knew the ways of the theatre in America and overseas. Her preface to *Altorf* predicted that the United States "will one day revive the sinking honour of the drama." After noting the decline of English tragedy and its replacement by "stage tricks and fine scenery," she declared that "there is not a stage in England from which the dramatist might breathe the sentiments of an enlightened patriotism and republican liberty. In America alone might such a stage be formed; a stage that should be, like that of Greece, a school of virtue—where all that is noble in sentiment, generous and heroic in action should speak to the hearts of a free people."

Frances Wright was a passionate and sensitive prophet even if it took more than a century to bring her prediction close to reality. In most of the nineteenth century, when America produced novels and essays comprising a remarkable literary coming of age, the theatre offered mediocrity and worse. There were some exceptions, not significant enough to remain stageworthy beyond their time but amusing and instructive to reexamine. The vast majority deserve their oblivion.

Urged on by Andrew Jackson, who declared that "it is time that the principal events in the history of our country were dramatized, and exhibited at the theatres on such days as are set apart as national festivals," writers produced a rash of historical works. They were occasional pieces, dashed off for holidays and other celebrations, and their standard of competence was, if possible, even lower than that of other plays. They dealt with Indians like Metamora and Pocahontas, explorers like de Soto, with colonial history, events of the Revolution, and the fight against the pirates in the Mediterranean. Later contemporary currents were noticed in plays that dealt with the competition between the political parties, the war with Mexico, the Mormon migration, the rush for California gold, and, of course, the burning issue of slavery. The first stage version of *Uncle Tom's Cabin* appeared in 1852 in Troy, New York. In time the *Uncle Tom* show assumed the proportions of a national industry that blanketed the nation before the end of the century and was ubiquitous well into our century. In theatres, under tents, in "improvements" that provided two Topsys and two Little Evas, the nation's insatiable appetite was fed with endless versions and variations. Many born in the early years of the twentieth century had their first exposure to the living theatre in the form of an *Uncle Tom* show. And when these spectacles became ludicrous, they were embellished with obvious hokum and were played for laughs.

In the manner of Royall Tyler's Jonathan in 1787, playwrights, managers and leading performers made capital out of a succession of simple but shrewd, comic but triumphant characters. James H. Hackett, one of our early native comedians, introduced Nimrod Wildfire, a juicy frontier character. Like Forrest, Hackett saw to it that no one but he had possession of the manuscript, and no copy of the play itself, *The Lion of the West*, written by James Kirke

Paulding, remains. Nimrod Wildfire evidently was a herald of the hillbillies who still infest the American entertainment scene.

After Nimrod came a host of native comic characters: Jonathan Ploughboy, the honest, simple farmer, who remained a fond figure of the American stage for half a century; Zachariah Dickerwell, a peddler from Vermont; Jedediah Homebred, Yankee farmhand; Solon Shingle, country teamster; Industrious Doolittle, Solomon Swap, Solomon Gundy, Lot Sap Sago, Deuteronomy Dutiful and Aminadab Slocum. Not content with the exploits of these laugh-provoking figures in their native land, authors and managers transported them to foreign shores. In 1841 there was a play called *Yankee in Poland.*

Since the cities were mushrooming, plays began to reflect their streets and people, but the treatment was romantic, maudlin, superficial and vastly exaggerated. There were plays about crooks and plays about lovable men of the people. Mose the fireman, appearing in a red shirt, plug hat and turned-up trousers, tickled New York when he first walked out on a stage at the Olympic in 1848 in F. S. Chanfran's *A Glance at New York,* and he had a remarkable run of 70 nights. He was too good to lay aside, and in sequel after sequel, he ranged beyond New York and carried on his adventures in foreign lands.

Of the attempts to reflect the social scene in comedy the most effective was Anna Cora Mowatt's *Fashion.* It had its premier at the Park on March 24, 1845, and scored an instant success, holding the stage for 20 successive nights. The dissenting opinion of Edgar Allan Poe, published in the *Broadway Journal* several days after the opening, had little or no effect on the pleased public. Poe thought that *Fashion* was "hackneyed." He wrote, "The day has at length arrived when men demand rationalities in place of conventionalities. It will no longer do to copy, even with absolute accuracy, the whole tone of even so ingenuous and really spirited a thing as *The School for Scandal.* It was comparatively good in its day, but it would be positively bad at the present day, and imitations of it are inadmissible at any day. . . ."

Having blasted *Fashion* for its "deficiency in verisimilitude—in natural art—that is to say, in art based in the natural laws of man's

heart and understanding," Poe, who went to see it performance
after performance, put in a good word for Mrs. Mowatt's play:

It must be understood that we are not condemning Mrs. Mowatt's comedy in particular, but the modern drama in general. Comparatively,
there is much merit in *Fashion* and in many respects . . . it is superior
to any American play.

Let us glance at the play itself. Here is an excerpt from the opening scene in which Zeke, the new Negro servant, consults with
Millinette, the supercilious French maid, in the home of the par-
venu Tiffanys:

ZEKE: Well, now, Missy, what's your own special defunctions?
MILLINETTE: I do not understand, Monsieur Zeke.
ZEKE: Den I'll amplify. What's de nature ob your exclusive services?
MILLINETTE: Ah, oui! je comprends. I am Madame's femme de cham-
bre—her lady's maid, Monsieur Zeke. I teach Madame les modes de
Paris, and Madame set de fashion for all New York. You see, Mon-
sieur Zeke, dat it is me, moi-même, dat do lead de fashion for all de
American beau monde!
ZEKE: Yah! yah! yah! I hab de idea by de heel. Well now, p'raps you
can 'lustrify my officials?

I hope you have the idea by the heel. Mrs. Tiffany, Mrs. Mowatt's
foolish, affected matron, appears and inquires for the new valet.
"I'm rather sorry that he is black," she observes, "but to obtain a
white American for a domestic is almost impossible; and they call
this a free country." Thou shouldst be living now, Mrs. Tiffany,
and seeking any kind of domestic service. Representative of the
enduring virtues is Adam Trueman, seventy-two, just come from
Catteraugus "to see you and yours" and "strong as a hickory and
every whit as sound."

"Let me tell you, Sir," Mrs. Tiffany tells him, "that liveries are
the fashion," whereupon bluff, upright Trueman retorts, "The
fashion, are they? To make men wear the badge of servitude in a
free land—that's the fashion, is it? Hurrah for republican simplicity! I will venture to say now, that you have your coat of arms, too!"

When Jolimaitre, a valet masquerading all too transparently as
a count, ticks off Trueman with "Where did you say you belonged,

my friend? Dug out of the ruins of Pompeii, eh?" that worthy demolishes him with "I belong to a land in which I rejoice to find that you are a foreigner."

Good old Trueman! How he must have brought cheers from the throats of honest burghers, perhaps even fashionable ones able to point the finger at others, not themselves. His style is pious and a bit high-flown but hardly without point:

Fashion! And pray what is fashion, madam? An agreement between certain persons to live without using their souls! to substitute etiquette for virtue—decorum for purity— manners for morals! To affect a shame for the works of their Creator! and expend all their rapture upon the works of their tailors and dressmakers!

At the end, Jolimaitre, revealed as an impostor, expresses his disappointment "in America, where you pay homage to titles while you profess to scorn them—where Fashion makes the basest coin current—where you have no kings, no princes, no nobility. . . ."

Trueman promptly sets him right: "But we *have* kings, princes and nobles in abundance—of Nature's stamp, if not of Fashion's— we have honest men, warmhearted and brave, and we have women —gentle, fair, and true, to whom no title could add nobility."

Do you see why the audiences were delighted with Mrs. Mowatt's play? Nor was it deficient in showmanship. In the fourth act it provided a ball with the party dancing the polka and the couples promenading arm in arm to supper at an elegant table. Although in the minority, Poe, of course, was right. The plot of *Fashion* is elementary, the dialogue obvious and the humor crude. But compared with the carpets, ottomans, chandeliers and conservatories of other "inane and despicable" comedies, *Fashion,* Poe recognized, had some right to success.

Because it ridiculed the pretentious ways of the world in a time when the theatre was not given to criticism, it was comparatively tolerable, even to persons with standards, like Poe. To us it reads like a naïve period piece. In 1924 it was revived at the Provincetown Theatre in New York, eventually moved uptown and had a run of 235 performances.

Why? Because the play was mocked outrageously. The absurdities that the passage of fourscore years had made archaic were further exaggerated. The comedy in *Fashion* was embellished into a lampoon of the play and its time. The actors, in the words of John Corbin, drama critic of *The New York Times* in 1924, trumpeted their asides at the audience through their hollowed palms and played a veritable hopscotch across the stage. The audience laughed because it felt superior, but it was not—and could not—be seeing Mrs. Mowatt's work as she and her audience saw it.

Apart from *Fashion,* Mrs. Mowatt deserves a word. At fifteen she was married, at eighteen she incurred symptoms of tuberculosis; after her first husband's financial reverses she did not hesitate to become the breadwinner, first as a writer and then as an actress, a career in which, without preliminaries, she made a deep impression, even on an exigent observer like Poe. She appeared in London, where *Fashion* was presented to divided opinion. She returned to America to act and to tour, enduring the freezing steamboats, the numbing stagecoaches and the rattling railroads to keep her scheduled appointments. She was a woman of determination and courage. Her credentials of respectability helped the theatre on its path to acceptance as a tolerable, even honorable profession.

CHAPTER VII

STARS AND SPECTACLES

As it was in the beginning and as it largely is now, the theatre in the first half of the nineteenth century was a commercial enterprise. It had to support itself or go under. The emphasis inevitably was on players rather than plays. After the interregnum of the War of 1812, when the importation of English players slowed to a trickle, the influx broadened into a stream. Theatres, which were as subject to fire as the populace to epidemics, disappeared overnight and were replaced in a few months. The Park, most stable and respected in New York in its various incarnations, grew to a capacity of 2,000. The Bowery, which became the seat of Edwin Forrest's power, had accommodations for 3,000, and the price scale separated the refined element in the boxes from the vulgar crowd in the pit. Philadelphia retained its autonomy and character as a theatrical community until 1825, when the center of talent and influence shifted permanently to New York.

The dominance of New York became a fact despite the growing population elsewhere, despite the presence of theatres and companies in other parts of the country and despite the increase of touring by managers and companies whose hardihood and intrepidity matched those of the pioneers. In New York there were new theatres like the Chatham Garden and the Lafayette as well as the Bowery to challenge the primacy of the Park, and later came the

Olympic and others and for a few months in 1845 Chapman's Floating Theatre, called the Temple of the Muses, which, fortified by a well-equipped bar, was moored on the Hudson River off Canal, Chambers and Delancey streets. In New York the showboat was a curiosity; on the rivers of the West it was a handy way to reach audiences in a wide area.

Not everyone rejoiced as the theatre spread its tentacles farther north on Manhattan. When Thomas S. Hamblin, a restless manager, cooked up a scheme in 1845 to raise $100,000 for a new theatre by borrowing $1 from each of 100,000 persons in return for scrip guaranteeing a dollar's worth of admission to his finished house, the *Broadway Journal* jumped on him.

"We should regret exceedingly," said an unsigned editorial, "to see a theatre erected in Broadway, more especially such a theatre as Mr. Hamblin would probably put up. Considering the effect which theatres invariably have in the neighborhood where they have been built, we should expect that the owners of the property would protest the erection of one in that noble thoroughfare."

Warming to his subject, the writer—was it Poe or one of the other editors, C. F. Briggs or H. C. Watson?—went on to give us a contemporary's disenchanted picture of the theatre as the century approached its midpoint:

The little Olympic is probably the best conducted theatre in the city; but we see it surrounded by dram shops, billiard rooms, and other equivocal resorts for the profligate and idle. We see no necessity of making a theatre a drinking house, a gambling house and a something else house, as well as a play house, but there seems to be the real unities of the drama, and pea-nuts and punch are as essential concomitants to the acting drama as tin foil and rouge. It is one of the strangest things in life, that every institution has been modified by time excepting the theatre. It is just as dissolute now as it was in the days of Charles the Second. Though governed by no laws, and its professors reckoned as vagrants, it is one of the most conservative institutions among us. . . . Mr. [Edmund] Simpson is the only man in New York who has remained unchanged during the past twenty years, and his theatre is the only building in the city which has not been renovated. All the churches have been remodeled; preachers have changed their style, their theology, and their habits; society has suffered a dozen revolutions; the whole order of living has been reversed; we have altered our food, drink, habits and even our speech; cotillions have gone out, and the Polka has come in; finger glasses and silver forks have become common in hotels; drunkenness has grown fashionable; the national name has been changed; new streets have been built; Texas has been annexed; cheap books have been invented; hanging is almost abolished; the Croton river runs through the streets;—but Mr. Simpson and the Park remain the same, as unchangeable as the eternal sphinx of the desert. He looks as gloomy and saturnine as he used to look when he played Charles Surface in a claret colored coat and straw colored shorts; and his theatre is as dingy, as English, and as expensive as ever. The filthy saloons, with their red moreen curtains and yellow refreshment sellers remain unchanged, and probably will remain so for the next century; and the same plays are presented on the stage that were witnessed by our grandmothers and our grandmothers' grandmothers. There is no church in christendom half so conservative as the theatre: there are isms in every thing but the drama, which has never known a schism. Mr. Dinneford, to be sure, got up a Greek tragedy the other day, which was stepping backward a thousand years or two, instead of moving forward, as any one must do who would produce a sensation in the drama; and it appears that he lost twenty-five hundred dollars by his devotion to the classics, which should be a caution to other managers to let the classics alone.

We have no reason to believe that Mr. Hamblin would break adrift from the legitimate drama, or that he would do any better in Broadway than he has heretofore done in the Bowery; and therefore we would rather see him fail than succeed in his present undertaking: not that we wish him any ill as an individual, but as a manager he cannot but do harm in the community. He has had a large theatre under his control for many years, but he has done nothing to elevate the drama or correct the corrupt tastes of his audiences. If Mr. Hamblin must have a theatre, let him by all means stick to the Bowery. He would be a fish out of water in Broadway, and his theatre would mar the beauty of our magnificent thoroughfare.

We shall have a theatre in New York by and by, we have no doubt, that will reflect the manners of the people and satirise their vices, but it must be under the control of a manager to the manor born.

Show business was bursting into flower. The competition for the dollar spent on entertainment was intensifying. Potpourris including animal acts and other novelties made their appeal, and they led to what came to be known as variety and vaudeville. Minstrel shows were in the offing when T. D. Rice, a comedian, did a comic act based on an old slave whom he called Jim Crow; his routines in blackface were so popular that he became famous as Jim Crow Rice. In 1843 a quartet that included Dam Emmett, the man who wrote that superbly jaunty tune, "Dixie," performed in blackface as the Virginia Minstrels and within a few years minstrel shows, with their interlocutors and their comic end men, Mr. Bones and Mr. Tambo, were everywhere, in some cases bloated in size, in the American tradition of inflation, to companies of forty.

In 1825 Italian opera made a splash at the Park when the Garcias were brought from Europe with the active help of Lorenzo da Ponte, once Mozart's librettist and now a very old man teaching Italian at Columbia College. In 1835 P. T. Barnum began his operations—one almost says depredations—as showman and salesman extraordinary, starting with freaks and curiosities, foraging into theatrical ventures and dazzling coups like the importation of Jenny Lind and making it tough for other merchants of entertainment to keep up with his resourcefulness and gusto.

Increasingly the theatre placed its reliance on the drawing power of an actor or on some breathtaking spectacle. In 1816 gaslights, probably the first in an American theatre, were installed in Philadelphia's Chestnut, and the novelty stimulated attendance. In 1830 *The Railroad,* a play by George Washington Parker Custis, son of George Washington's stepson, contrived to have a locomotive roll onto a Philadelphia stage, an effect that caused the audience to gape with pleasure, especially when the engine whistle tooted as it made its exit.

Do you regard horse opera as an invention of the silent films and a preserve of television? In 1824 the Park Theatre in New York came up with an unexpected hit that ran for 42 performances, a stunning achievement in those days. Called *The Cataract of the Ganges,* it was a melodrama in which the leading lady rode her horse to safety with a formidable leap across a cataract.

A few months later the Park had another triumph, which registered 30 performances, and this one, *Cherry and Fair Star,* was a forerunner of spectaculars with music that led through *The Black Crook* to the *Ziegfeld Follies*. The *Mirror* of January 15, 1825, offered a description of the fantastic mélange of effects assembled for the delectation of wide-eyed theatregoers. The first scene opened on "the avis grove or fairy abode." One saw a forest with a waterfall in motion. The waterfall, by the way, caught fire and burned, thanks to backstage carelessness, but the audience sat and watched as if the blaze were planned. In view of the high incidence of theatre fires in those days, one can only marvel at the audience's assumption that things were going according to plan. The opening scene was embellished by birds of various plumage, which warbled happily when the fairy queen descended "in her ambient car." In other scenes there were such marvels as an Etruscan villa and a tree that bloomed and unfolded its broad leaves to the sun, the port of Cyprus with galleys riding in the harbor and with water seemingly covering the entire stage as a Grecian galley carrying leading players sailed in and off "amid the acclamations of the spectators on the ramparts"; an enchanted wood, a fairy vision, a dragon spitting fire, a huge magical butterfly that carried the heroine off the stage and a frozen Caucasian mountain which changed to a temple of icicles and then to the palace of Cyprus.

One can see why the box set with its simulation of rooms and attention to details of furnishings made so great an impression when it was used for Dion Boucicault's comedy *London Assurance* in 1841 at the Covent Garden in London and the Park in New York. The comedy was regarded as the best of its time, which is ambiguous praise, but the production became epochal. Hit-or-miss staging that employed any bit of furniture or prop that happened to be handy became as intolerable as stereotypes of setting. The mounting of *London Assurance* fixed a new standard for "great verisimilitude," and the sight of rich drawing rooms that faithfully followed models one could visit, if one were lucky or rich or well-born enough, in fine London or New York homes delighted playgoers for decades.

But spectacular effects or believably sumptuous ones were not sufficient to keep the audiences coming. Nor were many of the plays, old or new, compelling enough. Actors were the chief attraction, and the star system began to fasten its grip on the theatre. A star named Lydia Kelly insisted on being paid in cash at each performance, and there were nights when there was nothing left for the others in the company. Dependence on big names undermined companies that had been sustained on common effort, for once a theatre offered the public the temptation of a star it risked disaster when the great name was withdrawn.

Walt Whitman, writing in the Brooklyn *Eagle* in 1846 and 1847, railed repeatedly that "one of the curses of the Park, and indeed of nearly all theatres now, is the star system." Yet he hailed the art of those actors he admired so enthusiastically that, willy-nilly, he contributed his meed to the system he loathed.

Like Poe, Whitman had a dream of what the theatre should be. Lamenting the fact that the drama "had been kept absolutely stationary for a hundred years, while its sister arts have rapidly flitted by and left it out of sight," Poe evoked in 1845 a vision of a drama of the future:

The next step may be the electrification of all mankind by the representation of a play that may be neither tragedy, comedy, farce, opera, pantomime, melodrama or spectacle, as we now comprehend these terms, but which may retain some portion of the idiosyncratic excellence of each, while it introduces a new class of excellence as yet unnamed because as yet undreamed-of in the world.

And Whitman, who campaigned against puffery by reviewers who "were the slaves of the paid puff system" or who were not granted the freedom to speak what they knew to be the truth, lashed at the debased state of the theatre. How contemporary his jeremiads sound!

"Of all 'low' places where vulgarity (not only on the stage, but in front of it) is in the ascendant, and bad taste carries the day with hardly a pleasant point to mitigate its coarseness, the New York theatres (except the Park) may be put down . . . at the top of the heap!" he wrote. "The Park, once in a while, gives a fine play, performed by meritorious actors and actresses. The Park is still very far, however, from being what we might reasonably expect in the principal dramatic establishment of the metropolis. It is but a third-rate imitation of the London theatres. It gives us the cast-off dramas, and the unengaged players of Great Britain; and of these dramas and players, like garments which come second hand from gentleman to valet, everything fits awkwardly. . . ."

Whitman envisioned the theatre's purification in terms of national affirmation:

English managers, English actors, and English plays . . . must be allowed to die away among us, as usurpers of our stage. The drama of this country *can* be the mouth-piece of freedom, refinement, liberal philanthropy, beautiful love for all our brethren, polished manners and elevated good taste. It can wield potent sway to destroy any attempt at despotism—it can attack and hold up to scorn bigotry, fashionable affectation, avarice and all unmanly follies. Youth may be warned by its fictitious portraits of the evils of unbridled passions. . . . New York City is the only spot in America where such a revolution could be attempted, too. With all our servility to foreign fashions, there is at the heart of the American masses there, a lurking propensity toward what is original, and has a stamped American character of its own. . . .

As to the particular details of the system which should supplant theatricals as they now exist, . . . that effort must be made by a man or woman of no ordinary talent—with a clear comprehensiveness of what is wanted—not too great a desire for pecuniary profit—little respect for old modes and the accustomed usage of the stage—an *American* in heart and hand. . . . The assistance of writers of genius will of course be required. . . . Until such a person comes forward, and works out such a reform, theatricals in this country will continue to languish, and theatre be generally more and more deserted by men and women of taste . . . as has been the case for eight or ten years past.

Whitman was right about some of the "unengaged players of Great Britain." But he was wrong, too, for America benefited from seeing the best England had to offer. Edmund Kean, most glamorous actor of his time, made his first visit to the United States in 1820 because he had got himself into an awkward personal situation at home. He turned the trip into an enormously profitable affair. Paid 50 pounds a performance plus a share of the profits, he played *Richard III, Hamlet, Othello, The Merchant of Venice* and Payne's *Brutus* in New York to tremendous excitement, and his take was more than 100 pounds a night. He was triumphant in Philadelphia and Boston and in a return engagement in New York. In May he went back to Boston where he ran into serious trouble. Attendance was poor, probably because Bostonians considered the season over, and Kean refused to go on one evening when he saw how sparsely the theatre was occupied. Boston felt insulted; Kean's offense haunted him when he tried another American tour in 1825. The scandal of his amorous adventures, which led him to leave England for this second tour, did nothing to make his path easier. He was obliged to apologize to the American public for his private behavior and to beg for sympathy and understanding.

Nevertheless, Kean's two American visits were important in raising the public's sights. The great star of London's Drury Lane was a magnetic, tempestuous performer. A contemporary said of him, "He is but a small man and from the gentleness of his manners no one would anticipate the actor who excels in bursts of passion." If you study Kean's portraits, you are impressed by the long nose, fiery black eyes with their intense look and the curly black hair. The paintings suggest a man possessed by demons, and his acting, evidently uneven, could erupt in demonic fashion. Americans no doubt had a chance to appreciate Coleridge's dictum that seeing Kean on the stage was like reading Shakespeare by flashes of lightning.

In 1821, Junius Brutus Booth, father of the acting family that made political as well as dramatic history, reached America. He appeared first in Richmond and was hailed enthusiastically. At the Park in New York he began as Richard III, and the comparison with Kean, whose performance Booth's resembled, was not to Booth's credit.

James William Wallack, founder of another honorable theatrical family in America, arrived in 1818, to make his debut as Macbeth. He was only twenty-four when he came, but he had good looks, talent and intelligence. He grew corpulent but never lost the "suavity and polish" of his "private manners," as a contemporary account put it. "It is true," wrote the *Albion* some years after his American debut, "that some of his former brilliance and fire is diminished, but we have in its stead a more chastened and more accurately delineated character." For more than four decades he was a prominent actor and manager. He was evidently one of the former Englishmen Whitman had in mind, yet several years after Whitman's diatribe Wallack took over Brougham's Lyceum, refurbished it and named it Wallack's and began several decades of scrupulous productions. Nothing like this theatre, according to Odell, "had existed in New York previously to 1852, nothing quite like it existed after 1880."

It is difficult to sort out from the conflicting testimony of contemporaries just what were the virtues and vices of the acting in New York. George Templeton Strong, an intelligent New Yorker who kept a diary faithfully, observed in 1859, after an evening at a French play by French players, "They tell me it's second- or third-rate French acting, but it is far above our standard in good taste, simplicity, attention to detail, and naturalness or reality."

The English-born comedian Charles Mathews, the younger, pleased Strong in 1857. "He is far the first of the actors I've seen, quite free from conventionality and stage manner. All his pieces, moreover, seem refined and wholesome." His good opinion of Mathews' acting did not keep Strong from thinking harshly of his personal life, as this entry the next year reveals:

Apropos of individual folly, Charles Mathews has just married that showy little piece of harlotry, Mrs. Lizzie Weston Davenport, with whom he's been playing at Burton's, and who's just divorced on her husband's suit. He's quite betwattled and fascinated by her. The marriage is a mere nullity, but before it was solemnized, the lady had shewn her lover, as she had shewn many others, that she cared little for forms and ceremonies. It's a pity, but I suppose his first wife, Me. Vestris [Lucia Elizabeth Vestris, a theatre manager in her own right] was not much better.

Mathew's father, Charles Mathews, had arrived in the United States in 1822 and had been hailed by the *Post* as "a genuine son of Comus, exhibiting talents of the first order." He had won fame in England in a one-man show called *At Homes*. He would begin quietly, seated at a table, illustrating aspects of English or Continental life with a song or anecdote, gradually shift to the impersonation of a variety of characters, including the use of ventriloquism.

One imagines that a modern counterpart, in versatility and variety, would be a solo performance by Danny Kaye.

In 1822 Stephen Price, the manager of the Park, thought that Mathews' *At Homes* would baffle New Yorkers. He preferred to introduce his new star in plays and farces, and he was right. Mathews, according to the *Post*, "acquitted himself in such a manner as to produce not only universal delight but no small surprise." When he tried *Trip to Paris*, which was one of his *At Homes*, he was, as he wrote his wife, "sorry for it." The theatre was "quite as large as that of Covent Garden" and "too full to obtain the sort of silent attention" that he required.

The stars were many in the years before the Civil War. A rising group of native-born actors included James H. Hackett, Edwin Forrest, E. L. Davenport, Charlotte Cushman and, later, Edwin Booth.

Charles Kean was disappointing to start with. Philip Hone, another indefatigable diarist, could not "perceive that he inherits any great proportion of his father's genius." The *Mirror* saw a resemblance to the fiery Edmund "in the roll of the eye, the sneer of the lip and the whole contour of the face and form." He became, according to Odell, "by dint of hard work and scholarly attainment, one of the most distinguished of English players and producers." But hear Whitman: "He has not that indescribable facility of fitness to the character . . . not the least particle of the 'divine fire' which all real artists have." As for Ellen Tree, Charles Kean's wife, Whitman was severe:

Of the lady truth will not allow much more favorable mention. . . . She *was* a young woman of genius. [Now] she is merely the frame and thews of that time, with none of its pliant grace, its smoothness, its voluptuous swell—(merely ex-Tree and *not* extra).

About Charlotte Cushman there was no disagreement. A native of Boston and of a good, though impoverished family, she tried singing, lost her voice and went into acting. At twenty-one in 1836 she faced a New York audience, a tall, plain girl with little prospect of success. Her style was subdued, which marked it immediately from the flamboyant techniques in fashion. In 1845 she went to

England for five years and returned as the most famous tragic actress of the English-speaking stage. In her early stage career she played male roles like Romeo. "Her homely features and lack of feminine charm," said Odell, "drove her to masculine characters; her success in them helped to perpetuate throughout the best years of the century the very bad custom of female Romeos, Hamlets, etc." One wonders today, in an age when we are all amateur psychoanalysts, whether Miss Cushman's motives and drives were that simple. Looking at a contemporary lithograph of her, one sees a round face, wide-set eyes, straight brows, small mouth, smooth hair parted at the center—a pleasant, intelligent face on a sturdy body.

Whitman was her devoted admirer. "She is *no* 'second Siddons'; she is *herself,* and that is far, far better," he exclaimed. "From what we have seen and heard, (and we consider ourselves no 'chicken' about stage matters) Charlotte Cushman is ahead of any player that ever yet trod the stage. Fanny Kemble, Ellen Tree, Miss Phillips, etc.,—Macready, Kean, Kemble, etc.—all had, or have, their merits; all played well, and their acting has afforded many an intelligent man and woman a rich treat. But Miss Cushman assuredly bears away the palm from them all. . . . She seems to identify herself so completely with the character she is playing; she loses, for the nonce, every attribute, except those which enter into the making up of what she is to portray."

On and off the stage these players exuded personality. Fanny Kemble was evidently a redoubtable character. In later years she moved through New York's social circles like the flagship of a fleet. Married to Pierce Butler of Georgia, she preferred to be addressed as Miss Kemble rather than Mrs. Butler. George Templeton Strong notes his reaction to her in 1859 when she appeared in a one-woman reading of Shakespeare's *The Tempest:*

She is fat, but not comely. . . . Vocal resources wonderful. She has half a dozen voices in her; drew a separate stop for each character; produced a deep, sullen brute roar and snarl for Caliban that seemed an impossibility from any feminine windpipe. Prospero's tone was grand, and nothing could be more tender and gentle than her Miranda. Her tipsy Stefano was transcendant . . . and all her comedy was rendered with a spirit of fun I did not in the least expect.

The passions and furious loyalties that stars of the stage could rouse in this era are epitomized in the rivalry that led to the bloody Astor Place Theatre riots in 1849. The actors involved were Edwin Forrest, chief American tragedian, and William Charles Macready, greatly admired English tragedian. Both men made their first New York appearances in 1826—Forrest as a twenty-year-old Othello and Macready, particularly successful as a mature, tragic Macbeth. Forrest was handsome of face and figure; his look was Byronic and he cultivated the body beautiful with a regimen of exercise. While admiring his attributes of robust force, deep and penetrating voice and carefully calculated movements, and acknowledging that he was "a deserved favorite of the public," Whitman warned of the danger that he has "become identified with a sort of American style of acting" and that "the crowd of vapid imitators may spread all the faults of that style." Whitman distrusted acting that sought to "tickle the ears of the groundlings." He warned against "the loud-mouthed ranting style—the tearing of everything to shivers."

We are left in little doubt of the essentials of Forrest's style, even when we read William Rounseville Alger's biography commissioned and approved by the actor.

Forrest, Alger tells us, "disliked essentially bad or ignoble characters. . . . He loved to stand out in some commanding form of virtue, heroism or struggle, battling with trials that would appall common souls, setting a great example and evoking enthusiasm. This was his glory." In describing his impersonation of Richelieu, Alger said, "Never was transition more powerful than from the minor wail of lamentation with which Forrest here began to the glorious eloquence of the climax, where his vocal thunderbolts drove home to every heart the lesson of conscious greatness and courage." His Hamlet, Alger opined, "stirred the soul like the grandest chords in the Requiem of Mozart, thrilling it with sublime premonitions of its own infirmity."

Forrest's style, in short, was all thunder and lightning, compounded of contrivance and effect—a style that, I am sure, would be regarded today as a caricature of acting. Macready, on the other hand, was closer to our spirit. Whitman called Macready's "the mental style" and he reported that the actor "touched the heart, the soul, the feelings, the inner blood and nerves of the audience. The ordinary actor struts and rants away, and his furious declamation begets a kind of reciprocal excitement among those who hear him. We have known the time when an actual awe and dread crept over a large body assembled in the theatre, when Macready merely appeared, walking down the stage, a king. He was a king—not because he had a tinsel-gilded crown, and the counterfeit robe, but because he then dilated his heart with the attributes of majesty, and they looked forth from his eyes, and appeared in his walk."

If Forrest was overbearing and egotistical, Macready was severe, aloof and patronizing. Returning to the United States in 1843 after a long absence, he took turns starring in classic tragedies at the Park with Wallack, Forrest and J. B. Booth. The next season Macready's Hamlet was coolly received and he confided in his diary that he had played "in defiance of the dullest audience" and had been obliged to contend with "the coarse, vulgar wretches that are the editors." However, he consoled himself with earnings of 5,000 pounds in a year's American tour.

Forrest sought to storm London in 1845 and fell short of glory. He and his friends were convinced that Macready was responsible for hostile receptions. Thereafter his hatred of his rival deepened. When Macready was announced to play Macbeth at the Astor Place Theatre on May 7, 1849, Forrest billed himself in the same role on the same night at the Bowery. Forrest's adherents made a rout of Macready's performance. The speeches were drowned in the shouting, hissing and whistling. The actors were pelted with eggs, fruits and vegetables. Chairs were flung onto the stage and asafoetida was tossed down from the gallery.

Macready prudently decided that he would play in New York no longer. But leading citizens, headed by Washington Irving, were outraged and appealed to him to complete his engagement. Macready agreed to appear on May 10, and the battle front was broadened and intensified along class lines. George Templeton Strong, who represented the respectable elements and whose home was not far from the Astor Place Theatre, described Forrest's supporters as "the Unwashed" from "the Bowery side."

Macready managed to complete the performance, but the riot

outside the Astor Place Theatre could only be quelled with the help of the police and the militia. The casualty list was worthy of a skirmish in a full-scale war—22 killed and 36 injured. Strong, a spectator, wrote in his diary the next day that it was "a real battle, for the b'hoys fought well and charged up to the line of infantry after they had been fired upon. Prospects of a repetition of the performances tonight on a larger scale, for the blackguards swear they'll have vengeance. The houses of the gentlemen who signed the invitation to Macready to perform last night threatened. . . . I'm going up now to clean my pistols, and if possible to get my poor wife's portrait out of harm's way."

A pamphlet was published by H. M. Ramsey immediately after the riot. On its cover were these angry words:

Account of the Terrific and Fatal Riot at the
    New York Astor Place Opera House
        on the night of May 10, 1849 with the
Quarrels of Forrest and Macready
    Including all the causes which led to that
        AWFUL TRAGEDY!
Wherein an infuriated mob was quelled by the Public Authorities
    and Military with its mournful termination in the
    SUDDEN DEATH OR MUTILATION OF MORE THAN
    FIFTY CITIZENS
    with full and authentic particulars
LET JUSTICE BE DONE THOUGH THE HEAVENS FALL!

To give you an idea of the emotions that inflamed the contending forces, here are excerpts from the pamphlet:

On the night of the tenth of May, 1849, the Empire City, the great metropolis of the Union, was the scene of one of those horrors of civilization, which for a time make the great heart of humanity stop in its beatings. In the darkness of night, thousands of citizens were gathered in a central square of the most aristocratic quarter of New York—gathered around one of its most conspicuous and magnificent edifices, the Astor Place Opera House. . . .

Around this edifice, we say, a vast crowd was gathered. On the stage the English actor Macready was trying to play the part of MACBETH, in which he was interrupted by hisses and hootings, and encouraged by the cheers of a large audience, who had crowded the house to sustain him. On the outside a mob was gathering, trying to force an entrance into the house, and throwing volleys of stones at the barricaded windows. In the house the police were arresting those who made the disturbance—outside they were driven back by volleys of paving stones.

In the midst of this scene of clamor and outrage, was heard the clatter of a troop of horses approaching the scene. "The military—the military are coming!" . . . Further on was heard the quick tramp of companies of infantry, and there was seen the gleam of bayonets. A cry of rage burst from the mob. The appearance of an armed force seemed to inspire them with a sudden fury. They ceased storming the Opera House and turned their volleys against the horsemen. Amid piercing yells and execrations, men were knocked from their horses, the untrained animals were frightened, and the force was speedily routed, and could not afterwards be rallied to perform any efficient service.

Now came the turn of the infantry. They marched down the sidewalk in a solid column; but had no sooner taken up a position for the protection of the house than they were assailed with volleys of missiles. Soldiers were knocked down and carried off wounded. Officers were disabled. An attempt to charge with the bayonet was frustrated by the dense crowd seizing the muskets. . . . At last the awful word was given to fire—there was a gleam of sulphurous light, a sharp quick rattle, and here and there in the crowd a man sank . . . with a deep groan or a death rattle. Then came a more furious attack, and a wild yell of vengeance! Then the rattle of another death-dealing volley. . . . The ground was covered with killed and wounded—the pavement stained with blood. A panic seized the multitude, which broke and scattered in every direction. In the darkness of the night, yells of rage, screams of agony, and dying groans were mingled together. Groups of men took up the wounded and the dead, and conveyed them to the neighboring apothecary shops, station-houses, and the hospital.

The horrors of the night can never be described. We looked over the scene that misty midnight. The military . . . were grimly guarding the Opera House. Its interior was a rendezvous and a hospital for the wounded military and police. Here and there around the building . . . were crowds of men talking in deep tones of indignation. There were little processions moving off with the dead or mutilated bodies of their friends and relations. A husband, uttering frenzied curses, followed his mortally wounded wife to the hospital. An aged mother found her only son . . . in the agonies of death. Many a wife sat watching at home, in terror and alarm for her absent husband. . . .

Succeeding generations of Americans have been stirred to frantic exhibitions of anger and adulation, but not even the Frankie Sinatras, Johnny Rays, Elvis Presleys or the Beatles have got the public that whipped up.

CHAPTER VIII

THE PENDULUM SWINGS

Fᴿᴼᴹ ɪᴛs ʙᴇɢɪɴɴɪɴɢs the United States was a mighty releaser of energies, and in the second half of the nineteenth century its driving forces erupted as if propelled by the unimaginable thrusting power of the next century's split atom. The sources of these energies were diverse: the increased tempo of industrialization, the vast frontiers that remained to be opened, the infusion of a steady stream of immigrants fleeing hunger and oppression and seeking work, food, liberty and individual dignity. The Civil War consumed men and substance and left ugly lesions that even now remain to be plucked out, but it did not stay the country's pressure to expand. Nor did scandal, corruption, maladministration, or the gigantic plunders of the robber barons. Booms and busts alternated with what was regarded in those years as the inevitability of death and taxes. Some grew rich, honestly as well as dishonestly, while many more remained mired in poverty and ignorance. Self-interest vied with idealism and often triumphed.

The theatre reflected the temper of the land and its people. It grew in size and spread across the continent as the population multiplied and settled the wide plains, high mountains and relatively virgin West Coast. When the iron rails were joined to knit the country after 1869, the theatre quickly took advantage of the better opportunity to penetrate everywhere. Stars had found it expedient and profitable to travel from one permanent company to another. Now it was possible to move entire troupes with all their equipment as units. Thus the self-contained touring attraction, usually a single play led by a star supported by a company assembled to keep cost low rather than standards high, became the pattern.

The results were unfortunate but unavoidable, given a theatrical life based on individual enterprise and the necessity to make a profit. Stock companies had provided a focus of local pride and a center where actors could learn their craft. Since these were repertory groups, performers had a chance to play all sorts of roles, from classic to contemporary. When they could not afford to retain the services of stars except for guest engagements, they began to collapse under the impact of the traveling troupe's competition.

The man held responsible for devising the idea of touring a complete company in a single work was Dion Boucicault, that remarkably fertile theatre figure of the nineteenth century. He left his imprint on many aspects of our dramatic life—as writer, actor, manager and propagandist. As a playwright he had every reason to wonder how he could outsmart the literary and theatrical pirates, and when the notion came to him to move plays from town to town as a package, he quickly embraced it.

Like a number of American-born playwrights, Boucicault was in the forefront of the struggle to get laws passed protecting the work of playwrights. Robert Montgomery Bird and George Henry Boker had seen to it that such bills were presented in Congress, but in 1856, thanks to Boucicault's joining the battle, a copyright law finally was passed. It gave the author "along with the sole right to print and publish the said composition, the sole right also to act, perform or represent the same." The law, unfortunately, was pitted with loopholes. It required only the filing of a title and not the full text. Tricky operators found that it was possible to evade the intent of the law by stealing the characters, situations and lines of a play simply by labeling them with a fresh title. Nevertheless, the legislation was a useful first step, for it acknowledged legally the author's right in his own work—a creative product achieved a preliminary sanction as property.

As the nation grew, theatres mushroomed. It became a matter of pride for any community, large or small, that fancied its position in its region, to have its own "op'ry house." Some were crude affairs. Others, like those thrown up in booming mining centers of Virginia City, Nevada, home of the Comstock Lode, Aspen, Colorado, and Central City, Colorado, were well equipped, comfortable and attractive in the manner of Europe's provincial theatres and opera houses.

In Boston a grand new theatre, to replace the Federal burned out in 1852, was opened on Washington Street in 1854. It had accommodations for 3,000 patrons, elegant lobbies and staircases, convenient lounges, a large and modern stage and a cut-glass chandelier as impressive as any in Europe's famous pleasure domes. For almost half a century this theatre was the platform of the elite in the performing arts. Here in the late 1860's one could encounter a *Macbeth* in which Edwin Booth played Macbeth in English while his Lady Macbeth, Fanny Janauschek, spoke in German. In succeeding generations only opera would tolerate such mixtures with a Chaliapin singing Boris in Russian at the Metropolitan while the rest of the cast sang in Italian or with a Leonard Warren singing Rigoletto in Italian at the Bolshoi in Moscow while his Russian colleagues sang in their own tongue.

In Salt Lake City the Mormons reared a theatre in 1862 that not only was the most impressive building in the young community but may very well have been the nation's first structure dedicated to Thespis put up by a church. Henry Miller, the actor, called this house "a Cathedral in the Desert," and it became for half a century a favorite stopping place for the great and near great of the theatre. Here in one of the earliest stock companies was Annie Adams Kiskadden, and here her daughter, Maude Adams, less than a year old, made her debut on a stage in her mother's arms.

Out in the roaring frontier towns the stage came in with the prospectors, the adventurers and all the other eager men who dreamed of striking it rich. In San Francisco shows were put on in saloons. A former taxi driver from New York, Thomas Maguire, erected a 2,000-seat theatre over his Parker Saloon, a resort for drinking, pleasure and gambling, in 1850, and called it the Jenny Lind, though the prima donna never honored its premises or ever set foot in California. The miners, gamblers and hard-bitten men would slog through the mud from the raw, glittering saloons and cheap boardinghouses and sit through the polished elegancies of *The Rivals* and the soaring periods of *Hamlet* and *Macbeth*. They saw the elder Junius Brutus Booth, a wild, gloomy, introverted player in the last troubled months of his life, and his son, Edwin, hardly out of his teens, who wandered through the mining towns, playing the banjo and appearing in a blackface version of *Box and Cox*. They saw the gaudy Lola Montez who, after her well-publicized romantic adventures with King Ludwig of Bavaria, father of Richard Wagner's fervent admirer, brought her flashy and shocking entertainment, *Lola Montez in Bavaria,* to New York and then to the West Coast. Her spider dance and other flamboyant routines had drawn packed houses, largely made up of men, in New York. Why not in turbulent San Francisco with its predominantly male population and its gusto untarnished by an excess respectability? Lola was burlesqued by an actress named Caroline Chapman, and she moved to Sacramento where, living in temporary semiretirement, she helped young Lotta Crabtree, later to be known only as Lotta, to start an extraordinary theatre career that led her from the rugged pioneer communities to the limelight in New York. Within a couple of decades after 1850 and the first lurid theatrical splash, San Francisco had become a proud dramatic center for its own company and for touring ensembles.

The temper of the flourishing times can be gauged by looking at New York even as the Civil War was still taking its toll. On November 25, 1864, the three Booth brothers appeared at the Winter Garden in *Julius Caesar,* probably for the only time on the same stage in the same play. Edwin played Brutus, John Wilkes was the Mark Antony and Junius Brutus Jr. was the Cassius. Impressed by the event, James Gordon Bennett's New York *Herald* celebrated the city's cultural progress. Making the usual allowances for civic hyperbole, one finds in the *Herald*'s editorial a sense of New York's expanding cultural frontiers.

The public amusements of this city for last night were of a very note-worthy character for their number, variety and excellence. Not that last night was so much richer in this respect than our nights usually are. It was rather a fair representative of the excellence and high stand-ard of our public entertainments, and the occasion was noteworthy in so far as it affords a fair occasion to point out how much New York is ahead of other cities in this respect. First on the list stands a represen-tation of one of Shakespere's plays. No playgoer has seen Shakespere presented with attraction more likely to draw and charm the true lover of the drama since the days when Shakespere himself appeared in his own plays. Three parts in the tragedy of Julius Caesar were personated by actors of the first merit—a thing that can hardly be seen in any city but ours. Only English cities could hope to rival us in this; and England does not now possess three tragedians, or even one, comparable to any one of the Booths. Moreover, if there were three men of such ability on the British stage, audiences would hope in vain to see them together in one play.

The editorial listed the other attractions on view that night: the opera, a performance at the Broadway Theatre "with Mr. Owens, the comic"—that is, John F. Owens, who that fall became a national hero on the strength of a Yankee named Solon Shingle in a play called *The People's Lawyer;* performances at Wallack's, the Olym-pic and Niblo's; "the usual variety of negro minstrelsy at the sev-eral halls devoted to that species of popular, national and original music and fun"; a "good circus performance"; a German theatre, and "though we did not have it last night, we do have it twice a week, an admirable performance in the French language."

And the editorial concluded prophetically:

All these entertainments were well patronised. . . . These facts all point to the conclusion that New York is growing rapidly in art as it has grown in commerce; and they seem to promise that at no very distant day it will be the art capital of the world. We will produce entirely our own actors and plays, our singers and operas. All the novelty that will charm in other cities will go from ours, and every impulse of life that shall stir the histrionic or lyric world will originate there.

This was not a new note of patriotic pride. Some years earlier—in 1852, to be exact—New York had manifested its nationalistic satisfaction in the accomplishments of a native son when Edwin Forrest carried out an impressive undertaking at the Broadway Theatre. For 69 nights he appeared in virtually all his great roles from the classics to the romantic tragedies written for him by fellow Americans. After the Astor Place riot, he had become a rallying ground for patriots and superpatriots. He—or the Broadway Theatre management—signalized an awareness of the occasion by embellishing the playbills with the American flag. His performances constituted, as Odell observed, "the most remarkable engagement ever up to that time carried through in an American theatre by a tragedian." No one else attempted such a retrospective run, not even Booth in his own theatre, which he opened at Sixth Avenue and 23rd Street in 1869 and which had such unheard-of modern devices as elevators that could lift a whole set into place on the stage from the preparatory resting spot below and so much space over the stage that drops could be hung and lowered without wrinkle and distortion.

New York knew what it wanted. In 1857, a year of panic, when the prices of theatre tickets had to be lowered and when nearly every box office suffered, Burton's Theatre managed to prosper by offering big names—Edwin Booth, John Brougham, Mr. and Mrs. E. L. Davenport and the unanimously admired Charlotte Cushman —in a series of Shakespeare revivals.

But the pendulum of taste was beginning, almost imperceptibly at first and then with stately deliberation, to swing away from poetry and romantic tragedy. A new realism slowly crept into the theatre. It was, during the greater part of this century, a superficial realism, tending toward sentimentality, homely familiarities and tear-soaked melodrama. It bore no resemblance, save in a distantly related case like Herne's *Margaret Fleming*, to the tough-minded realism that Ibsen detonated into a genteel theatre. Although he was the center of fierce polemics in Europe, Ibsen did not make much immediate impact on our theatre. The first American performance of *A Doll's House* took place in 1883 in Louisville when the play was still called *Thora*, introduced by Helena Modjeska, the actress from Poland, whose accent was as puzzling as the play was disturbing. The role of Nora served Minnie Maddern for her

Museum of the City of New York

Lewis Hallam Jr., 1740–1808

Interior of the John Street Theatre, built in 1767

Museum of the City of New York

Portrait of Eugene O'Neill in 1921 by William Zorach

reentry to the stage in 1894 after a four-year retirement following
her marriage to Harrison Grey Fiske. Returning as Mrs. Fiske, she
proved not only that she could play serious drama with brilliance
and penetration but also that Ibsen's uncompromising realism had
a place in a commercial theatre dedicated to easy entertainment.

Mrs. Fiske returned to Ibsen again and again in the early decades
of our century, and eventually the earnest commitment which the
Norwegian dramatist represented made deep invasions of our
drama. By then it was not only Ibsen but also Shaw and Chekhov
whose influence counted. But in 1900, it was possible for the New
York theatre to grant *The Master Builder* the ineffable boon of a
single performance.

If the pendulum eventually swung hard the other way, the point
from which it began to move may be pinpointed as 1853, the year
in which Boker wrote *Francesca da Rimini*. First produced at the
Broadway Theatre in New York in 1855, this romantic tragedy returned to the stage in 1882 in a highly successful revival by Lawrence Barrett and in 1901 Otis Skinner, who had supported Barrett
twenty years earlier, starred in it.

Francesca da Rimini, like its author, is worth more than a cur-
sory glance. While Boker's contemporaries attempted poetic diction that harked back to the great age of English drama, he was
more successful with it than any nineteenth-century American
writer.

Boker, well born and raised in an environment of comfort, leisure and learning, chose a literary career from predilection, not
necessity. However, it was not an easy career. When his comedy,
The Betrothal, was produced in London in 1853, it was poorly
done and savagely maltreated by the press. Boker thought that it
"was unusually successful with the audience" and blamed the harsh
criticism on "the gall of my brother dramatists." He thought that
"the play still stands as a monument of English injustice" and he
believed that the motive for hostility "was fear lest I should get a
footing on their stage."

Despite his independent means, Boker found the frustrations of
the theatre hard to endure. He resented the meager financial rewards received by the writer. He turned eventually to poetry, and

later to diplomacy, serving in the 1870's as Minister to Turkey and then as Envoy Extraordinary and Minister Plenipotentiary to Russia. He used blank verse flexibly and naturally, though he fell into clichés. A patrician, he had quick and warm sympathies for the humble. Indeed, the warmth of his emotion led him into well-intentioned oversimplifications, which harked back to attitudes like Thomas Hood's, who sang in *The Song of the Shirt* the miseries of the new working poor of industrialization, and which looked forward to the proletarian theatre of the 1930's.

As one reads *Francesca da Rimini,* one is struck by its instinct for garish theatricality. Where its style is embarrassingly overblown to us, it clung to its appeal late in the nineteenth century at a time when the high-flown manner was fading in popularity. The role of the deformed, powerful Lanciotto, betrayed by Francesca and by Paolo, the brother he adores, allows for the tearing of a passion to tatters. If E. L. Davenport, the first Lanciotto, was "mechanical and melodramatic," Barrett and Skinner in later years moved their audiences. One can imagine how Lanciotto's explosion would work in an undiscriminating theatre responsive to ample gestures and unabashed emotionalism:

> Curses upon my destiny! What I—
> Ha! I have found my use at last—What. I. *(Laughing)*.
> I, the great twisted monster of the wars,
> The brawny cripple, the herculean dwarf,
> The spur of panic, and the butt of scorn—
> I be a bridegroom! . . .
> Now in the battle, if a Ghibelin
> Cry, "Wry-hip! Hunchback!" I can trample him
> Under my stallion's hoofs, or haggle him
> Into a monstrous likeness of myself;
> But to be pitied,—to endure a sting
> Thrust in by kindness, with a sort of smile!—
> 'S death! it is miserable!

Lanciotto's wild exuberance when he thinks that the beauteous Francesca will not withdraw her marriage vow sounds like parody, but it emotionated the romantically inclined:

Now, I'll speak plainly, for a choice like thine,
Such love as women never felt,
Love me! Then monsters beget miracles,
And Heaven provides where human means fall short.
Lady, I'll worship thee! I'll line thy path
With suppliant kings! Thy waiting-maids shall be
Unransomed princesses! Mankind shall bow
One neck to thee, as Persia's multitudes
Before the rising sun! From this small town,
This center of my conquests, I will spread
An empire touching the extremes of earth!
I'll raise once more the name of ancient Rome;
And what she swayed she shall reclaim again!
If I grow mad because you smile on me,
Think of the glory of thy love; and know
How hard it is, for such a one as I,
To gaze unshaken on divinity.

The denouement with its unsurprising portion of disaster seems to us, whatever the effect on its contemporaries, vastly inflated. Note, for example, Francesca's last speech, addressed to the murdered Paolo:

Here, rest thy head
Upon my bosom, Fie upon my blood!
It stains thy ringlets. Ha! He dies. Kind saints,
I was first struck, why cannot I die first?
Paolo, wake! God's mercy, wilt thou go
Alone—without me? Prithee, strike again!
Nay, I am better—love—now. O! *(Dies)*.

Not only Francesca and Paolo were dying. So were, though they took a long time to breathe their last, all the fancy gestures of an essentially imitative theatre.

CHAPTER IX

REALISM OF A SORT

In 1855, the year of the introduction of *Francesca da Rimini* at the Broadway, Tom Taylor's comedy *Still Waters Run Deep* scored at Burton's. It was a comedy by this Englishman, *Our American Cousin,* which two years later presaged and shaped the new taste. This play was the making of Laura Keene as a manager, and it established Joseph Jefferson III and Edward Askew Sothern, father of the E. H. Sothern, as stars. Of Miss Keene, actress and manager, Jefferson later recalled that "as the treasury began to fill," she "began to twinkle with little brilliants; gradually her splendour increased, until at the end of three months she was ablaze with diamonds." In his diary George Templeton Strong wrote on November 20, 1858: "The play is very good. One Jefferson was admirable as the Yankee hero. The fair and sinful Laura, though less fresh and dashing than she was some five years back, is fascinating still."

It was Jefferson who prevailed on Laura Keene to produce the play after it had been rejected by Wallack's. He realized that the role of Asa Trenchard, the American cousin, had fine possibilities for him, but no one could have predicted the pleasure that the part of Lord Dundreary as played by E. A. Sothern would give. Sothern did not like the obviously written role and, perhaps in despair, turned himself with his skipping, stammering and sneezing into a comic-strip Englishman. That did it. The play held the stage from October 18, 1858, to March 25, 1859, a fabulous run in its time.

Then there was Boucicault, whose agility as a man of the theatre led him to use the stage in a variety of profitable ways. In *The Poor of New York,* which capitalized on the feelings generated by the panic of 1857, he appealed unashamedly to the easiest emotions. He pitted the dastardly rich against the virtuous poor in settings that seem blatantly theatrical to us but were eye-opening and exciting to audiences—a sumptuous home, a miserable tenement, a bank, a burning building, a snowstorm.

This was realism in its day. To us it is childish in characterization, obvious in plotting, parodistic rather than real. Indeed, two musical comedies based on this play were produced off Broadway in recent years—*The Banker's Daughter* and *The Streets of New York*—both seeking to draw merriment from treating Boucicault in his own terms.

With his instinct for the time, Boucicault took up the issue of slavery in *The Octoroon,* produced at the Winter Garden on December 5, 1859. Unlike Harriet Beecher Stowe, Boucicault did not set out to make propaganda. His main purpose was to put on a good show. He probably detested slavery, and as a shrewd stage craftsman he was aware of how effective a slave auction would be. His mind no doubt reinforced his heart in persuading him of the value of a passage in which Zoë, his octoroon heroine, broods on the shame of her blood. Never one to parcel out his effects, he included a noble redskin, the burning of a Mississippi riverboat and the sale of a gracious old plantation. When the Phoenix Theatre revived *The Octoroon* in 1961, we smiled indulgently at tears described as "honest water from the well of truth." We grinned at lines like: "You are illegitimate, but love knows no prejudice"; "Work is the salt that gives savor to life"; "I'd rather be black than ungrateful"; "I'll have her if it cost me my life" and "Must we immolate our love on her prejudices?" We found it hard to realize that this stuff could be taken seriously. How will our descendants feel about some of our successes?

Boucicault, who was born in Dublin, lived in France and functioned ably in the London theatre, and first came to the United States in 1853. His wife, Agnes Robertson, achieved fame as the heroines in his plays. His writings embraced original plays as well as adaptations from here, there and everywhere. An actor himself, Boucicault did not hesitate to play a role no one else would chance. Thus in his *Jessie Brown, or the Relief of Lucknow,* he took the part of the villain, a role so hateful that no other actor would play it. He dramatized Dickens' *The Cricket on the Hearth* and *Nicholas Nickleby.* He put together *The Colleen Bawn,* the most successful play New York had yet had on an Irish theme. "For the first time real Irish life was placed upon the stage," says Quinn, but this judgment becomes highly suspect when Quinn goes on to say that Boucicault's Irish life was "as far from the burlesque of his predecessors as it is from the sugary sentimentality of his successors in the romantic Irish play or of the grotesque satire of *The Playboy of the Western World.*"

Boucicault returned to London in 1860 and reappeared in New York in 1872. While in England, he made an adaptation of Washington Irving's *Rip Van Winkle,* in which Joseph Jefferson III became a national institution. Introduced at the Olympic Theatre in New York on September 3, 1866, this *Rip Van Winkle* made Jefferson the most beloved comedian of several generations of Americans.

The agility of Boucicault's mind was astonishing. He appreciated the sentimental value of *La Vie de Bohême,* which later served Puccini so famously, and he turned it into a play called *Mimi.* He saw the value of attempting a drama on a Civil War theme. The biggest success of his second American stay was *The Shaughran,* a play based on the Fenian rebellion of 1866. The title, a word that Boucicault coined from the Gaelic to mean a wanderer, referred to the principal character, Conn, whom the program described as "the soul of every fair, the life of every funeral, the first fiddle at all weddings and parties," and Boucicault himself played this rollicking rolling stone.

It was not Boucicault, however, who perpetrated the most egregious of our tear-soaked epics. *Uncle Tom's Cabin,* which had it first successful production in 1852, achieved the zenith of its incredible vogue after the Civil War. *Ten Nights in a Bar Room* made its initial appearance in 1858, and for decades thereafter was the happily lachrymose hunting ground of stock companies and touring troupes. That specimen of rank sentimentality, *East Lynne,* turned up at the Winter Garden in March 1863. Lucille Western, its star, may not have been much of an actress, but have there been superior businesswomen in the theatre? She paid $100 for all the rights, and at a profit of $350 a night reaped a bumper harvest. The melodramatic sob stories multiplied. *The Two Orphans* thrived with other pieces of that ilk, until absurdities like *Bertha, the Sewing Machine Girl* and its weeping sisters turned the genre into a laughingstock. While we laugh at these tear-jerkers, let us shed a tear in memory of some of the hacks who ground out the horrible stuff. Specifically, let us mourn for poor J. B. Howe, the Englishman engaged by the New Bowery's manager to be house dramatist at £8 a week and who found, when he got to New York, that his signed contract called for $8 a week. By mid-century the theme of the noble savage, the Indian, had been used so often with a straight face that in 1853 John Brougham, a comedian, who operated his own New York theatre, could ridicule it in a play called *Pocahontas, or the Gentle Savage.*

Swashbuckling costume melodrama had its vogue. *The Count of Monte Cristo* took New York by storm in mid-century, and in 1883, when James O'Neill, father of Eugene, assumed the leading role of Edmond Dantes, it acquired a new longevity.

The appeal of a flamboyant spectacle was established on September 12, 1866, when that progenitor of the gaudy musical, *The Black Crook,* became the rage of New York. Its preparation was an accident. A large troupe and an abundance of ingenious scenic effects had been imported from Europe for a ballet performance at the Academy of Music. When the Academy burned down, the manager of Niblo's Garden, with its seating capacity of 3,000, grafted the displaced performers and equipment onto a melodrama by Charles M. Barras.

Everything about *The Black Crook* was unprecedented, according to contemporary accounts. The money spent on it: The *World* guessed $50,000, the *Times* said $25,400; even the lower figure was staggering. The nature of the success: *The Black Crook* ran for 16 months and grossed more than $1,000,000. The stage: Its like, said the *Times,* "was never seen in this country before. Every board slides on grooves and can be taken up, pushed down or slid out at will. The entire stage may be taken away; traps can be introduced at any part at any time." And the girls, most of all the girls: There were 100 of them and they wore costumes considered daring.

"New York has never enjoyed the presence of so beautiful, varied, efficient, facile, graceful and thoroughly captivating a corps de ballet as the one herein introduced," cried the *World* ecstatically. "We have had great danseuses, in consignments of one—Elssler, Montez, Cerito, Cubas—but never, according to history, a regiment of lithe, active beauties bent on turning old heads by kicking their heels high in air. Mention of no such precedent can be found in Valentine's veracious Manual of Manhattan.

"It is not necessary to pause here for an ethical discussion of this interesting subject. Everybody knows how shocking a Parisian ballet must be, from hearsay, and therefore everybody is going to Niblo's post haste to learn from actual observation. . . . Nor . . . is it our journalistic province to pen roseate adjectives in favor of this matchless feast of natural beauty prepared for the enthusiastic student of anatomy. It is enough to repeat briefly that Niblo's Garden has become, in a single night, a vast paradise of houris, to which the Turks of fashion and the devotees of form are freely admitted between the precious hours of 8 and 12."

The *Evening Post,* stuffier and more prudish, commented, "Such a vision of beauty has rarely been seen on any stage—beauty perhaps less concealed than would be deemed proper by those of strict views as to where dresses should begin and end."

The whodunit achieved prominence, if not the silky smoothness of later manifestations of the genre, in *The Ticket of Leave Man,* a play by the Englishman Tom Taylor, which introduced to the American pantheon of fictional favorites the figure of Hawkshaw the detective. Hawkshaw bestrode the stage of New York's Winter Garden most of the 1863–64 season and he helped Mr. and Mrs. W. J. Florence, actor-managers, to become almost as well known as himself.

Melodramatic suspense was served up with steaming savor by Augustin Daly, a theatre man with better credentials to respect. As critic, manager, director and playwright, he was a dominant figure in the last four decades of the century. He had a hand in the writing or adapting of about ninety plays, finding his material in English, French and German originals—Wilkie Collins, Trollope, Sardou, Dumas, Meilhac and Halévy, Gustav von Moser, Julius Rosen and Franz and Paul von Schönthan. He wrote original works like *Horizon* which attempted to capture the feel of the frontier and which brimmed over with outrageous corn-bits like the Indian attack at night and like the heroine's being looked after by the so-called bad man after the murder of her worthless father. He was a producer who stressed ensemble rather than stars and who, with his instinct for discovering and developing young performers, opened the way to a host of new stars. Under his direction Ada Rehan and John Drew became a famous comedy team. He had the temerity to take a company to London where his success was so great that he established his own theatre to match his New York house, and he ventured with his company onto the continent. When he revived Shakespeare, he restored passages that for generations had been eliminated. He produced the works of Bronson Howard, who proved that the writing of plays could be a profession for an American. Known as "the autocrat of the stage," Daly was one of the line of versatile American stage personalities from Dunlap to Belasco. He attempted to make sense out of the irrationality of the commercial theatre. He organized an association of managers, which he hoped would exchange actors and reduce competition. Did he, without meaning to, open the way to the formation of the theatrical combines that held the theatre in a vise at the turn of the century? He had taste, but he was not above using any device to grip and shock his public.

In *Under the Gaslight,* his first original play, produced in 1867, he attempted to be realistic in the Boucicault manner. The shocker was a scene at a railroad crossing. A wounded soldier who protects the heroine is tied to the tracks by the blackmailing villain. While the audience sweats out the imminent arrival of the train, as thousands of spellbound moviegoers were to do in the cliffhangers of a half century later, the heroine is locked in a signal house after a breathtaking escape from the river and her evil captors. Finally, when the audience has had about all the suspense it can stand, she breaks out and looses the soldier's bonds.

Boucicault, no slouch at hocus-pocus, paid Daly the compliment of imitation with a similar scene in *After Dark*. But Daly was not flattered. He brought suit and won; the hair-raising bit was exclusively his. Imagine what his estate would have earned if it could have pursued the makers of the Pearl White and Eddie Polo serials and of countless feature-length movies, Western and otherwise, in which blackhearted villains bound lovely, fragile heroines and brave, virtuous heroes to railroad tracks.

Daly was one of many new playwrights in this epoch. No one appeared in the United States who could be compared even remotely with the best emerging in Europe—Ibsen, Strindberg, Shaw and Chekhov. Some highly regarded American writers braved the stage—with indifferent results even by the prevailing criteria. William Dean Howells, the novelist, had a respectable success with *A Counterfeit Presentment*, produced in 1877 by Lawrence Barrett. Henry James wrote patronizingly to his brother, William, "I am very glad that Howells' play seemed so pretty on the stage."

Henry James was a poor prophet, for in that letter he added, "For myself . . . it has been long my most earnest and definite intention to commence at play-writing as soon as I can. This will be soon, and then I shall astound the world!" Even *Guy Domville*, best received of his plays, was no triumph. It remained for others long after his death to make viable stage works out of his stories: *The Innocents* out of *The Turn of the Screw*, *The Heiress* out of *Washington Square*, and *The Aspern Papers* out of the novel of the same name.

Thomas Bailey Aldrich flirted with the theatre and produced a number of one-act pieces, most of them farces, whose chief virtue was their familiar and natural settings—a parlor or sleeping car on a railroad train, an elevator, a tea or dinner party.

The new "realism" whose principal spokesmen were Bronson Howard, Edward Harrigan, Steele Mackaye, William Gillette, David Belasco, Clyde Fitch and Augustus Thomas, was a matter of superficial details. The characters, even those regarded by thought-ful critical contemporaries as deeper and more faithfully realized than the old stereotypes, were clichés. The plots smelled of the stage rather than of truth. The gains, such as they were, reflected at least a professed intention to deal with people, events and the world as they were instead of with an imaginary, flowery, heroic and re-mote past.

Bronson Howard's first success, *Saratoga,* produced by Daly at his Fifth Avenue Theatre in 1870, was a farce about an amiable New Yorker, a man-about-town, involved with four women, all of whom appear in a big scene in his parlor in Saratoga. The scene was titillating to theatregoers in 1870, but it would be tame stuff to us, even with the vulgarisms added for the English version called *Brighton,* which led William Archer to complain that "ordinary modesty, not to say delicacy of feeling, is apparently a thing un-known and undreamt of among them," meaning the Americans.

Howard not only made money but also brought dignity to the profession of playwriting. He helped to amend and improve the copyright laws, and in 1891 was instrumental in founding the American Dramatists Club, which eventually led to the formation of the Dramatists Guild. His successes included *The Young Mrs. Winthrop,* a play about matrimony; *The Banker's Daughter,* the story of a woman who marries unwisely and suffers the loss of a child; *The Henrietta,* a satirical treatment of high finance, which provided a cheerful outlet for the comic talents of William H. Crane and Stuart Robson, and which grossed almost $500,000 in a 68-week run; and *Shenandoah,* a Civil War play. Produced in Bos-ton in 1888, where it won little approval, *Shenandoah* was brought to New York, and produced, slightly altered, by a new manager named Charles Frohman, to enormous success with a cast headed by Wilton Lackaye, Henry Miller, Viola Allen and Effie Shannon.

In his early plays Howard used asides, soliloquies and other passé devices. But even his later plays remain terribly dated. Glance through *Shenandoah* and you cannot help but smile at its naïveté. Here you have a story of war dividing friends and lovers but never affecting their gallantry or purity of heart. "You are a Northern girl," says one character to another, "and I am a Rebel, but we are sisters." A son who disgraces his family restores its honor by an act of bravery under an assumed name, and he has a farewell scene with his father, the General, who does not recognize him, which must have drenched sentimental eyes.

The chivalrous tone would make us blush or giggle. Colonel Kerchival West, northerner, stands before a prisoner, Gertrude Ellingham, southerner and his betrothed.

GENERAL BUCKTHORN: . . . Col. West. I command you! Search the prisoner.
KERCHIVAL: General Buckthorn—I decline to obey that order.
BUCKTHORN: You—you decline to obey my order! *(Moves down to him fiercely)*.
KERCHIVAL: *(Apart)* General! It is the woman I love.
BUCKTHORN: *(Apart)* Is it? Damn you, sir! I wouldn't have an officer in my army corps who *would* obey me, under such circumstances. I'll have to look for those despatches myself.
KERCHIVAL: *(Facing him angrily.)* If you dare, General Buckthorn.
BUCKTHORN: *(Apart)* Blast your eyes! I'd kick you out of the army if you'd *let* me search her; but it's my military duty to swear at you.

Edward Harrigan had his finger on the public pulse. He had begun by writing sketches for vaudeville and eventually expanded his best-liked basic characters into full-length plays. With his partner, Tony Hart, whose real name was Anthony Cannon, he performed in a succession of oeuvres devoted to the joys and sorrows of Dan and Cordelia Mulligan. The first of these was *The Mulligan Guard Ball,* produced at the Theatre Comique in New York in 1879, which ran for 100 nights. Sequel followed sequel—*The Mulligan Guard Chowder, The Mulligan Guard's Christmas, The Mulligan Guard Surprise, The Mulligan Guard Nominee, The Mulligans' Silver Wedding* until, with *Cordelia's Aspirations,* the former Irish immigrants, the Mulligans, tried and failed to make the move uptown. Harrigan played Dan Mulligan, corner grocer, and Hart impersonated Cordelia, his wife. The "realism," in short, was close to burlesque, and the interspersed songs were another remove from reality. Yet Harrigan's plays had their roots in the homely concerns of his audience. To us they are the analogues of television's situation comedies conditioned by musical comedy.

Charles Hoyt, who served as a drama and music critic as well as that new thing, a columnist, on the Boston *Post*, dealt with everyday scenes and people in a series of farces, adding an occasional seasoning of songs. His *A Trip to Chinatown* ran at the Madison Square Theatre for 650 performances in 1891, 1892, and 1893. If the play is forgotten, two interpolated songs are not—Percy Gaunt's "The Bowery" and Charles K. Harris's "After the Ball."

The frontier had its share of interest. Do you think that Davy Crockett is the exclusive preserve of Walt Disney and recent generations of youngsters? A play called *Davy Crockett* by Frank Hitchcock Murdoch appeared in 1872, and for years it served as a popular vehicle for Frank Mayo and later for his son, Edwin Mayo.

Bret Harte and Mark Twain tried to memorialize the West in *Ah Sin*. Its main character was the "heathen Chinee" of Harte's verse. The eminence of the authors could not make a success of this patchwork. The best thing about it was Twain's curtain speech on opening night at Daly's in 1877 when he declared dryly that the piece was "intended rather for instruction than amusement," and continued:

For the instruction of the young we have introduced a game of poker. There are few things that are so unpardonably neglected in our country as poker. The upper class knows very little about it. Now and then you find Ambassadors who have a sort of general knowledge of the game, but the ignorance of the people at large is fearful. Why, I have known clergymen, good men, kind-hearted, liberal, sincere and all that, who did not know the meaning of a "flush"; it is enough to make one ashamed of our species.

Then Twain descanted on the play's history in production:

When our play was finished, we found it was so long, and so broad, and so deep—in places—that it would have taken a week to play it. I thought that was all right; we could put "To be continued" on the curtain, and run it straight along. But the manager said no; it would get us into trouble with the general government, because the Constitution forbids the infliction of cruel or unusual punishment; so he cut out, and cut out, and the more he cut out the better the play got. I never saw a play that was so much improved by being cut down; and I be-

lieve it would have been one of the very best plays in the world if his
strength had held out so that he cut out the whole of it.

Twain might joke, but he and Harte no doubt were saddened by
the luck of Joaquin Miller, a Californian, whose plays of the West
won the great popularity they had hoped for. His work, *The
Danites in the Sierras,* came into New York some days after *Ah Sin*
was withdrawn and swept the town with the crude energy of its
plot and the wildness of its setting.

A rare quixotic and touching figure was Steele MacKaye, a man
of endless curiosity and ingenuity. As an actor he studied new techniques in France and was so profoundly convinced of the necessity
of rigorous and coherent schooling that he founded the first acting
school in America, later to become the American Academy of Dramatic Art. As an imaginative technician, he brought the latest
mechanical devices into the theatre; when he obtained control of
the Madison Square Theatre in 1879 he remodeled it to include
an elevator stage, folding seats, modern ventilation and overhead
lighting, which Thomas A. Edison helped to install. As a manager
he was up and down, and as playwright he was enormously successful and pitifully unlucky with one play, *Hazel Kirke.* For *Hazel
Kirke* opened at the Madison Square in February, 1880, and ran
for almost two years and then was played repeatedly on tour and
in stock. But the careless and exploited author earned little or
nothing from it, for he bartered away his rights in a merciless contract with his backers.

Hailed in its time for naturalness and simplicity and for the remarkable absence of a villain, *Hazel Kirke* is reticent and natural
only in comparison with the theatrical truck of its time. Its efforts
at humor are pallid; here is a joke uttered by Pittacus Green, a
cheerful, seemingly foolish eccentric, played by Thomas Whiffen:
"A brute with a long nose generally has some scents about him, ha,
ha, ha!" The story, placed near a mill in England's Lancashire, tells
of sweet, lovable Hazel and her stern father, Dunstan, who demands
that despite her love for another, she must marry the squire who
has saved him and his mill. The outcome turns on a legal technicality, the invalidity of a Scottish marriage performed on English

soil. In the end the unrelenting father is blind, broke and remorseful, and all is dissolved in satisfactorily miserable tears.

More impressive as a playwright was James A. Herne, who began in the theatre as an associate of Belasco in San Francisco. He had ideals and a philosophy. A liberal, and advocate of Henry George, he wanted to tell "the truth about real people." He wrote about fishermen and farmers and tackled themes that had some pertinence for his day. In *Shore Acres* he opposed the tory and the radical in a humble, rural setting. In *The Reverend Griffith Davenport* his hero was a Virginian who, in the heat of the Civil War, remembered to be faithful to his Christian beliefs and to support the fight against slavery when those near and dear to him pulled him the other way. In *Margaret Fleming,* which Howells acclaimed as "an epoch-making play," he coped openly with a problem not considered proper in polite circles—the study of a wife able to confront the truth that her husband has had a child by another woman and to make him accept her awareness of it. There are touches of sentimentality and melodrama—Margaret Fleming, the heroine, is in danger of blindness from glaucoma, and at the third-act curtain, she is about to breast-feed the other woman's child. One can understand why the first audiences in 1891 were shocked, and why the leading role, so shrewdly written, made an effect. Herne's wife, Katherine, was the first Margaret Fleming; in later revivals, their daughters, Chrystal and Julie, undertook the role.

The careers of William Gillette, David Belasco, Augustus Thomas and Clyde Fitch colored the closing decades of the nineteenth century as well as impinged on the twentieth. Gillette was another shrewd man of the theatre. He believed that on stage it was more important to concentrate on what characters did than on what they said. His adaptations and original plays covered a variety of subjects from the strictly theatrical and enormously successful like *Sherlock Holmes,* in which his playing of Conan Doyle's detective became a symbol of a theatrical era, to works like *Held by the Enemy,* an attempt at a serious drama of the Civil War, and *Secret Service,* an example of the well-made play of its time. In his acting style—in addition to his own plays he appeared in others like Barrie's *The Admirable Crichton*—he represented a new taste for reserve out of which dynamism could explode impressively.

Belasco to us is a legend, redolent of the affectation and meretriciousness of the theatre at its ripest. If you are old enough to remember him or if you study photographs of his elder-statesmen years in his clerical garb, you have the sense of a man who played a part so long that he became the part and forgot the man. But the image he offered of himself in the 1920s, when to a suddenly young, reinvigorated theatre he looked like a costumed anachronism, made a mockery of a fascinating early career.

A child of youthful, brawling, colorful California, Belasco began by learning every aspect of the theatre. He played a dwarf in *Rip Van Winkle*, served as prompter, assistant stage manager and stage manager and was versed in technical and business problems. He made contributions to lighting, pioneering the use of colored silks and gelatin slides. As manager and director, he became an exponent of a stage dedicated to minute and rich veracity of detail, an approach that served as his admired signature for many years until it became old-fashioned fussiness and bombast. It is forgotten that he could also be illuminatingly simple. In 1888, long before the advocates of economy and directness brought their ideas to realization, he produced Sophocles' *Electra* with unusual spareness and reticence. He had a flair for exotic and surefire situations, characters and effects, and as a result his plays, nearly all collaborations, combined elements geared for success. With Henry C. De Mille and John Luther Long, he wrote winner after winner. With the former he turned out *The Wife, Lord Chumley, The Charity Ball* and *Men and Women;* with the latter he wrote *Madame Butterfly,* a fat role for Blanche Bates; *The Darling of the Gods,* with an equally fat part for George Arliss, and *Andrea,* with a starring role for Mrs. Leslie Carter, a society woman who began as a non-actress and whom Belasco, by sheer tenacity and willpower, turned into a star. He also collaborated with James A. Herne and Franklyn Fyles, and his works included *May Blossom, The Heart of Maryland* and *The Girl of the Golden West.*

Belasco was a maker of stars; he plucked David Warfield out of burlesque and helped to convert him into a leading actor. He was also a determined fighter for his rights. When the trust closed in on independent producers who would not do its bidding, he stubbornly built his own theatres in Washington and New York. Although he lived until 1931 and some of his great successes, like *The Return of Peter Grimm* with David Warfield, came long after the new century, he was essentially a creature of the nineteenth century. Viewed in the context of that exuberant and ingenuous theatrical era, he was a force to reckon with.

Augustus Thomas, however, was in some ways ahead of his time. He believed in a theatre of ideas at a time when Ibsen and Shaw had made scarcely any impact on the American stage. In *Alabama* he wrote about a Southerner who could think nationally rather than regionally. Stirred by the Pullman strike, he tackled the subject of capital and labor in *New Blood*. In *The Capitol* he sought to deal with financial and religious effects on politics. In *The Copperhead,* a 1918 success about the Civil War with Lionel Barrymore in a gratifying role, he tried to capture a sense of the simplicity and dignity of unostentatious patriotism. Outraged by Prohibition, he tilted at it in *Still Waters* in 1925. If you read *The Witching Hour,* which arrived in 1907 and scored a great success, you will find that, though the theme is occultism, Thomas managed to inject his viewpoint. When Jack Brookfield, the gambler, who is the hero, is chided for the lavishness of his way of life made possible by his vocation, he replies, "You might say that, if I'd earned these things in some responsible business combination that starved out all its little competitors—but I've simply furnished a fairly extensive entertainment—to eminent citizens—looking for rest."

But Thomas, despite his admirable intentions, was no more than a skillful craftsman reflecting the undemanding standards of his time. He could write shrewd entertainments like *In Mizzoura,* with a juicy part for the beloved comedian, Nat Goodwin, and viable plays employing local color like *Colorado* and *Arizona*. To us *The Witching Hour* is merely a tricky, meretricious business. Although it behaves as if it will investigate the mysterious powers of the mind, it is full of hokum.

Clyde Fitch, born in 1865 and dead in 1909, was the golden boy of the century's turn, and in a way his career suggests the great changes that were impending. Slight of physique, independent in manner and dress even as a student at Amherst, he got his start early when Edward A. Dithmar, drama critic of *The New York Times,* recommended him to Richard Mansfield, the capricious star, who wanted someone to write a play for him centered around Beau Brummel. Mansfield was a difficult man to work with, as his first success proved. Preparing for the performance that made him a star—an old rake in *A Parisian Romance* produced by A. M. Palmer in 1883—he secretly worked out a multitude of effects and sprang them unexpectedly on his colleagues as well as the audience on the opening night.

Fitch quickly mastered his bright, fashionable, superficial techniques, and earned a million dollars in a time of the hard dollar and no income taxes. He could be, even for his period, a perfect cornball; witness *Barbara Frietchie,* a vehicle for Julia Marlowe. He could shock; witness *Sapho,* a vehicle for Olga Nethersole, which the police closed down in 1900 because the hero carried the girl upstairs with malice aforethought. He could be acerbic in *The Climbers* about money and society.

In 1901 he bestrode the New York theatre. Four of his plays— *The Climbers, Barbara Frietchie, Lovers' Lane,* and *Captain Jinks of the Horse Marines,* the comedy that lifted the lovely, young Ethel Barrymore to stardom—were running simultaneously to sold-out houses. His own favorite was *Major André,* which lasted two weeks.

Read *The Girl with the Green Eyes,* produced in 1902 with young Lucille Watson as Maggie, an attractive and honest maid secretly married to a Yale lad of good family, and you will note that Fitch is dipping his small toe, ever so gingerly, into the waters of serious drama. But his study of jealousy turns out to be thin and glib. The preoccupations of the time are ticked off with surface humor. "We've come to do Europe and the Holy Land," says a character, "in five weeks for $400—but I don't know, seems as if I'm getting awful tired—after jes' seven days." "Going to Brooklyn," says another, "is the sort of thing one talks about and dreads for days." When Jenny seeks to charm her young man out of a pet, she does a takeoff on Eliza crossing the ice and then she requests him to play the "Floradora Sextette" on the pianola. The young man's curtain speech has to be read to be believed, "There's one thing stronger even than jealousy, my Jenny, and that's love. THAT'S LOVE!"

Maude Adams, writing to Fitch after an illness of his, advised him to seek out a place where he could encounter "common life," and to seize the chance to find "new turns of mind." In his last years, he attempted more ambitious themes—*The Truth*, an effort to study the problem of a born liar, and *The City*, produced posthumously, which sought to show the influence of a harsh urban way of life on simple people from the country. It is not too much to say that these plays bore very faint marks of the Ibsen revolution. It is noteworthy that *The Truth* failed in New York in 1907, when Clara Bloodgood played the leading role. Several months later Marie Tempest appeared in the play in London to enormous success, and only in 1914 with the charming Grace George as the lead did it achieve an American success. *The Truth* won respect for Fitch abroad; he was one of our first playwrights to receive such recognition.

◆◖◁

CHAPTER X

THE PLAYERS WERE
THE THING

THE PERSONALITY OF THE PLAYERS rather than their plays dominated the second half of the nineteenth century and the early years
of the twentieth. There were no film and television luminaries to
preempt and command the center of attention. Sports had not
achieved today's enormous popularity with a commensurate spotlight on the outstanding athletes.

First and foremost in public curiosity and affection were the
people of the theatre. If you turn the yellowed pages of the newspapers and periodicals of the time and glance at the stories and
illustrations, so decorous compared with today's racy, gossipy accounts and tantalizing photographs, you will find how large the
careers and lives of the players loomed in the public's attention.
Bound portfolios of the picture of actors were issued on a weekly
subscription basis, like magazines. I have been leafing through a
set published in 1894 by an actress named Marie Burroughs. In
each issue there were 20 neatly touched-up rotogravure prints of
eminent actors and opera stars. What is particularly amusing is that
Miss Burroughs unashamedly ran her own picture in nearly every
issue. In today's more sophisticated climate a transparently self-ad-

vertising product like this would have to be given away, one imagines, rather than sold.

Then, as now, stardom did not always reflect distinction of gifts and style. The public could be persuaded to offer its patronage and applause to performers who thrived on tricks and effects rather than art. An exhibitionist like Adah Isaacs Menken, who had a good figure and lots of nerve, could create a sensation in New York in 1862 by riding bareback and looking bare, though she wore pink tights, on a supposedly wild stallion—actually a domesticated mare —into a horrible death in the finale of *Mazeppa,* a trashy melodrama based on Byron's poem. The ranting of Robert B. Mantell in Shakespeare had adherents and customers a good deal less discerning than the admirers of Edwin Booth.

Of Booth's extraordinary qualities there can be no doubt. It is possible to listen to him in a Hamlet soliloquy, recorded with primitive equipment in the last years of his life, and to be absorbed by the sensitive and affecting nuances of the reading. There is ample eyewitness testimony to his accomplishments. Small and neat of figure, he had the skill, consciously developed, to create the illusion of height. Starting in Boston as a sixteen-year-old in 1849 in a minor role in *Richard III,* he served a long, hard and varied apprenticeship. When he undertook the inevitable Richard III at Burton's Metropolitan Theatre in 1857, at twenty-four, he was prepared for the responsibility of stardom. His Hamlet at New York's Winter Garden in 1864 was a sensation for its day, running an astonishing 100 performances. After his brother, John Wilkes, assassinated Lincoln, he left the stage for almost a year, returning only upon genuine, not trumped-up, public demand. He never spoke of his brother's horrible deed, but it shook him to his roots and deepened and darkened a sensitive nature.

In his own theatre, opened in 1869 and shut four years later, Booth worked to establish high standards. Playing under the management of others, he did not relent in his search for fresh insights. Contemporaries speak of the subtlety of his acting. Kitty Molony, who was a young member of his company and later wrote *Behind the Scenes with Edwin Booth,* felt that his "art of make-up was as ruthless as a modern painter's. It did seem as if he labored to dig out the ugliest traits of his character and paint them into his face."

Booth was most memorable for his Shakespeare. Of his Shylock, Kitty Molony thought it "was not intended for a type—not a composite of a race, but just a man who was a Jew. What was *hard* in his Jew was Shylock himself. It was not racial." There were critical reservations about his Macbeth, Othello and Lear on the grounds that his voice was not a pealing organ and his passions were not outsize. His Hamlet and Iago were regarded as unsurpassed.

If the American theatre has a patron saint among its actors, it is Booth. In "The Grave of Edwin Booth," Thomas Bailey Aldrich wrote:

> In narrow space, with Booth, lie housed in death
> Iago, Hamlet, Shylock, Lear, Macbeth.
> If still they seem to walk the painted scene
> 'Tis but the ghosts of those that once have been.

Booth's shrine—and he did not intend it for such an egocentric purpose—is the home fronting on Gramercy Park, which he bequeathed to The Players, a club centered in actors and the stage, which keeps his memory green and which pays a heartfelt tribute to him each year on Founder's Day.

Native actors who could achieve prominence and favor appeared in increasing numbers as the decades went by. Mrs. Fiske's career bridged the nineteenth and twentieth centuries. She founded the basis of a glamorous reputation in the former and secured it so firmly in the latter that she became a kind of nonpareil. Alexander Woollcott made a fetish of chanting her praises; others thought that it was her personality rather than her art that triumphed. Certain it is that her range and sympathies were wide. She could play light comedy and intense drama with equal felicity. To those who saw her performances as Becky Sharp and Tess in plays drawn from Thackeray's and Hardy's novels, they were shining memories of her scope. She knew how to be the *grande dame* on stage, but cared little about such a role off stage. A professional through and through, she summed up her craftsman's attitude in a remark to Woollcott, "As soon as I suspect a fine effect is being achieved by accident, I lose interest. I am not interested, you see, in unskilled labor."

Beginning with the highest and lowest of the nineteenth century —the classic repertory and such things as *Ten Nights in a Barroom,* she became a star in her teens, and never ceased to grow. She was, as Walter Prichard Eaton wrote justly in a tribute to her in *Theatre Arts,* "in the thick and forefront of two battles, the battle for modernism in dramatic art, and the battle for freedom in theatrical organization." In the early years of the twentieth century at a site where Gimbel's now stands she organized an ensemble Eaton remembered as "the best resident company New York had seen" up to the time of the Moscow Art Theatre's visit in 1923. With this troupe, which included George Arliss, John Mason, William B. West and Charles Cartwright, she presented Ibsen—and not solemnly—as well as other plays of merit.

If the United States has had a royal family of the theatre, it is one that goes back to a resourceful and indomitable woman who, born in England of a stage family herself, made her first appearance behind the footlights when she was merely a year old. She was Louisa Lane, and she came to the United States when she was seven. At thirty she married an Irish actor named John Drew, and in 1861 took over the management of the Arch Theatre in Philadelphia. For almost a decade she presided over one of the most admirable companies in the land. She had a gift for discovering young talent. She believed in hard work, discipline and a well-knit ensemble. By 1869 she had to make concessions to the demand for outside stars, and she brought in guests to appear with her company. Eventually, she resumed her own appearances outside her own theatre, touring with Joseph Jefferson in *The Rivals.* But for thirty years she was the guiding light of a theatre of her own. New York managers of the era, Daly, A. M. Palmer, Lester Wallack, Steele MacKaye, Laura Keene, and later the Frohmans, Daniel and Charles, perhaps generated more excitement from new plays and players, but Mrs. Drew's respect for her craft left a lasting mark on many who went on to other places in the theatre.

In her descendants she left another legacy that shed a glow on the theatre for decades. Three of her four children—Georgiana,

John and Sidney—became prominent actors. Georgiana married Maurice Barrymore, and their children, Ethel, Lionel and John, lit up the theatrical heavens in the first decades of the twentieth century.

Although travel was slower 100 years ago than in our jet-propelled age, the great and near-great of the theatre from all over Europe appeared frequently on American stages. Even then the traffic was both ways. There was one notable, necessary and shameful self-exile by an American. This was the case of Ira Aldridge, the Negro, who was born in New York but who had to go abroad to forge a career. At twenty-six, in 1833, he played Othello in London. At his death in 1867 at the age of sixty he was renowned all over Europe as a tragedian and was a friend of Tolstoi. But his compatriots did not even know of his existence. There was no place for a black man on our stage—except in puny, menial roles. White actors in blackface were all right for comedy, but a Negro for any measurable purpose, no.

The British Isles including Ireland sent a steady stream of guests as well as immigrants. James O'Neill, an Irish lad of seven when he first came here, struggled upward the hard way until he found the starring vehicle, *The Count of Monte Cristo,* that served him well and in the end consumed him and his future. We get a searing account of him in his son's pain-racked evocation of his family, *Long Day's Journey Into Night.* Helena Modjeska, who grew up in Poland, had a difficult language barrier to overcome in the United States, but her intelligence, power and sensitivity enabled her to play classic and contemporary roles in English with impressive effect. Annie Russell was born in Liverpool, grew up in Canada and won hearts in the United States with her delicacy and charm. Ada Rehan, born in Ireland, came here at five, won even more hearts with her laughing, endearing personality and acting gifts. Henry Miller, an Englishman, who was also educated in Canada, was an unforced, direct, versatile actor in comedy, melodrama and farce. Richard Mansfield reached the United States by way of Germany; he had a flair for the individual touch on the stage; he appeared in *The Devil's Disciple* in 1894, the first play by Shaw to be seen by an American audience, and he was a dashing Cyrano. Julia

Marlowe, inseparable partner of Sothern, was also English born,
coming here at the age of four, and she did her bit to spread a
knowledge of Shakespeare among us.

The great international stars like Rachel, Adelaide Ristori,
Sarah Bernhardt, Eleanora Duse, Tommaso Salvini, Coquelin,
Adelaide Neilson, Sir Henry Irving, Ellen Terry, Sir Johnston
Forbes-Robertson, William Hunter Kendal, and Madge Robertson
Kendal displayed their remarkable personal talents for American
audiences in guest tours. Indeed, Bernhardt's "farewell tours" became virtually the signature of her American fame. If she practiced
personal peculiarities, like keeping a young tiger as a pet and a
satin-lined coffin as one of the furnishings in her boudoir, the ec-
centricities were added to what contemporaries assure us was incomparable acting. Lily Langtry relied more on her head-turning
beauty than any special acting gift, but London and New York
were at her feet, and so were the men. Her attachment to Edward
VII would have been enough to assure her fame.

Although he was not an actor, Charles Dickens made a great
splash as a stage personality, when he came here for a season late
in 1867 to offer readings from his own works. If you remember
Emlyn Williams' performance as Dickens reading himself, you
have an approximation of the novelist's performance, just as Hal
Holbrook's one-man show as Mark Twain re-creates the atmosphere
and spirit of the American novelist as public performer.

But no performer can reconstruct the stir created by Dickens'
appearances in America. Writing almost two decades later, George
Dolby, his manager, recalled that by 8 A.M. of the day set for the
Englishman's American debut in Boston "the queue was nearly
half a mile long and about that time the employers of the persons
who had been standing in the streets all night began to arrive and
take their places."

For the first New York appearance the excitement was even
greater. "The line commenced to form at ten o'clock on the night
prior to the sale," Dolby recalled, "and here were to be seen the
usual mattresses and blankets in the cold streets and the owners of
them vainly endeavoring to get some sleep. . . . When the time for
opening the ticket office arrived, the police passed the word along

the line that 'four tickets only for each Reading would be sold to each person, and those only to people in hats.' The consternation amongst the speculators was great. They, however, were equal to the occasion, for in the lapse of a few moments they had collected all the hats they could from waiters and others in a neighboring restaurant . . . and by means of changing a hat for a cap at the entrance door to the ticket office, the speculators contrived to get into their possession the greater portion of the seven or eight first rows of seats in the hall. . . . Before the sale had progressed two hours the speculators were selling the best seats at enormous premiums."

Dickens evidently was a shrewd performer. He offered *A Christmas Carol* without diverging from what he had written, but when he got to the trial from *Pickwick* he "often strayed away from the actual text and indulged in the habit of an occasional 'gag,' " according to Dolby. Although these "occasional liberties" were the more enjoyed "as nearly every line of 'Pickwick' was as well known to the audience as to himself," there was at least one exception. Dolby reported a meeting with an angry man leaving the hall during the performance.

"Say, who's that man on the platform reading?" the stranger inquired.
"Mr. Charles Dickens," Dolby replied.
"But that ain't the *real* Charles Dickens, the man as wrote all them books I've been reading all these years."
"The same."
"Well, all I've got to say about it then is that he knows no more about Sam Weller 'n a cow does of pleatin' a shirt."

CHAPTER XI

NEW CENTURY, BOOM TIMES

THE THEATRE and allied entertainments such as vaudeville and burlesque had every reason to ring in the new century with rejoicing. In the next two decades they enjoyed a steadily expanding nationwide boom. From 1900 onward the spirit of American optimism, so precious because it assumes that anything is possible and so dangerous because it accepts the corollary that anything possible is desirable, swept nearly everything before it in a rosy glow of energy. Only in San Francisco, where all new theatres were wiped out by the 1906 earthquake, was there a temporary setback.

New theatres were rising everywhere. In New York there were twenty by 1903 and eighty by 1927. Winthrop Ames, gentleman from New England, put up the Little, now the Winthrop Ames, at his own expense in 1912, providing a fireplace in the foyer and a tearoom downstairs. As a gesture to gracious theatregoing, he had a string quartet in the intermissions, served coffee and tea and cake to the audience free, and coffee and sandwiches to the actors. In this "house for the elite," called "Ames's Folly," because it was too small to be profitable, he put on plays of some quality, again at his own expense. He provided a greenroom, where players could receive guests, a rare amenity that only Frohman's Lyceum boasted. On the other hand, the architect of the Little forgot to install an exit at stage right. But he was not alone in overlooking a theatre's needs. The Music Box originally made no provisions for a box office, and what is one to think of the layout of the Guild, now the ANTA Theatre, where the audience on arrival descends only to climb stairs?

Across the country stock companies were flourishing, with about 2,000 in existence by 1910. Road shows were ubiquitous, with casts close to the Broadway originals or, more often, diluted versions of glamorous successes. Best patronized were the tours led by great stars, and rare was the performer, however famous, who did not travel across the land. A profitable tour became as important in a producer's calculations as movie money decades later. Some plays were not even produced in New York if bookings could not be arranged for a post-Broadway trip, and tours were the equivalent of subsidiary and residual rights.

Other days, other customs, but in the American theatre there has been one constant—some species of commercial tyranny. In 1900 it was the ruthless theatrical syndicate, a monopoly established in 1896 by Marc Klaw and Abraham L. Erlanger, booking agents working out of New York, joined by Al Hayman and Charles Frohman, New York managers, and Samuel F. Nirdlinger and J. Frederick Zimmerman, Philadelphia managers. This group acquired domination of the vast majority of the country's theatres and ruthlessly imposed its demands on producers and performers. A few fought back. Belasco refused to accept the trust's dictates. Great stars like Mrs. Fiske, Mansfield, Jefferson and O'Neill played under canvas and in sports arenas rather than swallow demeaning terms.

The Shubert brothers—first Sam in 1900, then Lee and J. J.— came down from Syracuse and entered the lists. They acquired theatres, devised their own booking arrangements, and presently built an empire strong enough to crush competitors. The change was, of course, largely of persons and names, not substance. Indeed, it was almost fifty years before the United States Government, through its antitrust activities, worked out a consent decree with the Shubert organization, which reduced but hardly liquidated its capacity to affect the character and quality of the commercial theatre.

Moves toward centralized power were also going forward in vaudeville and burlesque. The United Booking Office headed by B. F. Keith and Edward F. Albee established for some years almost impregnable dominion over vaudeville, and tight circuits for the booking of burlesque shows were established. Show business in all its manifestations was triumphantly in the ascendant, but as in any era of good times, there was the further question: Good times for whom? The manipulators might grow rich, and a few stars might prosper, but the rights and hopes of others were abused. Vaudeville performers, especially those on the lower rungs, were exploited shamefully, and in their anger and discontent formed a union known as the White Rats, which sought improvements in salaries, bookings, and working conditions. This movement was crushed, only to rise later with renewed force and greater success. In 1913 the performers in the theatre, many underpaid, overworked and shabbily treated, founded a union, Actors Equity, which the producers treated indifferently or cavalierly. In 1919 Equity struck and shut down the theatres to affirm its right to speak for all the actors, from the highest to the lowest.

Some producers shouted, "Starve them out!" A few, especially the charm boy, George M. Cohan, declined to go along with Equity and formed the Actors Fidelity League. The actors, supported by most of the glamorous names, demonstrated on the streets, carrying placards. They made passionate speeches and entertained the crowd without fee. For almost a month there were no performances in the theatres. In the end the producers gave in and signed contracts with the actors' union that granted the recognition that for six years had been withheld. Only Cohan declined to join Equity, and the union, eschewing rancor, let him round out his career in the theatre without a membership card. Until 1960 the producers and Equity were able to come to terms peaceably, but in June of that year another strike darkened the Broadway theatres, this time for less than two weeks before a settlement could be arranged, and an undamaging one flared for a few hours in 1964.

Vaudeville was a highly developed entertainment as well as a remarkable training ground for the theatre. Comedians, singers, jugglers, lariat twirlers, all sorts of performers who achieved distinction as actors in comedy, farce, musicals and even tragedy learned how to catch the attention of an audience, how to pace themselves, how to adapt themselves to crisis in this exigent school of the stage. The roster of vaudeville graduates is almost endless. Think of W. C. Fields, the Marx Brothers, Ed Wynn, Eddie Cantor, Bobby Clark, Walter Huston, Bob Hope, Danny Kaye, Eddie Foy, Sr. and Jr., Bert Williams, George M. Cohan, Norah Bayes, Elsie Janis, Joe Jackson, Will Rogers, Frank Tinney, Frank Fay, George Burns and Gracie Allen, Weber and Fields, Chic Sale, Fred Allen, Bert Lahr, Willie and Eugene Howard, Gypsy Rose Lee and her sister, June Havoc, Joe E. Brown, Pat Rooney, Fred and Adele Astaire, Al Jolson, Fannie Brice, Jack Benny, George Jessel, William Gaxton, Joe Cook, Milton Berle, James Barton, Phil Baker, Edgar Bergen, Jimmy Durante, Irene and Vernon Castle, Ray Dooley, Irene Franklin, Anna Held, Paul and Grace Hartman, Raymond Hitchcock, Victor Moore, Lillian Roth, Fred Stone, Bill "Bojangles" Robinson, Jimmie Savo, George White and Charles Winninger.

The list could go on and on. The graduates of vaudeville, and some of the good ones who came out of burlesque, like Phil Silvers, filled the musical theatre for several generations. They formed a pool of talent from which the new mediums, radio and television, drank thirstily.

Vaudeville, or variety, as Tony Pastor, the impresario, preferred to call it, had its roots in the remote past and counterparts in France and England. Pastor conferred respectability and prestige on it with his famous theatre on 14th Street, which he opened in 1881 and in which he presented turns that would not outrage the family trade. Koster and Bial's Music Hall, first on 23rd Street and later on 34th Street, offered beer and vaudeville—with many of the turns imported from the London music halls. With the development of the vaudeville chains, this form of entertainment grew into an American institution. When William Morris, the agent, was tangling with the potent Albee in the battle for bookings, he even managed to get the help of President Theodore Roosevelt, the original trustbuster. Unable to find a theatre for Harry Lauder, whose Scotch burr in comic songs and patter warmed countless American hearts, Morris persuaded the President to intercede. Lauder was booked into Washington, and Roosevelt underlined his interest by attending.

Vaudeville was so powerful and widespread an entertainment medium that the founding in 1905 of the trade paper *Variety* by Sime Silverman, a young, fearless critic of the medium, might be termed a monument to its importance. Silverman established his weekly because he wanted to speak honestly of the acts in the field, and he had the integrity to stand up against the Keith-Albee octopus.

Vaudeville's principal houses offered matinee and evening performances every day, and its front-line house, where it achieved its finest hours, was New York's Palace, built and opened in 1913 by Martin Beck, owner of an impressive variety circuit in the West. From 1913 until 1932—and its final years were wan reminders of the glorious past—the Palace was the Taj Mahal of vaudeville. To a performer it was the pinnacle of achievement. To a youngster growing up in New York it was a theatre to visit on special occasions. I remember that as a teen-ager in the early twenties I haunted the neighborhood theatres in Brooklyn to catch matinees of vaudeville shows. Although I fought and bled with Wilbert Robinson's hapless, inane Dodgers and on a pleasant Sunday afternoon could not resist the teasing, tormenting battleground at Ebbets Field, I would elect, more often than not, to blow my pocket money on a vaudeville show. The Dodgers could be agonizing, but a balanced variety bill would be pleasure and, if the bill offered a comedian I worshiped, I could look forward to bliss.

The stock companies, like vaudeville, cultivated audiences as well as performers, and were even more important as training grounds for the stage. Largely self-contained units, they used the same corps of acting talent while they changed the play each week. The burden of preparation and performance was heavy, one week's rehearsals for each show, while another piece was on the boards. It was a breathless, indeed half-baked system, visible today in many summer theatres. But it taught a multitude of actors to be practical and flexible. Managements often were heedless and inept and pro-ductions catch-as-catch-can, and in setups of this kind young actors acquired mannerism and faults that would haunt their careers. Some of the nation's 2,000 stock companies were run conscien-tiously, but even the best found it difficult to compete with road shows led by glamorous stars. With the development of full-length silent movies the resident companies began to disappear, and the talking film provided the coup de grace. Although the work done by these companies was often shoddy, their disappearance was a grievous blow to the theatre. Young performers lost a practical school and laboratory, which the films and television have not re-placed, and a potential audience lost a proving ground of its own, which the screen and TV have taken over but not replaced.

Despite the abundance of theatrical activity in the early years of our century, there was little reflection of the new content and tech-nique emerging in Europe. In 1887 André Antoine had founded his Théâtre Libre in Paris and had turned to experimental works that stressed naturalism and truth; here Strindberg achieved his first great success with *The Father*. In 1889, Strindberg attempted to form his own company in Copenhagen, with only slight success, but in 1907 founded his Intimate Theatre in Stockholm and made it an effective forum of his own plays. In 1889 Otto Brahm brought the serious-minded, naturalism-oriented Freie Bühne into being in Berlin. In 1891, Paul Fort launched his Théâtre des Arts in Paris, and in the same year J. T. Grein organized the Independent Thea-tre in London and presented Shaw for the first time. In 1892 Lugné-Poë began his Théâtre de l'Oeuvre in Paris. The Moscow Art Thea-tre, led by Stanislavsky, came into existence in 1898 and discovered its great playwright in Chekhov. The very next year Yeats and Lady Gregory led in the foundation of the Irish Literary Theatre, which became the Abbey in 1904. Max Reinhardt started his Kleines Theater in Berlin in 1902, took over the Deutsches Thea-ter in 1905 and organized his Kammerspiele in 1906. Jacques Copeau was to come along with his seminal Théâtre du Vieux Colombier in 1913. Other forces for rebirth and innovation were at work. Adolphe Appia, the Swiss designer, had begun to proclaim his theories in 1895, and Gordon Craig made his first large public impact in 1902.

It would be foolish to say that these movements with their fierce dedication and their power to attract those who cared about the stage as an art had no effect on Americans. Earnest and devoted men and women could hear the vibrations from abroad and dared to think of bold new possibilities, but it was some time before they made themselves felt.

Cheek by jowl with new productions in the New York theatres were frequent visits of repertory companies from abroad to complement the native ones. An astonishing diversity of troupes in the year after 1900 offered special repertories for periods of several weeks to several months: Sothern and Marlowe; Mme. Réjane and a French company; Robert B. Mantell and his company, Ellen Terry and an English company, Ben Greet and his English Players, Ermete Novelli and an Italian company, Olga Nethersole and a company in a repertory of her favorite roles, Vera K. Komisarzhevsky and a Russian company, William Gillette and colleagues in a series of his admired roles, Sarah Bernhardt and a company, supported in one season by Lou Tellegen, matinee idol and early film star; John E. Kellerd and a company, Herbert Beerbohm Tree and his English troupe, Forbes Robertson and Gertrude Elliott leading their company; the Abbey Theatre, in its first visit in 1911; Donald Robertson and his company; Granville Baker's English company with its accent on Shaw, Holbrook Blinn and his company, Arnold Daly and his company; Grace George and her company, a season of German repertory with a company starring a turbulent newcomer from Germany, Rudolf Schildkraut, who represented the best of Reinhardt's Berlin theatre.

Ardent spirits were beginning to urge a native theatre that would aim for prestige as an art as well as commercial success. Then, as now, the emphasis was on production for profit. Then, as now, the intelligent critics bemoaned a dearth of vigorous, adult writing. There were attacks on the preeminence of the star, and indictments of those who did not deserve the laurel. There were complaints about the hasty erection of more theatres than New York needed and about the failure to fill them with worthwhile projects.

It is possible to cite events and trends that look deplorable to us and to cry somberly that they sum up a mindless age. At the same time one can adduce testimony that argues the opposite.

Glance at some Broadway hits of the first two decades of the century. As 1900 dawned *Ben Hur* was the show of the hour, and an actor named William S. Hart was in it. Another costume dramatization, *Quo Vadis,* turned up in the spring in two different productions. The novel *David Harum* became a play and vied with Herne's *Sag Harbor* for suffrage of those who liked rusticity on the stage. Mrs. Carter in *Zaza* was a Belasco special, and *Floradora* with its storied sextette led the musical stage. In the next two decades many great successes leaned heavily on charm, sentimentality, melodrama and corn. Among them were *The Wizard of Oz, Babes in Toyland, The Squaw Man, The Warrens of Virginia, Alias Jimmy Valentine, Get-Rich-Quick Wallingford, Rebecca of Sunnybrook Farm, Kismet, Potash and Perlmutter;* a typical A. H. Woods-produced bedroom farce, *Up in Mabel's Room;* and Frank Bacon's sentimental *Lightnin',* which set a record for its time with a New York run of 1,291 performances.

New stars were in the ascendant: Maude Adams in *Peter Pan* and *What Every Woman Knows;* Ethel Barrymore in another Barrie winner, *Alice Sit-By-the-Fire,* and in Maugham's *Lady Frederick;* brother John in Schnitzler's *The Affairs of Anatol,* Galsworthy's *Justice* and Du Maurier's *Peter Ibbetson;* Mary Pickford and Lillian Gish in Belasco's production of Rostand's *A Good Little Devil;* Laurette Taylor in *Peg o' my Heart,* Ina Claire in *Polly with a Past,* Lenore Ulric in *Tiger Rose,* Ruth Gordon in *Seventeen* and Jane Cowl in *Smilin' Through.* In 1908 Theodosia de Coppet appeared in a Molnar melodrama, *The Devil,* but achieved fame as a national seductress in the silent films as Theda Bara, while in 1909 a tot named Helen Hayes first trod a stage in a bit role in *Old Dutch,* a Herbert operetta.

There were, it was true, other offerings. Ibsen was being performed with increasing tenacity. Hauptmann's *The Weavers* with its trenchant look at the conflict between capital and labor was produced in 1915. Shaw was frequently represented; indeed, he had a remarkable showing in 1905. Arnold Daly and Mabel Taliaferro introduced *You Never Can Tell,* which earned a gratifying run of 129 performances, and Robert Loraine appeared in *Man and Superman* for 192 performances. Daly presented a two-month season of *Candida, The Man of Destiny, How He Lied to Her Husband, You Never Can Tell, John Bull's Other Island* and *Mrs. Warren's Profession,* which was new and which got Daly and Mary Shaw, his leading lady, into court. Although the newspapers inveighed against this offense against decency and morality, the case was thrown out.

Commercialism in the theatre, then as now, was not exclusively crass. It made room for lively and provocative plays, but there is no shadow of doubt that it lavished the bulk of its attentions and substance on flashy, empty rodomontades that would sell.

CHAPTER XII

REAL STAGY LIFE

A STEP FORWARD in the development of a responsible school of American dramatic writing was the appearance of William Vaughan Moody. Some students of the American theatre hold that *The Great Divide,* presented on October 3, 1906, with Henry Miller and Margaret Anglin at the Princess Theatre in New York, marked our dramatic coming of age. Others deny Moody the honor of writing the first American play that could be taken seriously and insist it belongs to Eugene O'Neill and *Beyond the Horizon,* which had its first production in 1920. Intransigent judges will not even concede this honor to O'Neill, and the most uncompromising analysts, who choose to dwell only among masterpieces, are not yet ready to doff their berets to any American.

To one who reexamines Moody with an awareness of the mechanical, sentimental and crude stuff that was current, *The Great Divide* and *The Faith Healer,* his only other commercially produced play, are a mild, but not large advance. In intention Moody was ahead of his contemporaries. A teacher of English literature and a poet, he was a considerable cut above the fabricators of the run-of-the-mill plays. He had standing as a man of letters, and in those days American writers of his inclinations avoided the theatre.

Even before 1900 his plays were gestating, and although he occupied himself with poetic drama like *The Masque of Judgment,* he faced up to commercial exigencies. After meeting some professional playwrights, he called them "capital chaps" and observed that "the great thing about them is that they get their things played, and that sort of thing, begad, begins to appeal to me," though he had not turned "quite recreant to his ideals." Nevertheless, *The Great Divide* won an immense commercial success. *The Faith Healer,* produced in 1910 in New York by Henry Miller, had no such luck.

By our standards, *The Great Divide* is obvious and transparent. In its own time it did not impress all of Moody's contemporaries. Those were the innocent days when Americans, in their eagerness to have native plays of distinction, were on the qui vive for the Great American Drama. The epithet was pinned on Moody's play by hasty commentators, but the critic of *The New York Times* pointed to faults in the play's construction and denied that any play could be designated as the Great American Drama.

The Great Divide confronts a woman who represents the Puritan inhibitions of the East and a man with the bursting, independent spirit of the new West. The opening scene, in which Ruth Jordan is left alone in her brother's cabin in the great Wild West and is attacked by three half-drunken men, now is embarrassingly corny. Her weariness with the effete East and her longing for a primitive mate are also hard to take. The willingness of Stephen Ghent, one of the three brutes, to save her, if she pays his price, is another cliché of the Western. Not to outrage respectable tastes, that price was designated as marriage. However, in the published version of the play, there was no allusion to marriage. The real Moody is heard in Ghent's attack on outworn standards:

Our law is joy, and selfishness; the curve of your shoulder and the light on your hair as you sit there says that as plain as preaching.—Does it gall you the way we came together? You asked me that night what brought me, and I told you whiskey, and sun, and the devil. Well, I tell you now that I'm thankful on my knees for all three! Does it rankle in your mind that I took you when I could get you, by main strength and fraud? I guess that most good women are taken that way, if they only knew it. Don't you want to be paid for? I guess every good wife is paid for in some good coin or other.

Does this sound old-fashioned? It is, of course. But it is easy to see why *The Great Divide* blew into the theatre like a breath of fresh air. And Moody had the integrity to see to it that both characters changed and grew—the man as well as the woman—and that the inevitably happy ending made some sense.

In *The Faith Healer,* which Moody had contemplated before *The Great Divide,* he tackled the conflict between love and work, between belief and disbelief, between the rational and the occult. Plays touching on the mysteries of the mind were to follow, but in 1910 *The Faith Healer* was daring. It reflected a viewpoint that was fresh in American optimism—honest, rather than stagily contrived.

Was 1906 the pivotal year some scholars say it was? The only other American play of 1906 with any claim to attention is Langdon Mitchell's *The New York Idea.* I saw a revival of it several years ago by the Harvard Summer Players, admittedly an amateur group, not to be compared with the original cast of Mrs. Fiske, George Arliss, Emily Stevens, Marion Lea and John Mason, nor with a 1915 revival headed by Grace George. By uncompromising artistic standards *The New York Idea* is a trifle. By today's standards of fashionable comedy, *The New York Idea* is as quaint in its social posture as a Currier and Ives print. But for its time, it was social comedy that hinted at the spirit of the new century. Our specimens of this dramatic species differ in degree, not in kind.

The ingredients now look like those of slick-magazine fiction. Divorce and remarriage comprise the daring subject matter, sweetened to be inoffensive. Mrs. Karslake, who has impetuously divorced her gallant, handsome husband, still loves him, and in the end the decree turns out to be defective and the divorce is invalid. Thus we have the happy ending required by consumers of sugary fiction.

Stage writers were influenced by Moody and perhaps a little by the new novelists like Stephen Crane, Charles Norris and Theodore Dreiser. They began to recognize that man and his world deserved an honest look in the theatre. Valid themes were adumbrated by writers who wished to broaden the theatre's content. But nearly always these themes were compromised by a softness of attitude or a confusion of ideas and technique.

Sticky romanticism was the undoing of Edward Sheldon, who emerged from George Pierce Baker's bold Harvard experiment in academic recognition of the drama. Sheldon began with audacious ideas and failed them. In 1908, at twenty-two, a year after his graduation from Harvard, he made his debut in New York with *Salvation Nell,* and his first commercially produced play was a success, thanks in no small measure to its star—Mrs. Fiske. The play set out to be realistic about the corner saloon, the slums and their inhabitants, but did not follow through on the implications of its theme and naturalistic setting.

In *The Nigger* Sheldon fixed on a theme whose relevance has certainly not diminished. Early in the first act his protagonist, Philip Morrow, a decent Southerner who stands for law and against lynching, declares his belief in the purity of blood, "white's white and black's black," and in the separation of the races. It turns out, however, that he has a touch of Negro blood himself. His antagonist, a whiskey manufacturer, threatens to disclose Philip's secret. Now governor of a southern state, the hero must decide whether he shall let himself be blackmailed into silence and insure his personal happiness or acknowledge the truth and thus sacrifice everything —his position and the woman he loves. Sheldon resolved his theme in a haze of romantic self-abnegation. The real issue he had raised was forgotten as he bathed the audience in syrup.

With the best will in the world one cannot help but write off Sheldon as a playwright who, for all his awareness of urgent social problems, was essentially a slick, commercial fabricator of romanticism. His gallantry as a human being, however, was extraordinary. Disabled by a crippling illness, he ceased to write on his own in later years; yet upon his death in 1946, he was mourned not only for his acknowledged work but for his contributions to the plays of others. He helped a host of young writers, collaborating helpfully with some, on *Bewitched* with Sidney Howard (1924); on *Lulu Belle,* the story of a Negro prostitute, a big Lenore Ulric role in 1926, with Charles MacArthur; on *Dishonored Lady* with Margaret Ayer Barnes, which provided Katharine Cornell with a fat role in 1930.

Percy MacKaye, the son of Steele, spent a long lifetime seeking to wean the theatre from commercialism. A friend of Moody, he regarded the stage as a place for aspiration and vision.

In *The Playhouse and the Play*, published in 1909, he wrote, with the passion of the prophet, "And so today, though Puritan has departed and Satan has lost his anathema, and though the people once more flock back in multitudes to the playhouse, yet they no longer enter it as a public temple; new generations have forgotten that ever it was one, for they find it occupied by private merchants; and the joy of life which they view there is no longer dedicated to the common aspiration."

His best piece was *The Scarecrow,* much less pretentious than the elaborate poetic masques he later undertook. Here he presaged the freedom of imagination that another generation of Americans was to discover in native folk drama. *The Scarecrow,* produced at Harvard in 1909 and in Middletown, Connecticut, late in 1910, did not have much success on Broadway in 1911. In his adaptation of Nathaniel Hawthorne's story, *Feathertop,* MacKaye changed the characters and made additions of his own. He added human sympathy, he said, for the sake of irony.

Set in a seventeenth-century Massachusetts town, *The Scarecrow,* which MacKaye called "a tragedy of the ludicrous," invests the theme of witchcraft with a touch of humanism. The Yankee variation on the Devil is cynical and charming. The apt son of a theatrically imaginative father, Percy MacKaye, employed effective stage devices to capture a mood. When his Devil sits down to the spinet, he produces a weird chorus of cawings. With delicacy of touch MacKaye uses black magic to turn a scarecrow into a suitor for the hand of a girl, and then invokes love, with sensitive simplicity, to exorcise the Devil and turn the diabolical creation into a man. Once the miracle has been passed, the scarecrow, converted to humanity, falls dead. In the play's final words, MacKaye concentrates his proud affirmation, "But a man!"

Rachel Crothers, who wrote with success for more than four decades, used the stage to articulate the case for woman's freedom.

When the battle was won, she did not shrink from poking fun at the liberated woman's pretensions. Her work had sanity and humor, often sophistication and maturity. Although she did not dig deeply into questions of marriage, the new place of women, the rebellion of the young, she was always timely and bright. In the late thirties she could be amusing and a hit in a comedy about the Oxford Movement, *Susan and God,* with the enchanting Gertrude Lawrence to charm one and all. She could also toss off cheerful trifles like *Expressing Willie.* Her producer usually was John Golden, but she supervised and staged most of her own plays.

Clare Kummer brought a light approach to her work, notably in *Good Gracious, Annabelle,* and *Rollo's Wild Oats.* Jesse Lynch Williams in *Why Marry?* tackled marriage with some maturity and intelligence and won the first Pulitzer Prize in 1917. Owen Davis, who ground out melodramas like *Tony the Bootblack* and *Nellie the Beautiful Cloak Model,* the way a pulp writer might turn out cheap fiction, in the twenties could change direction and offer *The Detour* and *Icebound* and then collaborate with his son, Donald, in the dramatization of Pearl Buck's *The Good Earth,* and Edith Wharton's *Ethan Frome.*

In a way Booth Tarkington, immensely popular and adroit in applying his skills to the stage, summarizes the mood of the theatre before the upheaval of the twenties. His *Beaucaire,* a vehicle for Richard Mansfield, filled the stage with costume elegance in 1911. In 1919 at the dawn of a new epoch, his *Clarence* beguiled theatregoers. No one can deny that the cast assembled by George C. Tyler, the producer, was a winner, with the warm and lovable Mary Boland, the young and artful Helen Hayes, the disarmingly adolescent and awkward Glenn Hunter and the winning, youthful Alfred Lunt as Clarence.

Although a bloody world war had just been fought, the age of innocence was in full bloom. The sixteen-year-old Bobby remarks to Clarence, "Listen, do you think when a man's taken advantage of a woman's inexperience and kissed her he's bound to go ahead and marry her even if he's in love with another woman?" Forgetting what today's sixteen-year-olds are like, do you think they were that simple in 1919? The girls all fell wholesomely for Clarence—

the teen-ager, her mother, the little housemaid, the pretty governess. Clarence himself, in the easy comic tradition, was the likable
simpleton who turned out to be an important entomologist and
who, more resourceful than anyone in sight, could solve every
problem.

The comedy, if you read it now, is transparent, but its counterparts still thrive. Laughs are derived from confusion about Clarence's surname, which naturally turns out to be Smith, and from
a strange word like "coleoptera," which shrouds "beetles" in mystery for ever so long. You can depend on Tarkington to extract
every smirk from the foolishness of adolescence. At the end the
teen-ager refuses to say goodbye to Clarence: "I won't! I hate engaged men! I hate 'em, I hate 'em, I hate 'em!" And the play's last
line might well serve as an epitaph for an era's fraudulent innocence, "Oh, Clarence!"

CHAPTER XIII

OPERETTAS AND FOLLIES

Lᴏɴᴅᴏɴ, as Henry Arthur Jones, the English playwright, complained, may have been a happy hunting ground for musical production in 1906, but New York had 33 that year, beginning with George M. Cohan's *Forty-five Minutes from Broadway,* with its hit tune, "Mary Is a Grand Old Name."

Mindful of the most distinctive of our musical plays with their tightly knit plots, smoothly integrated songs, choreographed movement and painstakingly cast, staged and designed productions, we are tempted to look down on musical theatre in the nineteenth century and the turn of the twentieth. We think of it as an ornate reflection of a simple-minded world, and it was, but it had its compensations.

It is true that our musical theatre was a long time in forming a profile of its own. In the nineteenth century it was largely a matter of pastiches, parodies, *ad hoc* assemblages of popular, appealing materials. It was manifested in part in minstrel shows, variety and plays like those of Harrigan and Hoyt with their admixture of songs. *The Black Crook* was an accident, an extravaganza that was successful by chance, and its brazenness alienated the respectable public. Popular musical theatre of grace and gaiety came from Europe in the works of Gilbert and Sullivan, Offenbach, Suppé,

Johann Strauss. *Pinafore,* first revealed in Boston in 1878, swept the nation, with almost a hundred companies performing it in one season, including five in New York.

Gilbert and Sullivan as well as the French and Austrian operettas were charming, stylish and proper. The pieces from the Continent might have intimations of naughtiness, but they were the nice sort. Women could freely patronize them, and even children could be taken to them without danger of sullying their pure, impressionable young natures. Operetta was the rage, and it was only natural that America should turn out its own brand.

A Victor Herbert operetta became an annual staple. The 1906 contribution, *The Red Mill,* had succeeded the 1905 *Mlle. Modiste,* which gloried in the radiant and sweet-voiced Fritzi Scheff and in the romantic "Kiss Me Again." Miss Scheff was back in *The Prima Donna* in 1908. *Naughty Marietta* boasted Emma Trentini and such hit tunes as "Italian Street Song," "I'm Falling in Love With Someone" and "Ah, Sweet Mystery of Life."

Later Rudolf Friml and Sigmund Romberg stood out among a host of writers who ground out the expected product until in the twenties we got *Rose-Marie* and *The Vagabond King* from the former and *Blossom Time,* which "immortalized" as it vandalized Franz Schubert, from the latter.

Were the stories in the long line of American operas as artificial as those from Europe? Were the characters as papier-mâché? Hardly anyone objected so long as the performers had personality, the costumes were colorful, the scenery was picture-postcard pretty and, most important of all, the songs were caressing and lilting.

The best-minted operettas still came from Europe. None was more successful than *The Merry Widow* which arrived in New York in October 1907, after a huge European triumph. Lehár's songs swept everything before them. Its waltz planted the kiss of death on the rigid drills and marches that had been favorites of some of our musicals. Two Tin Pan Alley writers did a takeoff called "I'm Looking for the Man Who Wrote the Merry Widow Waltz." Ethel Jackson as the widow and Donald Brian as Prince Danilo were the romantic couple of theatregoers' dreams, as the operetta racked up an astonishing run of 417 performances.

The incredibly versatile George M. Cohan typified a thoroughly native American style and endeared himself with it. Breezy and relaxed, he epitomized the song-and-dance man. Imagine someone who combines the gifts of Bing Crosby and Fred Astaire, and you have a notion of Cohan. Add his gift for the common touch in a plot, a song or stage business and you can see why his musical theatre from *The Governor's Son* in 1901 won so many hearts. Yet his shows did not amass the long-run records we are accustomed to. *Little Johnny Jones,* in 1904, had only 50-odd performances, despite its unforgotten songs, "The Yankee Doodle Boy" and "Give My Regards to Broadway."

Jerome Kern and Irving Berlin, who were to figure prominently in the transformation of the musical theatre, began to contribute a song to a musical comedy here or a revue there. Kern did his first complete score for *The Red Petticoat* in 1912. By 1915 he was collaborating with Guy Bolton and by 1917, when *Have a Heart* appeared, P. G. Wodehouse had joined the team, which produced a huge success like *Oh, Boy* and a fresh work like *Leave It to Jane.*

Berlin reached the Broadway stage when he did a specialty number for the 1910 *Ziegfeld Follies* and followed with "Ephraham" and "Woodman, Woodman, Spare That Tree," for the *Follies* of 1911; by 1919 his gifts to the *Follies* were "Bevo," "Mandy," "A Pretty Girl Is Like a Melody," "You Cannot Make Your Shimmy Shake on Tea" and "I'm the Guy Who Guards the Harem." That *Follies* was regaled by Eddie Dowling, Mary Hay, Ray Dooley, Johnny Dooley, Marilyn Miller, Bert Williams, Van and Schenck, Eddie Cantor and Billie Dove.

In 1906 the *Follies* had not yet been born. The first arrived in 1907, ushered in by Florenz (né Florence) Ziegfeld, whose name and product became a byword for the gaudiest and most glamorous Broadway showmanship. If you are old enough, as I am, to have seen the versions produced in the 1920's, you will remember the extravagance of the décor, the lavishness of the costumes, the statuesque beauty of the girls, the titillation of the draping and undraping and, to be plain about it, the unevenness, if not downright absence of glowing entertainment.

But when Ziegfeld put together the first of these revues, which were to become a standard for himself and competitors to aim at, he was merely assembling a show for Klaw & Erlanger, to be presented on the New York Theatre roof, which was called resplendently the Jardin de Paris. This roof auditorium had its own roof of corrugated iron, open at the sides for a breath of air. The opening was on July 8, 1907, and one can imagine the effect of a heat-absorbent roof on a non-air-conditioned auditorium during a New York heat wave. Ziegfeld naturally began with a line of generously curved Anna Held girls. Julian Mitchell, staging the show, took pains to move and group them. The featured beauty was Annabelle Whitford, and she had a turn as the Gibson Bathing Girl. Appearing in bloomers, blouse and stockings, she must have seemed naughty and enticing. But the first *Follies* also behaved like a topical revue. It poked fun at Anthony Comstock and John D. Rockefeller Sr.

The first *Follies* required only $13,000 and had a weekly operating budget of $1,800. These costs, incredibly modest by our standards, were not insignificant in 1907. The show was not hailed by the critics and it had trouble paying its way. It moved from the Jardin de Paris to a real theatre, the Liberty, and added Norah Bayes as a star, but it earned a profit only when it went on tour.

Fervent show-business sentimentalists have bathed the *Follies* in nostalgia, implying that they summed up an age, and in a way they reflected part of its spirit. They responded to the longing for conspicuous luxuriance, which we satisfy today after a fashion on our enormous Cinemascope and Panavision screens and in such ostentatious conglomerations as the Christmas and Easter shows at Radio City Music Hall. They offered, in their gorgeously formed, dressed and posed girls, corporeal visions of idealized beauty. These annual revues were splashy, gaudy, tantalizing and eye-opening. More often than not they also remembered to be entertaining.

Examine the record of the *Follies* until Ziegfeld died in 1932. Even when their blood was running thin, they had infusions of the iron of earthy comedy and vibrant song. In the early days the shows abounded in a vitality that outshone the veneer of production elegance. One can guess at the effect made in 1908 by Norah Bayes and Jack Norworth singing their own song, "Shine On Harvest Moon." One may smile patronizingly, but one may be sure that in 1909 the ineffably beauteous Lillian Lorraine and her sisters in charm enchanted the men in the audience when they came out in knickers and tossed baseballs over the footlights as they sang "Come On Play Ball With Me." Were Miss Lorraine and her companions any easier to resist the next edition when, seated in billowing skirts on swings, thy soared over the front rows, singing "Swing Me High, Swing Me Low" while bells on the swings tinkled the melody and the girls flung flowers into the eager hands of the customers?

Ziegfeld looked constantly for new dances. One year it was "The Pensacola Mooch," a kind of shuffle. At the dawn of the jazz age it was a volatile dance performed to a spirited song called "I Want to Learn to Jazz Dance." He knew that a new, popular step could be a marvelous salesman for his shows.

Long before 1922, when he adopted the slogan, "Glorifying the American Girl," Ziegfeld had made the *Follies* the constant, resourceful Broadway pioneer in displaying the female of the species. His tableaux vivants were always teasers; eventually they turned so literal that they lost their mischievous gleam. It is difficult, of course, to see much fun or invention in a 1915 turn like "A Girl for Every Month of the Year," but with a dazzling beauty impersonating each month, Ziegfeld could offer gorgeous girls in a parade of pulchritude. No wonder rich swains thronged the stage door and became the sources of tantalizing gossip.

They seem naïve now—these Ziegfeld enticements: Anna Held flying in, via a short filmed sequence, as a comet in the year of Halley's Comet; Ann Pennington as "September Morn," the year of the Armory Show of modern painting; Annette Kellerman, the shapely swimmer, in her famous one-piece bathing suit; a stunning underwater sequence devised by Joseph Urban; Irene Castle, enchanting with her inciting come-hither walk; Ina Claire, young and matchlessly beautiful, having a whirl at songs and impersonations.

Best of all, at least in retrospect, were the comedians: Fannie Brice, who entered the *Follies* in 1910 and sang a song, "Goodbye,

Becky Cohen," by an unfledged writer namer Irving Berlin; Bert
Williams, the inimitable Negro performer, who as a tramp in rags
or man-about-town in tails, could sing and act and tell jokes that
seemed coined on the spot; Ed Wynn, flutteringly and shrewdly
silly; W. C. Fields, once a juggler, who could write a funny skit for
himself and partners and who, in one *Follies*, bounced a billiard
cue off Wynn's head for the perfectly understandable reason that
Ed was taking larcenous title to his laughs; Will Rogers, who
twirled a lariat and commented with genial nasal irony on the
day's news, like a harbinger of our stand-up comedians; Leon
Errol, of the rubbery legs; Eddie Cantor, of the bulging eyes and
bouncing song style.

By 1913 Ziegfeld was able to move into the shining and opulent
New Amsterdam Theatre, where he remained until his Ziegfeld
Theatre opened on Sixth Avenue in the glum depression days just
before his death. It is difficult for us to recapture the glamour of
42nd Street between Seventh and Eighth Avenues when it was a
thoroughfare of hits and the heart of Broadway and the New Amsterdam was the queen of houses. Here, on the roof, Ziegfeld instituted his *Midnight Frolics*, which he ran from 1915 to 1922, and
they were the forerunners of modern floor shows in the large caba-
rets and night spots and a trial arena for future *Follies* stars. Walk
down the tawdry thoroughfare that 42nd Street has become, with
the once-grand New Amsterdam serving, like its neighbors, as a
grind house for old films at low prices, and look at the cheap stores,
the pinball alleys and the low characters who infest the sidewalks
and you sigh for the degradation wrought by the headlong years
and careless men.

Ziegfeld's extravagances were legendary. He spent hundreds of
dollars on the silk for cushions, and with a regal gesture jettisoned
a set that cost thousands. He spared no expense to get stars or writing talent or directors or designers, and he attracted gifted newcomers. He had George Gershwin as a rehearsal pianist in 1918.
In the twenties he brought in large name bands.

Compared with the costs of a handsome musical today, his expenditures, if you do not take into account the difference in the
value of the dollar, do not seem outlandish. The *Follies* of 1918

cost $100,000. The 1921 edition, however, came to $250,000. By the twenties he sensed that book shows were the wave of the future, and he produced some, with varying results, even as he continued his *Follies*. One of the most successful was *Sunny*, which starred the delectable Marilyn Miller. His most significant was *Show Boat*.

CHAPTER XIV

PRESSURE FOR CHANGE

IT IS ALWAYS TEMPTING to simplify history, to select a man, work and date and proclaim them as a turning point. For the American theatre the magic year is supposed to be 1920, and the work *Beyond the Horizon*. The first full-length O'Neill to be produced, it was presented at the Morosco, on February 2, 1920, by John D. Williams, once associated with Charles Frohman, and a man of independent taste and judgment. No matter that George Jean Nathan, the critic, brought the piece to Williams's attention; a Broadway producer had recognized and endorsed O'Neill's arrival.

Beyond the Horizon did mark a notable change. In the light of today's uncompromising frankness of language and unsparing probing of character, it is tame. But in the context of its own time, its honesty was a tonic after decades of realism confined to literal and trivial details of stagecraft. The characters were not good or bad guys, saints or sinners, and their problems were treated with a reach for the harsh truth.

Ruth, the girl who chose the wrong brother, was brought to life in all her dissatisfaction, resentment and bitter defeat; there was no glossing of "the sad humility of exhaustion." Andy, the brother who had gone away, returned in disillusion; all he "found in the East was a stench." Robert, the brother who stayed home, could only console himself that the "wonders of the world happened on the other side of those hills," for he was defeated by the meanness of his environment.

What impressed people eager for a new voice to lead the American theatre out of its wilderness of mediocrity now strikes us as essentially sentimental. Suffering from an incurable disease, Robert at the end scanned the horizon and exulted that at last he was free, "free to wander on and on—eternally! . . . And this time I'm going! It isn't the end. It's a free beginning—the start of my voyage! I've won to my trip—the right of release—beyond the horizon! Oh, you ought to be glad—glad—for my sake!"

This was a reversion to romanticism; it had a sophomoric ring; it was rhetorical rather than true. In 1920, however, the play was like a refreshing breeze in a stale front parlor, grandly and excessively furnished but airless because the windows were tightly sealed. But it could not fairly be designated as the theatre's coming of age.

Influences for maturity had been at work a long time. Intelligent, if isolated, voices had spoken up before the turn of the century, and were joined by new, more numerous, even more ardent ones. After Herne there had been Moody and Percy MacKaye and Josephine Peabody and other writers of aspiration. Actor-managers like Henry Miller, E. H. Sothern and Margaret Anglin, managers like Harrison Grey Fiske, Winthrop Ames and later Arthur Hopkins espoused aims beyond the conventional and plushy. Teachers like George Pierce Baker with his Workshop 47 at Harvard and Frederick H. Koch at the University of North Dakota and the University of North Carolina were eager to open new windows and to look beyond the confining commercialized limits.

The preparation for the revolution of the twenties occurred in a multiplicity of ways and places. Enthusiasts for a mature drama formed the Drama League in 1910, which published the *Drama Quarterly* until 1931. In 1912 the Little Theatres began to sprout: the Toy Theatre in Boston, headed by Mrs. Lyman Gale; the Chicago Little Theatre, led by Maurice Browne and Ellen Van Volkenburg, and the Little Theatre shepherded by Ames in New York. They were followed by a host of others, and they reflected an improbable commingling of idealism, practicality, snobbish estheticism and social climbing. At their best they accomplished useful things, and at their most ludicrous were pretentious and inept. Their absurdity was memorialized by *The Torchbearers*, a farce that was a 1922 success and introduced George Kelly as a playwright.

Since the new plays and new writers did not make their full impact until the twenties, it is easy to overlook the preparatory stir. The Provincetown Players came into existence in 1915, and the Washington Square Players materialized in the same year. This was also the year when Irene and Alice Lewisohn helped to launch the Neighborhood Playhouse at the Henry Street Settlement, and Stuart Walker started his Portmanteau Theatre at the Christodora Settlement House. In 1916 Gilmore Brown founded the Pasadena Playhouse, and in the same year the Cleveland Play House came into being. In 1916 Sheldon Cheney started what became the serious magazine *Theatre Arts*. The Theatre Guild arrived in 1918.

These groups and movements provided the bubbling activity that expressed a vast ferment underneath. The United States was slowly discovering the new ideas and trends that had appeared in Europe. Travelers brought back news of change and upheaval abroad, and energetic voices at home attacked the hypocrisy and injustice of our social institutions and the stuffiness of our artistic institutions.

The war speeded change. Since Theodore Roosevelt and his "manifest destiny" we had been flexing our muscles, like a world power to be, but we were hesitant about openly assuming the responsibilities that go with power. Despite our losses in the war, we turned away from an active role of leadership in the councils of nations, rejecting Woodrow Wilson and the League of Nations. By our very political abstinence, we played a larger part in the making of future history than we realized. Although we refused to look outward on the world political arena, we reveled in our strength and resources. As we plunged into the twenties, we were like giants capable of prodigies. In sport we entered the era of the legendary champions—Babe Ruth, William T. Tilden, Robert T. Jones Jr., Jack Dempsey. Prosperity, we were assured, would be ours alone and eternal, with a chicken in very pot and two cars in every garage.

Not all Americans were subdued by this illusion of bumptious materialism. Some stayed at home to protest its false foundations and falser values: Sinclair Lewis was not a great novelist, but in *Main Street* and *Babbitt* he had the clear, truthful eye of a moralist. Other Americans exempted themselves from domestic felicity and became expatriates, railing at the noisy, sprawling loudmouth of a native land from the cafés on the Left Bank. In 1932 Elmer Rice in his play *The Left Bank* made the valid point that home was where the intelligent American belonged.

The ground swells foretelling changes in the theatrical landscape were rippling and heaving before 1920, but for the commercial theatre, largely centered around Broadway and happily preoccupied with more rushing business than usual in the booming twenties, the tremors were negligible. The effort to establish a repertory company at the New Theatre on Central Park West in a new home that later became the Century Theatre had failed after two seasons, starting in 1909, and obviously there was no threat in such an organization.

Privately supported and idealistically conceived, it was dilettantishly high-minded. Its company enlisted well-known, even distinguished names, like Sothern and Marlowe, Grace George, Rose Coghlan, Louis Calvert, Ferdinand Gottschalk, Annie Russell, Olga Nethersole and Frank Gillmore, but its policy had no core of esthetic conviction. The plays included classics as well as contemporary pieces like Galsworthy's *Strife,* Sheldon's *The Nigger,* Besier's *Don,* Pinero's *The Thunderbolt,* three by Maeterlinck (*Sister Beatrice, The Bluebird,* and *Mary Magdalene*) and an act from Ibsen's *Brand.* The repertory was varied but revealed no passionate commitment to a school or philosophy and, with only Sheldon's play to speak for America, was painfully deficient in native content. The theatre moreover was too large and acoustically defective.

A consuming drive can be more creative than a fat checkbook, as the Provincetown group began to prove on Cape Cod in 1915. These ardent spirits had plays of their own to write and on paper;

they wanted to act, design and create. They included George Cram Cook, Susan Glaspell, Mary Heaton Vorse, Wilbur Daniel Steele, John Reed, Robert Edmond Jones and Hutchins Hapgood.

Mary Heaton Vorse, back from a trip to bleeding Europe, found that "America did not want to think about war in the summer of 1915." As she recalled in *Footnote to Folly:*

Provincetown was very gay and full of life. The year before we had acted a play by Neith Boyce called *Constancy*. Now we organized the Provincetown Players and began giving plays on my fish wharf. We had a building fifty feet by a hundred with a door at the back which opened on the sea. I contributed a curtain which had been our curtain in the attic of Amherst, where as children we had given plays. We gave a play by Wilbur Daniel Steele and *Suppressed Desires* by Susan Glaspell and a satire on the conflict between the new school of art and the old which was then raging in Provincetown.

We made our own benches and our own scenery. The first performances were lighted by oil lamps. Four people in the wings held lamps, beside them four more with buckets of ashes.

Suddenly everyone took to writing plays. The beginning of the Provincetown Players was an organic thing like a plant growing. No one said, "Come, let's found a little theatre." We had no idea that we were to help break through the traditions of Broadway and revolutionize and humanize the theatre of America.

They were not entirely unknown, these organic growers. Jones, for example, had just revealed his mettle in designs for Granville Barker's production of Anatole France's *The Man Who Married a Dumb Wife*. They welcomed newcomers with talent. The next summer they introduced the first of O'Neill's work to be performed publicly—the one-act pieces, *Bound East for Cardiff* and *Thirst*, and the following winter they took over a converted stable on Macdougal Street in New York's Greenwich Village and as the Playwright's Theatre began an exciting career that lasted until 1929. O'Neill was their shining contribution. Besides his short pieces, they produced *The Emperor Jones, Diff'rent, The Hairy Ape, All God's Chillun Got Wings* and *Desire Under the Elms*. They introduced Paul Green's *In Abraham's Bosom*. They were the magnet for men and women who made a difference on the

American theatrical and literary scene: Edna St. Vincent Millay, Floyd Dell, James Light, Jasper Deeter, Kenneth Macgowan, Walter Huston, Cleon Throckmorton and Donald Oenslager. They also offered foreign plays by writers like Strindberg and Schnitzler, largely ignored in the United States.

The Washington Square Players began not in Washington Square but on East 57th Street in the aptly named Bandbox Theatre, commencing early in 1915 with one-act plays by Lawrence Langner, Edward Goodman, and Maeterlinck. For the *Interior* by Maeterlinck, there was a magically evocative set created with Robert Edmond Jones's help for $35. The admission charge was 50 cents; performances took place twice a week for several weeks. No one, of course, was paid. The next season there were three performances a week, and salaries of $25 were parceled out. In a sense these performances were the precursors of the weekend enterprises that one encounters in various parts of the country today where amateur, semiprofessional and even professional theatre people struggle to provide their communities with plays that the road shows and better-heeled professional units are neglecting.

By the end of their second season the Washington Square Players could undertake two full-length plays—Maeterlinck's *Aglavaine and Sélysette* and Chekhov's *The Sea Gull*. The vanguard of New York's theatre public rallied to them, and the Players transferred their operations to the Comedy Theatre for the third season, and here they virtually took on Broadway in head-on competition. They could not afford to be so carefree as in the past, and had to seek plays of stature. They turned to Shaw, Andreyev and Ibsen, and to American playwrights like Zoë Akins, Philip Moeller and Lewis Beach, to a designer like Lee Simonson and to talented young actors like Roland Young, Katharine Cornell, Rollo Peters, Frank Conroy, José Ruben and Glenn Hunter.

The Washington Square Players became the nucleus of the Theatre Guild. Meeting late in 1918, some of these Players formed the new organization, with a board of managers that included Langner, Simonson, Peters, Moeller, Helen Freeman, Helen Westley and Justus Sheffield, and later Theresa Helburn and Maurice Wertheim were added.

The Guild formally introduced itself at the Garrick Theatre in 1918 with Jacinto Benavente's *The Bonds of Interest*. The working capital had been $1,000, and when the second production, St. John Ervine's *John Ferguson,* opened in May, the treasury held $19.50. Happily, *John Ferguson* caught on, and the Guild's future was assured.

The climate into which the new group plunged was recalled in 1936 in the introduction signed by Moeller, Langner, Helburn, Armina Marshall, Westley and Alfred Lunt for *Theatre Guild Anthology:*

It had happened that the Guild dropped its idea into fertile soil in 1918. It took root in an unusual state of unrest which had begun to take form in the American theatre shortly after the turn of the century and which, with the end of the World War, had grown to dangerous proportions. The organized drama was in the hands of commercially minded producers whose eyes were intent upon the box-office. They dominated the drama to the extent of imposing their own idea of what the public wanted upon helpless theatregoers.

Playwriting had been reduced to a formula. Producers refused to permit violation of the formula in fear of failure. It was almost impossible to penetrate the stone wall with a new idea. If playwrights were unwilling to write the usual "happy-ending" drama, their chances of a hearing were slight. There were exceptions, of course, but they were few.

The Guild set out to give itself and its public continuity with a subscription plan. But in that first year it had 135 subscribers. Eventually it built up a subscription list of 25,000 in New York and an additional 25,000 outside New York.

If *John Ferguson* set the Guild on the right path, *Heartbreak House* in 1920 firmly fixed its course for the next decade. Shaw could not find a producer in London or New York for this glittering attack on war, which he had begun in 1913 and had withheld until after the war's end. Finally, he let the Guild produce the play—on his carefully designated terms. With characteristic alertness he would not let the Guild open *Heartbreak House* until the third week in November. To Theresa Helburn he wrote, as Langner recalled in his book, *G. B. S. and the Lunatic,* that "the Theatre is so out of touch with politics that it never even knows a Presidential election is on until it finds that the public is not paying the slightest attention to it and *won't* until the Monday following the first Tuesday in November relieves its mind as to who will be President next year." Explaining that he was "inexorable" against an earlier opening, he went on to remark that "very thankful you will be to me for having saved you from a disastrous blunder. You will be wiser four years hence. This is your first election. I forgive you for not being aware of the danger."

Heartbreak House ran for 125 performances, sufficient in 1920–21 to insure financial as well as artistic success.

Beyond the Horizon and *Heartbreak House* both arrived in 1920. What better proof that this was the year of a crucial upturn in the maturity of the American theatre? Yet in the *Theatre Arts Anthology* one finds a review by Kenneth Magowan, published in July 1919, which indicates that romantic and realistic forces were tugging the New York theatre in different directions.

The brave new world did not suddenly appear like Minerva out of the brow of Jupiter, on a given day, month, year or decade. The new, vigorous groups had begun to flex their muscles before 1920, and there were other signs of hope. In 1918 Arthur Hopkins produced a season of Ibsen—*The Wild Duck, A Doll's House* and *Hedda Gabler*—with Nazimova. And in 1919, besides *Clarence, Up in Mabel's Room* and a high-society drama like *Déclassée* by Zoë Akins with Ethel Barrymore, there was a somber production of Gorki's *Night Lodging* (*The Lower Depths*), produced by Arthur Hopkins with a cast that embraced Pauline Lord and a young performer named Edward G. Robinson.

The truth is that the exciting, progressive changes were currents that flowed and eddied in the midst of a broad, roaring stream that carried the usual portion of familiar debris along its swift course. In the twenties the New York theatre reached its quantitative apogee. Never before had there been so much activity, bad, good or indifferent. In the 1920–21 season there were 157 productions. The total climbed each season until it reached a peak of 280 in 1927–28, when 200 were new plays. Even in the 1929–30 season, blighted in its first months by the black days of the stock market crash, there were 240 productions.

This was the last fine fever of indiscriminate Broadway production. Outside New York the pace was not comparable. The competition of the movies was taking its toll. By 1920 there were 15,000 movies houses in the land, an increase of 6,000 in ten years. Concurrently the houses available for road shows and stock were diminishing as these theatres were converted into movie houses. The twenties were the era of lush movie homes, those garish Turkish, Moorish, Venetian and Renaissance palaces designed for thousands; in these plush houses pretentious stage shows supplemented the films, and thus a severe blow was being delivered not only at the live play and musical but also at variety's two-a-day.

The rise of the films was inevitable and not entirely deleterious. Touring in any case had ceased to become the concern of all the leading players. Famous stars whom the out-of-town public wanted to see dodged the strains of travel, and road companies were staffed with second-raters. The cost of touring a play rose, as the railroads charger higher rates to transport actors, sets, props and costumes. Not every community had the right kind of house for a play of intimate proportions. Most of the theatres, built in the post-Civil War afflatus, were the Op'ry House sort, meant for grand spectacles, mostly musicals, and audiences rarely filled these large houses. Ironically, now that the big musical bulks so large, huge houses are again going up outside New York.

As the traveling professional shows and the resident professional companies dwindled, there was an efflorescence of little theatres in America. In 1925 the Drama League of America registered 1,900, and drama departments were set up increasingly in the colleges and universities. The directors of the little theatres and college drama departments often were more truly committed to drama of aspiration than the professional theatre. They undertook works that Broadway ignored or rejected. They revived plays that had been commercial failures. They inspired a few fresh, young talents who achieved impressive places in the American theatre. But, in sum, these theatres made no lasting impact on their communities. Although their intentions were honorable, they generally lacked stamina, support and continuity. They served, and still do, as a pleasant diversion and social outlet for unpretentious amateurs. Occasionally they included dedicated spirits who did not know how to channel their visions and energies, and some made arty noises that their work did not warrant.

CHAPTER XV

BUSINESS AS USUAL—AND DIFFERENT

I~N THE CASCADE~ of Broadway production in the twenties, with its heartening new works and impressive new talent, the main motif was business as usual. It has been suggested repeatedly that the silent movies in the twenties satisfied the large, undiscriminating public's craving for the obvious, sugary and vapid and that the living theatre was liberated for better things. Alas, not true, any more than in later decades when the talking pictures, radio and television became the great mass mediums. It is, of course, indisputably true that much of what these mass mediums offered was banal, showy and soporific. Nevertheless, the live theatre devoted an unconscionable amount of its attention, time, effort and money to trash. So it was in the booming twenties when the theatre was coming of age; so it is in the 1960's when it fancies itself an adult; so, unhappily, it probably will always be.

Possibly the crudest fabrications of the twenties would not have a chance today. *Abie's Irish Rose,* for example. Could it get by when television gives this sort of stuff away or the movie houses sell it at modest prices? One likes to think not, but then one recalls a simpleminded monstrosity like *The World of Suzie Wong,* which managed to rack up a two-year run in the fifties, and one is not so sure.

It is certain, however, that the theatre is no longer the preserve of every sort of popular entertainment, especially that which appeals to the lowest common denominator. Glance through the archives for the season of 1921–22, the one in which *Abie's Irish Rose* made its appearance not long before the term's end. Among the 196 productions were *Tarzan of the Apes, Bulldog Drummond,* a revival of *The Squaw Man,* and girlie shows like the *Ziegfeld Follies,* George White's *Scandals, The Greenwich Village Follies* as well as others lower in taste and quality.

Even in the early twenties, *Abie's Irish Rose* seemed implausible. How many smart Broadway operators had a chance to acquire a piece of this gold mine just before its New York arrival and in the weeks when it struggled to gain a foothold! Indeed, *Abie's Irish Rose* got a start only because its author, Anne Nichols, who had once been an $18-a-week chorus girl, poured her savings into it. It obtained the Fulton (now the Helen Hayes) Theatre to open in because on May 23 tenants for an empty house were scarce. After some uncertain weeks, it moved shakily to the Republic on 42nd Street, no doubt because the Fulton thought it had a better prospect for the new season. *Abie's Irish Rose* remained at the Republic until October 22, 1927, incredibly accumulating 2,327 performances, to be outdistanced in the next decades only by *Life With Father* (3,224), *Tobacco Road* (3,182) and *My Fair Lady* (2,557).

Let me confess that, being young and snobbish in the twenties, I did not consider *Abie's Irish Rose* worth my time and money. I am sorry, though not inconsolably; it might have been educational after a fashion. Recently I read the play and could not believe that any audiences, however naïve, could swallow it. Its plot is childish, its characters puerile and even its ear for Jewish and Irish comic dialects monstrously false. Were standards lower in the twenties? They must have been. How else can we explain the records *Abie's Irish Rose* piled up—the performances by road and stock companies and the total audiences of 11,000,000, which paid $22,000,000 for the privilege of laughing and rejoicing as love conquered all for a Jewish boy and an Irish girl?

Was *Abie's Irish Rose* the extraordinary exception, or was it just luckier than a multitude of empty, dull-witted, offensive productions that arrived unsung and departed unmourned during the turbulent twenties? Look at the hits. There were thrillers like *The Bat* by Mary Roberts Rinehart and Avery Hopwood, *The Cat and the Canary* by John Willard and *The Trial of Mary Dugan* by Bayard Veiller. There were melodramas, some lurid and sexy in an old-fashioned way like *White Cargo* by Leon Gordon and *Ladies of the Evening* by Milton Herbert Gropper, and some fast, gaudy and loud like *Burlesque* by George Manker Watters and Arthur Hopkins, *Chicago* by Maurine Watkins and *Broadway* by Philip Dunning and George Abbott. There were farces like *The Nervous Wreck* by Owen Davis, *Cradle Snatchers* by Russell Medcraft and Norma Mitchell, and *It's a Wise Child* by Laurence E. Johnson. There were sentimental domestic comedies like *The First Year* by Frank Craven, *The Old Soak* by Don Marquis, *Seventh Heaven* by Austin Strong and *Tommy* by Howard Lindsay, and there was brassier or more sophisticated stuff like *Is Zat So?* by James Gleason and Richard Taber, *The Fall Guy* by Abbott and Gleason, *Gentlemen Prefer Blondes* by Anita Loos and John Emerson and *Strictly Dishonorable* by Preston Sturges, which had some sophistication and which brought into the theatre a former New Jersey cop named Edward McNamara, who played a disenchanted, worldly New York cop so winningly that he became a show-business legend. There was drawing-room comedy, mostly superficial in its aim and glancing in its effect, like *Enter Madame* by Gilda Varesi and Dolly Byrne, *The Green Hat* by Michael Arlen and *The High Road* by Frederick Lonsdale. There was a romantic and speculative exploration into the supernatural like John L. Balderston's and J. C. Squire's *Berkeley Square,* based on a Henry James story, with Leslie Howard as the elegant and quizzical star.

Because the Broadway theatre was so avid for product in the twenties, it opened its doors wide to the foreign drama. The Theatre Guild feasted on the untapped riches. From 1919 to 1929 it presented 47 plays from abroad—a cornucopia of Shaw, including the premiers of *Back to Methuselah,* which had to be performed one part at a time on three successive nights, and *Saint Joan;* plays by Georg Kaiser, Ernst Toller, Franz Werfel, Tolstoi, Andreyev, Evreinov, Ibsen (*Peer Gynt*), Strindberg (*The Dance of Death*), Claudel (*The Tidings Brought to Mary*), Capek, Molnar (*Liliom* and *The Guardsman,* the former youthfully romantic with Joseph Schildkraut and Eva Le Gallienne and the latter gleamingly mischievous with Lynn Fontanne and Alfred Lunt), Lenormand, Courteline, Verhaeren, the provocative anti-war *Merchants of Glory* by Pagnol and Nivoix, Copeau's version of Dostoevski's *The Brothers Karamazov,* Amiel and Obey's *The Wife with a Smile* and Ernest Vajda's *Fata Morgana.* Not all masterpieces, but a far more exhilarating repertory than the most progressive individual managers produced. Even the Shuberts made periodic safaris to Europe and brought back alive their share of promising, often profitable and occasionally worthwhile game.

It is impossible, without turning these pages into a thicket of titles, to list all the importations that poured into the New York and American theatre in the twenties with the headlong impetuosity of a spring freshet. But to grasp the diversity offered in New York, recall the more exciting things, those one wishes one had not missed or, having seen, one could see again:

Nikita Balieff's remarkable Russian vaudeville known as *The Chauve-Souris,* Pirandello's *Six Characters in Search of an Author* with Margaret Wycherly and young Florence Eldridge; the Moscow Art Theatre led by Stanislavsky himself in ensemble performances that shook the noisy, bustling New York theatre, leaving a wash that is still coloring our methods; André Charlot's British *Revue of 1924,* which introduced to America the light-footed Jack Buchanan, the joyously comic Beatrice Lillie and the radiant young Gertrude Lawrence; the spectacular Max Reinhardt production of Karl Vollmoeller's *The Miracle;* Wedekind's *Erdgeist* or *The Loves of Lulu,* as it was known here; Noel Coward's *The Vortex, Hay Fever* and *Easy Virtue,* all in one season, and his revue, *This Year of Grace,* with himself and Bea Lillie in another; O'Casey's *Juno and the Paycock, The Plough and the Stars* and

The Silver Tassie; the Moscow Art Theatre's Musical Studio with its *Lysistrata* and its dazzlingly dramatic *Carmen* known as *Carmencita and the Soldier;* Bourdet's honest study of homosexuality, *The Captive,* which was ruled off the boards after 160 performances by Mayor James J. Walker's administration; Maugham's *The Constant Wife,* with Ethel Barrymore, and *The Letter* with Katharine Cornell; Moscow's Habima Players in the brilliantly orchestrated *The Dybbuk;* the Spanish Art Players in Martinez Sierra's tender *The Cradle Song;* a German company in Reinhardt productions led by Alexander Moissi, Paul Hartmann, Hans Thimig and Tilly Losch, in Hofmannsthal's treatment of *Everyman* and in an appallingly lush *Midsummer Night's Dream;* R. C. Sherriff's *Journey's End,* England's understated disenchantment with war; Michio Ito's Players from Japan and Mei Lan Fang and his company in Chinese classics.

The twenties stimulated a burst of cooperative ventures. The Actors Theatre was created in 1922. Known first as the Equity Players, this group grew out of the actors' union, Equity. At the outset financing came in part from Equity; the first board of directors was named by Actors Equity Council, and the membership of 150 was drawn from Equity.

Plunging directly into the Broadway maelstrom, the Actors Theatre presented ten plays in its first season, among them *Roger Bloomer,* the first produced professionally by John Howard Lawson, a passionately committed playwright, who believed in using the theatre to state his socially oriented ideas and was one of our ablest practitioners of expressionism. Jesse Lynch Williams's *Why Not?,* a sequel to *Why Marry?,* and Rachel Crothers' farcical *Expressing Willie* were also on the program.

Not content with its formal productions, the Actors Theatre gave special matinees devoted to experimental works. In its third season the cooperative added plays from abroad, offering *Candida, Hedda Gabler* and *The Wild Duck,* the last with Blanche Yurka and Henry Travers in a memorable production staged by Dudley Digges.

A cooperative based on actors, especially good ones in demand, rests on shifting sands. In principle the performers are eager to join their peers in fine work, and quite a few are willing to make sacrifices for an ideal. But flattering offers to this player or that constantly obtrude, and since not everyone has the character to turn down a more glamorous part or a lot more money, nor can everyone afford to do so, the troupe's continuity is bound to be undermined. The Actors Theatre disbanded after its third season. In its relatively brief whirl, it did a little to set higher standards.

Then there was the Dramatists Theatre, which flared up ardently though briefly. Helped by Otto H. Kahn, banker and capitalist, it dedicated itself to social comment with a leftist viewpoint. The New Playwrights Company, as this venture called itself, was in operation only for three seasons, and was the forerunner of the hard-hitting Theatre Union of the thirties. There has been much talk about Britain's "angry young men" who charged the London theatre of the fifties with a new social fervor, but they were hardly the first group of angry young men to shake the drama by its throat. The New Playwrights Company of the twenties had plenty to be angry about, as the plays it produced indicate. Among them were John Dos Passos' *The Moon Is a Gong,* Upton Sinclair's *Singing Jailbirds,* Paul Sifton's *The Belt,* Lawson's *Loud Speaker,* Em Jo Basshe's *Earth* and Michael Gold's *Fiesta.* These spoke for labor, for the foreigner, for the Negro just as strongly as they inveighed against the dehumanization of workers on assembly lines and the shoddiness of an America dominated by slogans of "prosperity."

There was the American Laboratory Theatre, which sought out foreign as well as native plays that no one else attempted, including Jean-Jacques Bernard's *Martine,* Cocteau's *Antigone,* and an early drama of poetic intent by Lynn Riggs, *Big Lake.* Under the guidance of Richard Boleslavski and Maria Ouspenskaya, former members of the Moscow Art Theatre, who chose to make America their home, this enterprise cultivated an earnest searching respect for stage techniques according to principles they had absorbed from Stanislavsky.

In a gallant reversion to the glamour and magnetism of the great star who served as his own manager, Walter Hampden set up shop in an old theatre north of the busy Broadway arena, gathered a company around himself, and presented a series of productions, mostly classics, starring himself. Among them were *Hamlet, Othello, An Enemy of the People,* and two examples of old-fashioned romanticism, Arthur Goodrich's *Caponsacchi* and Rostand's *Cyrano de Bergerac.* Tickets cost a little less than the generality of Broadway plays. As a young New Yorker I was swept up by the panache, swordplay and romance of a *Cyrano,* even as I suspected that Hampden laid on movement and emotion thickly and that his supporting troupe could not match the sonorous grandiloquence of his style. Do you think I cared? The play was very much the thing.

So its was at Eva Le Gallienne's Civic Repertory Theatre, where the aim was for searching and integrated performances. It is hard to realize how much this theatre accomplished in its brief but gloriously busy career, which began in 1926 and ended in 1932, done in by the depression.

Miss Le Gallienne, a glamorous young figure after *Liliom,* was in her twenties, beautiful, and pursued by producers. But another Molnar success, *The Swan,* did not fulfill her ideals of theatre. She could draw no personal satisfaction from doing the same part over and over, month after month without end, though the earnings and acclaim were large.

Three decades later Miss Le Gallienne had not changed. Still dedicated to repertory, ensemble playing and distinguished plays, she sparked the creation of a new touring National Repertory Company and barnstormed with it across the land. In 1926, bent on creating such a theatre, she knew the plays were there to be done and she believed the actors could be found. Her task was to generate financial support, and this she suceeded in doing.

Recently she recalled that among her backers who would not allow themselves to be identified was one who contributed $50,-000. Otto H. Kahn, who could not say no to a worthwhile idea in the arts, lent Miss Le Gallienne $10,000, and she remembered that to repay him she rode the subway to Mr. Kahn's Wall Street offices with an envelope holding ten $1,000 bills.

Seeking a theatre, Miss Le Gallienne discovered that her conviction that ticket prices must be scaled at a $1.50 to attract a large, unserved, hungry public was a huge stumbling block. Not one of Broadway's 80 houses was available for rent; the owners frowned on Miss Le Gallienne's projected ticket scale. Even Hampden, away on tour, would not let his house. In the end, the Civic Repertory Theatre set up shop in a huge, decrepit barn of a house on West 14th Street. But when the curtain went up on a shimmering performance of *The Cherry Orchard*, irradiated by the special glow from Nazimova's Ranevskaya, the size, shape and smells of the theatre faded into irrelevance. Indeed, for the Civic Repertory's purposes the theatre had its practical value. Its backstage space was so enormous that 40 productions could be stored. The seating capacity was large enough to make the $1.50 top practicable rather than hopelessly quixotic, and the deficit did not become unmanageable until the depression.

As is so often the case in the arts, the chief subsidizers of the Civic Repertory were the artists themselves. The young, dedicated actors worked at minimum. The highest salaries, paid to Nazimova and Egon Brecher, were $400 a week, certainly a living wage but a measly fee compared with the salaries in four figures commanded on Broadway in the twenties by a luminary of Nazimova's eminence.

In its arduous, difficult, enriching six years the Civic Repertory presented 1,581 performances of 34 plays, some the great works of dramatic literature—Chekhov, Shakespeare, Molière, Goldoni, Ibsen, Benavente, Tolstoi, Sierra, the Quinteros, Dumas and Schnitzler. There was a fanciful production of *Alice in Worderland*, and a highly successful one of *Peter Pan*. Miss Le Gallienne's vision was admirable and her energy formidable. As one of thousands who benefited, I am grateful. Such dedicated spirits and such imaginative enterprises are just as desperately needed in our so-called age of affluence.

In a time of ferment new forces throw up new ideas, new organizations and new men and women to speak and act for them. The changes in atmosphere and direction may also affect established careers, turning them into different and more rewarding directions. An Owen Davis surmounted a career of hack writing with ambitious, serious plays. A John Barrymore stepped from

polished, teacup drama to a Hamlet that achieved the longest run
in Broadway history until Richard Burton's in 1964. Critics like
James Huneker and George Jean Nathan became more influential;
a new, vigorous group developed, led by Alexander Woollcott,
Stark Young, Brooks Atkinson, Robert Benchley, Heywood Broun,
John Mason Brown, Joseph Wood Krutch, Barrett H. Clark and
George Freedley.

Most important, of course, were the new playwrights. The best
of them expressed the change of climate in the American theatre.
Their realism was not merely the kind that lavished loving attention on the detail of a room or a street or on technical magic like
storms or fires; it did not seek to imitate or outdo nature but to
choose minutiae of reality that shed light on character and emotions. Characters tended to be recognizably human, not sugared
or soured in accord with mechanical, old-fashioned notions of the
theatre of what human beings are like. Facile divisions into heroes
and villains were cast aside for subtler distinctions. Clichés of plot
became laughing matters. Violence and shock remained in the playwright's armory, but attempts were made to have them serve an
integral function. For the most intelligent of the new playwrights
the old patchwork of timeworn situations and threadbare characters did not suffice, nor did the easy assumption that it was enough
to be a glib and softheaded moralist.

As Alan S. Downer observed in his meaty little book, *Fifty Years
of American Drama,* the playwrights "pulled down the revered
stereotypes which had been his dependable guides: the inviola-
bility of marriage, the sanctity of mother love, the heroism of war,
the respectability of commerce." Playwrights, in short, stopped
glimpsing life through the rose-colored spectacles of the old, un-
troubled, cloying staginess but looked at life itself. They tried to
see men and women as they were, hoping to make theatregoers
more deeply aware of themselves and their potentialities. They
looked at the social organism as it was and attempted to report its
secret workings and hidden truths. They looked into their own
hearts and dared to dream fragile and noble dreams. They attempted new forms, following fresh paths opened by European
experimenters and seeking to open new ones of their own. They

looked at the simple folkways of remote byways and sought to convey their freshness and simplicity. They dared to laugh raucously and uproariously at pretensions and excesses, inviting Americans to see themselves as others see them. They were not afraid of poetic visions and a reach for poetic language.

The achievements of these playwrights varied from writer to writer and from play to play. But what they accomplished they did not do alone. The actor found new inspiration in the enlarged and deepened demands on his talents. Where performance had so often been an end in itself, it became a servant and helpmeet of an idea—the playwright's. The director began to assume a new importance. Before the twenties one rarely finds him mentioned in the program credits. Now he became a vital member of the team. He was a good many years away from becoming, as he did increasingly after the middle forties, the dominant figure, so that people spoke ominously of "a director's theatre" and of a new tyranny that had to be overthrown.

CHAPTER XVI

EUGENE O'NEILL

Foremost among the playwrights who revolutionized the theatre in the twenties was O'Neill. He held that position in his day, and even in retrospect, when his stock has fallen, he still holds it. No one can doubt how high he aimed.

O'Neill came closest to realizing his soaring visions in three plays after the twenties—in *Mourning Becomes Electra, The Iceman Cometh* and *Long Day's Journey Into Night*. But the torrent of plays that appeared on the stage in the twenties revealed him as a writer who would not confine himself to a single style, who insisted on exploring new stage techniques and attempting to recover the validity of ancient ones. The variety of his plays that reached the stage in the twenties expresses better than any other corpus of American drama the energy, diversity and enthusiasm of the period.

In *Beyond the Horizon,* as in some of the one-acters about the sea, particularly *Bound East for Cardiff,* O'Neill wrote plainly about grimy lives, with a sympathy and understanding that were fresh but with strong traces of the school of "oh-the-pain-of-it" sentimentality. But there was no blinking the eagerness of the playwright's reach. Although *Beyond the Horizon* did not have a long run, it was well received by the critics and serious public. Its refusal to deny everything it had said all evening to provide the customary happy ending was in itself a novelty of considerable consequence, especially as a gesture of conviction by an American playwright. "From 1920 onward," wrote Barrett H. Clark in his and George Freedley's *A History of Modern Drama,* "in spite of periodic interference from the police, the vice societies and the church, playwrights were able to treat almost any subject that appealed to them, without compromise and with almost complete frrankness."

The Emperor Jones, ostensibly about a Negro trapped by his own fears, was an impressionistic tone poem about man of any color or shape caught by the primeval terrors within him. With its beat of the tom-tom that starts, as O'Neill instructed, "at a rate exactly corresponding to normal pulse beat—seventy-two to the minute—and continues at a gradually accelerating rate from this point uninterruptedly to the very end of the play," it was hypnotic theatre, a tour de force of sound piled on movement to create tension. As played on Macdougal Street and later uptown by Charles Gilpin and Paul Robeson, it was immensely compelling. Louis Gruenberg's operatic version produced at the Metropolitan Opera in the thirties with Lawrence Tibbett as the Emperor Jones could not, with its singing voices and full orchestra, match, let alone transcend, the effect O'Neill got with tom-tom and spoken voice.

Diff'rent was the third O'Neill play produced in 1920. Revived in the sixties, it was awkward in structure, old-fashioned in dialogue and melodramatic in denouement. Although it harked back to Strindberg, it curiously presaged the plays of two and three decades later in its attempt to examine the frustrations of a repressed woman. Skimpy in exposition and shaky in development, *Diff'rent* was not a fully realized play and did not deserve to be a success, but even in its flawed form it trod on forbidden American ground. One can understand O'Neill's irony when he wrote to Nathan, "Well, it's rather reassuring. I had begun to think I was too popular to be honest." From our perspective it is incredible that the police regarded *Diff'rent* as a moral blot that ought to be wiped out of the theatre.

One after another came the O'Neill plays, some popular successes and some failures at the box office. Some were marred by the author's difficulties with intractable themes and a few achieved their aims. Among the ineffective and all but forgotten pieces were *Gold* (1921), *The Straw* (1921), *The First Man* (1922), *Welded* (1920), *The Ancient Mariner* (1924), first of the plays to use masks, *The Fountain* (1925), and *Dynamo* (1929), an intense but abortive assault on the machine as a sole object of faith.

Anna Christie (1921), like *Beyond the Horizon,* won a Pulitzer Prize. Pauline Lord triumphed as the loose, bad daughter of the tough, old seafaring man who had assumed that he had kept her out of temptation's way by leaving her on the farm, far from "dat ole davil, sea." Her regeneration at the play's end was sharply criticized, and O'Neill, defending himself in a letter to *The New York Times* against the insinuation that he tacked on a happy ending, wrote, "The sad truth is that you have precedents enough and to spare in the history of our drama for such a suspicion. But, on the other hand, you have every reason not to believe it of me." The tang of a seaside saloon was caught in this play, and later it was to be developed more fully and profoundly in *The Iceman Cometh.*

There was no dispute over *The Hairy Ape* (1922), which the Provincetown Players produced. Here O'Neill used an expressionistic technique, as he had in *The Emperor Jones.* Accused of imitating the German Expressionists, he pointed out that both plays had been written before he saw his first expressionistic work, Kaiser's *From Morn to Midnight.* With Louis Wolheim as the brokennosed, brutish Yank, *The Hairy Ape* etched baldly the contrast between the classes. Mildred, the glamorous brat, representing the spoiled rich looking for sensations among the oxlike workers in the bowels of a ship, would be ridiculous to us today, even as a symbol. And Yank, symbol of "unknown, abysmal brutality, naked and shameless," would be equally hard to credit, for unionized laborers in the most menial, dirtiest jobs are nowhere near so hopelessly displaced as Yank. For that matter, incidental details are no longer true; note Yank's remark to his shipmate about the sidewalk on Fifth Avenue, "Clean, ain't it? Yuh could eat a fried egg offen it." The feeling for the cleansing, if dangerous, sea was there, as evidenced by an old sailor's nostalgic speech: " 'Twas them days men belonged to ships, not now. 'Twas them days a ship was part of the sea, and a man was part of a ship, and the sea joined all together and made it one."

The protest against violation of that unity of man and nature remains an enduring aspect of *The Hairy Ape*. On the stage the play had impact. Even on the printed page, where its diction is dated, it has fire.

Striking and provocative as were O'Neill's plays in the twenties, they have not retained their validity and power. Yet one has only admiration for the playwright's endless quest—his determination to grapple with themes from which the squeamish were likely to turn away and his tireless search for fresh dramatic devices that would liberate his thought.

In *All God's Chillun Got Wings* he was ahead of his time and yet insufficiently prophetic of the new ideas that were to come. In his treatment of a mixed marriage, between a Negro played by Paul Robeson and a white girl, the aspiration of the black man to seek a life in which the color of his skin did not weigh him down was described as hopeless. O'Neill's heart as usual was in the right place well ahead of his time, but his hopelessness was, praise be, premature.

In *Desire Under the Elms*, produced by the Provincetown Players at the Greenwich Village Theatre in November 1924, which moved uptown and played there until the following October, O'Neill dealt frankly with sensuality and lust on a New England farm. Walter Huston made something memorable of the unyielding old Eben who brought home a young wife. In a revival by the Circle in the Square almost forty years after its premiere, the dramatic structure proved to be elementary. Its simplicity and bareness had become a species of naïveté. But its flaming sincerity helped it across unsophisticated shallows. In its time *Desire Under the Elms* was a shocker. The police intervened, and the issue was taken to court, where the adult community prevailed and the production was permitted to continue.

With *The Great God Brown*, produced by O'Neill himself with Kenneth Magowan and Robert Edmond Jones, the playwright moved into an intensified symbolic style. To differentiate between what the characters are and feel and what the world thinks they are and feel, O'Neill used masks. Thus Dion Anthony, the artist, wore the mask of the attractive, sophisticated poet and dreamer for his wife, Margaret, who loved him as his mask revealed him, and he dispensed with it for Cybel, the prostitute, who perceived the frightened, sensitive man he really was. The play was mysterious and mystifying; yet it ran for 171 performances and was the conversation piece of the early months of 1926. In retrospect it cannot be said that O'Neill achieved what he sought, for he meant his play "to be mystically within and behind [his characters], giving them a significance beyond themselves, forcing itself through them to expression in mysterious words, symbols, actions they do not themselves comprehend. . . . It is Mystery—the mystery any one man or woman can feel but not understand as the meaning of any event— or accident—in any life on earth."

Nor did he succeed in *Strange Interlude,* a blockbuster of a script, which was produced in the same year as *Marco Millions,* a work that failed in 1928. In the sixties both were revived, *Strange Interlude* by the Actors Studio Theatre as its first production and *Marco Millions* by the Lincoln Center Repertory Theatre as its second.

Marco Millions remains a hash of romanticism and symbolism designed to attack the materialism of society. The theme remains valid, though the point is made too obviously and elaborated for our tastes.

Strange Interlude, which flourished for more than a year after its première in January 1928, was the talk of the town. Its length and boldness made news. Here was a play consisting of three full-length plays each containing three acts. One went to it in the afternoon, stopped after the fifth act for a long dinner interval, as one does at Bayreuth's Wagner rites, and returned for the final four acts. At the first night fastidious theatregoers arrived in short dresses and business suits and went home to change into long gowns and dinner jackets for the second half.

Strange Interlude created all sorts of new problems. Because of difficulties in mounting, an unexpected delay cropped up before the opening. The critics had received copies of the script in advance, a rare procedure then as now, and Alexander Woollcott, drama critic of the *World,* wrote a sharp, unfavorable article for the magazine *Vanity Fair.* To the embarrassment of the *World,* the issue carrying Woollcott's disapproval appeared on the stands before the opening, and Herbert Bayard Swope, managing editor, decided that Woollcott should not review a play he had already condemned in print. Dudley Nichols, then a reporter on the *World* and later one of the rare film writers of talent, was assigned to the job, and he wrote a laudatory review that helped *Strange Interlude* on its way. At the buffet served during the intermission, Woollcott, who nevertheless attended the opening, was in one of his most waspish moods.

Even if Woollcott had contributed a negative opinion in the *World,* the chances are that *Strange Interlude* would have flourished. Not only were other reviews highly favorable but the size of the play and the distinction of a cast led by Lynn Fontanne were sufficient to make the production an Event.

In a more limited way that is what happened in 1963 when the Actors Studio Theatre's revival headed by Geraldine Page was produced. Again it was an Event. The older generation wished to revisit its youth; a new generation wanted to see what the excitement had been about. Thirty-five years after the première the excitement seemed unwarranted. *Strange Interlude,* with its soliloquies, asides and nine acts, was uncomfortably windy. The soliloquies had occasional validity, the asides none. The thoughts expressed proved to be so commonplace and predictable that they became a source of unplanned laughter. The motivation for the selfishness and neuroticism of Nina Leeds around whom these nine acts are built seemed incredible. It was impossible to believe that her failure to marry a young aviator could be responsible for all that bitchiness. It was impossible to care enough about Nina Leeds, for she lacked the size to support a drama of this magnitude.

Yet in certain scenes one could see why the play held the public's attention. O'Neill had learned to use the theatre strikingly. The end of the sixth act remained magical—the moment when Nina reaches her highest triumph. Three of her men—her good, foolish husband, her intense, honorable lover and her spinsterish father-substitute—surround her in her living room like contented pawns paying homage to their queen. There is a hush, the calm of Nina's overwhelming satisfaction and the men's adoration. To end the act there is reminder that Nina's young son, yet another man, waits for her; the playwright has gashed a serene paradise with a blade of irony.

Lazarus Laughed, written before *Strange Interlude,* used masks and indulged in high-flown philosophy. Even if it was garrulous and pretentious, it is difficult to understand how the work of a man riding the crest of unparalleled success could be ignored by the commercial theatre. But so it was. In 1928 only the Pasadena Playhouse cared to risk it.

In 1931 came *Mourning Becomes Electra.* Using the *Oresteia* of Aeschylus as his point of departure, O'Neill composed this trilogy of a New England family playing out its destinies like figures in the Greek tragedy. O'Neill's agents of destiny were not fate or the gods but the forces in man himself. With Alice Brady as Lavinia, the Electra figure, and Nazimova as the Clytemnestra figure, the three plays in one—*Homecoming, The Hunted* and *The Haunted*—built into an evening of compelling theatre and intense emotion.

The production of *Mourning Becomes Electra,* suggest Arthur and Barbara Gelb in their massive and comprehensive life of O'-Neill, was the climax of his career. O'Neill apparently regarded it as his best work, but added, like the self-critical artist he was, that he was also "deeply dissatisfied" because "it needed great language to lift it beyond itself. I haven't got that." Touching—and true.

Like *Strange Interlude, Mourning Becomes Electra* was an adventure in playgoing with a long intermission after the first play for dinner. It was an Event, but not so fashionable as its predecessor, even if the play itself was a better-rounded achievement. The novelty had worn off, and for the sensation seekers there was, after all, only the play.

With *Ah, Wilderness!* in 1933 O'Neill found relief in warm, domestic comedy—a marked change of pace after vast travails. George M. Cohan was winning as the wise and tolerant father, and so was Will Rogers who played the role on the West Coast. Call it O'Neill's sentimental journey back into his youth, a journey untinctured by the corrosive bitterness in *Long Day's Journey Into Night*.

After the failure of *Days Without End* in 1934, O'Neill relapsed into silence. But he was wrestling with immense projects. He worked on a cycle of plays, first nine, then eleven, that would trace a "continuity of family lives over a space of 150 years." As far as the public is aware, the survivors of that project are *A Moon for the Misbegotten, A Touch of the Poet* and *More Stately Mansions*. The first two were produced in New York in the fifties. Helen Hayes, Kim Stanley and Eric Portman could not make *A Touch of the Poet* more than fitfully interesting. Wendy Hiller and Franchot Tone could not bring to life *A Moon for the Misbegotten*. When I saw a production at Spoleto in 1958, played with considerable force by Colleen Dewhurst and Richard Kiley, I felt that this unfinished and unresolved work might better have been allowed to rest in peace. A final posthumous play, *More Stately Mansions,* edited by the Swede J. Gierow from a truncated play, was mounted reverently in the sixties in Stockholm where O'Neill has always been a dramatic god.

In *The Iceman Cometh,* produced with indifferent success in the forties and revived off Broadway at the Circle in the Square with marked success more than a decade later in a production that projected Jason Robards Jr. into prominence, O'Neill returned to the bums, drunks and human leavings of his earliest plays. The mood was more intensified and more somber. Although O'Neill was holding fast to the conviction expressed in *Beyond the Horizon* that man could not live without his illusions, he was expressing it in a purified, though not more laconic form because O'Neill never mastered the art of spareness and concentration. Even in his most searing play, *Long Day's Journey,* played unforgettably in the fifties by Fredric March, Florence Eldridge, Jason Robards Jr. and Bradford Dillman, he could not refrain from piling detail upon agonizing detail as he stripped away layer upon layer of self-delusion. For in "this play of old sorrow, written in tears and blood," O'Neill faced up to his own dead. As a man who believed that man must perish without illusion and hope, he sought, in this uncompromising autobiographical drama, to purge himself of false illusions and to confront the truth of himself and his heritage.

Long Day's Journey was to have lain untouched for many more years, by the author's wish, but his widow, Carlotta Monterey O'Neill, sanctioned the performance sixteen years after its completion. One cannot quarrel with this decision. O'Neill's parents and brother, so mercilessly portrayed, no longer required protection, and even if they had, the drama transcended personal reminiscence. Grant that it is long, repetitious and awkward in expression; nevertheless, it is charged with a deep and true tragic sense.

Hughie, a one-acter, had a posthumous New York première late in 1964. Very closely allied in theme to *The Iceman Cometh,* indeed a study of a down-and-out Broadway hanger-on who, like Hickey, cannot live without his pipe dreams, it is almost like a sketch for the bigger play.

How does O'Neill assay in the perspective of time? He is still the best we have produced. But he does not rank with the great masters, not because he lacked the language but because his view of men and life was muddied by immature romanticism. To his honor it should be said that he was not content with threadbare forms, but there were plays in which the new techniques or the revised treatments of old techniques were too fancy and too cumbersome. He mistook size for grandeur; he resorted to grandiloquence when he should have spoken simply. But he helped to give the playwright new freedom and dignity. Without polemics or self-advertisement, he remained unswervingly faithful to the tragic truth of the human predicament. It was fortunate that he won a heaping measure of money and fame, for he never wrote a line unsupported by his profound and humble belief in his high mission.

❖❘❮❖

CHAPTER XVII

NEW VOICES IN THE TWENTIES

O'NEILL WAS NOT the only American playwright to step forward front and center in the twenties. Elmer Rice belongs high on any list of Americans who fought to make the theatre a forum for truth telling and ideas. It is fashionable today to dismiss him as a technician who had a theatrical flair and who from his first success, *On Trial,* produced in 1914 when he was in his early twenties, had a flashiness that caught the eye of the unreflecting. It may be granted that Rice was an uneven dramatist, that he had troubles fleshing out his ideas in terms of vivid, fallible, complex human beings, but he sought honorably to report the real world in all its turbulence, aspiration and hypocrisy, and he had a lively awareness of the nature of politics, economics and the maneuvers that passed for statesmanship.

His expressionistic play of 1923, *The Adding Machine,* tilted at a dehumanizing, materialistic society. In a fine Theatre Guild production Dudley Digges as Mr. Zero and Helen Westley as his nagging wife were ciphers who had once been human. Never long on the humor that stems from warm, human comedy, Rice nevertheless laughed sardonically through *The Adding Machine.* Mrs. Zero's nonstop monologue, which occupies four columns in a printed version, was bitter and funny as a tirade at a husband who has not risen above bookkeeper. The nameless, numbered couples representing Mr. Zero's shrunken cosmos were summed up frighteningly in their commonplace chattering. Mr. Zero's long speech in the court of justice had a lot to say about the life of a man who has kept books for 25 years: "Eight hours a day, exceptin' Sundays. And July and August half-day Saturday. One week's vacation with pay. And another without pay if you want it. . . ."

Today's working hours are a lot shorter, and fringe benefits are a new and comforting economic factor, but Rice foresaw the future in which machines would replace men. Eventually Zero died, went to the Elysian fields and was sent back to earth—a soul to be used again and again, a soul to be debased into mindless servitude. Rice was scathing about the prospects of the revenant, including what the schools would teach him and his offspring: "There they'll tell you the truth about a great many things that you don't give a damn about and they'll tell you lies about all the things you ought to know—and about all the things you want to know they'll tell you nothing at all."

In *Street Scene,* his huge 1929 success, Rice used the strident tactics of melodrama to organize honest observations and comment on the way poor people huddle, brawl, pleasure and destroy themselves in the heedless, impersonal city. The play was shot through with sentimentality and resorted to the sensationalism of violence to achieve a dramatic wallop. Nevertheless, I respect its basic probity. Although it did not offer searching character studies, it orchestrated a representative group into a truthful, exciting, brooding picture of a time and a milieu.

There were more strings to Rice's bow than flashy dramatizations of social observation. He could write light comedy, as in *See Naples and Die;* sentimental drama, as in *Dream Girl;* shrewd reportorial plays, like *Counsellor-at-Law,* which in 1931 was a popular vehicle for Paul Muni. In his work for the Federal Theatre, and in his later plays, like *Judgment Day,* in which he reacted strongly to the encroachments of the Nazi conspiracy, he was a playwright who sought not simply to entertain but to rouse the conscience of his fellow Americans. I treasure him for that.

Maxwell Anderson's reputation also burgeoned in the twenties.

He, too, felt a strong pull to use the theatre to comment on politics
and world affairs. After his solo effort, *White Desert* of 1923, he
joined with Laurence Stallings to set off one of the decade's theatrical explosions. *What Price Glory?* was a comic, yet forthright
look at war as it is. With its brawling and ribald Captain Flagg and
Sergeant Quirt, played to the hilt by Louis Wolheim and William
Boyd, the stage's romantic notions of war were swept away. Anderson and Stallings, of course, were hardly the first to look unspar-
ingly at the grim face of war. To name but two classic examples
—Euripides had been savage in his indictment in *The Trojan
Women* several millennia earlier, and Shakespeare had written
with disenchantment in *Troilus and Cressida* several centuries earlier. But this was something new in the twenties, even if we see
now that *What Price Glory?* had its own species of romanticism.
In the hills of Italy, the hedges of Normandy, the jungles of Asia
and atom-bombed Hiroshima and Nagasaki, war was infinitely
meaner, dirtier and more brutalizing than the comparatively honest accounts of World War I had made it out to be.

On his own Anderson wrote *Saturday's Children,* a sentimental,
decent little comedy about early married life, which won a lot of
hearts in 1927. Then, stirred by the blatant miscarriage of justice
in the Sacco and Vanzetti case, he joined Harold Hickerson in an
indictment, *Gods of the Lightning,* in 1928. Anderson's conscience
was haunted by this case, and he returned to it in *Winterset* some
years later. His most ambitious work was to come in the thirties
and forties, but in the late twenties he began to brood over the
theatre's earthbound style and envisaged the day when it would
grow wings. He set himself the task of doing his part toward that
end. "If we are to have a great theatre in this country," he said,
"somebody has got to write verse, even if it is written badly. It is
at least a beginning."

Unlike the playwrights of consequence who appeared in the
twenties and continued to write in the following decades, George
Kelly belonged largely to the decade in which the American theatre made its leap forward. With less than a handful of plays he provided his share of impetus. After *The Torchbearers* in 1922, he
followed with two notable studies—*The Show-Off* in 1924 and

Craig's Wife in 1925, the former an examination of presumption and brashness that, despite its broadness of style, was truly founded on an aspect of American character, and the other a sharp dissection of a compulsive female driven to dominate who ended by possessing only the objects around her.

One of the attractive new voices belonged to a young man whose natural graces and talent were reminiscent of Edward Sheldon twenty years earlier. A product of George Pierce Baker's Harvard Workshop, Philip Barry, like Sheldon, knew the world of comfort and shared its easy graces, and like Sheldon, his natural gifts were rewarded by early success. He became a suave writer of high comedy. Luckier than Sheldon, he arrived on the scene when a playwright could go beyond simpleminded plot and characters. The ground was prepared, the audience more hospitable to an advance in sophistication. Barry could even venture beyond a shining dramatic package into more ambitious territory of thought and fancy.

Hardly out of college, he scored a success with his Harvard Prize play, *You and I*, in 1925. In quick succession came *The Youngest, In a Garden, White Wings, John, Paris Bound* and *Holiday*, the last two among the most popular comedies of the twenties. In all these pieces, in a fairly subtle, yet basically romantic theme like *In a Garden* or in fantasy like *White Wings* or his natural métier, high comedy, Barry wrote with lightness and smoothness. His dialogue sparkled; it was in the vein of the period, like the best pages of the sprightly new magazine, the *New Yorker*. The themes of his most characteristic and successful comedies, though not probing, reflected intelligence and good breeding.

I recall the charm and spirit of *Paris Bound* as it was played at the Music Box in the late twenties. Many years later as I reread the play, I was saddened by its essential thinness. Like so many of Barry's comedies, this one was preoccupied with the mystery of a marriage. The secret to him was always in a fundamental spiritual communion, which no passing transgression should affect. In *The Animal Kingdom* some years later Barry offered the other side of this coin, that a true spiritual harmony might be the one unsanctified by legal union. These were valid theses, but they also were self-evident—or do they seem so now in our freer moral climate?

Paris Bound now is too slick and pat. The heroine, on the verge of submitting to an intense composer as her revenge on a husband who has strayed, is saved by the bell. Three noisy friends arrive at the crucial moment. They chatter while the angry composer suddenly thinks of an ending for his ballet score and bangs the piano relentlessly. This flurry helps build a busy theatrical scene. At its height the heroine realizes how narrow her escape from infidelity, and at last she understands and is prepared to forgive her husband.

It is a typical American ploy in this type of comedy to invoke the peril of sin and to evade it in the nick of time, to titillate and to remain "moral." In this respect *Paris Bound*, like Barry's other high comedies, was modish and flimsy. But it was commercial in the twenties, and its descendants continue to flourish.

If Barry's high comedy bowed to the necessity of ultimate innocence, S. N. Behrman's plays did not. Despite their surface of gaiety and wit, their content was serious. In a career remarkable for durability and vigor Behrman deepened content and refined his workmanship.

The Second Man, produced by the Theatre Guild in 1927 with Lynn Fontanne, Alfred Lunt, Earl Larimore, Margalo Gillmore and Edward Hartford, proclaimed the arrival of a playwright who could mask wisdom in brightness. I remember the glow of the play and the performance, and as I reread it now I rediscover its laughter and intelligence. The protagonist expresses the delightful self-critical turn of the author's mind. Clerk Storey is a writer who is too intelligent to be slick and not talented enough to be great. "I'll be—what I've always wanted to be—a prosperous dilettante—I assure you I'm perfectly serious now. What this country needs is a dilettante class, interested in art with no desire to make money out of it. . . ."

The two sides of Storey are objectified by the two women who would have him—the rich widow, who offers him wealth and security and the chance to be the kind of dilettante he admires, and the girl, who offers him youth, beauty and ardor. He does not make the romantic choice. He takes the older woman, for Behrman's comedy is mature.

"Life is sad," says Storey, "I know it's sad. But I think it's gallant to pretend that it isn't."

In 1929 Behrman was represented by a new play of his own, *Meteor,* a study of an *enfant terrible* of a producer, who might have been modeled on the tempestuous Jed Harris, and by an ingratiating dramatization of *Serena Blandish,* a novel by Enid Bagnold, an English lady of quality who was to emerge many years later as a playwright of fancy and urbanity, spiritually close to Behrman.

Like Barry, Sidney Howard was a young writer who came away from G. P. Baker's Harvard Drama Workshop with an awareness of the needs of professional craftsmanship in the theatre. Like Barry, he contributed almost annually to the Broadway seasons of the twenties. He blended idealism with an eye for reality. He could write comedy, but mostly he sought to be a social critic. He emerged as a playwright who mattered in *They Knew What They Wanted.* Though overheated in its emotions and undermined by sentimentality, the play had gusto and excitement. If its colors were largely primary, they were laid on with boldness. Pauline Lord, Richard Bennett and Glenn Anders are still vivid in my memory for the credibility they brought to a story that, were it not for Howard's conviction, could easily have sounded like the melodramatic theatricality of a generation earlier.

In his next three plays Howard's social awareness was translated more surely into tough-minded character. There were unconvincing passages in *Lucky Sam McCarver, Ned McCobb's Daughter* and *The Silver Cord,* but each had a spine of sharp observation. Lucky Sam McCarver, speakeasy owner, was in the mold of Regan in Sheldon's *The Boss,* without sloppiness at the edges and softness at the core. He knew how to take care of himself in a world of cheap values; and Carlotta, the self-indulgent socialite, was viewed without blinkers. In *Ned McCobb's Daughter* rural Maine was caught with some honesty. *The Silver Cord* was a lethal treatment of a smothering mother. Mrs. Phelps, played in 1926 with insidious, chilling sweetness by Laura Hope Crews, now seems transparently characterized compared with searing portraits of her breed that our theatre has offered. A line like her "My two beaux! My two jealous beaux!" as she stands with her two sons is now too obvious, as is the irony when she remarks, "I don't like mothers who keep their sons tied to their apron strings" and ". . . I may have my faults but I'm not selfish. I haven't a selfish hair in my head." But Howard put forthright words into the mouth of Christine, the honest and indignant daughter-in-law: "You belong to a type that's very common in this country, Mrs. Phelps—a type of self-centered, self-pitying, son-devouring tigress, with unmentionable proclivities suppressed on the side." Equally potent is Christine's speech to her husband: "But the fact remains, Dave, that she did separate you and me last night and that she separated us because she couldn't bear the thought of our sleeping together . . . grown man that you are, down, down in the depths of her, she still wants to suckle you at her breast!" And there is the final mordant line by Robert, the son who cannot wrench himself free and who is, in the author's words, engulfed forever—"Yes, Mother!" Shades to come of Tennessee Williams, William Inge and how many others!

In the bracing atmosphere of the twenties the American playwright found that new areas of imagination were open to him. Plays embodying the folk spirit of communities not yet caught up in urbanization and sophistication could be written without the patronizing simplemindedness. Not that the advance in an acclaimed play like *Sun-Up* by Lula Vollmer, who had been raised in North Carolina and who brought the play with her when she took a job as a box-office treasurer at the Theater Guild, was so great as its period thought.

It is difficult to repond to a play of this kind as its contemporaries did. The know-nothings of the Deep South are still with us, but now frantically on the defensive, against a new, militant enlightenment. Even the most primitive are no longer totally shielded from the world, for they have been exposed to films, radio and television, which have been homogenizing our customs and standards and robbing formerly remote regions of their local mannerisms and insularity.

It may have been credible in 1923 when *Sun-Up* was new that the mother would say, "Where *is* France?" and that Rufe, her son, would reply, "I don't know. I heared it wuz 'bout forty miles t'other side o' Asheville." Today we cannot believe that any characters anywhere in the United States would not recognize "The Star-Spangled Banner" and that a preacher would say, "Reckon it's one of them new hymns I don't know."

Rufe's tussle with the Army is innocence incarnate, and reading the play, we are incredulous. Yet the same kind of character, converted to comic hokum, was the foundation for a success of the fifties, *No Time for Sergeants*. To the discriminating in the twenties *Sun-Up* had a rugged simplicity that appeared to be a fresh look at truth. First produced by the Provincetown Theatre, it moved uptown, and with Lucille LaVerne as the Widow Coyle, it ran all in all for a year. To us it is utterly simplistic.

In Abraham's Bosom, Paul Green's Pulitzer Prize winner, which the Provincetown Playhouse presented in 1926, is a folk play that stands on solider ground. The quaintness of its customs and characters is not its main business, and its folk setting is merely the background for a study of a man of Negro blood who seeks vainly to realize his potentialities as a human being. The play is melodramatic and prolix, but retains its passion and sense of aspiration.

In Abraham's Bosom was hailed as a play that saw the Negro from the inside out, unlike *The Emperor Jones,* which used the Negro as a generalized symbol. That is perhaps how it looked to the twenties, just as *Porgy,* Dorothy and Dubose Heyward's dramatization of his novel, seemed like a marvelously fresh evocation of Negro life as it is lived in Catfish Row of Charleston, S.C. The Theatre Guild performance staged by Rouben Mamoulian with its striking use of Negro spirituals was certainly stirring, as I well remember. But these were picturesque fictions that gratified a white society's notion of Negro life. Now that the Negro is finding his own spokesmen in the theatre and is telling us what it is like from the region of his mind, the report is not quite what the white man had supposed it to be even in his most liberal and generous moments.

The stage commodity that flourished most joyously in the twenties was comedy—not only a new type of polished comedy but also earthier models. Robert E. Sherwood in *The Road to Rome* achieved his first success in 1927. He was to turn serious without losing his sense of humor, but here his major objective was laughter based on a civilized man's sporting with history.

Two men who did as much as anyone to shape the tough, boisterous, fast-moving side of the American theatre achieved prominence in the twenties—George S. Kaufman, tall, rumpled and saturnine, and George Abbott, tall, elegant and impassive. They came to the theatre from different directions, Kaufman through his work on a newspaper and Abbott through college dramatics, but both became the complete professionals. Both were sure-handed collaborators as writers; both learned to stage plays with faultless precision and command of timing that multiplied the laughter and excitement in a script, both could take a whirl at acting, both were dependable doctors to sick productions. Both were at home in musicals as well as straight plays. Abbott, if anything, was slightly more versatile, for he could put his hand successfully not only to farce, at which he was a master, but to satire, melodrama and social comment. Kaufman at the outset revealed an unexpected flair for fantasy. Since so much of the work both men did was collaboration, credit for certain aspects of their achievements belongs to their various collaborators. But in both cases there was a firm foundation of professionalism. Both were important to the commercial theatre decade after decade—Kaufman almost until his death in 1961 and Abbott well into the sixties.

Kaufman's affinity was for broad, hearty American humor with its affection for a tall story, exuberant action and laughter based on a kick in the pants and a pratfall on a banana peel. It is an American style of humor that goes back to the nineteenth century, to our literature, notably Mark Twain; to our theatre, notably Harrigan; to the minstrel show, to variety and burlesque. Kaufman, of course, was not its only exponent. A host of writers, directors and performers has been at home with it. But Kaufman was one of its most skillful practitioners. Being an intelligent, skeptical man, he turned it to occasionally trenchant purpose, making it the vehicle for comment on our madder customs and institutions. Despite the occasionally keen-edged, often extravagant ridicule he heaped on persons, institutions and politics Kaufman was not a satirist who hurt, embarrassed and changed society. Indeed, his

style of lampoon should not be called satire at all. But gusty, robust, burlesque it was, and it added to the pleasure of theatregoing.

The works he had a share in writing and doctoring rarely retain
their old punch and exuberance. In revival they are dated. But in
work after work he and his collaborators adumbrated a sense of
adult values, no matter how sophomoric were the antics on stage.
Construction and characterization were often slapdash, but always
the tone was decent and humane. He was a useful, civilized citizen
of the theatre. Kaufman would have snorted at any attempt to con-
fuse him with art, but in his multifarious roles he arrived at a high
standard of craftsmanship.

Kaufman's first success was *Dulcy,* written with Marc Connelly,
the first of a long and distinguished line of collaborators. They
based their story on a character invented by Franklin P. Adams, the
F.P.A. of "The Conning Tower," then in the New York *Tribune,*
later in the *World* and for many years a rallying point for bright,
young writers. Dulcy was the prototype of the stupid, well-meaning
female, and in 1921 lifted Lynn Fontanne to stardom. The next
year Helen Hayes and the Kaufman-Connelly team joined in *To
the Ladies,* distilling humor and mild comment from another domestic situation, this one in which the wife, unlike Dulcy, had the
wit and resourcefulness to bail out her husband. The collaborators
had a subject that was ripe for their talents in Harry Leon Wilson's
spoof of the early films, *Merton of the Movies,* and with Glenn
Hunter in the lead this was another 1922 winner. The next collaboration, *The Deep-Tangled Wildwood,* in 1923 was a flop, but in
1924 the two came back with their last and best joint effort, *Beggar
on Horseback.*

In view of Connelly's later work, his gentle fantasy about a meek
clerk, *The Wisdom Tooth* (1926), and the overwhelmingly successful *The Green Pastures* in 1930, it is a safe guess that fancy, whimsy
and tenderness were his forte and that he brought these qualities
to *Beggar on Horseback.* Winthrop Ames deserves credit for suggesting to Kaufman and Connelly that they use Paul Apel's *Hans
Sonnenstössers Höllenfahrt,* a German expressionist piece, as their
point of departure.

Beggar on Horseback had unexpected freshness. It poked fun at business, the assembly line, the worship of success. It used the technique of dream sequences with imagination and verve. Like nearly all of Kaufman's satires, this one was so broad that it was inoffensive. The conflict between business and art was managed in fantastic terms that are obvious to us today, as the social comment in *Babbitt* and *Main Street* is thoroughly transparent. Cady, the business man, played by that memorable embodiment of snorting pomposity, George W. Barbier, was projected with more amusement than contempt. There was something disarming in his proud boast, "Yes, sir! I suppose I'm the biggest manufacturer in the world of overhead and underground A-erial widgets." Surely one of the authors of *How to Succeed in Business Without Really Trying* remembered *Beggar on Horseback*, for the articles manufactured in this musical fable of big business are, of all things, widgets. Not A-erial widgets. Just widgets.

The representative of art was a composer named Neil McRae, played by Roland Young, another of my agreeable memories. He, like the composer in *Paris Bound*, was the stock genius who would write the great symphony if he would just get down to work. But *Beggar on Horseback* made no pretense of literalism. It was imaginative, if not original, in its use of theatrical devices. In Neil's dream in Part One, butlers multiplied from 2 to 4 to 6 to 8 to 10 to 12. When he dreamed that he had killed the four Cadys—Pa, Ma, Son and Sis—as the end of the first half neared, he saw the reporters arriving—note that half the newspapers mentioned are now gone— "The *Times!* The *World!* The *Post!* The *Globe!* The *Sun!* The *News!*" Newsboys rushed down the aisles crying, "Extra! Extra! All about the murder!" As the audience turned to look, the curtain fell and the newsboys distributed copies of *The Morning-Evening*. In the second half there was a pantomime, "A Kiss in Xanadu," for which Deems Taylor supplied the music, and a distorted jury trial that was, in a mild way, a precursor of the daft one that the English playwright, N. F. Simpson, put into *One-Way Pendulum*, almost forty years later.

Kaufman's one solo attempt, *The Butter and Egg Man*, did not amount to much. He never again was without collaborators. In the twenties, collaborations began to pour out as if from an assembly line. With Edna Ferber, he did *Minick* and *The Royal Family,* the ebullient spoof of the Barrymores; with Herman J. Mankiewicz, *The Good Fellow;* with Alexander Woollcott, *The Channel Road,* based on Maupassant's *Boule de Suif;* with Morrie Ryskind, *Animal Crackers,* a dervish of a musical for the moonstruck Marx Brothers; with Ring Lardner, *June Moon,* a clattering spoof on Tin Pan Alley, today dated, yet I have fond memories of a wonderfully foolish moment when Harry Rosenthal as the window washer who has eavesdropped on the business of fabricating song hits steals into the office to try out a tune of his own. I am as fond of this moment as of the one in Neil Simon's recent *Barefoot in the Park,* in which the telephone repairman, accidentally privy to an altercation between a young couple, listens sympathetically as the husband demands that his wife bring him a glass of milk and when she declines, murmurs helpfully, "Can I get it for you?"

Abbott did not hit his stride in farce until the thirties. But his contributions in the twenties were formidable. One of the mad specimens of the decade, *The Front Page,* came from other heads. With Osgood Perkins and Lee Tracy as a ruthless managing editor and a resilient star reporter to body forth the frantic and funny inventions of the authors, Ben Hecht and Charles MacArthur, the controlled madcap direction was supplied by Jed Harris. But Abbott's future was foreshadowed in his staging of John V. A. Weaver's tough, sentimental *Love 'Em and Leave 'Em,* in his participation in *Broadway* and *Chicago,* fast, hard-boiled melodrama; *Spread Eagle,* an attempt to satirize war and revolution in a Mexican setting; and *Coquette,* an earnest and moderately effective effort to skewer a southern type, in which Helen Hayes gave a virtuoso performance of sugared malice.

It was a mad, turbulent, wonderful decade—exciting things could happen side by side with utterly implausible ones. The Theatre Guild, in the buoyancy of its growth, maintained for several seasons an acting company in plays like Werfel's *Juarez and Maximilian, Ned McCobb's Daughter, The Silver Cord, Pygmalion, The Doctor's Dilemma, Major Barbara, The Second Man, Strange Interlude, Marco Millions, Right You Are If You Think*

You Are, Mr. Pim Passes By, Volpone and the Copeau-Crone version of Dostoevski's *The Brothers Karamazov.* In major and minor roles this company brought together men and women who were to have a potent influence on the theatre, not only as players but in other capacities: Lynn Fontanne, Dudley Digges, Henry Travers, Philip Loeb, Edward G. Robinson, Clare Eames, Cheryl Crawford, Harold Clurman, Margalo Gillmore, Sanford Meisner, Morris Carnovsky, Earl Larimore, Elizabeth Risdon, Eliot Cabot, Laura Hope Crews, Helen Westley, Reginald Mason, Armina Marshall, Beryl Mercer, Edward Hartford and Winifred Lenihan.

It was a decade in which a notorious creature of horror tales, Dracula, the vampire, played by Bela Lugosi, made his bow on Broadway, where he had a long run. Mae West paraded her blatant, yet antiseptic brand of sex in *Diamond Lil* while the police brought complaints against *Volpone.* The evils of sin and the titillations of temptation were made exciting in *Rain* with Jeanne Eagels as the fatalistic seductress, Sadie Thompson. In Edgar B. Davis, a Texan, the theatre had not merely an angel but an archangel, for he caused J. Frank Davis's *The Ladder,* an odd concoction about the soul and its reincarnations, to run for 789 performances, inviting audiences to attend free when the paying public would not support the propagation of the theosophical faith.

Although Broadway buzzed with activity, there were in 1928 and 1929 the familiar lamentations of bad seasons, and the chichi thing to do was to take the ferry to Hoboken, dubbed the "last seacoast of Bohemia," where one dined, drank beer and felt superior to Boucicault's *After Dark* played grimly for laughs, in a production masterminded by Christopher Morley.

On April 18, 1927, a play was produced that, in itself, would not receive more than a footnote, if that. Samson Raphaelson's maudlin *The Jazz Singer,* with George Jessel in the title role, lasted for 18 performances. But converted some time later into the first successful talking film with Al Jolson in the main role, it tolled the tidings to a commercial theatre that would never again be like that of the twenties.

CHAPTER XVIII

MUSICAL THEATRE IN
TRANSITION

IN THE MUSICAL THEATRE the twenties were also the decade of transition. The historic landmark was *Show Boat,* which opened at the Ziegfeld Theatre on December 27, 1927.

Knowing observers were unaware of how this occasion would bulk in history. How could anyone foretell what directions any theatrical form would take? Since the prophecy of *Show Boat* was not crystallized until the forties, *Show Boat* might easily have been a sport.

Change, however, was in the wind, though it was hard to detect as the twenties began. Victor Herbert, chief confectioner of Broadway operetta, was still functioning. His muse was tarnished by war, revolution and inflation and by age and repetition but, like a large section of the public, it harked back to golden memories. In 1920 he was represented by two shows, *My Golden Girl* and *The Girl in the Spotlight,* and in 1922 by *Orange Blossoms.* In 1921 and 1923 he contributed songs to the *Ziegfeld Follies;* for the latter edition he wrote to words by Gene Buck, his longtime friend and admirer, a couple that were perfectly titled to serve as a nostalgic nosegay for lost dreams—"That Old-fashioned Garden of Mine" and "I'd Love to Waltz Through Life With You." The last by Herbert on Broadway, *The Dream Girl,* arrived in August 1924, stayed for 117 performances and in effect closed an era.

Others worked the vein of simpleminded stories, tepid comedy and lush melodies with notable success. Rudolf Friml picked up the baton without loss of a stride. In 1924 he was represented by *Rose Marie,* with its "Indian Love Call" call-all-all-alling its audiences to linger in the never-never land of operetta, and in 1925 by *The Vagabond King* with its "Song of the Vagabonds" sounding its virile summons to all good men and true.

Sigmund Romberg was firmly in the arena when the old gladiator, Victor Herbert, finished his labors. In 1921 came *Blossom Time,* which had 516 performances the first time around and toured in duplicate companies. Whenever the Shuberts were in trouble or doubt, they fell back on *Blossom Time.* Second only in popularity was Romberg's *The Student Prince in Heidelberg,* to give it the dignity of its full title, which arrived in December 1924, and had 608 performances in its first run plus repeated revivals as well as long stretches of touring. In 1926 Romberg wrote the tunes for *The Desert Song,* and one of his collaborators was Oscar Hammerstein II, who was engaged in those very months on *Show Boat.* Two weeks after the Broadway opening of *Show Boat* came a new Romberg operetta called *Rosalie,* which contained several songs by George Gershwin. With associates like Hammerstein, Romberg had a hand in *New Moon* in 1929, with its rousing "Stouthearted Men" and he was still braving Broadway in the fifties, but in spirit he belonged to the age that *Show Boat* and its successors made passé.

At the other end of the spectrum was George M. Cohan, also still functioning in the twenties. *Little Nellie Kelly, The Rise of Rosie O'Reilly, The Merry Malones* and *Billie* were in his early style—fast-moving, yet relaxed; modern, yet corny; breezy, yet sentimental. If Herbert was the full-voiced sorcerer with pulsating strings to add opulence to the empty romances, Cohan was the carnival pitchman whose manner seemed without guile and whose audiences, well aware of his shell game, would have him employ no other. In the twenties the manner was still there and so was the personal magnetism when he appeared in a work of his own, like *The Merry Malones,* but the works had grown pallid. Fresh talents were taking over, and the Cohan technique looked—and was—old hat.

Somewhere between the lush operetta style and the casual, thin Cohan approach was the larger part of the musical theatre of the twenties—busy, exuberant, sumptuous, occasionally rowdy. This type of musical, though it appeared side by side with a multiplicity of revues like the *Follies, Varieties, Scandals, Artists and Models, Brevities, Nifties, Frivolities,* many of which were spawned hopefully and died quickly, was also an outgrowth of these revues. Many aspired to follow the Ziegfeld model with its opulent production numbers, its spectacular effects, its beautiful unclothed girls, and its songs and comedy. Book musicals were growing in popularity. The book did not have to be ambitious, and not many who wrote or produced bothered their heads about an integrated work in which book, songs and action were a unity. A book show with the bare ribs of a story was enough. Hardly anyone went beyond the building of a skeleton, and credibility was not important, for audiences had not been taught to expect a great deal. The main objective was to make room for a romantic star or a popular comedian.

Star vehicles were the main business of the musical theatre, and Jerome Kern was most skillful at crafting them. *Sally,* a lavish and immensely successful Ziegfeld production of 1920, typified the genre. It was designed for Marilyn Miller, who had glorified several *Follies.* The book told a transparent little Cinderella tale about a girl who rose from humble beginnings to become a *Follies* luminary. Taking no chances, Ziegfeld included two established comedians, Leon Errol and Walter Catlett, and got Victor Herbert to supply music for a pretentious finale, a "Butterfly Ballet." Kern's score was generous, and he enhanced it by rescuing from his trunk rejected numbers written for other musicals, "The Church 'Round the Corner" and "Look for the Silver Lining."

In 1925 Kern, now allied with Hammerstein, was still assembling commercial products in the shape producers thought the public wanted. That year there was *Sunny,* another Marilyn Miller vehicle. This time Jack Donahue, Clifton Webb, Mary Hay, Cliff Edwards and Pert Kelton abetted the lovely star, and Charles Dillingham, the producer, spared no expense to enhance them all. The authors patched together their show as if assembling material for performers signed before a word or note was on paper, and the formula served its purpose. Why not? Didn't Kern's bags of goodies include "Who?", "Two Little Bluebirds," "D'Ye Love Me?" and "When We Get Our Divorce"?

The archives are filled with the remains of any number of these professional paste-up jobs. The sumptuous display pieces have long since disappeared from my memory, but I still recall with the glow of youth the shows that were the points of departure for the rich, uninhibited comic spirits of the twenties.

I fondly recall *Poppy,* which opened in September 1923, and which offered that princely contemner of the standard virtues, W. C. Fields, nose not yet so proudly bulbous as it was to become but honestly on its way. Fields impersonated Professor Eustace McGargle, grifter, gambler and con man extraordinary, who found himself in the unexpectedly tender role of foster father to Poppy, an abandoned waif, played by the adorable Madge Kennedy. Fields brought up his charge to be his assistant and to learn the arts of fortune-telling. When they drifted into Poppy's home town in Connecticut, the Professor heard of an unclaimed inheritance and announced that Poppy was the lost but rightful claimant. Never mind that Poppy, dear, good child, refused to join in the Professor's swindle. Never mind that Poppy, in a twist that could enter the long-arm-of-coincidence stakes, turned out to be the heiress. What lingers in the mind is Fields huffingly resplendent as con man. In this work Arthur Schwartz and Howard Dietz, who were to play a part in changing the face of the musical theatre, had their first song in a Broadway musical—a number called "Alibi Baby."

I have equally fond memories of *The Cocoanuts.* I admit that in 1925 when this harebrained panic arrived I was uncommonly predisposed to laughter, but it is not mere nostalgia that makes me think it was one of the funniest routs I ever saw. For low-down, knockabout goings-on this one took the cake as well as the cocoanuts. It marked the undisputed establishment of the Marx

Brothers as clowns in a style of their own. They had been in something called *I'll Say She Is* the year before, put together in somewhat rickety fashion around their vaudeville routines. In *The Cocoanuts* they improved the dementia of their raucous vaudeville acts, and this time they had the benefit of a book written by George S. Kaufman. Of course, Kaufman could not recognize what he had written; there is a legend that once in the show's run he murmured in stunned appreciation that Groucho had articulated a line exactly as the author had set it down.

The story, if anyone cared or could follow it, had something to do with the Florida real estate boom. Groucho ran a hotel in a phony development with lunatic meretriciousness, taking time off from his confusing discussions of future transactions with Chico to manhandle the cool and distant dowager, Mrs. Potter. Meanwhile Harpo slinked about making himself useful by filching the silver, disemboweling the guests' mail, blowing the horn attached to his stick, grinning his infinitely guileless grin and taking off like a lustful satyr after any well-shaped doe in sight. The fourth brother, Zeppo, who remained in the family act as long as a permanent straight man could be asked to endure it, behaved valiantly as a juvenile lead, singing songs that a composer of no small talent or standing provided.

Irving Berlin's principal tunes for *The Cocoanuts* were "A Little Bungalow," "We Should Care," "Lucky Boy" and "Minstrel Days." But who remembers them? Who remembers Berlin or Kaufman as architects of this furious assault on sanity? I didn't until I checked the records. But I remember the Marx Brothers, and the recollection leads naturally to the querulous complaint of oldsters of every age that comedy isn't what it used to be. Well, it isn't, you know. However, I don't believe that comedy went out with the vehicles for the likes of the Marx Brothers, Fields, Wynn, Clark & McCullough, Lahr, Cook and the other joyous comic spirits. Although later decades may have had less to make merry over, they produced their votaries of merriment.

In the large, the twenties were concerned with formula works. The breakthroughs are always the exception, and a new, winning idea is quickly followed by imitators, who fix another formula.

Eugene O'Neill's *Beyond the Horizon*. Edward Arnold is on the right.

O'Neill's *Strange Interlude*. Seated are Lynn Fontanne and Earl Larimore.

Original members of the Theatre Guild. Left to right: Lee Simonson, Theresa Helburn, Philip Moeller, Helen Westley, Maurice Wertheim, and Lawrence Langer

Theatre Guild's production of Elmer Rice's *The Adding Machine,* 1923, with Dudley Digges as Mr. Zero

Theatre Guild production of Sidney Howard's *The Silver Cord*, 1925. Left to right: Earl Larimore, Laura Hope Crews, and Eliot Cabot

George S. Kaufman and Marc Connelly's *Beggar on Horseback* with Roland Young

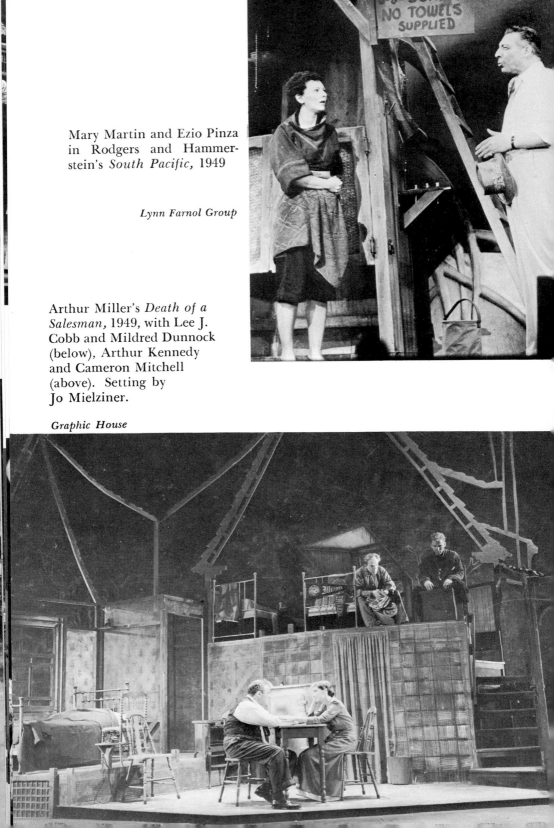

Mary Martin and Ezio Pinza in Rodgers and Hammerstein's *South Pacific*, 1949

Lynn Farnol Group

Arthur Miller's *Death of a Salesman*, 1949, with Lee J. Cobb and Mildred Dunnock (below), Arthur Kennedy and Cameron Mitchell (above). Setting by Jo Mielziner.

Graphic House

Carson McCullers' *Member
of the Wedding*, 1950, with
Julie Harris and
Ethel Waters

Graphic House

Tennessee Williams' *Cat on a Hot Tin Roof*, 1955, with Barbara Bel
Geddes as Maggie and Ben Gazzara as Brick. Direction by Elia Kazan.

Friedman-Abeles

Enid Bagnold's *Chalk Garden*, 1955, with Gladys Cooper, Fritz Weaver, Betsy Von Furstenberg, and Siobhan McKenna. Setting by Cecil Beaton.

Giraudoux's *Tiger at the Gates*, 1955, with Leo Ciceri, Leueen McGrath, and Michael Redgrave

With the benefit of hindsight, we can see that *Show Boat* was an immense breakthrough.

The quality of *Show Boat* was not anticipated. The first-line critics did not even review the opening. Not that I blame them; I would have done as they did. Brooks Atkinson for the *Times* and Percy Hammond for the *Tribune* were at the first night of Barry's *Paris Bound*. With 200 and more openings a season, there were frequent conflicts; some nights there were four and five openings, and the first-line critics had to make hard choices.

The second men did not disgrace their newspapers. John Byram in an unsigned review for the *Times* called *Show Boat* "just about the best musical piece ever to arrive under Mr. Ziegfeld's silken gonfalon" and went on to observe, "If these three contributions—book, lyrics and score—call for a string of laudatory adjectives, the production compels that they be repeated—and with a short tiger." Richard Watts Jr. in the *Tribune* hailed the new work as "a beautiful example of musical comedy."

Show Boat was a great success. It had 575 performances, which was impressive for the twenties, and then toured for seven months. Ziegfeld revived it several years later, and it rang up another long run. It has been revived repeatedly and has been filmed several times. The book may seem excessively romantic to us today, but its fusion of music and action is still admirable. We have grown accustomed to musical comedies that begin without an overture and even with a bare stage, and we may forget that in the twenties it was all but imperative to raise the curtain on a line of attractive chorus girls mincing or prancing through an opening number. *Show Boat* had the temerity to start with a gang of Negro dock workers lifting huge bales of cotton and bemoaning their hard lot.

Show Boat contained Kern's loveliest score. To recite the names of some of the songs is to say everything: "Ol' Man River," "Make Believe," "Can't Help Lovin' Dat Man," "Why Do I Love You?" and "Bill," written for *Oh, Lady, Lady!,* a 1918 musical, but withdrawn because of its unusual layout and dark mood and exhumed for Helen Morgan. These songs have had a long life of their own apart from *Show Boat.*

With a cast that included Norma Terris, Howard Marsh,

Charles Winninger, Edna May Oliver, Jules Bledsoe, Miss Morgan, Sammy White and Eva Puck, a typically sumptuous Ziegfeld production made magic out of the romantic Edna Ferber novel. But when Kern had first read the novel and imagined it on the stage, hardly anyone agreed with him. Miss Ferber thought he was out of his mind, and it was only when he explained that he was not thinking of thinly clad girls, baggy-pants comedians and the rest of the formula that she let him have the rights. Oscar Hammerstein, whose private vision of the possibilities of musical theatre had ranged well beyond the conventional, needed only a single telephone call from Kern to take on the task of writing the book and lyrics. Both men were assured by the knowing professionals that they had embarked on an impossible enterprise. Could any story be less promising? Two miserable marriages; Negroes bewailing their unhappy lot; a touch of miscegenation. There was much headshaking; there always is on Broadway, a mixture of concern for men gone wrong and a secret hope that they would stay wrong. Ziegfeld agreed to produce, tried to back down, then saw it through.

By the time it reached New York, *Show Boat* was set. It came from tryouts in Pittsburgh, Washington and Philadelphia, trailing rumors of excitement, and for the period it had a formidable advance sale.

It would be well, however, not to lose perspective. Viewed from our vantage point, *Show Boat* is not as revolutionary as it once looked. Its unusual subject matter was made palatable by its sweetening and showmanship. "Ol' Man River," which made Edna Ferber predict, when Kern played it privately for her, that it would outlive all the participants in the piece, remains a fat, solid folklike tune, but compared with the chain songs and the Negro songs of protest that later gained considerable currency, it is tame.

Indeed, considered in the long perspective of history, *Show Boat* is not a revolution at all. It only seems so in the context of the Broadway popular theatre. Several centuries ago there were opera buffas in Italy that set gay, comic stories dancing brightly to music. In the latter part of the eighteenth century a composer named Mozart fashioned musical theatre of coherence and integration and filled it with music whose radiance has never been surpassed. What are *The Marriage of Figaro* and *Così Fan Tutte* if not sublime musical comedies? What is *Don Giovanni* if not comedy and drama fused by deathless music into musical theatre of the highest order? Without going beyond the usual musical-comedy staples of comedy and romance, what are Rossini's *The Barber of Seville* or Donizetti's *Don Pasquale* and *L'Elisir d'Amore* and Verdi's *Falstaff* and Johann Strauss's *Die Fledermaus* and all the Gilbert and Sullivan gems and Prokofiev's *The Love of Three Oranges,* to name but a few examples, if not musical comedy of a very high order? I do not seek to diminish the significance of *Show Boat*. But it is salutary to weigh its achievement in the balance of longer values.

Show Boat was the foremost achievement of the popular American musical theatre in the twenties. But the excitement of new ideas and fresh talent made itself felt in other shows from the very first years of the decade. How could it be otherwise? These were the years when men like George and Ira Gershwin, Vincent Youmans, Richard Rodgers, Lorenz Hart and Cole Porter were coming to the fore and taking their place beside Irving Berlin, Kern and Hammerstein.

As an antidote to the opulent revues, assembled according to formula, the decade threw up a number of brash, intimate ones. For his new theatre, the Music Box, Irving Berlin instituted the *Music Box Revue,* which had editions in 1921, 1922, 1923, 1924. Not pinchpenny affairs, they were handsomely and imaginatively designed and staged; they were so resourceful technically that it became a matter of wonder when a performer just walked out instead of materializing from some mysterious spot in the set. "Say It With Music" was Berlin's theme song for the revues, and the four were studded with hit songs: "Everybody Step," "They Call It Dancing," "Crinoline Days," "Pack Up Your Sins and Go to the Devil," "Lady of the Evening," "Will She Come from the East?", "Learn to Do the Strut," "Tell Me a Bedtime Story," "The Waltz of Long Ago," "Little Butterfly," "Don't Send Me Back to Petrograd," "Listening" and "Rock-a-Bye Baby." The sketches were bright, and the talent exceptional, including William Collier, Sam Bernard, Miriam Hopkins, Charlotte Greenwood, Grace LaRue,

William Gaxton, Clark & McCullough, Frank Tinney, Joseph Santley, Robert Benchley (doing his immortal "Treasurer's Report"), Phil Baker, Grace Moore, Fannie Brice and Berlin himself.

The *Grand Street Follies* was brasher and a lot less expensive. It set a fashion for intimate revues. Begun at the Neighborhood Playhouse in 1922, it had new editions throughout the twenties. It poked shrewd fun at theatre, opera, ballet and at a variety of reigning favorites. It described itself at the very outset as "a lowbrow show for high-grade morons," and it brought forward such new names as Albert Carroll, Aline McMahon, Dorothy Sands, Paula Trueman, Jessica Dragonette, Joanna Roos and a young hoofer named James Cagney. Among its composers were Arthur Schwartz and a young man named Randall Thompson who went on to become the head of the Curtis Institute, a distinguished teacher at Harvard and a respected composer of serious music.

The Garrick Gaieties in May 1925 was another eruption of talent. It was an offshoot of the Theatre Guild, enlisting the cooperation of young actors who had worked in that organization's productions. The Guild was to help put it on but ran short of money in erecting its own theatre on West 52nd Street. The new revue was scheduled for two Sundays, caught on, and presently was on its way to a six-month run.

Richard Rodgers and Lorenz Hart, both champing at the bit after getting some songs into *Poor Little Ritz Girl,* a 1920 affair that leaned most heavily on Romberg, finally got a chance and filled the revue with snappy and lilting songs, including such fragrant ones as "An Old-Fashioned Girl," "April Fool," "Manhattan" and "Sentimental Me." For another edition the following year they provided such winners as "Mountain Greenery," "What's the Use of Talking?" and "Keys to Heaven." Hart's intricate and amusing lyrics had the literacy of W. S. Gilbert's verses and the brashness of young America, and Rodgers had a melody for every mood and unexpectedly witty turn of phrase.

The performance of the "hitherto unknown youngsters," as Benchley called them, was as surprising and pleasing as a good deal of the lively, impertinent material. In the two editions were such performers as Sterling Holloway, Romney Brent, James Norris,

June Cochrane, Betty Starbuck, Edith Meiser, Philip Loeb, House Jameson, Hildegarde Halliday, Lee Strasberg, Rose Rolanda, Alvah Bessie, Libby Holman, Sanford Meisner and Bobbie Perkins. I remember how startled I was to discover at a performance in 1925 that a member of the male chorus was uncommonly familiar. I studied the program and found the name, Felix Jacoves, and the next morning in a class at De Witt Clinton High School there sat Felix in the next seat as unconcerned as if he had not been disporting himself on a stage the night before. He had never uttered a word about his spare-time occupation.

Having started to roll, Rodgers and Hart were like a mountain torrent. By the end of 1929 they had collaborated on nine musical comedies, with Herbert Fields as their most frequent book writer. They had their share of flops, like *Betsy, She's My Baby* and *Chee-Chee*, but even in the failures they flexed their muscles and made new trials of strength. Thus *Chee-Chee* in 1928 was meant to be novel, with every note of music speeding the progress of the piece and with nothing to be inserted merely for effect. The program did not even list all the musical numbers, explaining that some were very short and "so interwoven with the story that it would be confusing for audiences to peruse a complete list."

Into all their works of the twenties Rodgers and Hart poured an unceasing flow of songs, many of which fill the memories of nostalgic theatregoers and are played and sung often enough to be familiar to the younger set. In *Dearest Enemy* (1925), there was "Here in My Arms"; in *The Girl Friend* (1926), "The Blue Room"; in *A Connecticut Yankee* (1927), "My Heart Stood Still" and "Thou Swell"; in *She's My Baby* (1928), "You're What I Need"; in *Present Arms* (1928), "You Took Advantage of Me"; in *Spring Is Here* (1929), "With A Song in My Heart"; in *Heads Up* (1929), "Why Do You Suppose?"

Like Rodgers and Hart, George Gershwin and his brother, Ira, were to make their most important contributions in the thirties. But they were men of talent, and George, overflowing with ideas, was ambitious to break out of the conventional molds. However, in his shows of the twenties he accommodated himself to requirements. For George White's *Scandals,* he provided such songs as

"On My Mind the Whole Night Long," "South Sea Isles," "I Found a Four-Leaf Clover," "I'll Build a Stairway to Paradise" and "Somebody Loves Me." For a happy musical like *Lady, Be Good!* (1924), through which floated Fred and Adele Astaire while Walter Catlett provided comedy, George and Ira packed "Hang On to Me," "So Am I," "Fascinating Rhythm," "Oh, Lady Be Good!," "The Half of It, Dearie Blues," "Little Jazz Bird" and "Swiss Miss." Dropped from this show was "The Man I Love," which refused to make a home for itself in later musical comedies, yet managed to carve out a lasting career. For *Oh, Kay!* (1926), graced by Gertrude Lawrence and Victor Moore, the Gershwins provided "Dear Little Girl," "Maybe," "Clap Yo' Hands," "Do Do Do," "Someone to Watch Over Me" and "Fidgety Feet." For *Funny Face* (1927) with the Astaires and Victor Moore, they turned out " 'S Wonderful," "Funny Face," "High Hat," "Let's Kiss and Make Up," "He Loves and She Loves," "Tell the Doc," "My One and Only" and "The Babbitt and the Bromide." In 1925 they contributed to a musical comedy called *Tell Me More!* which began life on the road under the title of *My Fair Lady,* and included a song of that name.

Eager to do something different, Gershwin attempted for the 1922 *Scandals* a 20-minute jazz opera. With words by B. G. DeSylva, it was called *Blue Monday,* and in a raw, tentative way it was an intimation of *Porgy and Bess.* In the *Scandals* it was a puzzle, and its white performers in blackface did not help. Years later, the piece was retitled *135th Street,* and I saw a production. It had only momentary flashes of interest. An audience bent on the predictable pleasures of a *Scandals* would naturally be put off by an experiment of this kind, and understandably it was dropped from the *Scandals* after the opening night.

If Gershwin was disappointed, he was not discouraged or deterred. He knew where he wanted to go musically. With the help of Paul Whiteman, he produced at Aeolian Hall in February 1924 a jazz work for orchestra that did not have to run the initial gamut of a Broadway audience. *Rhapsody in Blue,* with Gershwin himself at the piano, scored an immediate triumph. To my mind it is still Gershwin's best work, for in it he concentrated his strong feeling for the jazz idiom and his remarkable melodic gift into a form that did not have to make allowances for the routine requirements of the musical theatre of its time.

Because of premature illness, Vincent Youmans had a short career. He did little to change the nature of the conventional musical comedy, but he deserves a note of fond remembrance for helping to infiltrate formula with freshness and gaiety. For a big success like *Wildflower* (1923), he wrote "Bambalina"; for *No, No, Nanette* (1925), "Tea for Two" and "I Want to Be Happy," both with Irving Caesar. In *Hit the Deck*, which he produced himself so that he could incorporate the ingredients he thought best for a show, he had the rousing "Hallelujah!," the first song he had ever written, dating back more than a decade to when he was a young man in the Navy.

Like the other bright young men of the twenties, Cole Porter languished outside the charmed circle of the major theatre composers for years before getting full scope for his talents. He contributed "I've a Shooting Box in Scotland" to a 1916 failure called *See America First* and he had songs in *Hitchy-Koo* in 1919, including "Old-Fashioned Garden," and in the *Greenwich Village Follies of 1924,* including "I'm in Love Again" and "Two Little Babes in the Wood." In 1928 he was finally established with *Paris,* in which Irene Bordoni and Arthur Margetson turned his "Let's Do It" into a delight of that season and many others to come. In the next year Porter was back in *Fifty Million Frenchmen* with songs like "You Do Something to Me," "You've Got that Thing," "Find Me a Primitive Man" and "You Don't Know Paree" and, in the final days of the twenties, when *Wake Up and Dream* came along, he was represented by such new numbers as "I Loved Him But He Didn't Love Me," "What Is This Thing Called Love?," "I'm a Gigolo" and "Looking at Love."

Porter was independently well-to-do and amused himself in the first years of the twenties abroad with the international set when the theatre was indifferent to his gifts. But once he was accepted, he became one of the men who transformed the naïve musical theatre. Not a product of Tin Pan Alley, he abjured the corn so commonplace among its practitioners. His lyrics were literate and blithe; his ideas were mischievous as well as adult; his rhymes were full of surprising turns of imagination and wit, and his tunes reflected the spirit of the words in their sprightliness and polish. Like Gershwin and Rodgers, Porter was not ashamed of a touch of musical literacy.

There were other writers and works in the twenties reflecting an eagerness to enlarge the musical theatre. Lew Henderson, a skillful tunesmith, joined in 1927 with B. G. DeSylva and Lew Brown, lyricists, in a fast and furious entertainment called *Good News*, which paid its respects to college football and romance. Though formula musical theatre, it had a winning vitality, thanks in part to songs like "Varsity Drag," "Good News" and "The Best Things in Life Are Free." The next year the Henderson-Brown-DeSylva team had a hand in *Hold Everything*, with Bert Lahr as a hilarious pugilist, and their songs included "You're the Cream in My Coffee" and "Don't Hold Everything." In 1929 they contributed to *Follow Through*, a formula job about golf, country clubs and, naturally, love. "Button Up Your Overcoat," "You Are My Lucky Star" and "I Want to Be Bad" were the hits of this show.

Even in conventional treatments of orthodox subjects, authors, directors, choreographers and performers blazed with vitality. The twenties served notice that the old soundings of the musical theatre would not do, that fresh ones would have to be taken and that the charts would never be the same again.

CHAPTER XIX

TWIN MENACES

THE STOCK MARKET CRASH of October 1929 sounded the knell of prosperity. Who would have thought in the grim weeks, months and years that followed, with their shrinking employment, bread lines, apple peddlers on street corners, their misery and despair, that an unbelievable age of affluence would evolve in several decades and provide two cars in most garages as a matter of course and lobster as well as chicken for a lot of pots?

The October crash, of course, did not at first seem as grim as it became. Although it was alarming, men of power and substance assured the world that it would pass, like a short, intense fever. To demonstrate their faith in the status quo, they invested huge sums in stocks at prices that, though falling, were still inflated. Plans made as if the boom could not be followed by a bust were carried out. It took a little time for the inevitable attrition to become starkly noticeable.

This was especially true in the theatre. Although there is no barometer more sensitive to shrinkage than the public's ready cash, the theatre did not experience an instant contraction of production or patronage. Something like 240 shows, including revivals, were presented in New York during the 1929–30 season. Producers bravely went ahead with their commitments. Only in the second half of the season did they begin to cut back as people frequented the theatre less and less. There were fewer hits, profits were reduced, salaries were cut, rentals were trimmed, more and more houses remained dark. Reflecting the determination of the business community to shore up confidence by talking confidently, the theatre made gestures of self-assurance. The Shuberts rushed a season of operetta, mostly Victor Herbert, into the breach.

The theatre's difficulties stemmed not only from the financial disaster. The evolution of talking pictures was an almost equally ominous threat. The film studios, which were forced to plunge into this terra incognita, seemed at first more panicky at the ingenuity man had wrought than grateful for the new means within their grasp. They scrambled in a competitive flurry to engage actors who could speak and playwrights who could write. Although *Once in a Lifetime,* Moss Hart's and George S. Kaufman's contemptuous salute to the new Hollywood dawn, was exaggerated and fantasticated, it was sufficiently founded on fact to reflect valid truths. In the last glorious days of the silent films, which coincided with the peak of the boom in the twenties, even good pictures, as Glogauer, the play's fatuous film tycoon declared, could make money. Now the problem was to make any picture in the new, articulate medium, and since the theatre was a place where actors talked, it was obvious that the theatre had to be raided.

Broadway old-timers still bemoan the inroads that Hollywood made on theatre talent in those days, as they inveigh against television for feeding on the soil cultivated so patiently by the theatre. And it is true that a host of writers, directors, designers and actors dashed out to the lotus land to embrace huge salaries, easy living and a ruthless abuse of their skills, gifts and integrity. But I am not sure that Hollywood should be denounced automatically as the villain and the living theatre as the outraged heroine.

The theatre, in its abounding prosperity of the twenties, was not notably concerned with the integrity of new talent. Opportunities were made for it, but they were chancy and erratic. The theatre on the whole did not differ greatly from cinemaland in its overriding concern with making a dollar. If Hollywood corrupted with its blandishments of riches and luxury, it was because there were men and women eager to be corrupted. I do not even think that one can cast stones at writers, actors and directors who chose Hollywood because it offered substantial rewards rather than a theatre that became an increasingly precarious place for anyone to function or earn a living. It was possible, after all, for a man of character to decline extravagant offers and to remain in the theatre; O'Neill did not dash off to the Gold Coast to lave his hands in great urns of gleaming metal. It was also possible for a man of character to defend his integrity even in Hollywood; William Faulkner took its money and retreated to Oxford, Mississippi, unscathed. It is possible, in short, to sell out anywhere—and it is possible, but infinitely more demanding, to stand firm even in the films and television as well as in the theatre.

The theatre, of course, is freer. It always has provided, like the printed word, a haven and a forum where one can speak what is in one's heart without the imperative to tailor one's words and visions to the lowest common denominator. By an unexpected, though perfectly logical, twist of fate the theatre became bolder than ever before, as a result of the depression and the development of talking films.

Leafing through the records of the period, one repeatedly encounters the names of new authors who went straight from a Broadway debut to a Hollywood contract complete with options and escalated salaries. Not many of their plays amounted to anything. They lasted for a week or a month and were gone. Had they persevered, several of these writers might have developed into capable and perhaps successful playwrights. Some became key figures in films, writing scripts that were slick, attractive and commercial and moving up in the Hollywood pecking order to become producers, directors and major executives. A very few even made the trek back to the theatre and proved that they knew something about craftsmanship.

No one will ever be able to strike a balance of what the theatre lost when the films became a competitor for talent any more than one can now say how much television harms or helps in the nurturing of writers, directors and performers. What is beyond question is that both mass mediums of entertainment have reduced the theatre's paying public. On this point, too, theatre people prone to look for a silver lining deluded themselves. With the frivolous, superficial, dull-witted audience lost in good riddance to the light-weight films, the theatre—so the thesis went—could devote itself to the invaluable core of the adult and the intelligent, and this group, to be counted in the thousands, remained faithful to the living stage. But theorize as you may, the ineluctable fact is that the flighty, pleasure-loving public has continued to be a powerful maker of the stage's enormous successes. Thin domestic comedies, teasing sex plays, rowdy farces, melodramatic thrillers and mind-less musicals have always had a far larger market than plays of stature and quality.

During the depression, the consolatory words were spoken often, "Now only the good plays will have a chance." It wasn't so. Good, earnest ones had the usual troubles. Plays with something to say had a somewhat better chance to get a hearing, but this improve-ment owed much to the zeal of young, dedicated people willing to make sacrifices for a meaningful theatre.

Looking at the figures for Broadway production during the thirties, one sees how the twin menaces—the depression and films —emaciated the theatre. In the 1930–31 season there were 190 pro-ductions, a drop of 50 compared with the previous season. By 1938–39 the tally was 80 new productions. In December 1930 it was unmistakable that the theatre on Broadway was wilting like a flower past its bloom. The depression was omnipresent—in the newspapers, on the radio, in people's talk. Producers might bewail the deplorable psychological effect, but the prescription of a self-appointed medicine man like Coué, "Every day in every way I feel better and better," just wouldn't work. The crisis could not be wished away, it was constantly there to be felt, smelled and en-dured.

Producers and theatre owners bestirred themselves to do things they should have been doing long before. A determined effort was made to revive the road in the hope that it would replenish shrink-ing Broadway receipts. Plans to build subscription audiences in cities outside New York were promoted. Indeed, early in the thirties an improbable miracle occurred—the Shubert and Er-

langer interests lay down together like the lion and the lamb (make
your own choice of who was which) and formed the American
Theatre Society.

Three of the most responsible forward-looking producers
mounted a war on ticket speculation. This was more than a decade
after Marc Klaw had solemnly assured a 1918 Senate committee:
"There are no ticket scalpers any more, they have been legislated
out of existence." Is it odd to hear of ticket speculation in a time
of economic stringency? No odder, you may be sure, than the city,
state and national flare-up in recent years when the theatre was
struggling through some of its most painful seasons, artistically
and economically. For even in the worst of depressions or sourest
of seasons, several shows always thrive famously on Broadway.
Their tickets are what the trade calls hot, and in the eagerness of
the customer to get his hands on them the speculator finds a profitable pasture in which to graze.

The initiative of Arthur Hopkins, Brock Pemberton and Gilbert Miller in organizing a war on scalping led to the founding of
the League of New York Theatres. For a few breathless weeks it
looked as if a greater miracle than the snuggling of lion and lamb
would be passed; an entire menagerie might choose to live in
amity, like Noah's passengers. The producers talked as if they
shared the same lofty objectives. Presently dissension broke out.
The brokers got into the fight. The fate of the League seemed in
doubt, and although it has persisted, it often acted and sounded
as if it would collapse.

Cooperation among producers did not preclude individual difficulties. If solvency was precarious in more substantial businesses
in the early thirties, why expect the theatre, so sensitive to every
fiscal wind that blows, to be above the battle? Arthur Hammerstein, son of the redoubtable Oscar I, impresario extraordinary
of opera, variety and other forms of show business, and uncle of
Oscar II, equally redoubtable as a writer for the musical theatre,
went into bankruptcy. Two failures led to his downfall, the second
a musical called *Ballyhoo*, with no less a funnyman than W. C.
Fields. A. H. Woods, who had made a fortune out of bedroom
farce, followed into bankruptcy. The loudest tremor to shake the

theatre was the announcement that the Shuberts with all their holdings of theatres in and out of New York had gone into receivership. Lee Shubert and the Irving Trust Company were declared the receivers, and the Shuberts were encouraged to find ways of producing and filling their theatres. Neither the theatrical community nor the business world could contemplate the abandonment of the stage. The bankers wished to preserve their equity in the property, and it was important for morale to keep this area dedicated to laughter, gaiety, brightness and excitement alive and functioning.

To keep going, the Shuberts negotiated a loan from, of all places, the Reconstruction Finance Corporation. Always active as producers as well as lessors of theatres to other producers, the busy brothers stepped up their schedule. Like other business leaders determined to demonstrate that they were not giving up, they were eager to get product into their showshops. They imported London hits; they produced American plays; they supported a series of Gilbert and Sullivan productions; and in the usual last resort they trotted out *The Student Prince* and *Blossom Time*.

The mob, as the gangsters are known, latched onto the theatre momentarily, beguiled by its glamour and thinking it was a soft touch for easy money. They backed a musical, *Strike Me Pink,* starring Jimmy Durante. In the garish tradition of thugs, the mob had tough-looking representatives on the scene. A swarthy mugg would accompany an actress to a designer's studio, order a costume and pay for it in cash with a big bill peeled off a fat roll. If the musical had thrived, who knows what effect the mob would have had on Broadway. But the critics slapped down *Strike Me Pink,* and the mob decided that the theatre was entirely too risky.

Heywood Broun, once a drama critic himself, who was, whatever critic baiters of all periods may say, indestructibly softhearted and generous, bestirred his shaggy bulk to organize a cooperative revue. He prevailed on his friends to contribute songs and sketches, helped to assemble a company and appeared on the stage himself. Thanks to the interest drummed up by this unconventional approach to show business, the revue called *Shoot the Works,* which unfortunately was not so good as its intentions, ran for eleven weeks. At least two of its graduates achieved a sort of fame decades later—George Murphy as film star cum politico and Imogene Coca as a comedienne who brightened the early days of television.

A good deed by a former drama critic did not spare his successors, heirs and assigns in criticism. A speech in the halls of Congress denounced the critics as the villains undermining the welfare and prosperity of the theatre, even as other termites, never congressional ones, constantly eat away at the pillars of this great republic. Representative William Sirovich, New York Democrat, was the statesman who delivered the attack. There was nothing novel in it, of course, except the place of its delivery. It is hard to believe that Sirovich's fellow congressmen were much concerned with the theatre's fate. Indeed, a few years later when the Federal Theatre Project was making a nationwide effort to create work and to rebuild the living theatre, many of these congressmen fussed much more over a few boldly expressed ideas.

During the 1932–33 season, when Franklin D. Roosevelt was winning his first election as President and preparing to take over the leadership of a country on its knees, half of New York's theatres were dark. There had been a subsidence in the flurry of productions in the previous two seasons by people who thought that they ought to have their fling in the theatre now that everything—actors, sets, stage crew, the house itself—was cheap. These bargain hunters had inconveniently forgotten that a production must be appealing and entertaining as well as inexpensive to produce, and nearly all of the hastily assembled ventures splashed down the drain. Playing it safe, producers resorted to revivals in the 1932–33 season, which was the nadir of the depression. Low-priced enterprises became commonplace. The Jolson was renamed the Shakespeare Theatre, and a cooperative troupe presented fifteen of the plays in 249 performances at 25 cents to $1 a ticket. Some weeks the actors had salaries; other weeks they got nothing for their labors, yet were less miserable than those who were idle.

Veterans observed the deflation in salaries, royalties and profits and predicted bravely, if lugubriously, that an era had ended. The day of the $3, $4, $5 and $6 was over, they said. If ever a crystal ball was clouded, this one was.

Spirits were not raised by the resounding fiasco at Radio City where S. L. Rothafel, better known as Roxy, who had achieved a reputation as a demon showman in the twenties, put on a gala opening at the Music Hall that laid a bigger egg than any prehistoric bird. The fancy variety show that had been assembled for the opening was hastily dismantled, and the theatre was converted into a movie palace with a policy of first-run films plus pretentious stage shows. It is a policy that has proved more durable than most things in show business. The stage show, which has gone the way of all flesh in most other movie houses, has continued to flourish, and the concept of the movie palace itself in all its ostentation and vulgarity has been abandoned nearly everywhere, but not war, nor revolution, nor affluence, nor the population explosion affects the Radio City Music Hall. As for the second Radio City theatre, somewhat smaller than the Music Hall and originally destined for opera, it was used fitfully for theatre, operetta and musicals and finally was demolished and the space converted to income-producing office space.

The plight of theatre people, like that of millions of other unemployed Americans, was desperate. Rachel Crothers was one of a group that organized the Stage Relief Fund to raise funds for needy theatre workers' most urgent bills for food, gas and electricity, physicians and medicine. Selena Royle, an actress, led the way in founding the Actors' Dinner Club, where meals were served at $1 apiece to those who could afford to pay and without charge to theatre people who couldn't. During one grim winter 150,000 meals were served, 120,000 of them free.

A time of terrible suffering, the depression was also an era of regeneration and rededication. Valuable forces, ignored when things appeared to be going well, were released. New people with vigorous ideas and flaming ideals found ways to be heard, and older men and women who had been submerged or obliged to conform spoke with freshly acquired authority. The left, ranging from a few inches beyond the center all the way to the extremes of militant Socialism and Communism, found plays, players and stages and lashed out at things as they were. In the twenties men like O'Neill, Elmer Rice and John Howard Lawson had raised questions and thrown harpoons at noisy, complacent materialism. With the profit system's promises in tatters in the early thirties, its very foundations came under attack. Some of the blows were as wild as they were naïve, but it was an exhilarating epoch in the American theatre— the most provocative and exciting, in my judgment, that this country has ever known. We have matured and are developing saner and more orderly dramatic institutions, but never were there so much passion and commitment in the theatre.

CHAPTER XX

IN THE COMMERCIAL
MAINSTREAM

THE THEATRE even found a wry theme song for the depression. "Brother, Can You Spare a Dime?" turned up in *Americana* in 1932–33, hoping to induce a consoling smile. Although the theatre changed under the goad of the depression, the pursuit of small thrills and thin pleasures did not cease.

As the thirties arrived, Broadway was faring well with the usual commercial successes—comedies in which titillating seductions were being interrupted just before surrender, farces in which rowdiness and exuberance blew up storms of motion and laughter, melodramas in which action and suspense were more important than character or comment, and romances in which sentiment fluttered its tender, if not perturbing banners. Each decade has its product designed for easy success, and the variations are largely in quality and sophistication.

Early in 1930 the New York theatre was still prodigal of productions, and a variety of earnest, even ambitious, efforts pushed through to the stage. Robert E. Sherwood tried to say something about war in *Waterloo Bridge*. By way of Paris there came Marcel Pagnol's *Topaze*, a cynical view, characteristically Gallic, of politics and the urge to get ahead, with Frank Morgan a joy as a meek schoolteacher who adapts himself to the world as it is and becomes a rapacious, mendacious and successful man of affairs.

Most noteworthy in the first months of the thirties were *The Green Pastures* and *Hotel Universe*. The first, Marc Connelly's evocation of Roark Bradford's *Ol' Man Adam and His Children*, now is regarded nostalgically as an American classic. The second ranks as Philip Barry's most ambitious flight.

To appreciate how contemporaries felt about *The Green Pastures* one must think oneself back into the spirit of 1930. The news was bad and getting worse, and as if to counteract it, there shone on the stage a radiant innocence. Here was the Negro, simple and childlike as so many people liked to regard him, acting out his naïve account of the Bible stories. Here an angel, white eyeballs shining in a black face and wings sprouting from a white robe, could cry out, "Make way for de Lawd," and a tall, dignified, white-haired, dark-skinned actor, Richard Harrison, voice deep and resonant, could step forward and play the part not only creditably but also heartwarmingly.

When Connelly received the Pulitzer Prize for *The Green Pastures*, there was an outcry that Bradford had been shabbily neglected, and of course he deserved to be cited as the source of the playwright's achievement. But Connelly brought a great deal of his feeling for fantasy and warmth to his treatment, adding characters not in the original and expanding paragraphs into delicious scenes.

My recollection of this work in 1930 is total enchantment. But it no longer looms as "one of the noblest poetic dramatic works of our theatre," as Barrett H. Clark insisted some years later. And the reasons for Arthur Hobson Quinn's celebration of the work are the very ones that make me feel that *The Green Pastures* would not go down in the turbulent sixties. "To project the imagination of a race into the relations of God and man," wrote Quinn, "to dare the seemingly impossible and achieve success, might teach other playwrights that the Negro, in his wistful, exalted and emotional phases, is much better suited to the stage than when he is being exploited as the symbol of a struggle for racial equality." One could laugh and cry at the obtuseness of that sentence if one did not have a guilty feeling that a great many Americans long felt about the Negro that he was a treasure if only he retained his docile simplicity. In the mid-sixties, however, the black-skinned peoples of the world no longer are to be expressed in terms of folksy legend, and *The Green Pastures* now seems like a patronizing work—fond, endearing and tender, yet incontrovertibly and offensively condescending.

In *Hotel Universe* Barry, gay and touching fabricator of fragile tales for sophisticated theatregoers, attempted to arrive at a profound statement, as he did again almost a decade later in *Here Come the Clowns*. Neither of his most probing works came off. In both he sought an extended metaphor for man's search for God. In *Hotel Universe* a group of alienated people assembled on a terrace in southern France in a mysterious setting. Barry insisted that the two-hour play be performed without intermission or the fall of a curtain.

Each character, exploring his failings and frustrations, came into contact with Stephen Field, who helped each to understand himself and the illusions he needed. What and who was Field? Wisdom? Death? God? It did not matter. The point of *Hotel Universe* was that if we bravely face past events and emotions that blur or sicken our lives we may be able the better to endure them.

Hotel Universe produced a divergence of opinion. According to Burns Mantle, critic and annual historian of the theatre, the spiritually minded loved it, and the others couldn't understand it. It was not all that deep or difficult then, and is a lot less so now. Upon rereading it, one notices that its search for truth peters out into jejune mystical speculation. Barry's vision, like his philosophy, was mushy. It was equally fuzzy in *Here Come the Clowns,* even though this play was less vague about its parable of show folk. The hero, searching for God, learned that what he sought was to be found in the free will of man. The play abounded in symbolism, which, on reacquaintance in an off-Broadway revival 20-odd years after the première, I found too pat and transparent. Despite his eager reach, Barry was not gifted for the grasp of a high philosophical prize. He was not a thinker in drama, and when he tried to be, he gave off, despite his earnestness, an odor of artiness.

All through the thirties the normal traffic of the light, the thin, the sensational and the technically adroit passed along Broadway. Without disrespect for the skills that went into the writing, production and performing of these pieces and without minimizing the pleasure and thrills they generated, one finds it hard in the perspective of time to separate one from another, unless one has some special reason for remembering a character, a line or a situation.

How account for what clings to the memory? One of my cheerful recollections is of a moment in a musical of early 1930. I remember its name, *Simple Simon,* but only after looking at an old program did I recall that it had a book by Ed Wynn and Guy Bolton, that the songs were written by Rodgers and Hart and that they included "Send for Me," "I Can Do Wonders With You" and "Ten Cents a Dance," which Ruth Etting sang. What lingers in my memory, like a strong, unforgotten fragrance, is a scene in which Ed Wynn, his foolish face wrinkled in perplexity, walked out onto the large stage of the Ziegfeld, dragging a lariat. Noticing the length of rope in his hand, he giggled in embarrassment. "Either I found a rope," he murmured abstractedly, "or I lost a horse."

Another indelible memory is the romantic ardor of *The Barretts of Wimpole Street,* and this recollection has a double focus. In 1931 Rudolf Besier's dramatization of the love affair of Elizabeth Barrett and Robert Browning had an unexpected literate ecstasy, and for me—and many thousands—it glowed with fervor in Katharine Cornell's high-spirited, yet tremulous Elizabeth, Brian Aherne's vibrantly virile Browning and Charles Waldron's austere and rigid Father Barrett. I can still relive the exultation of that striking moment when Miss Cornell finally rose from her chaise longue, stood uncertainly for an instant and walked again hesitantly and bravely.

My recollection of this scene is intensified by the superimposition of another image thirteen years later, when I saw Miss Cornell and Mr. Aherne in the same play under radically different circumstances. I was thirteen years older and thirteen years less sentimental, but I was more deeply moved. For this time the theatre was the small, gemlike Opera House of Caserta near the Versailles-like park and castle that the Kings of Naples had created in imitation of Louis XIV's pleasure palace. Here the Allied Command in the Mediterranean had its headquarters, and here in the Opera House Miss Cornell and her associates began their tour for the troops. This time I watched *The Barretts* through the eyes of the soldiers who filled the theatre and who hung over the railings of its multitiered boxes, and when Elizabeth finally stood and walked on her own, I think my heart rose not only with her but also with the absorption of my fellow soldiers, some of whom had never seen a round actor or listened to such literate dialogue and who nevertheless were so stirred that they all but fell out of the boxes.

Do you remember *Grand Hotel,* Vicki Baum's cross section of flamboyant characters and melodramatic incidents in a great European hostelry? Herman Shumlin, a young producer who had begun his career the previous season with the taut, angry prison drama, *The Last Mile,* by John Wexley, was on his way to becoming one of the most intelligent, influential and tempestuous figures in the American theatre.

Noel Coward was at the top of his shocking, sophisticated bent in the thirties. With the glowing Gertrude Lawrence and a magnetic young Laurence Olivier, he appeared in *Private Lives.* With the mischievous Lynn Fontanne and Alfred Lunt he scintillated through *Design for Living.*

Barry turned out smooth, neatly made, comedies with their surface charm and fundamental sentimentality and softness of spirit. *Tomorrow and Tomorrow* deserted the drawing room for romance. *The Animal Kingdom* was back in the sophisticated world with Leslie Howard as the diffident, graceful hero. *The Joyous Season, Bright Star* and *Spring Dance* were topped off in 1939 by *The Philadelphia Story,* an ingratiating vehicle for the young Katharine Hepburn and a bright once-over of that favorite subject of sentimentalists, the rich girl full of rue.

George S. Kaufman was as reliable as the earth turning on its axis. With Moss Hart, who shared his older partner's professionalism, to which he added a particular stagestruck fervor, he rejoiced the thirties with a variety of efforts. After *Once in a Lifetime* came *Merrily We Roll Along,* a foray beyond farce and satire into a glimpse at what easy success and popularity might do to ruin a playwright. *You Can't Take It With You* was their affectionate hymn couched in farcical terms to the values of ordinary middle-class life, in which losing one's money or not having any seemed equally unimportant. This was a comforting if not penetrating thesis in a time when other, fiercer playwrights were determined to raise searching questions about the American way of life. Back in their happiest vein of farce-comedy, Kaufman and Hart did *The Man Who Came to Dinner* in 1939, a takeoff on Alexander Woollcott, now become town crier to the nation, with the bearded Monty Woolley as the imperious, interfering Sheridan Whiteside. With Edna Ferber the busy Kaufman early in the decade wrote *Dinner at Eight,* which, in a time of want, commented on the coupon-clipping idlers and social climbers in brisk, dramatic terms.

As if all this were not enough for one man, Kaufman had a hand in raising the age level of the musical theatre. With *Of Thee I Sing* (1931) Kaufman, abetted by Morrie Ryskind and the Gershwins, poked broad fun at Presidential campaigns, the Vice-Presidency, the Supreme Court, the Congress and other national foibles, and as in the earlier *Strike Up the Band,* the musical numbers were integral to the theme. The prophecy of *Show Boat* was being realized, not in romantic terms, but in the brash, exaggerated form of satire on the verge of burlesque.

In its time and place *Of Thee I Sing* was a joy. I remember with delight the opening scene with its campaign parade and its exuberant song, "Wintergreen for President," which in words, music and production—and wouldn't you know it, Kaufman was also responsible for the direction—caught the gusto af American politicking and commented on its foolishness. Such songs as "Love Is Sweeping the Country" and "Of Thee I Sing (Baby)" were in the impudent vein of this unbuttoned show which had William Gaxton as its breezy Wintergreen and the shy, friendly, droll Victor Moore as Alexander Throttlebottom, the Vice-President nobody knew.

Of Thee I Sing won the Pulitzer Prize, the first musical to receive this accolade, and although it was the year of *Mourning Becomes Electra,* the protests were not numerous. At the time I would have predicted that this musical would be one of our classics. Well, it was revived about two decades later, and, alas, it had aged. Grant that the production did not compare with the original, but after a devastating war, its satire was altogether too scattered and pallid. Only the score retained its luster; "Wintergreen for President," with its interweaving of "Tammany," "The Sidewalks of New York" and "Hail, Hail the Gang's All Here," was no longer germane to campaigning in a day when street rallies were being replaced by appeals on radio and television, but had become instead an evocation of a dying custom and therefore a nostalgic period piece, reminding us of a time when the theatre and we were young.

The creators of *Of Thee I Sing* brought in a sequel, *Let 'Em Eat Cake,* in 1933. The performers were much the same, and the tone of the work was darker and more biting. Gershwin's score was subtler and bolder, with harmonies and contrasts that were remarkably advanced for the popular theatre. Although the work expired in less than three months, Kaufman tried a contemporary political subject again in *I'd Rather Be Right,* which he wrote with Moss Hart and Rodgers and Lorenz Hart. In this one, which opened in 1937, George M. Cohan played Franklin D. Roosevelt with personal warmth, though he was not happy with the Rodgers and Hart songs, referring to the authors sneeringly as Gilbert and Sullivan.

As for Gershwin, he knew that there was no going back for him after *Let 'Em Eat Cake.* He wanted to press beyond the limits of Broadway musical comedy. His next and last work was *Porgy and Bess.*

Gershwin had been drawn to this subject in 1926 when, after reading the novel, he wrote to Heyward to tell him of his interest in converting it into a stage piece and was startled to hear that Mrs. Heyward was at work on a dramatization. The play's success did not alter Gershwin's belief that *Porgy* was destined for him. When he finally tackled this project so close to his heart, he spent eleven months in collaborating by mail with DuBose Heyward, while brother Ira worked on the lyrics. Gershwin required another nine months for the orchestration, which he refused to turn over to another man as is the invariable Broadway procedure.

Porgy and Bess opened in October 1935—a musical work of operatic pretensions launched in the mainstream of popular entertainment rather than in the opera house, which to a majority of Americans had always seemed a species of alien highbrowism.

The music as well as the drama critics had their say about *Porgy and Bess,* the latter reacting to it with greater warmth. It ran for 124 performances, but in view of its size, cost and pretensions, it had to be classified as a failure. However, it refused to remain one. In 1942 it was revived after considerable paring of the recitatives and tightening of the book, and did much better. In 1953 it was mounted most brilliantly of all, with Robert Breen's clean-cut, yet intensely dramatic staging and with a cast of extraordinary performers, led by Leontyne Price and William Warfield, who could sing superbly and act well enough. This version toured the world to unanimous hosannas.

With each revival, including more recent ones at New York's City Center, it has become more emphatically clear that *Porgy and Bess* is most impressive and affecting where Gershwin was true to his essential talent as a Broadway composer with audacity, rather than a longhair imitating Verdi—who, by the way, was anything but pretentious. The vivacity and sincerity of Gershwin's melodies invest the characters with tenderness and humor. The connecting tissue of recitative performs no organic function; it is merely empty aping of a style out of place in this milieu.

Had he lived beyond his allotment of thirty-seven years, Gershwin might have gone further in helping to transform the popular musical theatre, for he had the desire and the gifts and was perfecting the technical tools. Thanks to his sincerity of emotion, *Porgy and Bess* endures despite its now outdated white man's view of the Negro as a simple lovable child of nature.

The omnipresent George Abbott cut a huge swath through the theatre of the thirties. From his fast-moving, raucous workshop came such rousing farces as John Cecil Holm's *Three Men on a Horse,* Bella and Samuel Spewack's *Boy Meets Girl,* the Murray-Boretz *Room Service,* the Finklehoffe-Monks *Brother Rat* and Clifford Goldsmith's *What a Life,* the play that shot the schoolboy Henry Aldrich and his voice, Ezra Stone, into national popularity via the radio. Abbott had a hand in robust, realistic, melodramatic comedies like *Twentieth Century.* He moved into the musical theatre and directed—and probably touched up, where he was not credited openly with contributions to the writing of such successes as *Jumbo, On Your Toes,* and *The Boys from Syracuse.*

There is a tendency to think of Abbott, in the light of his record of hits, as the consummate professional of Broadway, interested only in what would work and make money and rarely concerned with a brittle, unprofitable concept like adventure and novelty. What else would you expect from a man so businesslike and efficient, a man who could play a key part in getting before the public thirty varied productions in a decade?

Take a look at the musical *On Your Toes,* and you discover that Abbott was not the enemy of new ideas. For in 1936 he joined with Rodgers and Hart in writing a book that told a tightly knit story and in inviting George Balanchine to become the choreographer. *On Your Toes* was the precursor of the revolution for which *Oklahoma!* generally gets all the credit. Its low-down, violent jazz ballet, "Slaughter on Tenth Avenue," danced unforgettably by Ray Bolger and Tamara Geva, was not a carelessly injected interlude but a concentrated extension of the story.

CHAPTER XXI

HOPE OUT OF DESPAIR

THE BEST CRAFTSMEN usually respond to the mood of an era. They do not sign manifestos, coin slogans or lead revolutions to bring new ideas and new approaches to the theatre, but being observant and intelligent, they adapt themselves to the most viable of the fresh ideas.

The burning zeal for change and the willingness to make sacrifices and to invest endless hours of toil come generally not from the established professionals but from the intense, idealistic newcomers. In the grim, straitened years of the early thirties the soil was ripe for protest and experiment. Routine opportunities in the theatre were drying up. Impatience with the mindless entertainment that made up the bulk of New York's theatre offerings was endemic. Out of this discontent there emerged eager, young theatrical organizations dedicated to the proposition that the theatre should be something more than a place to kill an hour or two. Most of these enterprises were oriented to the left politically, as was to be expected in a period when President Herbert Hoover was assuring the country that the economy, left largely alone, was bound to right itself, when families took refuge in huts improvised from packing boxes in pathetic communities called Hoovervilles, when the United States Army with Douglas MacArthur as Chief of Staff drove demonstrating World War I veterans out of their encampment in Anacostia Flats not far from the Capitol.

Most of the cooperative efforts established with reforming zeal by combinations of young professionals and amateurs fell by the wayside leaving no memorial to their high intentions. The Group Theatre and the Theatre Union made a striking impact, and the graduates of the Group influenced the theatre into the next three and four decades.

In a sense the Group was an offshoot of the Theatre Guild. Some of its members had appeared in Guild productions in the twenties, and some were Guild apprentices. A few, like Harold Clurman, had worked with the Provincetown Players. Clurman himself was reading plays for the Guild and appearing in bit parts in the bleak winter of 1930–31 when he broached the notion of a permanent ensemble to some of his friends. The idea was received with enthusiasm. As a trial gesture the young enthusiasts produced in the 1930–31 season Tretyakov's *Roar China!*, a play dealing with an uprising in China against the white foreigners, but it expired quickly.

Undaunted, they went ahead. They spent the summer of 1931 in Brookfield, Connecticut, some seventy miles from New York. Here in a barn, before barns, stables and carriage houses became summer refuges for theatre, they rehearsed, talked and nursed their hopes and ambitions. The only emolument was room and board, not to be sneezed at in 1931.

In addition to Clurman, there were two other directors, Lee Strasberg and Cheryl Crawford. Among the actors were Stella and Luther Adler, Franchot Tone, Morris Carnovsky, Mary Morris, J. Edward Bromberg, John Garfield, Elia Kazan and Clifford Odets. All in all, there were 31.

The Theatre Guild gave the Group its blessing as well as a small capital fund, and not only let the budding organization have the rights to Paul Green's *The House of Connelly* for its initial Broadway fling but also presented the production under its own name.

It was a bracing start, for *The House of Connelly* had adult qualities. It told an unsparing story of the decaying old South in a style blending naturalism and folk legend. Green refused to be confined by the conventions of the commercial theatre and persisted in bringing poetry, music and a free imagination into his dramatic works. Eventually he parted company with the professional theatre, calling it "an industry and not an art . . . a business run to the pattern of supply and demand," and devoted himself largely to folk drama like *The Lost Colony*, which was performed for years in a noncommercial Virginia setting. Using music extensively, he made *Johnny Johnson*, an evocative play about the madness of war, which the Group put on in 1936.

In *The House of Connelly* the old South revealed more than a distant kinship to rotting provincial Russia at the turn of the century as disclosed in *The Cherry Orchard*. Green's play had nothing like the stature of Chekhov's, but did more to illuminate the correspondences than the 1949–50 *The Wisteria Trees*, Joshua Logan's transplantation of Chekhov's characters into the tragicomic aristocrats of the Deep South.

The disintegrating gentry in *The House of Connelly* were contrasted with hard-working, canny Sid Shepherd who "grew up from poor white folks" and with the crude, incantatory figures of Big Sis and Big Sue. In Green's version these Negro women, who served as a primitive Greek chorus, crushed the life out of Patsy Tate, the girl to whom Will, the scion of the house of Connelly, was drawn. But the Group Theatre insisted on a more optimistic ending, and Green rewrote it and dispensed with the killing. The original conclusion was better, but I do not like it either, for it is unexpectedly violent and incredible, like a ritual killing in the jungle.

Favorably received, *The House of Connelly* ran for 91 performances, a respectable achievement for a new enterprise in the fall of 1931. The Group discovered the hard facts of failure in December when it presented *1931—*, Claire and Paul Sifton's angry arraignment of capitalism and rousing plea for social justice. For "a bad play" it had a stunning effect on audiences, but it lasted only nine days. John Howard Lawson's *Success Story*, another attack on capitalism, not expressionist but naturalistic, fared much better, for it had a run of 121 performances.

The Group was now an independent organization, economically, emotionally, and philosophically detached from the Guild. Its first production on its own, *Night Over Taos,* Maxwell Anderson's attempt to treat the Mexican War in poetic terms, folded rapidly early in 1932, but the success of *Success Story* was a tonic. And what seemed like full security arrived in September 1933 with Sidney Kingsley's *Men in White,* which rolled up 351 performances. As if to crown its triumph, the Group discovered within its own ranks a new playwright—Clifford Odets.

In the thirties after his explosive debut with *Waiting for Lefty,* Odets sounded and looked like a great white hope of American drama. In 1963, upon his death at fifty-seven, he was a sad, dim figure, puttering around in Hollywood and talking of new projects. The truth about Odets is that his gifts were not Olympian, and such as they were, he did not employ them to the full. Yet in 1950 he returned to Broadway with *The Country Girl,* an abrasive, touching study of an alcoholic actor and his disillusioned wife, played tautly by Paul Kelly and Uta Hagen, and in 1954 he was represented by *The Flowering Peach,* his last full-length play, with its quizzical look at Noah and the Ark, recommended for the Pulitzer Prize by the jurors and superseded by the Advisory Board, which conferred the award on Tennessee William's *Cat on a Hot Tin Roof.*

If any Odets play deserved a Pulitzer citation, it was *Awake and Sing!,* his first full-length work. It arrived in a season that brought forward the taut, intense *The Children's Hour,* the first Lilliam Hellman play on Broadway; Sherwood's *The Petrified Forest* and Elmer Rice's *Judgment Day,* but the Pulitzer Prize went to Zoë Akin's dramatization of Edith Wharton's *The Old Maid.* No wonder the New York drama critics decided in the fall of 1935 to make their own award to the best American play and in the spring of 1936 voted their initial plaque to Maxwell Anderson's *Winterset.*

In January 1935, *Waiting for Lefty,* agitated herald of Odet's theatrical flair, was tried out by the Group at a special Sunday matinee. A tour de force of theatricalism, *Waiting for Lefty* was a call to arms. Based on a strike by New York's taxi drivers the previous year, it described a meeting at which union members rallied to action without waiting for the missing Lefty. In this play young Elia Kazan flashed electrical sparks as a cabbie who took the center of the stage and thundered so passionate an appeal for strike support that members of the audience were all but incited to rise from their seats, seize placards and join the picket line.

While *Waiting for Lefty* played engagements at Sunday-night labor meetings—it required no sets and could be done on any platform—the Group rehearsed *Awake and Sing!* With a cast that included Carnovsky, the Adlers, John Garfield, J. Edward Bromberg, Phoebe Brand, Art Smith, Sanford Meisner and Roman Bohnen, and directed by Clurman, the play opened at the Belasco on February 19 and remained for 137 performances. Even then the melodramatic gestures of *Awake and Sing!* were unmistakable. In rereading it recently, I found a disaffecting sentimentality in it. But even now the play throbs with a sense of aching aspiration. For *Awake and Sing!* lived up to the author's promise, made in an opening sentence describing the characters, that all "share a fundamental activity: a struggle for life amidst petty conditions." The play still is a tender, impassioned hymn to the struggle, whether clear or inchoate, against poverty of purse and spirit. Its Jewish family in the Bronx—the well-meaning parents, the daughter who gets pregnant, the son who desperately wants a chance to break free, and the wise, interfering grandfather—would easily have become clichés were it not for Odet's brooding and laughing grasp of basic truth.

A spirit of hope, which paradoxically flamed more brightly in the somber thirties than in the later decades of affluence, sang through this play. To a cynical world the old man's advice to his grandson may sound embarrassingly ingenuous, but it was stirring in its day: "Boychick, wake up! Be something! Make your life something good. For the love of an old man who sees in your young days his new life, for such love take the world in your two hands and make it like new. Go and fight so life shouldn't be printed on dollar bills."

One may well wonder whether their author did not recall those lines wistfully as he vegetated in Beverly Hills, doctoring film scripts gone wrong and promising himself that he would presently return to the theatre.

Waiting for Lefty was coupled with another Odets one-actor and put on at the Longacre for a moderate run immediately after the acclaimed arrival of *Awake and Sing!* The Group followed with *Paradise Lost* late in 1935, a further glimpse at the decay of one section of the American middle class, but this one was a failure and Odets made the first of his forays into Hollywood. Back on Broadway in 1937, he scored his biggest commercial success, *Golden Boy*, a play about a young violinist who becomes a prize fighter. Again there was a sharp savor for the diversity of character, and again Odets wrote ardently, but here too, in the arbitrariness of the golden boy's violent melodramatic end, there were theatricalism and sentimentality. In the later plays *Rocket to the Moon, Night by Music* and *Clash by Night,* Odets was seeking and partially achieving some maturity of psychological insight. All these were produced by the Group before its dissolution in 1941.

Irwin Shaw, Robert Ardrey and William Saroyan were among the young playwrights introduced by the Group. Like *Waiting for Lefty,* Shaw's first effort, *Bury the Dead,* was a young man's furious outburst. Produced in 1936, it was alert enough to be aware that war might "begin tomorrow." It envisioned six slain soldiers, who would not lie in their graves until they had made clear to the living that war was terrible and unforgivable. *Bury the Dead* resembled *Waiting for Lefty* in being the fiery reflection of a new generation that was bringing into the theatre passionately held liberal convictions and stating them with exhilarating naïveté.

In *Siege* Shaw sought to convey his burning concern with the desperate rights and wrongs of the Spanish Civil War, but his heart outran his hand. A maturer play was *The Gentle People* (1939), another Group Theatre triumph, which Shaw called "a fairy tale with a moral." On the surface it is a tale of two old men who rise up and demolish a racketeer who has nearly destroyed them. As Shaw said ironically in the printed version of the play, "In it justice triumphs and the meek prove victorious over arrogant and violent men. The author does not pretend that this is the case in real life." But he hoped it could be, and he embedded his preachment in credible characters.

Like Odets, Shaw drifted away from the theatre, returning to it occasionally, but not with much luck. His career after the war was built largely around short stories, novels and films. A play with a viewpoint like *Children from Their Games,* which in 1963 lasted only a few days on Broadway, made one feel what a pity it was that the theatre could not keep him as its servant. There is no proof, of course, that men like Odets and Shaw would have grown into the powerful, dominating figures of our drama they promised to be if they had stayed with it. Indeed, the speculation is as wistful as it it is pointless. Why should a writer dedicate himself to an unpredictable institution, which gladly uses him when it is profitable and casts him aside when not?

The Group Theatre did not introduce Robert Ardrey, who made his bow with *Star Spangled,* but it produced two of his plays, *Casey Jones* and *Thunder Rock.* Although these plays, including a fourth, *How to Get Tough About It,* failed in New York, Ardrey gained some respect. *Thunder Rock* did not shout from a soapbox, but it joined the preachers of faith in the future with its account of a young man's rediscovery of the courage to fight for a sane world after running away from its stupidity and vanity.

My Heart's in the Highlands, produced by the Group in 1939, was, like *Awake and Sing!,* the tocsin for another great hope. William Saroyan brought into the theatre a personal way of looking at his characters and at life. *The Time of Your Life,* produced a few months later by the Theatre Guild, reinforced the first impression. Here was a man who could laugh with, not at, people, who could convey sentiment and skirt cloying effects, who could ignore the rules of the well-made play and hold the attention with a free-flowing style. But Saroyan did not change or go forward. What was fresh at the outset turned mannered and stale. The heedlessness of the commercial theatre could not be held responsible for his failure to develop; one might argue that the money and acclaim it laid at his feet was excessive and turned his head, but any other kind of theatre would have greeted him with open arms and generous rewards.

The cement of a common purpose that held the Group Theatre together began to crack as success beckoned some of its members into more remunerative activities like the films. Others accepted invitations to play and direct for other managements. The out-

break of fighting abroad and the imminence of American participation had their effect. In his story of the Group's adventurous
decade, *The Fervent Years,* Harold Clurman has honestly set forth
the good and the bad.

The Group might have lasted longer if by some miracle it could
have armed itself against the seductions of the commercial theatre.
By this I mean that its offerings lived and died like commercial
productions. Despite its fervor and dedication, the Group did not
establish a basis for continuity, with a subscription audience, a
home of its own outside the high-cost, high-pressure Broadway am-
bience, and a school for young actors. Only after the Group Theatre had vanished did some of its alumni, notably Lee Strasberg,
Cheryl Crawford and Elia Kazan, form the Actors Studio as a training ground for actors who had hardly any other place in America
to test and stretch their capacities. But for many years the Studio,
with no producing arm, was detached from the mainstream of
American theatrical activity.

The Theatre Union, liveliest and most hard-hitting of the avow-
edly left-wing companies, flourished for a few years as a theatre of
social protest. On 14th Street in the theatre abandoned by the Civic
Repertory it set up shop, and among its productions was *Stevedore,*
a play as hortatory as a union recruiting campaign. In this work by
George Sklar and Paul Peters the point was made that the best
hope for an improvement of the situation of the Negro in the South
was unionization. A European voice, which was to become loud
and influential, Bert Brecht, was introduced through Peters, who
did an adaptation of the radical German playwright's treatment of
Gorki's *Mother.* But it was too early for Brecht in America.

The thesis plays of the thirties, though not lasting art, reflected
a concern with the urgencies of the day that made the escape stuff
seem particularly anemic. John Wexley brought anger to *They
Shall Not Die,* his dramatization of the case of the Scottsboro boys,
incarcerated for years and threatened by the electric chair on a
trumped-up accusation. Albert Maltz attempted a dramatic statement of the hard lot of the coal miners in *Black Pit* (1935). Albert
Bein charged into the proletarian battle with *Let Freedom Ring*
(1935), a drama about southern mill workers.

In the long view, the Group Theatre's influence has been the more pervasive, but in the thirties there was no movement to compare with the scope and size of the Federal Theatre Project. For a time it looked as if this grand, wide-ranging experiment in national support of the arts would not only shake the country but change it permanently. That it did not do so is attributable in part to its very magnitude and even in larger measure to the forces that created it.

The Project came into being in mid-1935 as an activity of the Works Progress Administration, through which the New Deal and its principal administrators in this field, Harold Ickes and Harry Hopkins, sought to make jobs for a multitude of the unemployed. Hallie Flanagan of Vassar College was placed in command, and her account of its turbulent history in a book called *Arena* is still worth reading. Mrs. Flanagan had been a student at Grinnell College in Iowa when Hopkins was there, and because of Vassar's proximity to Hyde Park, where the Roosevelts had their home, Mrs. Flanagan's Experimental Theatre was favorably known to Mrs. Roosevelt.

Mrs. Flanagan took over in August, prevailed on leading figures of the commercial and amateur theatre to take part in a series of Washington conferences and by October had set up regional divisions. Production units were formed throughout the country. New York got six, since it had the largest reservoir of unemployed talent, but this preponderance of activity in one center became a source of irritation and contention in an undertaking that began with hostility and was pursued by rancor and intrigue.

Mrs. Flanagan and her staff pitched in as if they meant to change the world. Before mid-1936 the Project had 12,000 men and women on its payroll, half in New York. The pay, it should never be forgotten, was a bare subsistence. If the Government poured millions upon millions of dollars into the Project's manifold activities, it got back not only the satisfaction of putting people back to the work for which they were equipped but also unparalleled enthusiasm and devotion. Of course the Project had troubles and defects. Its accomplishments were uneven—incompetents, amateurs as well as professionals, found their way onto the payroll. It was riven by inner dissensions and riddled by outside attacks. The commercial managers, never at a loss to protect their own interests, complained that the Government was competing for plays and talent and was therefore undermining free enterprise. In and out of Congress the opponents of the New Deal flailed away at the Project as egregious boondoggling. The radical associations of some in the Project were assailed, and so were the plays with a liberal viewpoint. Elmer Rice, who agreed in September 1935 to direct the New York wing of the Project, left in January 1936 because censorship of the Living Newspaper was imposed by Washington.

Say what you will about it, the Project lived up to the conviction, stated by Mrs. Flanagan, that "the talents of these professional theatre workers, together with the skills of painters, musicians and writers made up a part of the national wealth which America could not afford to lose." The diversity and quantity of what it produced was staggering. Something like 1,000 plays—classics of ancient times and more recent vintage, new works, experimental efforts—were mounted, some routinely, some poorly and a few brilliantly. The offerings included pageants, operas, puppet shows, dance works, vaudeville shows and a circus. English was the main language, but there were presentations in other tongues. Special performances for children were arranged. The Negro, who had been largely a fringe worker in the theatre, was brought into all-colored units, and although this was not the answer to his desire for equality as an artist, it was a small step forward.

Most novel and successful of the Project's ventures was the Living Newspaper. Drawing on his knowledge of adventurous theatre along these lines abroad, Elmer Rice was responsible for the original conception, which had a double value: each production enlisted the services of hundreds of performers and each attempted to dramatize a pressing problem. Arthur Arent, the most effective writer in this form, was in charge of the team that fashioned *Triple-A Plowed Under* (1936) and he wrote *Power* (1937) and *One-Third of a Nation* (1938). These productions examined with driving energy and enthusiastic partisanship the problems of farming, natural resources and poverty. The Living Newspaper was not strictly objective. It editorialized as well as reported. But at its most partisan, it never went beyond the New Deal position. To a Republican, of course, who had seen Franklin D. Roosevelt bury Alfred Landon in a 1936 landslide, the Living Newspaper gave an infuriatingly unfair advantage to a President who had too many weapons for any opposition's comfort.

The unit headed by Orson Welles and John Houseman was one of the most fiery in the Project, combining a flair for the stage and a talent for making news. Its production of Marlowe's *Dr. Faustus* was striking, and its all-Negro *Macbeth* was flamboyant in intention and impressive in realization. It could also perpetrate *Horse Eats Hats*, a daffy version of Labiche's *Italian Straw Hat*, which would have given pause to sophomores on a tasteless spree. Its presentation of Marc Blitzstein's *The Cradle Will Rock*, an incendiary tract against the steel companies opposing unionism and, indeed, against capitalism itself, was the brand that burned away the tie between this unit and the Project.

Welles and Houseman suspected that their production might be headed for trouble, for they invited an influential audience to the final dress rehearsal at the Maxine Elliott Theatre. Their fears were well grounded. The routine wire from Washington authorizing the première did not arrive; instead the authorities moved in, closed the box office and forbade the use of sets and costumes. Welles summoned cast and crew to an emergency meeting in the ladies' powder room and promised that the première would take place. Although he had nothing but his optimism to go on, his faith was rewarded. The Venice Theatre, later the New Century, on 58th Street and Seventh Avenue, was made available. Jean Rosenthal, now the lighting expert and then a young member of the staff, found an upright piano and got it hauled to the theatre. Led by the cast, an audience marched uptown.

The performance was an incomparable amalgamation of split-second timing and improvisation. Alone on the stage at the piano sat Blitzstein, not certain as he began whether any actors would adopt Welles's suggestion to sit in the auditorium and come in on cue. Blitzstein commenced the first song and the words were seized from his mouth by the actress in a loge. An actor took up his theme from a place in mid-orchestra. Abe Feder, in charge of lighting, caught each performer in a spot. Not all of the company were prepared to risk their meager Project salaries, but most did. The piece moved forward irresistibly, and the audience seethed with excitement. Archibald MacLeish rushed backstage to hail the new day of the participating audience and was invited to top the occasion with a curtain speech.

Separated from the Project, Welles and Houseman formed the Mercury Theatre, which presented *The Cradle Will Rock* as one of its productions in a more orderly version of the style in which it had been done, *faute de mieux*, the historic night. At each performance the composer sat at the piano on a stage without sets, and the cast came forward for solos and ensembles. It was remarkable how effective this procedure was, proving once again that it is far better for the theatre to liberate the audience's imagination than to offer it literalisms of set, costume and action.

Ten years later I heard *The Cradle Will Rock* again, this time with its full orchestration conducted by Leonard Bernstein. But the old excitement could not be recaptured. The piece had become dated—as polemic and entertainment. The sense of triumph in a time of crisis and adversity was no longer there to add its spice.

Welles and Houseman attempted—and succeeded—in turning Shakespeare to rousing political account. Their production of *Julius Caesar* is still remembered as a remarkable experiment in converting a remote classic into a forceful contemporary comment. They dressed the players in the clothes of the thirties, and Caesar's resemblance to Mussolini was stressed. The conspiracy to overthrow him became a hotly contemporary precept in insurrection against dictators. But even if one objected to the Mercury Theatre's way with Shakespeare as a distortion, one was bound to acknowledge the theatrical excitement this bold, fresh approach created. The Mercury's *Julius Caesar* rang up 157 performances, still an impressive figure for a Shakespeare run on Broadway.

Like any hastily assembled, far-flung mass operation, the Federal Theatre Project stood sponsor for all sorts of plays, amateurish and professional, freshly written or long since composed and unproduced, simple and elaborate, bad and good. Among the more interesting were *Battle Hymn* by Michael Gold and Michael Blankfort; *The Cherokee Night* by Lynn Riggs; *Brother Mose* by Frank Wilson; *Chalk Dust* by Harold A. Clarke and Maxwell Nurnberg; *Class of '29* by Orrie Lashin and Milo Hastings; *Native Ground* by Virgil Geddes, a playwright who, despite unusual gifts, never achieved the work that seemed within his power; *Prologue to Glory* by E. P. Conkle and the Sinclair Lewis–J. C. Moffett dramatization of *It Can't Happen Here.*

It Can't Happen Here was the Project's most ambitious undertaking. To demonstrate what a nationally directed network of theatres could do to make an overwhelming impact with a play about the threat of native fascism, the Project had *It Can't Happen Here* produced simultaneously by twenty-one companies in seventeen different states. All twenty-one openings took place on October 27, 1936. One thinks of the parallel of a new film launched on the same day in movie houses across the land, but it was not the same thing. For twenty-one companies were bound to differ from one another in details of casting and staging; each built its own production.

By November 1938, the Federal Project was in deep political trouble. Martin Dies and his Committee on un-American Activities summoned Mrs. Flanagan and hinted that she was under Russian influence. The only basis for this innuendo was a visit to the Soviet Union more than a decade earlier to study its theatre. Using the tactics that became standard operating procedure for this committee, its inquisitors sought to spread the poison that the Federal Theatre Project was an arm of the Communist Party and atheistic and immoral to boot. No doubt there were Communists on the Project payroll, but the plays it produced hardly ever ventured beyond the position of the Democratic Party's liberal wing.

Congress would not be appeased. The Senate joined the hunt for the Project's scalp. Despite a wave of support from the public and the theatrical community, including many of its established professionals, the Project's appropriation was voted down. On June 30, 1939, it went out of existence.

As a huge emergency venture in making work, the Project accomplished its chief mission. Despite diffuseness, ineptitude and controversies, it was an exhilarating mass undertaking in the drama. It left a residue of experience still worth exploring in an intelligent discussion of what role, if any, government can and should play in the theatre. It made clear that assembly-line techniques are troublesome and that political control of a theatre supported even partly by government funds can be mischievous. It also proved that there was an appetite for living drama in many sections of the nation that the commercial theatre, centered on Broadway, did not satisfy.

It has been suggested sadly that the Project's greatest failure was not to resettle professional cadres in a score of cities outside New York and to encourage them to put down roots, thus benefiting themselves, the communities and the theatre as a whole. It would have been a wonderful thing to do, but the cities beyond New York were not yet ready to build their own companies on a high, professional standard. Even now when the job is being done, the pull of New York is an ever-present obstacle.

CHAPTER XXII

THE LOUD, RUDE, VIGOROUS
THIRTIES

I N THE HETEROGENEOUS SEASONAL FARE on Broadway new names of consequence were emerging. Thornton Wilder, whose *Trumpet Shall Sound* did not even reach Broadway in the twenties and who in the thirties adapted André Obey's *Lucrece* and Ibsen's *A Doll's House,* the first for Katharine Cornell and the second for Ruth Gordon, established himself with *Our Town.* Well known as the author of the novel *The Bridge of San Luis Rey,* he recalled the theatre to its pristine simplicity, invoking that intimate interchange of imagination between stage and audience that the cluttered, fustian theatre had forgotten. Whatever one's reservations about the enduring qualities of *Our Town,* one was grateful for a play that returned to first principles. At the outset the stage was bare, with the brick walls at the rear as a backdrop. Frank Craven walked out casually, introduced himself as the stage manager and began to talk, like a country philosopher to his cronies around the cracker barrel. All we needed to be in Grovers Corners, N. H., with the people in the story was to be told that we were there. A chair, a ladder, a table were enough to evoke a house or a drugstore, and the props could be moved openly, as in the Chinese theatre. Wilder had done nothing new; yet it seemed new. The truth, of course, was that *Our Town,* despite its charm and honesty, was perilously close to banality. The final act, with its figures from the grave noting ruefully that people on earth don't see and appreciate enough of the pleasures of living, seemed in 1938—and still does—a very small, bittersweet portion of comment.

Another Wilder work, *The Merchant of Yonkers,* a free treatment of a theme from a nineteenth-century Austrian play, was a flop in 1938, but some fifteen years later he reworked it into *The Matchmaker,* and it became a joy of the fifties with Ruth Gordon and Eileen Herlie; and *The Matchmaker* in turn was reworked a decade later into the musical *Hello, Dolly!* to become a rousing success of the sixties.

With *The Children's Hour* in 1934 Lillian Hellman proclaimed herself as a tough-minded, uncompromising writer. *The Little Foxes* in 1939 confirmed her claim to distinction as a playwright who knew how to construct a powerful edifice filled with tension, how to make people live and breathe on the stage and how to probe under the elaborate defenses and pretenses of men and women to get at the essential weaknesses and strengths. For all its tightness and intensity, however, *The Children's Hour* seemed contrived. In *The Little Foxes* the control was surer and the dramatic power greater as the author looked at life without sentimentality or illusion. Here, in the heart of the decadent South, was a family without scruples or pity. The strong dominated the weak, and the weak retaliated as craftily as they might. Here was a horrifying revelation of the nature of human aggressiveness and greed. No American playwright of our time had probed more devastatingly under the skin of a ruthlessly acquisitive society. Miss Hellman did not soften her portraits or observations to please a public unaccustomed to such unyielding truths; such was the measure of her discipline and integrity as an artist. One cannot forget the play, nor can one forget the malevolent fumes that steamed from the performances led by Tallulah Bankhead as Regina, a vicious vixen among the little foxes.

Another newcomer, Clare Boothe, wrote with sharp-tongued sophistication. Her plays had neither the intensity nor the moral fervor of Miss Hellman's. They had a sophisticated veneer and acerbity. *The Women* (1936) was malicious and bright about the wealthy, self-indulgent creatures who had nothing to do but amuse themselves and feed their vanities. *Kiss the Boys Goodbye* (1938) poked fun at the smart set. *Margin for Error* (1939) sought to comment satirically on the Nazi mentality. At most these plays were smart, skillful entertainments, though Miss Boothe might have become an incisive satirist in the theatre had her interests not led her elsewhere.

John Steinbeck, who had achieved repute with his novels, ventured into the theatre with *Of Mice and Men* (1937). Although this work appeared first as a novel, it was designed as a play, as the novel's pared form suggested. Though touching in places as well as theatrical, the play did not have a convincing inner life. The story of the itinerant who protected and then killed his dim-witted companion to save him from the punishment awaiting him for a maniacal murder had a contrived, melodramatic air. Steinbeck tried again in 1942 in *The Moon Is Down,* another play that had a novelistic counterpart. Again his heart was in the right place; again his playwriting appeared to be too pat for its own good.

In the thirties Howard Lindsay could not be called a new boy, for he had been actor and playwright for a number of years. However, the work preceding *She Loves Me Not* (1935) was formula comedy. *She Loves Me Not,* based on a novel by Edward Hope, was an advance in speed and skill, and it spread a good deal of cheer. Lindsay joined Damon Runyon in writing *A Slight Case of Murder,* a broad jape about beer racketeers, but this one failed on Broadway, only to become a great film success. With Russel Crouse he made a free adaptation of Clarence Day's stories about *Life With Father,* and this comedy, with Mr. Lindsay himself as Father Day and his wife, Dorothy Stickney, as Mother Day, ran for seven and a half years on Broadway to break every record and to become not only a warm memory for millions of theatregoers but a shining example of the theatre's unpredictability. Who would have guessed that this family comedy, neither sexy nor sophisticated, would flourish so famously?

Not far removed in genre was *The Male Animal,* which brought

James Thurber all too temporarily into the theatre. Collaborating with Elliot Nugent, he offered a cheerful comedy that laughed at the American alumnus and his devotion to football and at the same time had something to say about the values a university in a democracy ought to sustain.

Playwrights who had made themselves key figures in the twenties were all-important to the thirties. Maxwell Anderson was enormously productive. His determination to infuse the American drama with poetry, begun with *Elizabeth the Queen,* did not waver. Anderson often sought to bend his verse to contemporary purpose, and always he hoped to make it the instrument of a liberating grasp of character.

The range of Anderson's work in the thirties was impressive, even if his plays no longer are imposing. He wrote realistically as well as in verse, tackling both contemporary themes and figures of the past. In *Winterset* he set out to write tragic poetry on a contemporary subject, explaining in a preface that he was aware that "the great masters themselves never tried to make tragic poetry out of the stuff of their own times." But he felt that the challenge to say vital things greatly had to be met "if we are to have a great theatre in America," and he was blunt: "Our theatre has not yet produced anything worthy to endure—and endurance, though it may be a fallible test, is the only test of excellence."

Anderson did not meet the test. His poetic diction was too self-conscious and earthbound. His ideas and sensibilities were generous, and he had a keen appreciation of what would work on the stage. But even as one sat in the playhouse and watched his works when they were new, one had an uneasy sense that something was lacking. As I reread the plays, I feel the lack more strongly. The emotions and visions do not rise like flame from character and style but are attitudes imposed by the writer.

Look at *Winterset,* in which Anderson returns to the Sacco-Vanzetti theme. This time he seeks to purify the subject by eliminating much that is specific. The drama does have a fine passion for justice; it also has, alas, a superfluity of rhetoric. The long search by a son for the man guilty of a crime wrongfully attributed to his father reminds one a little of Orestes come to avenge the death of Agamemnon. But love refines the fury for vengeance out of him.

Read the speech of Mio, the son, to Miriamne, the girl he encounters in his search. It is an appeal for help in an effort to change his nature. He recalls the harrowing venom that has pulsed sullenly and incurably in his veins. He wants to be rid of it, to be whole again, to forgive at long last. He feels the first stirrings of an end of vindictiveness. He pleads with her to show him the way to a life without corrosive rancor.

Mio's speech is well and honestly written, yet it does not move me. The denouement, with Miriamne getting shot and crawling to Mio's side to die, is stagy. The fault may not be Anderson's but mine. I believe in such an ending in *Romeo and Juliet,* but it does not ring true for me in Anderson's play. Nor does Rabbi Esdras's final prayer over the dead pair on the glory of dying young.

They are ringing sentiments, these lines spoken by Rabbi Esdra. In apostrophizing Miriamne and Mio, whom he describes tenderly as "my son," he proclaims the proud potentialities within man to stand up against defeat without cringing or yielding and, if necessary, to perish without a gesture of submission. But fine as these sentiments are, they have a rhetorical flourish.

I sympathize just as little with the rhetorical flourishes in the historical plays. In *Mary of Scotland* Anderson let the ill-starred Mary have the last word. For in this play he caused Elizabeth to be the architect of Mary's poor reputation as a woman and ruler. The play is well made, the blank verse supple and theatrically effective. The direct encounter between Mary and Elizabeth imagined by the playwright is admissible dramatically, especially Mary's pathetic desire to believe the best of Elizabeth.

Anderson confers a touching humanity on Mary in those lines in which she addresses Elizabeth, not as an antagonist and queen but simply as another vulnerable woman, one who must suffer, as she does herself, from the subtle, ever-present fears of advancing age. In a moment of pathos Mary wonders if sympathy and friendship might not, after all, be possible between Elizabeth and herself. These are sensitive lines that reveal character with delicate simplicity. They help to give the main role, if not the play as a whole, a bittersweet taste.

Helen Hayes was touching as Mary and the play had a romantic glow, but on reexamination it seems to posture sentimentally rather than to live.

Yet I do not wish to underestimate Anderson's high aims and expertise as a dramatist. His plays in the thirties included *Night Over Taos,* a tribute to the simple nobility of an ancient past; *Both Your Houses,* thesis drama on corruption in government; *Valley Forge,* an evocation of the hard days of the Revolution and a vision of the future as Washington might have seen it; *High Tor,* an attack on the greedy vandals who would sacrifice natural beauty for personal profit; *The Wingless Victory,* a look at the destructive force of ancient prejudice; *The Masque of Kings,* a hymn to the brave new world as contrasted with the sad, ghostlike one of the Crown Prince of Austria; *Knickerbocker Holiday,* a lively fantasy with satirical overtones, in which Walter Huston was a joy and Kurt Weill's music, especially "September Song," added a touch of magic; and *Key Largo,* an attempt to deal with the Spanish Civil War. Even if one includes *The Star Wagon,* another fantasy and an unsuccessful one, Anderson's output in the thirties had spiritual reach, if not greatness.

Sidney Howard's tragic end in an accident on his Massachusetts farm in 1939 ended a career that might have exceeded the stature it achieved. Much of Howard's work in the thirties was adaptation. From the French of Marcel Pagnol he prepared *Marseilles* and from René Fauchois the amusing and successful *The Late Christopher Bean.* From Sinclair Lewis's novel he drew *Dodsworth,* and from Humphrey Cobb's *Paths of Glory* he fashioned a play that commented on war with ironic power.

Yellow Jack credited Paul de Kruif with being collaborator, but it was largely Howard's work. It deserved a better fate than its mild reception on Broadway. It was an achievement in dramatic terms, for it made palpable the events in the conquest of yellow fever, without descending into cheap melodramatic tricks. The study of character took second place to a theatrical and factual account of a vital scientific development; there should be a place in the theatre for vivid history.

Trickier and more successful was *Alien Corn* (1933), which

served as a vehicle for Katharine Cornell. With *Gather Ye Rosebuds,* written with Robert Littell, *Ode to Liberty, The Ghost of Yankee Doodle,* dealing with the impact of international tension and the threat of war on private lives, and *Madame, Will You Walk,* a fantasy that foundered out of town, the career of an honest, serious American playwright was terminated prematurely.

S. N. Behrman took his place as the best of our playwrights of the comedy of manners. His workmanship was so controlled and refined that it was easy to underestimate. Each work from his atelier had style and taste. In each there was, besides felicity of phrase, a sense of values. In *Brief Moment, Biography, Rain from Heaven, Wine of Choice* and *No Time for Comedy* one felt always the tolerance of a civilized viewpoint that was more than an agreeable mantle covering an acceptance of things as they are. Behrman, in short, mastered the craft of fusing entertainment and comment into indivisible theatre pieces. No American, not Barry nor Sherwood, ever surpassed him in this genre.

Consider *Biography* as a chiseled example of the Behrman style. Some of us remember how the beautiful Ina Claire floated and sparkled through this play as Marion Froude, warmhearted and tolerant woman of the world. Behrman's characterization was sharp and precise even as it moved the drama along its course. The author's descriptive phrases, like his dialogue, had a flavor. Note how he first described Marion: ". . . the tears of things have warmed without scalding her; she floats like a dancer's scarf in perpetual enjoyment of its colors and contours." And how gently wise and witty she could be. There was the moment when the aggressive young Richard Kurt talked her into writing her biography for a mass-circulation magazine for an advance of $2,000—remember, this was the depression when $2,000 was big money in the magazine world. Now that he thought the deal closed, he rose abruptly to go, and Marion exclaimed: "Well, you can't go away and leave me like this—alone with my life."

In contrasting the radical with the conservative viewpoint, Behrman took what he considered the humane middle ground, the side of decency and liberalism. But his instinct for the silken dramatic touch was faultless. Marion's cremation of the manuscript

of her biography is a case in point. It reminds one of Hedda
Gabler presiding over the obsequies of another manuscript, but
what a difference! Even when his comment was wry, Behrman remembered to smile.

Robert E. Sherwood, who came into his own in the thirties, had
something of Behrman's quizzical approach, but his humor tended
to be gustier. *Reunion in Vienna* was a prime example of the
writer's robust, playful manner, and Lynn Fontanne and Alfred
Lunt imbued its mischief with an unforgettable shimmer and
dazzle. With lightness of touch, Sherwood revealed the decay of a
gracious European way of life. In *The Petrified Forest*, which gave
Leslie Howard a graceful, yet pointed role, and precipitated Humphrey Bogart into fame with a pungent, melodramatic one, Sherwood was diverting and theatrical. But the attempt to be meaningful sputtered out in a sentimental and meretricious conclusion.

Being a thoughtful man of liberal ideas, Sherwood, who devoted
much of his time and energy to serving Roosevelt as a speech
writer, sought increasingly to use the theatre for comment and
inspiration. In *Idiot's Delight*, again with the Lunts whirling
through a European milieu, he was concerned with the imminence
of war. In the same year, 1936, he was represented by *Tovarich,*
his adaptation of Jacques Deval's playful glimpse at the world of
the White Russian refugees in Paris. In *Abe Lincoln in Illinois*
he wrote, with simplicity and directness, a tender, yea-saying
chronicle about Lincoln's life up to the point where he leaves for
his anguished destiny in the White House. With Raymond Massey
as Lincoln this play was a success in the 1938–39 season; indeed,
it provided the rocket power for a new enterprise, the Playwrights
Company, organized by Anderson, Howard, Behrman, Rice and
Sherwood as their own producing instrument that presumably
would free them from the pressures and caprices of Broadway. It
didn't, but for some years it gave them more freedom of movement
than playwrights usually enjoy.

Several seasons ago the Phoenix Theatre revived *Abe Lincoln
in Illinois* with Hal Holbrook bringing a winning, homespun
quality to the title role that was superior to Massey's performance,
and I was pleased to discover how neatly and warmly the play dis-

charged its duty of re-creating the feel of history. The scene of the debate between Lincoln and Douglas had a theatricality and vigor that were still fresh. I realized that *Abe Lincoln in Illinois,* though not a drama for the ages, was a well-conceived and vibrant exercise in history, and deserved to be revived from time to time, especially for young people. If we had a theatre with such a mission, Sherwood's play would rightfully have a place in its repertory.

A name that flared brightly for a season and then drifted away was that of Lynn Riggs whose *Green Grow the Lilacs* had the free, open gait and robust laughter of the Southwest. With Franchot Tone as the cheerful Curley this play seemed engagingly fresh in the dispirited early thirties, and in its musical guise as *Oklahoma!* it helped to brighten the war years more than a decade later.

Of sensation-mongering productions the one that took the prize for durability was *Tobacco Road,* Jack Kirkland's dramatization of Erskine Caldwell's novel. The irony of this play, which became a magnet for countless theatregoers avid for titillation and shock, was that at the outset it had some merit. Despite its crudity, it threw a garish light on the debasement of life in dark, neglected byways of the Deep South. Once it became clear that scatology and voyeurism were box-office, however, the guardians of this production's destiny added to its vulgarity and profanity, and nursed the strange theatrical manifestation into a seven-year run. Odd how many people, who otherwise did not go to the theatre, relished Henry Hull as Jeeter Lester, the old goat of a poor Georgia paterfamilias, and his favorite expletive, "Jeepers creepers," and Sammy Byrd as the lecherous son.

Interesting work from abroad, in addition to the significant plays produced by the Theatre Guild and Group Theatre, had a share in the theatrical scene. T. S. Eliot made his bow as a playwright with *Murder in the Cathedral,* and an impressive one it was in the Federal Theatre Project's production, which preceded any in England. Sean O'Casey, Paul Vincent Carroll, J. B. Priestley, Dodie Smith, John van Druten and Mordaunt Shairp, whose *Green Bay Tree* with Laurence Olivier in the cast dealt with homosexuality, another theme hardly tackled by the theatre, were among the British writers who brought stimulation and amusement to our stage. There also were Continental writers. Helen Hayes had a winning vehicle as the generous little usherette in Molnar's *The Good Fairy* just as several seasons later she had a virtuoso role as *Victoria Regina* in Laurence Housman's chronicle play. Franz Werfel's *The Eternal Road* provided the theatre with the kind of Biblical epic that has become the exclusive ostentatious province of the wide-screen movies, and they can have it.

That prince of foreign writers, William Shakespeare, got more attention on Broadway than he does now when he has become a festival hero in several Stratfords and in a variety of far-flung centers across the land. In one season John Gielgud and Leslie Howard offered New York their Hamlets, and while the former won the honors of the longer run, the latter earned the gratitude of connoisseurs who admired the subtlety of his interpretation. In a succeeding season Maurice Evans appeared in an uncut *Hamlet* that had the temerity to require almost six hours with a break for dinner just as if it were a nine-acter by O'Neill, and this too had a certain vogue. Evans's Falstaff in *Henry IV, Part I* did not thrive, however.

Katharine Cornell unwisely undertook to play Juliet as two decades later she manhandled Cleopatra. But if her judgment was misguided in these Shakespeare ventures, she rarely failed in her dedication to the theatre as a personal obligation. One of her most notable contributions was a tour of 75,000 miles in the 1933–34 season, when the country's morale desperately needed a lift, with *The Barretts of Wimpole Street* and *Candida*, two of her best vehicles, as well as *Romeo and Juliet*. Eva Le Gallienne, indomitable despite the collapse of the Civic Repertory Theatre in New York, took her company on the road for an extensive tour in the same season.

If the musical theatre of the thirties was dominated by Gershwin's finest achievements, *Of Thee I Sing* and *Porgy and Bess*, it marked the continuing high standards of old hands and the development of new.

Arthur Schwartz and Howard Dietz were the principal contributors to the sophisticated revues that Max Gordon presented at the Music Box. Remember *Three's a Crowd* with such ingratiating performers as Clifton Webb, Libby Holman, Fred Allen and Tamara Geva? Or *The Band Wagon* with Fred and Adele Astaire, Frank Morgan and Tilly Losch and a song like "Dancing in the Dark"?

Kurt Weill arrived on the scene. His masterly acrid, ironic score for *The Threeepenny Opera* set to Bert Brecht's version of John Gay's *Beggar's Opera,* lasted only twelve performances and had to wait until the fifties and Marc Blitzstein's English adaptation to become an off-Broadway perennial. But his songs for the Group Theatre's production of Paul Green's *Johnny Johnson* marked him as a man with an individual style, and his score for *Knickerbocker Holiday* reinforced this impression.

Harold Rome made an enormous splash with *Pins and Needles,* a manifestation of the explosion of unionism in the thirties. The Labor Stage, a wing of the International Ladies Garment Workers Union, produced this labor-oriented revue, which Rome and his associates had polished in several summers at Green Mansions in the Adirondacks under the guidance of Robert H. Gordon, a director and actor who had been a loyal member of the Civic Repertory Theatre. Produced in the union's auditorium, *Pins and Needles* proved to be a long-running delight with its bright, labor-oriented sketches, its disarming performances by union members and a sheaf of fresh tunes and lyrics that included "Sing Me a Song of Social Significance," "Sunday in the Park" and "One Big Union for Two."

I happened to hear Rome play and sing his songs at a private home in the long, weary months when he was seeking to get them produced in the New York theatre, and I was impressed. Some time later an acquaintance who worked in the Shubert office phoned me and said that her bosses were on the hunt for new talent in the musical field. As music editor of *The New York Times,* did I know any names worth recommending? I mentioned Harold Rome, and learned later that when the suggestion was relayed to higher authority it was rejected out of hand. "Why, the man is unknown," was the complaint.

For Jerome Kern it was his last decade in the theatre, but he ornamented it with *The Cat and the Fiddle,* which was graced by

"The Night Was Made for Love"; with *Music in the Air,* a return to operetta land with Oscar Hammerstein as traveling companion and with Walter Slezak and Reinald Werrenrath in the cast and with a lovely score led by "I've Told Every Little Star"; with *Roberta,* which spotlighted a young comic talent named Bob Hope and a couple of hits like "The Touch of Your Hand" and "Smoke Gets in Your Eyes"; and with *Very Warm for May,* Kern's swan song and a flop, which nevertheless included a song like "All the Things You Are."

Irving Berlin was relatively inactive, but he did two shows, in collaboration with Moss Hart. The book show, *Face the Music,* introduced "Let's Have Another Cup of Coffee." The revue, *As Thousands Cheer,* left a legacy of "Easter Parade" and "Heat Wave."

Rodgers and Hart did not slacken their pace. Besides *On Your Toes,* a milestone in the growing boldness of the musical theatre, and the topical *I'd Rather Be Right,* they collaborated on *Simple Simon; America's Sweetheart; Jumbo, Babes in Arms,* which had one of my favorites among the Rodgers and Hart numbers, "The Lady Is a Tramp"; *I Married an Angel,* which filched the lovely Vera Zorina from the ballet for the theatre; *The Boys from Syracuse,* which was as brash as its score was fresh, including "Falling in Love with Love," "Sing for Your Supper" and "This Can't Be Love," and in which Jimmy Savo, Teddy Hart, Eddie Albert and Ronald Graham joyously cavorted; and *Too Many Girls.*

Cole Porter shifted into high gear as he moved from *The New Yorkers,* a vehicle for Hope Williams, Ann Pennington, Frances Williams and one of my favorite madcaps, Jimmy Durante, to *Gay Divorce,* in which Fred Astaire was nimble grace incarnate and "Night and Day" was a stunning winner; to *Anything Goes,* which brought together Ethel Merman, William Gaxton and Victor Moore and spread laughter and melody with "I Get a Kick Out of You," "You're the Top" and "Blow, Gabriel, Blow"; to *Jubilee,* with such knockouts as "Just One of Those Things" and "Begin the Beguine"; to *Red, Hot and Blue,* with a song like "It's De-Lovely"; to *Leave It to Me!* with a new hoofer named Gene Kelly and Mary Martin, a young unknown who made a triumph out of a disarmingly antiseptic striptease as she sang "My Heart Belongs to Daddy"; to *Dubarry Was a Lady,* which brought together Merman and Bert Lahr and provided them with a chortling, robust duet called "Friendship."

The plush musicals of the century's first three decades were shrinking and vanishing, although in *The Great Waltz* the old tradition had a last shined-up, though boring fling. The trend was toward integrated musical theatre. No one could say that the raffish, burlesque-like *Hellzapoppin,* which Ole Olsen and Chic Johnson detonated in 1939, was a pointer toward the future. Compared with the sophisticated felicities of Rodgers and Hart or Cole Porter, it was a sock on the head with a clown's bladder. Yet somehow it was an appropriate expression of one of the moods of 1939. It spoke loudly and rudely for a nation that had regained its confidence but scanned the darkened international horizons with foreboding. As it ran on and on, its exploding firecrackers and bursting balloons were loud, senseless punctuations in a troubled nation's frantic pursuit of diversion.

❖❧

CHAPTER XXIII

IN THE WAR YEARS

F ROM THE DAY that Hitler's panzer divisions stormed into Poland and his bombers splintered a beleaguered Warsaw into rubble while a brave radio station defiantly but hopelessly broadcast a proudly Polish Chopin Polonaise, war conditioned the American theatre. Although the United States was not involved in the fighting until the attack on Pearl Harbor, its mind was on it constantly. Our young men were being drafted and trained; our merchant ships were traveling in the war zones; our government and the great majority of our people made no secret of their sympathies.

In the early autumn of 1939, the theatre, especially on Broadway, was busy and not without cheer. The World's Fair, in its second year, still attracted a host of visitors to New York. Business at box offices was good, for the depression had receded. Behrman had written *No Time for Comedy*, but comedy was very much in demand. *Life With Father, The Man Who Came to Dinner, The Male Animal* and *The Time of Your Life* were big hits.

Bizarre comedy, if you laughed heedlessly, was on display in John Barrymore's return after an absence of seventeen years, most of them in Hollywood making films, in a vehicle called *My Dear Children.* The once-admired matinee idol was deriding himself and his profession as he clowned, improvised and teetered on the edge of intoxication.

The accent was on unruffling entertainment. Milton Berle made an impression as a comedian in a farce called *See My Lawyer*. Gertrude Lawrence spread the glow of her personality over Samson Raphaelson's sophisticated *Skylark*. Flora Robson's grave dignity added to the appeal of a mystery drama from Britain, *Ladies in Retirement*. A newcomer named Danny Kaye appeared with Imogene Coca, Alfred Drake, Jerome Robbins and other young performers in *Straw Hat Revue*, put together at an adult summer camp.

Established personalities experienced variable fortunes. Ethel Barrymore played a ninety-seven-year-old in something that swiftly came and departed, obviously inevitable casting after her success as a centenarian in Mazo de la Roche's *Whiteoaks*. Helen Hayes had slightly better luck with *Ladies and Gentlemen*, a comedy of the juryroom, concocted by Charles MacArthur, her husband, and Ben Hecht. Maurice Evans played *Richard II*. Those endearing Irish actors, Barry Fitzgerald and Sara Allgood, appeared in a revival of O'Casey's raffish and keening *Juno and the Paycock*. Burgess Meredith and Ingrid Bergman were teamed in a return of Molnar's *Liliom*. *Romeo and Juliet* gloried in Laurence Olivier and Vivien Leigh.

The world's anxieties could not be kept out of the theatre. Ernest Hemingway's only play, *The Fifth Column*, dealt with the Spanish Civil War, but was a failure, and, alas, deserved to be, despite its awareness of the import of this prelude to Armageddon. The aging Bernard Shaw, still contentious and provocative, had grown garrulous in *Geneva*, which took a satirical look at Europe's problems. Dorothy Thompson joined Fritz Kortner, a German, in writing *Another Sun* which dealt with two actors driven from Nazi Germany, one of whom returned while the other remained to fight for a fresh career. Once again it was clear that goodwill could not substitute for good drama.

More touching was *Reunion in New York*, a revised version of an earlier revue called *From Vienna*, which brought together refugees from Hitler's Europe. By their very appearance, these performers were more pertinent than their material or the stuff being offered on other stages.

In stage terms the war at this point was most effectively dramatized for Americans by Robert E. Sherwood in *There Shall Be No Night*. Moved by the Russian attack on Finland, Sherwood wrote at white heat, and when the manuscript was finished, submitted it to the Lunts. They had just completed an exhausting 30,000-mile national tour in *Idiot's Delight, The Seagull* and *The Taming of the Shrew*, and had returned to New York in *The Shrew* for two weeks to raise $25,000 for the Finnish Relief Fund. They took the new Sherwood script with them on the train ride to Genesee Depot, their Wisconsin farm, thinking that it might be a possibility for the next season. When they reached Chicago, they wired Sherwood that they were turning back to begin rehearsals.

There Shall Be No Night, which the Lunts played with dignity and humility, touched the public nerve like no other work of the early war years. It laid its scene in the Finland of 1940, and through its protagonist, a man of enlightened simplicity, it declared its faith in the enduring power of those willing to die for their deepest convictions. When the play was presented in London the Finnish characters and setting became Greek, to mark Greece's struggle in defense of its integrity as a nation, and it was equally viable.

Two decades after the war's end, I wonder whether *There Shall Be No Night,* despite its honesty and humanity, would stand up as well as *Abe Lincoln in Illinois*. I have similar doubts about two plays by Lillian Hellman. I remember how moving was *Watch on the Rhine,* which described a decent German's struggle with a pursuing, vengeful Nazi agent and which brought home something of the hunted desperation of the victims of Nazism. I remember how Herman Shumlin's production and staging and the performance by Paul Lukas and Mady Christians, an actress of remarkable warmth and sympathy whose haunted Gertrude in Leslie Howard's *Hamlet* I shall never forget, shook me. Upon reexamination of the play, I find that its conflict is too pat. I never saw Miss Hellman's *The Searching Wind* on the stage, for I was abroad in the Army when it was being performed in New York, but I have gone over the text and, despite my admiration for the author's intelligence and viewpoint, I feel that its characters and conflict do not hold up. But I suspect I would have found it effective in 1944 in the theatre. In telling a story of a young American who loses a leg as a result of fighting in Italy, *The Searching Wind* condemned the good, well-intentioned people for their failure to speak out against Mussolini's coming to power in 1922, against the depredations of the new movement of Nazi bullyboys in 1923 and against the "peace-in-our-time" Munich mentality of 1938.

As the war went on, more and more pieces were preoccupied with it—some seriously, some amusingly and quite a lot simple-mindedly and opportunistically. Hardly a play or musical was without its men and women in uniform, its reference to shortages of housing, gasoline, and services, its attempt to invoke the scenes, sights and emotions of embattled individuals and nations.

In *The Patriots,* Sidney Kingsley, then a sergeant in the U. S. Army, wrote a well-constructed study of the conflict between Jefferson and Hamilton with Washington as the weary arbiter. In a play named *South Pacific* by Howard Rigsby and Dorothy Heyward, a Negro merchant seaman floated with a white man on a lifeboat after their ship was torpedoed and raised a question to be put more acutely after the war, "What has freedom done for me?" The play itself, unfortunately, was not nearly so apt.

The best of the war plays were, in plain fact, none too good. Several, however, communicated a sense of decency and honesty that justified their success. In *Tomorrow the World* James Gow and Arnaud d'Usseau imagined a twelve-year-old Nazi and a well-meant effort to reclaim him that failed as the fanatical boy, remarkably played by a youngster named Skippy Homeier, began to poison the democratic atmosphere. In *A Bell for Adano* Paul Osborn turned John Hersey's novel about the humane Major Joppolo, played with crusty warmth by Fredric March, into an immensely popular play; in showing that impersonal Army directives could be applied with humanity, this play was comfortingly civilized but, like the novel, not really probing. In *The Hasty Heart* John Patrick told of an embittered and gravely wounded young Scot in a hospital behind the Burma front who learned that the friendships forced on him by war could have unexpected meaning. In his adaptation of Franz Werfel's play, *Jacobowsky and the Colonel,* which dealt with the German invasion of France, Behrman contributed the wryest evocation in seriocomic terms of the civilized mind's quandary in a fanatical world, and Oscar Karlweis, a refugee from Austria, was altogether winning as the bedeviled, gallant little man, Jacobowsky.

The theatre raised questions, but the questions nearly always were sharper than the plays. Paul Green adapted Richard Wright's bitter novel, *Native Son,* and although it was contrived and melodramatic, it brought home fervidly the fury and despair of the Negro who destroyed and was destroyed by his inferior position in a white environment. It was in this play that Canada Lee, formerly a jockey, pugilist, fiddler and band leader, emerged as an intense actor.

Most amusing and lasting of the war period's plays was Thornton Wilder's *The Skin of Our Teeth.* Though not searching, it was a heartening tribute to the staying powers of the human species. In its striking theatrical staging by Elia Kazan and a delicious performance by Tallulah Bankhead, Fredric March, Florence Eldridge and Montgomery Clift, this play when new in 1942 won the hearts of many people and confused and annoyed many more. Its adherents, led by Alexander Woollcott, who as self-appointed town crier to the nation was making even more noise than he had as a drama critic, called it the finest play ever written by an American. Its belittlers described it as nonsense. On revisiting it recently I found it effective as theatre and as an optimist's tribute to man's indestructibility. But I wondered whether in the age of the H-bomb and missiles in space Wilder would still be so cheerfully certain about man's survival.

Although the number of productions did not come close to the triple figures of the twenties, business at the box office hummed. The national economy, fed by the tremendous war effort, was booming. A lot of loose cash—some no doubt black-market profits—was available for Broadway productions. Angels, theatrical genus, sprouted wings on all sides. The happy history of *Life With Father,* which paid its investors $35 for every $1, was the golden carrot that led a host of innocents into the theatre. Almost as golden was the story of *Arsenic and Old Lace,* a comedy by Joseph Kesselring produced by Lindsay and Crouse, which returned $7,400 for every $583.34 invested.

The customer with money in his hot little hands had relatively few places to spend it. What with rationing and travel restrictions, people not in the service stayed close to home, and they went to the theatre. Artistically the 1941–42 season was the worst in many years, but there was at least one success for every three failures. Indeed, in the 1944–45 season the ratio improved; out of 83 productions 24 were counted as hits, about a dozen, big hits.

In the musical field two works proclaimed a lifting of sights and a future in which the American product would emerge as the undisputed leader. These were *Pal Joey* (1940) and *Oklahoma!* (1943), both the work of Richard Rodgers, the first with John O'Hara and Lorenz Hart, and the latter with Oscar Hammerstein II.

In many ways *Pal Joey,* which opened on Christmas night, 1940, was a greater advance on what had preceded it than *Oklahoma!,* which arrived at New York's St. James on March 31, 1943. Rodgers put it accurately more than a decade later when he said this work "wore long pants, and in many respects forced the entire musical comedy theatre to wear long pants for the first time." It looked unblinkingly at a heel, a self-indulgent rich woman, and a sleazy world, and did not romanticize.

George Abbott brought his tough theatricality to the staging, and Gene Kelly, Vivienne Segal, June Havoc and young Van Johnson gave the characters the flinty, tinselly flash they required. Songs like "Bewitched, Bothered and Bewildered," "In Our Little Den of Iniquity" and "Take Him" had an edge. *Pal Joey* had 374 performances the first time around, though some influential opinion was repelled by its subject matter. Revived in 1952, it was hailed as a "classic" and rang up an astonishing 542 performances.

Oklahoma! had no trouble once it landed in New York, but it faced a plague of problems on a thorny path to its thunderous success. The Theatre Guild had fallen on painful days when it was ready to produce the musical made out of Lynn Riggs' play, *Green Grow the Lilacs.* Its once-bursting treasury was down to $30,000, and Lawrence Langner and Theresa Helburn might well worry that their once-epochal enterprise was on the verge of disintegration. Loyal backers declined to put up money. Titled *Away We Go*, the new musical did not impress the Broadway cognoscenti at its New Haven unveiling; some recommended closing there and then. The show moved to Boston; some changes were made, and the title was changed. Nevertheless, there were even unsold seats for the first night, unbelievable for an enterprise involving such eminent theatre folk. But with the opening shot the battle was won. As the curtain rose on a quiet stage on which sat Aunt Eller rocking herself, a young, healthy baritone offstage sang a glad hymn to being alive. The singer, Alfred Drake as the extroverted cowboy, Curley, strolled out, still singing, and with each verse of "Oh, What a Beautiful Mornin' " the audience's euphoria increased. This gesture of beginning with a hit tune was as nervy as Verdi's placing "Celeste Aïda" in the first scene of his opera. Like Verdi, Rodgers and Hammerstein were wise thrushes able to recapture their type of fine careless rapture, for they followed with "The Surrey With the Fringe on Top," "Kansas City," "I Caint Say No," "Many a New Day," "People Will Say We're in Love," "Pore Jud Is Daid," "Out of My Dreams," "All er Nothin' " and "Oklahoma!" The staging by Rouben Mamoulian, the sets by Lemual Ayers, the costumes by Miles White and the dances by Agnes De Mille, the performances by Joan Roberts, Celeste Holm, Lee Dixon, Joseph Buloff and Howard Da Silva conjured up magic. A full-length ballet danced by Joan McCracken, Bambi Linn, George Church and Marc Platt as the first-act climax was not only novel but also enchanting.

It is impossible to guess the effect of the simple optimism of *Oklahoma!* on a nation receiving grim reports from battlefronts in North Africa, Europe and the Pacific, or the impact of its novelty. As one sits through revivals two decades later one notices that the book is thin and that the folk spirit is show-business rather than authentic Southwest. *Oklahoma!* is not, after all, an enduring masterpiece. But the score remains rich and beguiling and the importance of *Oklahoma!* as a landmark has not dimmed.

Rodgers and Hammerstein moved further toward the integration of all the elements of musical theatre in *Carousel,* their adaptation of *Liliom.* They transplanted the locale from Budapest to a New England coast town; they gave the story a touch of optimism, and they made the music into a more significant element of storytelling. Once again the Theatre Guild was the producer, and Rouben Mamoulian the director. John Raitt as Billy Bigelow, the boastful carnival barker, and Jan Clayton as Julie Jordan, his touching, forthright girl, were not typed performers.

There were song hits in *Carousel* that became standards like the best in *Oklahoma!*—"If I Loved You," "June Is Bustin' Out All Over," "Blow High, Blow Low," "A Real Nice Clambake" and "You'll Never Walk Alone." The texture of this musical was more refined than that of *Oklahoma!* In a song like "You're a Queer One, Julie Jordan," which is not hit-parade material, and in the long "Soliloquy," which characterized in a way most musicals would not dare, Rodgers and Hammerstein stretched the bounds of the popular lyric theatre.

While the musical theatre moved forward, the drama, on the whole, played it safe, relying chiefly on writers established before the outbreak of hostilities. But in the 1944–45 season two significant names appeared.

Arthur Miller could hardly have had a less auspicious start. *The Man Who Had All the Luck* had a grand total of four performances, but there were some observers who thought that it was too hastily withdrawn and predicted better things from the newcomer.

Tennessee Williams made it with *The Glass Menagerie,* but only after a good deal of uncertainty. When the script was submitted by mail to Eddie Dowling, he was preoccupied with something called *The Passionate Congressman.* His wife, Ray Dooley, read *The Glass Menagerie* and insisted that her husband must do so, too. Dowling was taken with this "memory play." He approached the man who had agreed to back *The Passionate Congressman,* and suggested a switch, and marvel of marvels, the backer consented. The play was rehearsed in New York and opened in Chicago. In the cast were Laurette Taylor, playing with incredible incandescence, as well as Julie Haydon and Dowling. The Chicago critics greeted *The Glass Menagerie* warmly, but the public did not respond. For three weeks there were losses, while the critics urged their readers to see the play. Finally the production turned a small corner as enough business developed to keep going. But it was almost prize time in New York—the Pulitzer Prize and the New York Drama Critics Circle Awards were not far off—and the producers decided to come East at once. They were rewarded with the New York Drama Critics Circle award, though the Pulitzer Prize went to *Harvey*, Mary Chase's fable about the invisible rabbit whom Frank Fay made so endearing. For Laurette Taylor the role of Amanda in *The Glass Menagerie* was a crowning triumph. She encased its indestructible egocentrism in a shimmering mist of self-illusion. She was indispensable in creating a mood of muted poetry and heartbreak. I have seen the play in several revivals and have found it both callow and tenuous without her magic. But the revaluation of two decades later cannot vitiate the lift that the theatre derived from the appearance of a gifted new playwright.

CHAPTER XXIV

BRAVE PLANS — VAIN HOPES

AFTER A BITTER, grinding, unimaginably costly war, the theatre, like the nation, had every reason to expect happier days and nights. Victory was heady, and the Cold War was a phrase waiting to be invented. Energy was strong and further invigorated by men returning from war duties and eager to bring their gifts to the stage. Money was still abundant. What had the theatre, particularly its fount and center in New York, to worry about?

If it stopped to think, it might have realized that it had not shared the wartime prosperity. Hardly any of the profits were used as seed money. No permanent companies of consequence were formed in New York, no help was provided for such ventures in other cities, and the road, cramped by travel restrictions, fell off even further. The theatre had other reasons for nervousness beyond the normal tensions. Hollywood, itself jittery, reduced its spending on plays because it did not know what to expect. Television was on the horizon.

There were scattered, hopeful signs of constructive activity reflecting a sense of the responsibility that the theatre owed itself and the community. Late in 1943 New York had established the City Center of Music and Drama. The idea behind its founding was radiantly simple: a great city should have a home for the performing arts within the reach of the smallest budgets. With the active blessing of Mayor Fiorello H. La Guardia, Mecca Temple, a mosquelike barn of an auditorium, was taken over in lieu of tax arrears and turned over to a publicly owned City Center corporation. Newbold Morris, President of the City Council, became chairman of the board, and raised an initial operating fund of $65,000 from friends of the project, ranging from John D. Rockefeller Jr. to the labor unions.

Susan and God with Gertrude Lawrence served as the opening attraction. Prices ranged from 85 cents to $2.20. There were brief runs of Kingsley's *Patriots* with Walter Hampden and Cheryl Crawford's production of *Porgy and Bess*. The New York Philharmonic Symphony under Artur Rodzinski anointed the old barn with an inaugural concert, the Ballet Russe de Monte Carlo gave performances, and an opera company began operations.

Speaking of the new venture, the ebullient La Guardia said, "It has to succeed, because the players love it, the ushers love it, the public loves it. And what's more—it's good for them." Hailing "the awakening of a dream," the Mayor hoped "that my successor in five years will have a temple of art."

In its first years the City Center's drama depended on touring attractions and the availability of stars. The Opera Company established an identity early in the Center's history, and the New York City Ballet Company, creation of Lincoln Kirstein and George Balanchine, moved into the Center early in 1946 and became its most distinguished component. The Light Opera Company did not take shape until 1954. The Center did not have its own Drama Company until 1948. Meanwhile, it was able to offer its new audiences early in 1944 a revival of *Our Town,* and late that year Helen Hayes played *Harriet,* the Florence Ryerson-Colin Clements play about the little woman who wrote *Uncle Tom's Cabin,* and there was a special production of *Little Women.* In 1945 Eva Le Gallienne and Joseph Schildkraut appeared in *The Cherry Orchard,* Fred Stone in *You Can't Take It With You,* and Paul Robeson, José Ferrer and Uta Hagen in the *Othello* that had done so well on Broadway. A revival of *The Tempest,* with Zorina, Canada Lee and Arnold Moss, came for a while at the end of 1945, and in 1946 Maurice Evans's *GI Hamlet*.

The role of the drama at the City Center was becoming meager. A plan to organize a summer stock company in 1947 got no farther than a first production of *Rip Van Winkle*. By January of the next year the dream of a resident company was realized. With an initial gift from Richard Aldrich, Broadway producer, the New York City Drama Company came into being.

José Ferrer, the director, and Richard Whorf, the designer, assumed the principal roles in *Volpone*, the first production. Under Ferrer's leadership there were two spring seasons, which included notable productions of *The Alchemist*, O'Neill's one-acters assembled as *S.S. Glencairn*, a group of one-acters by Chekhov and Capek's *The Insect Comedy*. Maurice Evans took over the leadership of this drama venture in 1949 and produced, among other things, a delightful *Devil's Disciple* with himself and Dennis King which was so popular that it moved to Broadway, and an acclaimed *Richard II*. In the fifties under George Schaefer, who had been Evans's associate; then under Albert Marre and finally under Jean Dalrymple, the City Center's Drama Company mounted revivals of old and recent pieces, including one of *The Male Animal* with Elliott Nugent, Robert Preston and Martha Scott that returned to Broadway for almost another year. Leading lights of the stage worked at Equity minimums. During her stand as Blanche in a revival of *A Streetcar Named Desire* Tallulah Bankhead remarked that her pay was $85 a week, while her theatre maid received $100.

Although the Center was living up to its aims to provide professional theatre of respectable caliber at popular prices, it was in plain fact doing little more than assembling *ad hoc* productions. At no point did its theatre activities resemble the New York City Ballet or the Opera Company, both of which were developing new talent and opening opportunities for new creative figures. It always seemed to me that the City Center did not aim high enough in the theatre. I wonder if a vigorous, imaginative policy could not have helped to create and establish a permanent company dedicated to the classics. I know that money was always in short supply at the

Center, but an idea and a commitment can be more important than cash in hand.

In the months after the war another and theoretically more widely based organization roused itself to action, mindful that the theatre as an art with a national destiny was being neglected. For a few years the American National Theatre and Academy, known as ANTA, had a flurry of impressive activity. It had been chartered by Act of Congress in 1935, and when President Franklin D. Roosevelt signed his name to the charter it was imagined that automatically a new day had dawned for the theatre in America. But ANTA was soon submerged by the Federal Theatre Project's hurricanes of excitement.

In 1935 not one of ANTA's founders was an important theatrical figure. In 1937 Robert Sherwood, appointed to an Advisory Committee, which, *mirabile dictu,* embraced playwrights and actors, offered a plan for a National People's Theatre. This proposal envisaged touring productions of the classics and outstanding modern plays, but it remained, like so many other noble visions, words on paper.

In 1946 ANTA behaved as if it meant business at last. Its officers were largely of the theatre: C. Lawton Campbell, chairman; Vinton Freedley, president; Sherwood, vice-president; Gilbert Miller, treasurer; Rosamond Gilder, secretary. Robert Breen took over as an energetic executive secretary. The year before, with Robert Porterfield, founder of the Barter Theatre in Abingdon, Virginia, where for years audiences have bought their way into performances with contributions in kind rather than cash, he had drawn a plan for a National Theatre Foundation. Its objective was to stimulate the development of the theatre as an art, educational medium and civilized recreation for the great majority of Americans. The establishment of a graduate laboratory for young people who had completed their formal schooling was high on the agenda. Here fresh talent could develop under the guidance of the best professionals and become the nucleus of a National Theatre Company. Brave plans—and vain hopes!

ANTA did conduct a nationwide drive for members. It organized benefit shows, including the famous ANTA Albums that charged $100 a seat and were rife with glamour and sentiment. But apart from the Experimental Theatre, ANTA was addicted to *pronunciamentos* rather than accomplishment. Even its purchase in 1950 of the Guild Theatre, which it renamed the ANTA, did not mean a frontal attack on the major problems of a mature, artistic theatre.

For several seasons the Experimental Theatre was a concrete expression of the theatrical community's awareness that the heedless system of putting on only what could make a profit narrowed the drama's range and constricted its future. During the 1940–41 season Actors Equity and the Dramatists Guild had helped to found Experimental Theatre, Inc., with Elaine Perry, producer and director, as the president. The new unit produced *The Trojan Women* and a couple of American plays, but with the United States' entry into the war, it shut up shop.

Early in 1947, Experimental Theatre, Inc., was revitalized. ANTA took the lead, and received cooperation from Theatre, Inc., the Theatre Guild, the American Repertory Theatre and the Playwrights Company. Breen was the animating spirit. The small Princess Theatre was taken over. Gertrude Macy, a longtime associate of Katharine Cornell, was appointed executive producer. A subscription scheme of $15 for five plays was set up, and a firm policy of no free tickets, not even to critics, was fixed and followed.

In the first season five new plays were presented: *The Wanhope Building,* a fantasy by John Finch; *O'Daniel,* by Glendon Swarthout and John Savacool; *As We Forgive Our Debtors* by Tillman Breiseth; *The Great Campaign,* by Arnold Sundgaard; and *Virginia Reel,* by John and Harriet Weaver. No masterpieces in the lot; not even commercially viable stuff. But this initial season was the theatre's affirmation of a responsibility to its own future.

The second season had commercially attractive ingredients. Charles Laughton undertook to play the lead in his own adaptation of Brecht's *Galileo,* with Joseph Losey directing, and John Garfield assumed the principal role in Jan de Hartog's *Skipper Next to God,* with Lee Strasberg directing, which moved to a regular Broadway house for a run of about twelve weeks. *Ballet Ballads,* a fresh, experimental enterprise, with words by John Latouche and music by

Jerome Moross, also went on to wider success. An adaptation of Gorki's *The Lower Depths* by Randolph Goodman and Walter Carroll was staged by Alan Schneider. Richard Harrity's rueful one-acter about bums in Central Park, *Hope Is a Thing with Feathers*, which later vainly tried Broadway, shared an evening with Horton Foote's *Celebration.* E. P. Conkle's *Afternoon Storm,* and Halsted Welles's *A Temporary Island* completed an ambitious season.

But expenses outran income, which included $70,000 from subscribers and $2,000 each from Equity and the Dramatists Guild. It was other costs, not the actors, who ate up the money, for Garfield received $10 a week, and Laughton got $8. Laughton was miffed for another reason. Among the appeals to accept an invitation from Experimental Theatre, there was one from a well-known New York critic, who wrote his letter to the actor in a spirit of concern for the theatre's good. Once *Galileo* opened, the critic wrote forthrightly, as a critic must, and his judgment of Laughton's performance was not flattering.

In the 1948–49 season Experimental Theatre pulled in its wings. A committee led by George Freedley saw to it that seven new plays were put on twice for invited audiences, and one of these was a version of Louis O. Coxe's and R. H. Chapman's adaptation of Herman Melville's story, *Billy Budd.* At this point the play was called *Uniform of Flesh;* some seasons later it earned respect on Broadway as *Billy Budd.* In the 1949–50 season there was a mild activity, but it no longer had any value.

Theatre Incorporated began in 1945 flying banners of goodwill. According to its prospectus, it was to be a nonprofit, tax-exempt corporation, "committed to a sustained program of great plays of the past and outstanding plays of the present." Its income was to be "devoted to the continuation of such a program on a permanent basis; to the encouragement of young playwrights, directors and actors through a subsidiary experimental theater; to the utilization of the stage as an educational force, and to the ultimate development of a true people's theatre."

With Richard Aldrich as managing director, Theatre, Inc., plunged into activity as if it intended to live up to its prospectus.

It underwrote a visit by London's Old Vic, and it presented the first of what it hoped would be a series of first-class revivals—in repertory form—*Pygmalion* with Gertrude Lawrence and Raymond Massey. The production caught on; the planned short run was extended to almost half a year; the idea of repertory died before achieving life.

The Old Vic, however, demonstrated what repertory could be, particularly if a nation's leading players were willing to devote intervals in their careers to performing roles they cared about without the big money to be earned in the West End, on Broadway or in the films. With the Old Vic company on this visit to New York were Laurence Olivier, Ralph Richardson, Joyce Redman and Margaret Leighton. The repertory included both parts of *Henry IV*, *Uncle Vanya*, *Oedipus Rex*, with Olivier as a shattering king, and *The Critic*.

Eva Le Gallienne, who did not need to be persuaded or inspired, succeeded in getting another repertory enterprise started. This one was called the American Repertory Theatre. With the collaboration of Margaret Webster and Cheryl Crawford, a group of notable actors was assembled. Walter Hampden played Cardinal Wolsey in *Henry VIII*. June Duprez was in *What Every Woman Knows*. Ernest Truex played Androcles. Victor Jory, Richard Waring and Philip Bourneuf joined Miss Le Gallienne and Miss Webster in the acting troupe. *John Gabriel Borkman*, *Yellow Jack* and *Alice in Wonderland* were in the repertory. But the venture did not thrive; once again *Alice in Wonderland* staved off catastrophe. The gravest trouble was the intransigence of the theatrical unions—particularly the stagehands and musicians—in their refusal to give the enterprise any special consideration. *Henry VIII* required a large body of stagehands, and the company was obliged to employ the full contingent for the entire engagement, though during the Barrie and Ibsen plays some sat around idle. Add the public's reluctance to embrace repertory, and the brave enterprise could not survive.

Less glamorous but more durable was the Equity-Library Theatre, which came into being during the war. Under a partnership between the New York Public Library and Actors Equity, plays were mounted in auditoriums of the city's public library system. George Freedley for the library and Sam Jaffe for Equity shared in the administration, and John Golden made gifts of money. The objective was twofold: to give young stage folk an opportunity to work and learn and to bring live theatre to people who could not afford it. In its first season—1944–45—Equity-Library produced 37 plays. In 1946–47 it put on 56—an impressive record. The pace slowed measurably, but over the years this modest program has been, without fanfare, of some small benefit to many young hopefuls.

CHAPTER XXV

A NEW ERA — THE MUSICAL DOMINATES

As a victory season, 1945–46 should have been all sweetness and light. But there is no season when feelings are not exacerbated somewhere in the murderously competitive commercial theatre, and it is a rare one when someone is not firing away at the critics. This time the war was open and declared. Stung by rough reviews of his *Truckline Café,* Maxwell Anderson paid his respects to the critics in advertisements placed in the newspapers. His indictment read; "It is an insult to our theatre that there should be so many incompetents and irresponsibles among them. There are still a few critics who know their job and respect it, but of late years all plays are passed on largely by a sort of Jukes family of journalism who bring to the theatre nothing but their hopelessness, recklessness and despair." Orson Welles also fired away when *Around the World,* a musical that he created with Cole Porter, got its lumps, being called, among other things, "Wellesapoppin."

In the seasons following the war's end patterns were set for the fifties, sixties and, for all anyone can predict, far into the foreseeable future. The era of the producer who backed his judgment and enthusiasm with his own money was over. A new boy like Anthony Brady Farrell might whirl like an extravagant Roman rocket for a season or two, but eventually would tire of pouring hundreds of thousands into the theatre's gaping maw. Having wasted a large amount on a musical called *Hold It* as a starter, Farrell was determined to beat the game. He purchased Warner's Broadway and renamed it the Mark Hellinger, where he installed a new musical called *All for Love,* which got little encouragement from the press or public. Farrell decided to fight for his baby's life, and he kept the show running at a loss of $12,000 a week. Finally, he gave up—and the theatre communty estimated that his unrequited passion had cost him $2,000,000. Before leaving Broadway, Farrell, however, had the satisfaction of producing *Texas, Li'l Darling,* which, despite unfavorable notices, did well at the box office.

The business of financing shows became increasingly a matter of assembling a halo of angels with relatively modest sums to gamble. A few producers still were able to raise all the backing needed from a well-heeled elite. Others had to scrounge and sell shares to a multitude. Farthest out was a short-lived organization called Your Theatre, Inc., whose pitch was pared to essentials. It only asked its shareholders to buy a ticket, and to prove that it would not let any individual carry too large a burden it said it would sell only 24 shares to a customer. It attracted 3,000 subscribers whom it regaled with something dreadful called *Heads or Tails.* When the critics tore the play to shreds, Your Theatre, Inc., designated its own reviewers from its roll of shareholders and ran their admiring notices as advertisements.

The postwar period ushered in the era of the musical's dominance. *Oklahoma!* set producers, writers and investors to dreaming of similar glory and profits. The public caught the fever and eagerly bought tickets in advance so that it would not be shut out when a smash hit arrived. Theatre parties proliferated, and musicals were among their favorite buys. An advance sale of $300,000 for *South Pacific* early in 1949 was regarded as phenomenal, and the buildup for *Miss Liberty* a few months later was even more impressive. In response to an ad placed one Sunday in the *Times, Herald Tribune* and *News,* the production received mail orders with checks for an unbelievable $100,000. The public had learned after the success of *Kiss Me, Kate* and *South Pacific* that it would not be able to get tickets for months. It did not know that many of these hot tickets were sold at inflated prices running up to $100 under the counter and that the "ice"—the difference between the legal cost and the black-market payment—was distributed furtively among unidentified individuals who reaped huge dividends from the theatre's greatest successes. What the public did know was that it had to be forehanded if it wanted tickets for a *Miss Liberty* which looked like a sure success, since its authors were Robert Sherwood and Irving Berlin and its director Moss Hart. The advance exceeded $400,000, and the theatre community and the world at large marveled.

Miss Liberty was disappointing, and once it had exhausted its advance, it folded its tent and slipped away into the night. But musicals with promising components continued to rack up astonishing advance sales. For *The Sound of Music* which brought together Rodgers and Hammerstein, Lindsay and Crouse and Mary Martin in the late fifties, the advance was well over $2,000,000. *Camelot,* the Lerner-Loewe musical that followed *My Fair Lady,* brought in more than $3,000,000 before the first New York curtain. These huge sums, invested in 3 percent Treasury notes, could produce a neat profit for the theatre owner, and producers who did not share in the unexpected windfall complained, as they still do, that they were entitled to part of it.

The sources of the musical's widespread appeal were many and varied. With the end of wartime controls, the economy leaped forward. More people than ever wanted complete escape. More people enjoyed the easily accessible, generally unperturbing combination of story, color, song, dance and attractive young people. More people had more money. Conspicuous spending increased. Theatregoing on lavish expense accounts became a commonplace. The cost of tickets was no deterrent. Finally, the theatre was generally at its most sustained, professional best in the musical.

The great successes of the postwar years underlined the high standard being achieved by the musicals. Before the 1945–46 season's end, *Call Me Mister* and *Annie Get Your Gun* arrived. The first, although it looked like a farewell to soldiering, was at heart a spirited, yet nostalgic withdrawal from the pains and pleasures of being in uniform. Produced by a newcomer, Herman Levin, with sketches by Arnold Auerbach and Arnold Horwitt, it had Harold Rome's best songs since *Pins and Needles*. A bright young troupe directed by Robert H. Gordon included Betty Garrett, Jules Munshin, Lawrence Winters and Harry Clark, and it rejoiced in numbers like "Goin' Home Train," "Little Surplus Me," "The Red Ball Express," "The Face on the Dime," "South America, Take It Away" and "Along With Me."

Exuberant as only Broadway can be, *Annie Get Your Gun* gave Ethel Merman her best role. Still brazen and extroverted, she had as Annie Oakley powerful songs to belt out—"You Can't Get a Man with a Gun," "Doin' What Comes Natur'lly" and "I Got the Sun in the Morning." But she also had romantic numbers like "They Say It's Wonderful" and "I Got Lost in His Arms." Gratefully she remarked, "Irving Berlin made a lady out of me."

Berlin had never been in happier form, though it had taken a lot of persuasion to make him believe that he was the songwriter for this show. The producers, Rodgers and Hammerstein, had designated Jerome Kern as the composer, but he died before beginning the assignment. Berlin was unsure of his ability to adapt himself to an integrated musical. He had no need to fear. His overflowing score included "There's No Business Like Show Business," "The Girl That I Marry," "My Defenses Are Down," "I'm an Indian, Too" and "Anything You Can Do," which would have graced Cole Porter's literate, antic output.

The book by Herbert and Dorothy Fields, the staging by Joshua Logan, the dances by Helen Tamiris and the cast led by Ray Middleton that backed up Merman were among the solid forces that speeded the dominance of musical theatre.

The next season's principal winners were *Finian's Rainbow* and *Brigadoon*, which indicated that the musical theatre could embrace delicacy of fantasy and breadth of imagination.

Finian's Rainbow the work of E. Y. Harburg, Fred Saidy and Burton Lane, aimed for that rare thing in the musical theatre— social comment. It poked fun at burying gold, as the Government does at Fort Knox, and was sardonic about the stupidity of racism. Lane's tunes wedded to Harburg's lyrics caught the flavor of the theme. The promise of the future was celebrated in "When the Idle Poor Become the Idle Rich" and "The Great Come-and-Get-It Day." For the impish leprechaun, Og, played delightfully by David Wayne, there was "Something Sort of Grandish" and "When I'm Not Near the Girl I Love." Ella Logan, who imposed a Scots brogue on an Irish role without impairing its charm, had the enchanting "How Are Things in Glocca Morra?" and "Look to the Rainbow." Bretaigne Windust's staging, Michael Kidd's dances and Jo Mielziner's sets did no harm, either.

I don't know how *Finian's Rainbow* would stand up today, though I am sure that the score would hold its own in the best of company. I do know that *Brigadoon* upon revival in the sixties lacked the magic luster it had in the forties. For Alan Jay Lerner and Frederick Loewe, *Brigadoon* marked their arrival among the major teams. When it was new, this musical was fresh and fanciful and its attractive score included "Brigadoon," "Waitin' For My Dearie," "I'll Go Home with Bonnie Jean," "The Heather on the Hill" and "Come to Me, Bend to Me." With Robert Lewis directing and Agnes De Mille choreographing and with Marion Bell and David Brooks in the principal roles, *Brigadoon* was a sugared never-never Scotland just as *Finian's Rainbow* brought a whiff of a never-never Ireland to an imaginary American setting.

The vintage season was 1948–49. With *Kiss Me, Kate,* Cole Porter reached his zenith. With *South Pacific* Rodgers and Hammerstein were at the top of their form. The former ran for 1,077 performances, the latter 1,925. I do not begrudge the impressive figures established by *South Pacific;* I merely regret that *Kiss Me, Kate,* which I liked a little better, did not come anywhere near this record.

I can see why *South Pacific* outdid *Kiss Me, Kate.* The story that Hammerstein and Logan got from James A. Michener's *Tales of the South Pacific* had more romantic appeal, and there was dignity in the treatment of a middle-aged planter's love for a forthright young American nurse. But *Kiss Me, Kate* had an elegance, wit and distinction of style that no musical of its time matched.

Let us grant that Shakespeare is always a powerful asset, but let us credit Sam and Bella Spewack with making brilliant use of *The Taming of the Shrew* in their fable of actors on the road. Nor should we forget the gleaming skill with which Cole Porter used Shakespeare's words to enrich his lyrics. Alfred Drake and Patricia Morison knew how to be modern and timeless in their real-life and play-acting embodiments of the determined lover and his temperamental lass, and they had a lot of help from the wickedly innocent Lisa Kirk and the high-stepping Harold Lang in John C. Wilson's staging and Hanya Holm's choreography.

One has only to recall the titles of the songs to realize what a jewel of a score Porter had provided: "Another Openin', Another Show," "Why Can't You Behave?" "Wunderbar," "So In Love," "We Open in Venice," "Tom, Dick or Harry," "I've Come to Wive It Wealthily in Padua," "I Hate Men," "Were Thine That Special Face?," "Too Darn Hot," "Where Is the Life That Late I Led?," "Always True to You in My Fashion" and "Bianca."

It is almost impossible to believe that this rich musical, which opened on December 30, 1948, could be followed on April 7, 1949, by one almost as sumptuous. For Rodgers and Hammerstein adorned *South Pacific* with a score that included "Dites-Moi Pourquoi," "A Cockeyed Optimist," "Some Enchanted Evening," "Bloody Mary," "There Is Nothin' Like a Dame," "Bali Ha'i," "I'm Gonna Wash That Man Right Outa My Hair," "I'm in Love with a Wonderful Guy," "Younger Than Springtime," "Happy Talk," "Honey Bun," "Carefully Taught" and "This Nearly Was Mine."

It is doubtful that *South Pacific* could have been defeated with lesser casting, but it was inspired in its choice of Mary Martin as the lively, outgoing American nurse, Nellie Forbush, and Ezio Pinza as the middle-aged planter, DeBecque. When Miss Martin sang "I'm Gonna Wash That Man Right Outa My Hair," as she washed her hair six nights and two matinees a week under a streaming shower, one shared her annoyance and determination, and when she celebrated her happiness with "I'm in love, I'm in love, I'm in love with a wonderful guy," one felt like joining in this rapturous hymn of the happy heart.

The casting of Pinza for a musical seemed to Broadway, which looked on grand opera as the outlandish preoccuption of highbrows, as incredibly risky. The truth, of course, was that Pinza had been a distinguished singing actor for a generation. The man who could be a superb Don Giovanni, Boris Godunov, Figaro and Mephistopheles did not need the fears or patronage of show-business types. He could hold his own on any stage as an actor, and vocally he could make the average Broadway singer seem a poor, thin thing, indeed. Actually it was the right move for Pinza at the right time. I remember hearing him some months before as Don Giovanni when the once-magnificent, seamless, velvety bass-baritone was beginning to show signs of wear. In a musical even his second best would seem like glorious singing, and so it was when he sang "Some Enchanted Evening."

For years *South Pacific,* like *My Fair Lady,* was an international industry. I was in Florence on a summer's assignment in Europe in June 1951, when I had a telephone call from Hammerstein, who was in Bucks County, Pennsylvania. He had read a piece I had written about Boris Christoff, then appearing at the Florence Festival, and he called to ask whether the Bulgarian basso could sing in English. He was looking for a DeBecque for the London production, due to open that fall. Mind you, I had never met or spoken to Hammerstein. But when you need a DeBecque, you don't stand on ceremony. For the record, Wilbur Evans was in the Pinza role when *South Pacific* opened in London.

The last of the gaudy musicals to arrive in the forties was *Gentlemen Prefer Blondes,* which brought forward Carol Channing, who had been attractive but unknown in Charles Gaynor's revue, *Lend an Ear,* of the previous season. As the winsome Lorelei Lee of Anita Loos's story, this tall, congenial, outgoing girl made the most of the Jule Styne–Leo Robin score to spread gusty laughter with "Diamonds Are a Girl's Best Friend" and transparent innocence with "I'm Just a Little Girl From Little Rock." Overnight she was a star.

Since the musical was now the moneymaking king on Broadway, venturesome souls undertook ambitious works that let the music speak with more subtlety and breadth. Composers who were thoroughly educated musicians and who could, if they chose, do all their arranging and orchestrating found a place in the theatre beside the Tin Pan Alley lads whose forte was a simple melody. Leonard Bernstein had proved it could be done with *On the Town.* Now came a passable Comden-Green show, *Billion Dollar Baby,* staged by Abbott and with choreography by Robbins. Jerome Moross made generous use of Lully for a musical version of Molière's *The Would-Be Gentleman,* which starred that ineffable musical-comedy gentleman, Bobby Clark.

In the 1946–47 season Broadway made the leap into opera, undisguised and unashamed, when a production of Gian-Carlo Menotti's *The Medium,* coupled with his curtain raiser, *The Telephone,* moved down from the Brander Matthews Theatre at Columbia University. To Broadway's surprise this suspect form with the strong eerily dramatic ingredients of *The Medium* heightened by the raffishness of Marie Power's playing and the fierce intensity of her singing flourished for a number of months.

In the same season Kurt Weill attempted an ambitious version of Elmer Rice's *Street Scene.* With lyrics by Langston Hughes, Weill wrote music that required actors with trained voices, and the company included Polyna Stoska, Anne Jeffreys, Brian Sullivan and Norman Cordon. Unfortunately this version of *Street Scene* did not improve on the original. It did not go far enough toward fullness of musical expression. Weill was inhibited, I would guess, by the fear of alienating a public that regarded opera as an exotic.

Weill, always alert to an unconventional approach, next joined with Alan Jay Lerner to write *Love Life,* an imaginative work that deserved better than the lukewarm success it had. Produced by Cheryl Crawford and staged by Elia Kazan, this musical traced the essentially unchanging nature of love across the generations with wry, adult humor. The score had a touch of refinement—note a song like "Green-Up Time"—that did not make any impression on ears accustomed to more obvious strains.

With the failure of the expensive *Magdalena* in the 1948–49 season the move toward involving fine composers in the popular theatre suffered a severe setback. This musical had a score of unmatched inventiveness by the distinguished Brazilian composer, Heitor Villa-Lobos, but the book was dreadful. I cannot recall any Broadway score that had such lightness of touch, such variety of color, so much fantasy in its melodies. I remember a number called "The Broken Pianolita," which was like a free and joyous improvisation on the sounds that an automatic player piano would make if it went beserk and if a composer like Villa-Lobos were on hand to extemporize on the unpredictable broken chords.

In 1948–49 Benjamin Britten had an unmistakable opera, *The Rape of Lucretia,* performed first in the normal theatre channels of Broadway. Staged by Agnes De Mille, it failed. Not Britten's best work, it had a certain fire and distinction, but it was really out of its element in Broadway.

The musical theatre on Broadway reached its most ambitious operatic level in 1949–50. First there was *Lost in the Stars,* based on Alan Paton's affecting novel of South Africa. Maxwell Anderson did the book and oversimplified it into banality. Weill took the trouble to do his own orchestrations. Rouben Mamoulian staged the piece, and the cast was headed by Todd Duncan, Leslie Banks, Inez Matthews and Warren Coleman. There were some lovely songs, but they were isolated from each other, like numbers for an orthodox musical. Weill should have opted uncompromisingly for concentrated and continuous music expression.

Blitzstein and Menotti did not write down to Broadway in *Regina* and *The Consul. Regina,* based on *The Little Foxes,* was a much better piece than it got credit for being. If Blitzstein could not catch the savagery of the play's comment on human greed in his music, he did bring out elements of compassion that gave his version a different balance.

Regina, staged by Robert Lewis and performed by a company that included Jane Pickens, Brenda Lewis, Priscilla Gillette and William Wildermann, was a Broadway failure, even though it had more quality than many of the musical works that flourish in the commercial showshops.

The Consul, on the other hand, was a success. Menotti's work was opera without mitigation or disguise. The cast was full of trained singers, and young Thomas Schippers was in the pit, where he had a full orchestra. Although the story was melodramatic, its sympathy for the displaced and stateless was impassioned. And when Patricia Neway near the end of the second act sang "To This We've Come," with its piercing lament for man's indifference to man, one could feel an entire theatre's hackles rising with excitement.

◆《《

CHAPTER XXVI

FORGETTING THE WAR

T̲H̲E̲ ̲M̲A̲J̲O̲R̲ ̲E̲V̲E̲N̲T̲S̲ of America's postwar drama were the establishment of Arthur Miller and Tennessee Williams as writers of character and stamina.

Miller made the transition from *The Man Who Had All the Luck* to the probing *All My Sons* in two seasons. Despite faults in the structure and a lack of lift in the language—the latter was to remain a chronic Miller flaw—*All My Sons* spoke with fervor. An attack on the chiselers who lined their pockets in wartime even though the lives of fighting men were further endangered, it raised the moral issue that has haunted Miller in play after play—man's responsibility for his fellows. Ed Begley and Arthur Kennedy were in a cast directed by Kazan with his customary tensions, and *All My Sons* was a tonic in the 1946–47 season.

Death of a Salesman two years later was a more penetrating inquiry into the problem of responsibility. Freer in form than its predecessor, it examined the downfall of Willy Loman, salesman, a man of pathetic mediocrity who mouthed, lived by and was defeated by the empty slogans of a go-getting America. Again Miller had a lot to say about a heedless, destructive, materialistic society. This time he had written a notable play, if not a great one.

Much ink has been spilled over whether *Death of a Salesman* qualifies for the lofty designation—tragedy. It has been argued that according to the classic theory, tragedy must deal with a noble nature brought low, and that Willy Loman was a fumbling little man and no more. My own belief is that classic definitions exist to be stretched or broken. I cannot see why a humble man cannot be the protagonist of great tragedy. The trouble with Willy Loman is that he merely feels sorry for himself, and you sympathize with his plight because it is the plight of innumerable feckless men and women in an industrial, profit-oriented society. At least it was their plight before capitalism began to make modifications in its institutions to admit aspects of the welfare state, like reasonable pensions set up by contract with unions and widened and improved social security benefits. Willy, like his pitful kind, does not recognize the causes of his failure as a human being, nor does he assume responsibility for it.

Nevertheless, *Death of a Salesman* was an impressive reach for size. I felt that way in 1949 when it first appeared in the taut and humane production produced by Kermit Bloomgarden and Walter Fried, staged by Kazan, designed by Jo Mielziner, composed by Alex North and performed memorably by Lee J. Cobb as Willy, Mildred Dunnock as his wife and Arthur Kennedy as one of the sons. I have seen and read the play again in recent years, and feel it remains a strong and valid criticism of the way our system debases values and discards its victims.

Williams, the hardest-working and most prolific of our serious playwrights, has rarely been unrepresented on the New York stage since the success of *The Glass Menagerie*. Shortly after the war's end his *You Touched Me,* written with Donald Windham and based on a D. H. Lawrence story, had a run of 109 performances. It was a romantic comedy with an attractive part for Edmund Gwenn. The true voice of Tennessee Williams was heard, piercing and racking, in *A Streetcar Named Desire,* which lit up the 1948–49 season with its ferocity and intensity.

What *The Glass Menagerie* had said in a muted, sardonic way *A Streetcar* expressed searingly and furiously. Its Blanche DuBois, a neurotic and a nymphomaniac who lived in a world of fantasy, was an unsparing portrait of corrupted and corrupting womanhood. What made the play absorbing was not its stridency and sensationalism but the sense of truth it conveyed, and what gave it uncommon stature in a theatre given to small gestures and small, if not imitation, emotions, was its pity. Kazan's staging and the performance by Jessica Tandy as Blanche and Marlon Brando as the animalistic Kowalski intensified the impact.

With *Summer and Smoke* the next season it became increasingly clear, as, indeed, it has been transparent over the years, that Williams writes endless variations of the eternally baneful female. In *Summer and Smoke* she was inhibited and frustrated. In *A Streetcar* she was crippled by her fantasies and crippling in her passions. Elsewhere she would be consuming, lustful, frigid, demanding, intrusive, dominating—a creature wreaking malevolent vengeance on helpless males or one to be rooted out like a canker by self-defensive males, but rarely a balanced, fulfilled human being.

Williams writes as he must, and he describes a world that is real to him. Thanks to his power of characterization, his flair for the stage and his gift of phrase, he forces you to attend to him. But I often feel as if he were charming snakes. I admire his skill and respect his passion, but I go away sadly feeling that his is a special, hothouse world, only remotely my world.

For a time directly after the war it looked as if the New York stage was going to grow up. Shortly after the peace the holocaust remained on people's consciences. The returning veterans with their memories and their problems of readjustment kept it alive. Among the plays that turned up in the Victory Season nearly all had been written while the fighting was on, while men and women were still convinced that the world must be changed to wipe out the causes of national and international dissension and to root out injustice.

However, the public, despite its feeling that it must remember the agony and the losses, was weary of war. Arthur Laurents's *Home of the Brave*, mingling a war-induced shock and a psychiatric cure with bigotry in race relations, lasted only eight weeks. It was an interesting switch that in the successful film version the gravely scarred war victim, a Jew in the original, became a Negro.

Racial intolerance was on dramatists' minds, though none of

the treatments had real quality. The most successful, *Deep Are the Roots* by Armand d'Usseau and James Gow, considered what happened when a Negro war hero returned to an unchanged South and sought to realize his love for a white girl. The play's heart was in the right place, but the points were made by contrivance of incident and by stereotyping southern characters.

Comedy and romance aimed at comment on things of moment. In *State of the Union* Howard Lindsay and Russel Crouse had fun with the search of the Republican Party for a Presidential candidate who would look liberal but not be too liberal. Ralph Bellamy was capital in this one. In *Born Yesterday,* Garson Kanin wrote vivaciously about the dumb blond (Judy Holliday was a find in this role) who in an unexpected access of moral rectitude bedeviled her rich wheeling-and-dealing protector, played expansively and cholerically by Paul Douglas.

Of the established playwrights, Lillian Hellman's *Another Part of the Forest* went back twenty years in the lives of the Hubbards of "The Little Foxes" and with equal mercilessness showed them in the process of becoming what they became. In *Montserrat* Miss Hellman adapted a play by Emanuel Robles, which told unflinchingly of how innocents may be taken as hostages and killed. I remember Emlyn Williams as the sadistic inquisitor and especially Julie Harris, as a frightened, brave young girl, one of the six who chose to die rather than reveal Bolivar's hiding place. Again, a vital theme.

Maxwell Anderson came back after the exacerbations of *Truckline Café* with a winning approach to the Maid of Orleans in *Joan of Lorraine,* using a commonplace stock company as the background for an exploration of his notions about the character. Ingrid Bergman's beauty shone through this work. In *Anne of the Thousand Days,* Anderson invoked his verse style for a study of Anne Boleyn.

Elmer Rice surprised the public with *Dream Girl,* an escapist yarn about an attractive young girl who spent a lot of her time in a dream world. The play was offered to a number of glamorous figures in filmdom, and none could see it. Whereupon Betty Field, Mr. Rice's wife, took it on and turned it into a successful fantasy.

Moss Hart, adept at suiting the taste of the moment, fabricated a popular tale in *Christopher Blake* of the orphans of divorce—the children left unanchored by the parting of parents. In *Light Up the Sky*, Hart was back in his most comfortable milieu—show business—and in his most familiar vein—farce—and had another success.

Some new, welcome names drifted into the theatre. Already famous, Robinson Jeffers was represented by his retelling of the story of Jesus and Judas and by his version of *Medea*. In the latter Judith Anderson burned up the stage in the raging inferno of her performance.

The two who offered hope for the future were Carson McCullers and William Inge. Mrs. McCullers, it turned out, was a writer for the stage at second remove; her true calling was the novel. Nevertheless, *The Member of the Wedding* was a heart-warming play. Structurally it was infirm, but it had several enchanting characters, the most memorable being the young girl on the threshhold of adolescence who wants to be a member of the wedding. Julie Harris, turning herself into a clumsy, tender pre-adolescent, worked wonders of humor and sentiment with this child, and Ethel Waters as an understanding maid and seven-year-old Brandon de Wilde as a matter-of-fact little cousin helped to make magic out of this piece.

Inge arrived in the 1949–50 season with *Come Back, Little Sheba*, a harsh, compassionate view of a marriage held together by the memory of love and a horror of intolerable loneliness. Speaking of what it truly knew with candor, this was a work meant for —and at home on—the stage. Shirley Booth and Sidney Blackmer gave remarkable performances as the divided, yet inseparable couple.

If the American theatre in the postwar years did not receive as rich an infusion of new native writing blood as it needed, it gained immeasurably from the discovery of work from abroad. Priestley was still contributing an occasional play; I remember being entertained by *An Inspector Calls* for its blend of speculations about time and social responsibility. John van Druten, now resident in America, was constantly productive. Terrence Rattigan began to be a commercial factor. The Lunts, seeking a change of pace, glided through *O, Mistress Mine,* and two seasons later came *The Winslow Boy,* an attempt at an earnest character study. The two plays illustrated the basic nature of Rattigan's work: its slick technique and its overriding submission to theatricalism.

The significant importations from France were Jean Giraudoux, Jean-Paul Sartre and Jean Anouilh.

Giraudoux was one of the finest writers of our century. It is characteristic of our theatre's parochialism that Americans hardly knew his work before his death in 1944. It wasn't until the 1948–49 season that he appeared on Broadway with *The Madwoman of Chaillot.* Even then it was a near thing. For when this remarkable play translated by Maurice Valency, produced and staged by Alfred de Liagre Jr. with loving irony and humanity, designed by Christian Berard, and performed with shrewd and tender waywardness by Martita Hunt and Estelle Winwood, only three reviews the next day spoke up for it. Fifteen years later, when operating costs were much higher, it probably would have died before it could catch its breath. Given a chance, it slowly picked up enthusiastic spokesmen, won an audience and achieved a run.

For Giraudoux wrote with skepticism and high intelligence, mocking the pretensions of man and barely adumbrating a hope that somehow somewhere simplicity and wisdom might prevail. His style was in the high French tradition with its precision of diction and its gift for paradox and irony. It was—and unhappily remains—a style that a good many Americans find it hard to tune in on, particularly in the theatre where as a people we are uneasy with intellectual subtlety.

The proof of how we could despoil work of this order was the production of Giraudoux's *The Enchanted.* Broadway laid its rude, uncomprehending hands on a play of imaginative quality and robbed it of its point and refinement. This was one place where the George S. Kaufman touch was baneful. He directed Valency's adaptation as if it were a raucous farce, and the result was repellent.

Sartre made his entry in 1946–47 with *No Exit,* his investigation into the nature of a human hell. Although the cast included

Claude Dauphin, Annabella, and Ruth Ford and the direction was by John Huston, the play ran only 31 performances. *Red Gloves* turned up two seasons later in a Jed Harris production that the author disavowed from Paris, and only Charles Boyer, moving from the cinema to the stage, gained from this venture. Sartre was served more effectively off Broadway when *The Respectful Prostitute* with Meg Mundy in the lead was played by a group known as New Stages on Bleecker Street and then taken uptown to the Cort. New Stages tried again, with less luck, the next season with *The Victors*.

If Giraudoux was difficult for Americans, Sartre was even less concerned with the conventions of plot and characterization. He used the theatre as a forum for philosophical probing.

Anouilh, France's most adept writer of black comedy, was introduced just after the war when Katharine Cornell appeared in his simple adaptation of Sophocle's noble *Antigone*. Anouilh had written it during the war and it was produced in German-occupied Paris under the title of *Antigone and the Tyrant*. Why the Nazis let it take and hold the stage I shall never understand, for it was a fierce attack on dictators.

From Great Britain came *The Cocktail Party* by T. S. Eliot. It had a literary quality so rare on our stage that some hailed it as a towering masterpiece. It wasn't. It was, however, stimulating, civilized and, to some of us not prepared to accept Eliot's conservative vision of man and his salvation, rather irritating. But in the production staged by E. Martin Browne and performed by a cast headed by Cathleen Nesbitt, Irene Worth and Alec Guinness, *The Cocktail Party* was a reminder that the theatre need not be the exclusive playground of hacks.

Antique in provenance was *The Lute Song*, an adaptation of a 2,000-year-old Chinese classic by Will Irwin and the late Sidney Howard, which was turned into a success, thanks to Mary Martin's performance, R. E. Jones's sets, John Houseman's staging and the initiative of Michael Meyerberg, producer.

In every season there are the light comedies about domesticity, sex and other family matters, which amuse mildly and titillate even more modestly. After the war Broadway continued to seek the glib, remunerative victories and found or missed them according to the luck of the draw. In this category were pieces ranging from the boisterous hilarity of Thomas Heggen's and Joshua Logan's *Mister Roberts* to the dreary farce routines of Clair Parrish's *Maid in the Ozarks,* which was advertised as the "worst play in the world" and was rewarded for its impudence with 103 performances.

As always there were vehicles for stars:

The Lunts celebrated their 25 years together in S. N. Behrman's version of Marcel Achard's *Auprès de Ma Blonde;*

Robert Morley and Peggy Ashcroft were smooth and admired in *Edward, My Son,* fashioned by Morley and Noel Langley, which had a long Broadway run;

Cornelia Otis Skinner in a revival of Oscar Wilde's *Lady Windemere's Fan;*

Maurice Evans and especially the delectably mischievous Frances Rowe in a happy revival of Shaw's *Man and Superman;*

Katharine Cornell as stately as a dowager and as cold as an iceberg in *Antony and Cleopatra.*

The number of revivals and imports was symptomatic of the malaise infecting the commercial theatre. In the 1947–48 season there were 30 revivals out of 80-odd productions. The losses on Broadway that season were described as appalling. Forty-seven failures ate up 4½ million dollars, and even if the successes made as much or more, they were no comfort to investors who had no stake in them. The shock of these heavy losses brought pledges from producers and unions to cut costs. P.S.: They didn't.

There were a few earnest efforts to push the theatre out of its commercial rut. The Actors Studio, still young in 1948–49, attempted a first production. Bessie Breuer's *Sundown Beach* was a slice of life about fliers suffering from combat fatigue in a veterans' hospital, which quickly conked out, and the Studio did not produce again for almost fifteen years.

At the end of the forties television, though growing irresistibly, was still young. Not yet committed to the eternal scramble for ratings, it often essayed original drama and granted opportunities to new writers, directors and actors. But whatever the quality of its programs, its impact on the theatre by 1950 was unmistakable. There were only 62 productions in the 1949–50 Broadway season. The public would not even bestir itself to patronize plays the critics had recommended highly; it was a lot cheaper to stay at home and look at the home screen.

The shrinkage on Broadway led to a vacuum which Off Broadway sought to fill. In the late forties, it was still in its infancy. Although many works—new and old—were attempted, the productions were on an amateur, if eager, basis. Professionals appeared in some of these ventures, and Equity got up enough nerve to insist on minimum salaries of $5 a week. Groups like the American Negro Theatre in Harlem, the Associated Playwrights on Grand Street, New Stages and On Stage in the Village came into being. The fine old German actor, Albert Bassermann, with his wife, Elsa, played in his native language at the Barbizon-Plaza. Modeled after the Dallas theatre presided over by the indomitable Margo Jones, a theatre in the round was attempted at the Edison Hotel in New York on May 31, 1950, with Lee Tracy and Jane Seymour, established professionals, directed by Martin Manulis, appearing in a revival of George Kelly's *The Show-Off*. But the Off-Broadway idea was still some years from fruition.

CHAPTER XXVII

◆⟨C◆⟨C◆⟨C◆⟨C◆⟨C◆⟨C◆⟨C◆⟨C◆⟨C◆⟨C◆⟨C◆⟨C◆⟨C◆⟨C◆⟨C◆⟨C◆⟨C◆⟨C◆⟨C◆⟨C◆⟨C◆⟨C◆⟨C◆⟨C◆⟨C◆⟨C

SKIDDING DOWNHILL

THE NATION MOVED into an age of affluence in the first decade of the second half of the twentieth century while the theatre skidded downhill—as a business, as a form of communication and as an art. Despite some of the greatest individual successes of all time and despite a few works of style, size and quality, the mood was frightened and frantic.

The sources of attrition were many. From several hundred thousand television sets in 1947, the count in the fifties rose to scores of millions. If the theatre comforted itself with the hope that television would be a place where new talent could serve a remunerative apprenticeship, the reality was disenchanting. Drama on the airways became hopelessly stereotyped. Writers with a shred of talent were pulverized into mediocrity, required to grind out mechanized situation comedy, soggy mysteries, private-eye serials and Westerns. It is true that television gave actors, directors, designers and other hungry children of the theatre a chance to eat, but its lavish salaries and fees exacted a costly toll, for the medium rubbed out individuality, standardized impulses to freshness and disarmed and crushed the creative spirit.

I do not minimize or deny the infinite possibilities of television. It has been used from time to time for fine things. I can remember charming moments from Shakespeare. Plays of quality, great music, notable documentaries and exciting coverage of impressive and heart-stopping contemporary events have made television an inescapable part of our daily lives. It is possible that television—if and when we have a decently financed network independent of advertising and sponsors—someday will fulfill its promise. Then, indeed, it may be the good companion of the drama and the other arts.

For the time being television has drained away a large part of the theatre audience. In 1950 a committee representing the Association of Theatrical Press Agents and Theatrical Managers reported that fewer than 2 percent of the country's population attended the living theatre and that fewer than 1 percent of this public were under the age of twenty-five. By the decade's end the statistics probably were more disheartening.

Did the theatre do anything constructive to reverse its precipitous decline? Always apt at forming well-intentioned organizations with lofty titles, it organized the Council of the Living Theatre in 1950. Robert E. Sherwood was the president, and a couple of unhackneyed projects were undertaken—Robinson Jeffers's *The Tower Beyond Tragedy*, with Judith Anderson as Clytemnestra, and Edmund Wilson's *The Little Blue Light*. The Council arranged a celebration observing the 200th anniversary of the opening of New York's first commercial playhouse. Then, like other well-meaning groups, it fell into innocuous desuetude.

The status quo got a jolt in 1950 when the Federal Government through the Attorney General's office brought an antitrust suit against the Shubert organization and its United Booking Office. In 1956 the Government won its case in the Supreme Court, which ruled that the antitrust laws applied to the theatre. The Shuberts agreed to dispose of four theatres in New York and eleven in other cities, to stop restrictive booking practices and to eschew a financial stake in any ticket agency in any city with a Shubert house. The decision was a blow to the feelings of the Shuberts. Nevertheless, they retained ownership of 17 New York theatres, a half interest in an 18th and full control of six outside New York.

In the fifties they ceased to have any weight as producers. Their substantial influence was exercised through the power to determine whether or not to rent a theatre to a producer. Lee Shubert died in 1953, and his brother, J. J., became ill and inactive. J. J.'s son, John, who took over the management of the empire, was content to book shows, occasionally giving helpful concessions to a few, but rarely investing Shubert money. In the fifties the Shubert record, which had embraced a grand total of 520 productions in more than half a century, was down to four works—*Day After Tomorrow, Ti-Coq, Conscience* and *The Starcross Story,* none of any account commercially, let alone artistically.

This was not surprising. The Shuberts had never been a force in the nation's dramatic culture. In the days of the New Theatre, when New York first attempted repertory on an elaborate scale, Lee Shubert had been an associate in the business management of a high-minded, nonprofit undertaking. In later years, particularly in the twenties, the Shuberts were busy importers of European successes, and in the depressed early thirties they fought hard to keep theatre alive. But they made no contribution of significance toward raising standards, seeking out new talent and giving it the means and the encouragement to develop. They were businessmen in a commercial enterprise, dominant merchants for a time in the entertainment field. By the standards of show business they had great importance; by the measuring rod of art, none.

Perhaps I am too harsh. It should be entered on the credit side of the Shubert account that over the years they kept their theatres active as theatres. They could have sold some of their holdings, to be converted into garages, office buildings and luxury apartments. After the Music Hall and Center Theatre at Rockefeller Center, no new theatres were built in New York, except for those at the Lincoln Center of the Performing Arts, and these were made possible by huge public and private benefactions. For years it was argued that no theatres could be built profitably on the old basis, that stages and auditoriums must be part of a larger structure with dependable earning capacity. In the fifties New York's building code was amended to permit the construction of theatres surrounded by office and store space. At last, the cry went up, the hands of investors have been freed, and New York will get some new houses.

The cost of building skyrocketed, and no one felt that it would be profitable to devote a substantial amount of space in a new building to a theatre. The contraction of theatregoing and the rise of television caused a diminution in the number of theatres. By the fifties only 30 Broadway houses continued to serve as theatres. Many had become television studios; a few of these were turned back to the theatre late in the decade and in the early sixties. Even with 35 houses, New York's commercial theatre had too many for profitable year-round operation. Each fall there was a booking jam, but after the inevitable disasters, the jam evaporated.

Touring hit a new low in the fifties. A unit that set out bravely for a cross-country tour in 1950 would be lucky to complete half its schedule before *rigor mortis* set in.

In this extremity, a cooperative effort was launched by the Council of the Living Theatre, the Theatre Guild and the American Theatre Society to build subscription audiences in key cities. By the end of the decade there was a network of communities that would support touring Broadway productions on a guaranteed basis.

The contraction of touring was unfortunate for the performers, playwrights, producers and investors hoping for further returns from their New York enterprises, but gave added impetus to the establishment of regional theatres. In 1950 Zelda Fichandler and several other young people started their Arena Stage in Washington. In Houston Nina Vance, using the last few dollars in her purse to pay the postage of an initial mailing, launched the Alley Theatre. In San Francisco Jules Irving and Herbert Blau organized their uncompromisingly aspiring Actors Workshop. By the end of the decade an educational institution like U.C.L.A., through its Extension division, was cooperating in the creation and maintenance of the professional Theatre Group devoted to drama of quality. There were several regional playhouses with a long history going back to the twenties, like the one in Cleveland, which sought to be nearly all things theatrical to its community.

The Pasadena Playhouse had declined in quality, and Margo Jones's theatre in Dallas disappeared after her death.

For the new regional companies the early years were often desperate struggles. Being devoted to the theatre as a forum and an art, the hardy founding fathers and mothers had to fight to gain a foothold, to draw similarly dedicated people to their sides as collaborators, to find community support and to build an audience. Often they were on the ragged edge financially. Although they rallied a small, staunch public as a nucleus, the larger, theatregoing groups were slow to come around. The glamour of the stars and Broadway hits still dazzled too many people. A young, regional troupe was not likely to have the resources to put on performances with good enough actors in all the roles. The prophet is usually an unconscionable time winning honor in his own community.

By the end of the fifties the turn in the fortunes of these regional theatres was at hand. Local pride and support were increasing. Help in the shape of grants from foundations like the Ford was not far off. The Arena Stage could undertake a public campaign for funds to build a new, modern home—and carry it to fruition. Other communities, proud of their symphony orchestras, realized that the theatre was a cultural resource they had been indifferent to and undertook to support new permanent companies.

Despite their early difficulties and handicaps, the regional theatres committed themselves to the production of plays of quality. They were not interested in the Broadway hits—indeed, could not get them if they wanted them, for they were foreclosed to performance by other companies while road units toured and the inescapable film was being made and shown. The classics of the past and more recent times as well as American and foreign plays that had been neglected, unfairly rejected or badly produced occupied their efforts. They searched areas that the commercial theatre avoided and performed the works of playwrights like Brecht and Betti, whom Broadway did not bother with or could not turn to profitable account. They developed new talent, and gave young people who had vainly or unsatisfyingly tried New York a chance for fuller expression and further growth.

The competence and contributions of these theatres need not be exaggerated. They fumbled and stumbled. They undertook works they were not ready to cope with. They lacked the resources of time and knowledge to enlarge the powers of their young personnel. But they endured and won through. No one can begrudge the credit due to their founders and leaders. It is no detraction of their worth to observe that they filled a vacuum left by the shrinkage of the commercial theatre and the inadequacies of college and university drama departments.

The theatre in New York, of course, was reflecting the economic facts of life. The rising cost of labor and materials affected the theatre with staggering force. By the end of the fifties it was a commonplace that a one-set play with a small cast required $100,000 to raise the curtain on its New York opening. Capital expenditures for a musical ballooned past $300,000 and approached $500,000. Operating expenses moved up commensurately, and it was not unusual for a play to need a weekly income of $20,000 and a musical $40,000 to break even.

From these costs flowed grave results. The funding of shows became a cruel frenzy, especially for serious work. The package became more important than the play's imperatives. Producers felt bound to seek glamorous stars, gimmicks, sensationalism. Hucksters and packagers moved into the theatre, while the few producers with a viewpoint retrenched, quit or unhappily adapted themselves to the new, hopped-up ways.

It became a time of the smash hit or the abject flop, with no margin of maneuver between. A play and a musical or two would become the vogue—the must-see show for all those who run with the fashions. The expense-account set and the lavish spenders paid what the freight would bear for the hot tickets. They could usually write off as business expenses inflated prices on the black market. Undiscriminating theatregoers joined in the scramble for scarce tickets.

The biggest hit and money-maker in the history of the commercial theatre, *My Fair Lady,* which came along late in 1955, epitomized the hysteria. One could understand the willingness of wealthy individuals and of businesses with the freedom to write off such expenses to pay as much as $100 for these choicest of tickets.

The thundering success of *My Fair Lady*, which ran for six and a half years in New York to record-breaking receipts and continued to be a tremendous money-maker well into the sixties, accelerated the mischievous trends. The dream of untold riches gained on one show had become a reality. A host of hopefuls rushed onto the whirling merry-go-round to reach for the dazzling gold ring. Small investors brought forward their cash offerings to producers, hoping to get in on a killing. Purchasers of tickets in advance sought to guess which incoming show would be the magic winner. Theatre parties became outrageously important because sizable sums for worthy causes could be earned without trouble if a committee was foresighted or lucky enongh to sign up in advance for a hot attraction like *My Fair Lady*.

As the successes ran longer and earned more, the failures were instant and total. In the twenties, thirties and forties some shows struggled against unfavorable reviews to win a public. In the fifties such reversals became rare, if not impossible. Shows closed within a week, occasionally after the opening night. In the spring of 1958 an expensive musical called *Portofino* shut down after three performances. Early in 1959 *Juno*, Marc Blitzstein's musical version of Sean O'Casey's *Juno and the Paycock* starring Shirley Booth and Melvyn Douglas, called it a career after 16 performances. In 1959–60 the carnage was frightful: a revue called *The Girls Against the Boys* with Bert Lahr, Nancy Walker and Shelley Berman stayed alive for 16 performances, a musical called *Happy Town* lurched through five performances, and a piece called *Beg, Borrow or Steal* equaled this meager achievement, while the musical *Christine*, partly the work of a Nobel prize winner, Pearl S. Buck, sank without a trace after 12 performances.

The power of the critics, particularly those on the New York daily newspapers, grew out of all proportion. Producers hastened to take advantage of favorable reviews, proclaiming flattering phrases in or out of context in clamorous advertisements. Thus they conditioned the public to look for critical endorsement before venturing into a theatre.

Fred Fehl

he Diary of Anne Frank, 1955. In front are Gusti Huber, Joseph Schildkraut, and Susan Strasberg as Anne.

Samuel Beckett's *Waiting for Godot,* 1956, with Bert Lahr and E. G. Marshall

Eugene O'Neill's *Long Day's Journey into Night,* 1956, with Florence Eldridge, Bradford Dillman, Jason Robards Jr., and Fredric March

ANTA

ANTA

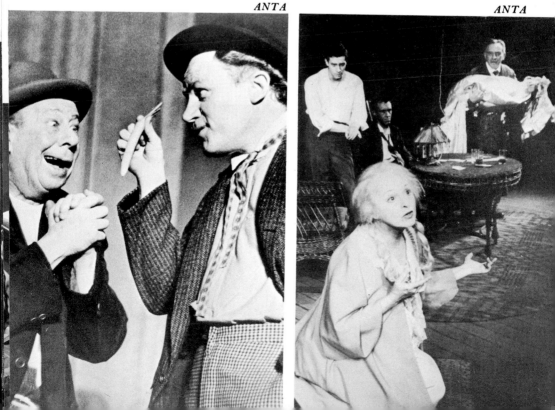

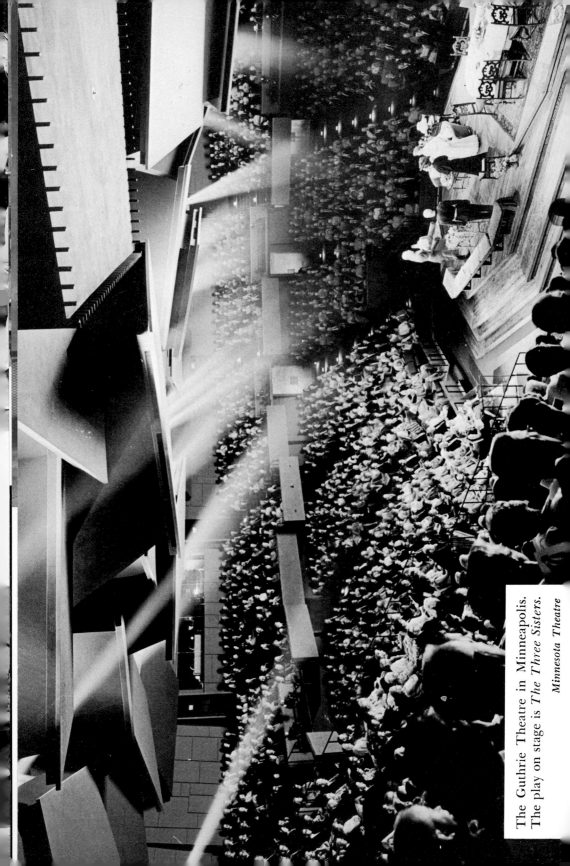

The Guthrie Theatre in Minneapolis.
The play on stage is *The Three Sisters*.

Minnesota Theatre

The public for its part would not invest in tickets for anything but sure things, and the way to be sure was to wait for a play or a musical with unanimous critical approval. Save for the habitual, independent-minded theatregoers, who form a hard core of the New York audience, the public would not commit itself until it thought a new show extraordinary. To be told that a play was entertaining, stimulating, provocative, worth attending for a fine scene or an unusual performance, was not enough. Superlatives of description and approval were required.

The exception, besides theatregoers who made up their own minds, was the theatre parties. The shows, largely musicals, which benefited from these parties, welcomed the large sums they poured into the box office before opening night. They were a hedge against the lethal impact of unfavorable reviews, assuring runs of a good many weeks and giving a production the time to find its own audience. But if theatre parties were good for a few offerings, their indirect effect on everything else was deleterious.

A purchaser of a ticket for a theatre party paid an inflated price, most of which was a tax-deductible contribution to charity. Much of the money spent on these tickets did not find its way into the theatre at all. People who might patronize eight shows a season went only to two.

But even the worst of commercial excesses were not so harmful as vicious influences over which the theatre had no control—the Cold War and McCarthyism. Both had a corrosive effect on the arts and amusements. The films, never too courageous, just rolled over and were the tamest of puppies. Television, which finally spoke up on C.B.S. through Edward R. Murrow and Fred W. Friendly, played it safe, and so did the press. A great democratic nation was terrorized into silence. Blacklists became a way of life.

The theatre, not to be pressured like the mass mediums, remained a small bastion of freedom of speech. But the right to speak freely was invoked with caution and hesitation. Arthur Miller dared to write a play on witch-hunting, *The Crucible,* and got it produced in 1952–53 when McCarthy was at the height of his career. The play, however did not achieve a long run. The trouble lay partly in the production: it was entirely too ponderous; Miller redirected one of the scenes during the limited run to make it simpler and more direct. The trouble was also in the luke-warm reaction of the critics to *The Crucible*. I concede that the play was couched in melodramatic terms and that its characters tended to be too uninflected, but I wonder whether fear did not keep people away from the theatre.

⊹€€⊹€

CHAPTER XXVIII

OF VIOLENCE AND FLUFF

It was not coincidence that in the 1953–54 New York season nearly all the hits were comedies. Apart from Herman Wouk's *The Caine Mutiny Court Martial,* which had elements of courtroom melodrama to give it theatrical punch, and Robert Anderson's *Tea and Sympathy,* the successes were *The Teahouse of the August Moon, Kind Sir, Solid Gold Cadillac, Sabrina Fair, Oh, Men! Oh, Women!, The Remarkable Pennypacker* and *Anniversary Waltz.* In *Teahouse,* John Patrick's play based on Vern Sneider's novel, a civilized point was made that even an occupying army must have some respect for the folkways of a strange island like Okinawa, but the essential mood was fairy tale, and the basic laughter was of the familiar army variety with Paul Ford making his mark as an apoplectic colonel and David Wayne contributing capital comedy as Sakini, an Okinawan factotum. Samuel Taylor's *Sabrina Fair* with Margaret Sullavan as charming as ever had a touch of style as a comedy of manners. But the other successes were in the Broadway tradition of gags and wisecracks. No need to look down one's nose at a Broadway specialty. But its predominance suggested that the public had little heart for large issues.

What the theatre got in abundance in the fifties was violence, which took obsessive, decadent forms. It was as if playwrights, embittered and turned cynical by what Dalton Trumbo called scathingly "the time of the toad," wished to slash out, stun and shock, if only to rouse a nation from complacency or apathy.

As if to sum up the dismaying decline in standards in the fifties there was the disparity between two plays by Lillian Hellman. At the decade's beginning there was *The Autumn Garden,* her subtlest and finest play. If it was not a success, the reflection is not on the author but on those who judged her and on a public unwilling to go and see for itself a notable, mature work by one of our leading playwrights. The word went out that *The Autumn Garden* was Chekhovian, as if this were some species of obloquy. The truth is that Miss Hellman was describing a southern—and American— way of life with something of the autumn's aching chill and glow. The form was firm and tight, as in all her plays, but was no longer charged with electricity that drew attention to itself.

Toys in the Attic came late in the 1959–60 season, which Brooks Atkinson justly described as one of the shabbiest of his 35 years as a critic. Compared with the stuff that had reached the stage, Miss Hellman's play was at least adult. Like all her pieces, it was well made, and was performed impressively by Maureen Stapleton, Anne Revere, Jason Robards Jr. and Irene Worth. But it was second-rate stuff. Its careful description of decaying southern life now appeared routine where in earlier Hellman plays it had blazed with controlled fires. One left the theatre with the sad feeling that Miss Hellman had enlisted in an alien milieu.

As the decade went on, Tennessee Williams's plays grew more violent and more sensational. He continued to be obsessed by neurotic females, but from the frustrated ones of the early plays he now turned to the furious devourers. In *The Rose Tattoo* he described a woman, played with earthy vitality by Maureen Stapleton, who had an immense relish of life. By the time he got to *Suddenly Last Summer* and *Sweet Bird of Youth,* he was writing about cannibalism and castration. In *Orpheus Descending,* a revision of his 1940 *Battle of Angels,* which never got beyond Boston, he dealt with mutilation by bloodhound in the lynch-law atmosphere of the South. His experience with *Camino Real,* an effort at nonrealistic drama, a failure on Broadway when produced in March 1953, was probably disheartening. This was a play that cried out to be free of the confines of the conventional proscenium stage—not a neatly made work but one that dared to be fresh and imaginative. It was also somewhat woolly in essential content. I found it more stimulating than the neatly limited efforts of writers who did not take risks. Something of Williams's fundamental gallantry of thought and style was summed up in the bittersweet speech of Esmeralda, the Gypsy's daughter:

God bless all con men and hustlers and pitch-men who hawk their hearts on the street, all two-time losers who're likely to lose more than once, the courtesan who made the mistake of love, the greatest of lovers crowned with the longest horns, the poet who wandered from his heart's green country and possibly will and possibly won't be able to find his way back, look down with a smile tonight on the last cavaliers, the ones with rusty armor and soiled white plumes, and visit with understanding and something that's almost tender those fading legends that come and go in this plaza like songs not clearly remembered, oh, sometime and somewhere, let there be something to mean the word *honor* again!

In *Cat on a Hot Tin Roof,* he was back in the style of *A Streetcar Named Desire. Cat on a Hot Tin Roof* had the intensity of *Streetcar* against a larger social background. Williams spoke openly of his preoccupation with homosexuality, and this motif was part of a broad frame of reference. Big Daddy, with his passion for domination and his fear of illness and death, and the characters around him were disturbing, exciting, authentic human beings on a steaming volcano fed by the pressures of their own natures. In Kazan's staging and the playing of Burl Ives, Mildred Dunnock, Ben Gazzara and Barbara Bel Geddes there were the clash of wills and the surge of emotions. This was Williams in his most exciting form as an alchemist, even poet of the stage. Here were temperament and theatricality; here also was the fury of the failure of a vision of life.

Sweet Bird of Youth five seasons later, though staged with familiar intensity by Kazan and played scorchingly by Geraldine Page as an aging, dissolute movie queen and Paul Newman as a spoiled, self-centered gigolo, was a febrile dilution of the old formula. Williams could still build conflict and tension and write passages that flared with individuality. But his voice was growing shriller. He had, in fact, reached the end of his line in violence and sensationalism.

William Inge, who seemed to be a product of the Tennessee Williams atelier of hothouse intensity, came forward with *Picnic*. There was no denying the brooding atmosphere of this play, particularly as Joshua Logan staged it. Sultriness flashing with heat lightning hung over it. Without denying its skill and power, however, I was uncomfortable in its presence. I found it hard to believe in the irresistible magnetism of the stranger whose masculinity reduced nearly every woman to compliant jelly. As in the Williams plays, women were pallid, helpless creatures or consuming Liliths.

Inge's next, *Bus Stop*, also implied that sex was the root of evil. This time, however, the viewpoint was comic and humane, darkened by the underlying loneliness of Americans drifting from space to barren space along a vast, indifferent landscape. Young Kim Stanley sparkled in the central character of a dancer on the loose.

The cry of loneliness began to turn inward in *The Dark at the Top of the Stairs*. This play of middle-class American life was lit up by a sub-theme—the suicide of a young Jewish boy in an overtly tolerant but covertly hostile environment. But the principal theme dealt with the nature of a youngster's attachments to his parents, and the author's obsession with the silver cord was further emphasized in *A Loss of Roses*, where the bond had grown twisted.

Robert Anderson's *Tea and Sympathy* seemed to announce a new playwright of worth. In its use of homosexuality as a dramatic catalyst, it was one of the pieces that set the new style of invoking this theme openly. What bothered me about this play, as I have been bothered by a number of others, was my feeling that, while the suspicions and charges of homosexuality were brought in to be opposed and dismissed, the essential preoccupation with the aberration undermined the work and the nature of its characters. Even the hushed ending, with Deborah Kerr ministering as mother-mistress to the bruised young man played by John Kerr, left a

double image—sensitive and touching on the one hand and contrived and theatrical on the other.

Anderson's next two plays did not match the achievement or
success of *Tea and Sympathy*. There was delicacy of feeling in *All
Summer Long* but no sense of energy. In *Silent Night, Lonely
Night*, the fires burned low and the words drifted in a murmurous,
uninflected flow.

In *The Time of the Cuckoo* Arthur Laurents described an
American woman's last fling in Venice, and Shirley Booth brought
humanity to the role. In *A Clearing in the Woods* Mr. Laurents
ventured into more unconventional territory. With Kim Stanley
as his protagonist, he attempted to follow an overwrought young
woman in a quest for her past. In a way this was a nonrealistic
theatrical equivalent of a patient's long monologue on a psycho-
analyst's couch. It did not work out, but it was an interesting try.

N. Richard Nash had a hopeful effort in *The Rainmaker*, in
which Geraldine Page was touching as a plain, intelligent girl
transfigured and fulfilled—at least temporarily—by a strange con
man. There was a note of breeziness that saved the play from pat-
ness. Nothing else of Nash's revealed so personal a flair.

Maxwell Anderson, still committed to exploring and reinter-
preting the past, attempted a play on Socrates in *Barefoot in
Athens*, but it was merely wordy. With *Bad Seed* he was successful
again. In adapting William March's novel, he dealt with violence
and horror in this story of an apparently innocent young girl who
committed three murders. Anderson's adherents might insist that
this was a study of congenital evil, but on the stage it was simply a
shrewdly made shocker.

Approaching the close of a long and earnest career, Anderson
tried an adaptation of Brendan Gill's novel, *The Day the Money
Stopped*, and watched it die after four performances.

Earlier in the decade two other shining careers had faded as
sadly and wanly. Philip Barry's last play, *Second Threshhold*, revised by his friend, Robert Sherwood, was presented posthumously
in the 1950–51 season and was a pathetic failure. Six seasons later
Sherwood's last effort, *Small War on Murray Hill*, was also pro-

duced posthumously, and its confrontation of Venus and Mars proved to be mild and ineffectual.

It was a decade marked by very little distinction in American playwriting. One of our most gifted novelists, William Faulkner, tried his hand with *Requiem for a Nun* in the 1958–59 season; despite Tony Richardson's staging, the piece was clearly not at home in a theatre. One of our honored poets, Archibald Mac-Leish, had a great success with *J. B.* The kudos it gathered were unwarranted. Although MacLeish used the English tongue with a poet's sinuosity and eloquence, his drama was hopelessly flawed. Not Kazan's tight, flaring staging, or Boris Aronson's imaginative circuslike set, or the performances by Raymond Massey, Christopher Plummer, Nan Martin and particularly Pat Hingle as a fervent Job could persuade me that this was great poetic drama.

Elmer Rice, still working at his métier, could not seem to please press and public any longer in *Not for Children, Grand Tour* and *Cue for Passion,* a curious effort to modernize Hamlet from a Freudian viewpoint. Sidney Kingsley made a shrewd adaptation of Koestler's *Darkness at Noon,* and then turned out a fast, noisy farce in *Lunatics and Lovers;* craftsmanship and commercialism still went scrupulously hand in hand, but the lift of the well-made *The Patriots* of wartime vintage was missing. Moss Hart wrote *Climate of Eden,* which leaned heavily on theatricality but did not thrive. William Saroyan, back on Broadway in 1957 after fourteen years, offered *The Cave Dwellers,* and was virtually unchanged in his wistful, breezy view of broken-down performers holed up in on abandoned theatre. John Steinbeck tried the theatre again with *Burning Bright* but was not quite at home in it. Nor was Pearl Buck in *A Desert Incident,* which was at least intelligent in warning against secret weapons that might destroy men. Paul Osborn, a skilled craftsman with a special aptitude for adaptation, turned J. P. Marquand's *Point of No Return* into a viable work.

Some writers did well with one work and could not repeat. Dore Schary had a surprise winner in *Sunrise at Campobello,* an earnest dramatization of the ordeal of Franklin D. Roosevelt stricken by polio, and Ralph Bellamy played the future President with impressive authenticity. Joseph Kramm produced a surprise success with *The Shrike,* a stark portrait of a horrible woman. Michael Gazzo wrote a shocker on drug addiction in *A Hatful of Rain,* which aroused people with its sensationalism in a performance by Anthony Franciosa, Shelley Winters and Ben Gazzara. James Leo Herlihy and William Nobel in *Blue Denim* dissipated their astringency by arranging a happy ending for their pregnant teenager. Morton Wishengrad wrote *The Rope Dancers,* an account of a sick, hate-filled woman, sullenly and ragingly played by Siobhan McKenna.

Although the fifties were not conducive to investigation of social problems, there were those who tried. Arthur Miller did an adaptation of Ibsen's *An Enemy of the People,* stressing the contemporaneity of its story of corruption in politics. But in *A View from the Bridge* he returned to the individual predicament, analyzing the problem of a decent longshoreman, who is laid low by an uncontrollable, guilty passion for his niece and by his own black ignorance. He seemed to be trying for the contemporary equivalent of Greek tragedy, but what emerged was something closer to Italian operatic *verismo.* Later he revised and lengthened the play and it was staged excitingly off Broadway by Ulu Grosbard, but it still struck me as fiery realism, *verismo* at its best, rather than tragedy of grandeur.

Jerome Lawrence and Robert E. Lee made a good impression as collaborators with *Inherit the Wind,* their colorful and dramatic documentary on the Scopes trial. These newcomers had been encouraged by Margo Jones in her Dallas theatre, and she joined in the Broadway production with Herman Shumlin, who staged it vividly. Paul Muni as the Darrow character and Ed Begley as the William Jennings Bryan figure brought conviction to this play with its dynamic second-act, courtroom fireworks.

The Negro, long either a subject of indifference or, at best, the concern of self-conscious white writers, began to speak for himself with greater force. Lorraine Hansberry's *A Raisin in the Sun,* a domestic comedy with overtones of emotion, some close to soap opera, was out of the ordinary in its warm, human way with Negroes whose problems, not unlike those of families everywhere, loomed so much larger simply because their skins were dark. With

Sidney Poitier, Ruby Dee, Diana Sands, Claudia McNeil and Louis Gossett, this play, staged by Lloyd Richards, was an unexpected hit.

For a brief euphoric time it looked as if the broadcasting world would be a source of new writers. Paddy Chayefsky, William Gibson, Gore Vidal and Robert Alan Aurthur went from the home screen to the theatre.

Chayefsky made the transition from the heady victory of *Marty,* his acclaimed TV play and surprise film hit, with *Middle of the Night,* a play about a middle-aged man's romance with a young girl, which revealed the author's keen ear for the way people talk and his relish for the minutiae of character. With Edward G. Robinson and Gena Rowlands in the principal roles, Chayefsky's first sortie onto Broadway was a success. So was his second, *The Tenth Man,* a free, modernized variation of *The Dybbuk.* Chayefsky wrote with warmth and humor of the old Jews who spent their time in the social communion of the synagogue, and Tyrone Guthrie handled the staging with his customary theatrical flair. But the play forfeited all right to respect with its phony ending. I speak of the moment when the rites of exorcism had been carried out with solemnity, the lights went out, and we heard a cry and the thud of a falling body. When the lights came up, we discovered that not the girl invaded by the dybbuk but her unbelieving, disturbed suitor had fainted. This was flummery worthy of an O. Henry short story in search of a surprise ending no matter how farfetched.

William Gibson scored with *Two for the Seesaw* and *The Miracle Worker.* In his book, *The Seesaw Log,* Gibson complained of the way in which casting and other production problems aborted his desires. But had Gibson had his way in all things, *Two for the Seesaw,* I think, would not have amounted to more than it was in the theatre—a modern, bittersweet, charming fairy tale, not especially believable, but made appealing by the disarming freshness of the complaisant Gittel. Anne Bancroft did wonders for Gittel in a performance that was crotchety and radiant; Henry Fonda was Henry Fonda, and Arthur Penn adroitly manipulated the trick staging.

In *The Miracle Worker* Gibson turned to documentary uplift, managing a combination of pathos and optimism in a theatrical combination hard to resist. Once again Anne Bancroft was a tower of strength, this time as a ferociously committed young Annie Sullivan who tamed the mute, deaf, blind child, Helen Keller, played with unforgettable intensity by little Patty Duke. Again Arthur Penn was the director, and his staging of the showdown struggle between Anne Bancroft and Patty Duke released enough histrionic fireworks to make any play newsworthy. It was easy to point out the hokum and melodrama in *The Miracle Worker;* yet, as a reconstruction of a memorable relationship, it was more than an arrant tearjerker.

Gore Vidal used a TV play, *Visit from a Small Planet,* as his entry into the theatre. Although its expansion was apparent, it brought freshness and humor into the theatre, especially in the performances of Eddie Mayehoff and Cyril Ritchard. And in *The Best Man* Vidal accommodated himself to the stage with shrewdness and high spirits. Writing of the infighting for a Presidential nomination, he caught the flavor of the contest between decency and skulduggery in comic, melodramatic terms. Vidal's use of a charge of homosexuality against one of the candidates struck me as contrived. Vidal later argued that there once was such an accusation against a candidate, but it was now chichi to make homosexuality a crucial element in drama. Staged by Joseph Anthony and played to the hilt by Melvyn Douglas, Frank Lovejoy and Lee Tracy, the comedy was refreshingly alert to the realities of politics.

Symptomatic of the state of American playwriting was the abundance of adaptations and readings. One of the most brilliant and enchanting events of the decade was the playing of the *Don Juan in Hell* section of Shaw's *Man and Superman,* without sets, costumes or action, by Charles Laughton, Charles Boyer, Cedric Hardwicke and Agnes Moorehead.

In their zeal to mine unexpected ores for stageworthy material, producers and writers turned in every possible direction. This trend reached its apogee when casual essays by James Thurber, staged by Burgess Meredith with a good deal of imagination and savor as *A Thurber Carnival,* proved to be the comic hit of the

1959–60 season. It had charm and sophistication as played airily by Tom Ewell and Paul Ford, and Don Elliott's score and his jazz ensemble added brightness. The plain fact, however, was that it was chiefly Thurber read aloud, hailed in the theatre because nearly everything else was so witless.

Not that adaptation is necessarily wrong or futile. One of the moving plays of the fifties was an adaptation. It is easy to minimize *The Diary of Anne Frank* on the ground that the emotion we brought to it seemed to magnify it as art. Although it was based on the facts of the furtive existence of the hunted Jews in Nazi-occupied Amsterdam, it was far from being a pedestrian documentary. In its modesty, honesty and tenderness it was beguiling as well as heartrending. Its people were brave and weak, selfish and crotchety in the unpredictable way that human nature in its erratic diversity dictates. Its story was about heroism of endurance in the face of grave peril and terrifying fears, yet it had no trace of heroics.

I am grateful to Frances Goodrich and Albert Hackett for their tact and sensitivity in making a play out of little Anne Frank's diary, and I remember admiringly the contributions of Kermit Bloomgarden, the producer; Garson Kanin, the director; and the luminous performances of Susan Strasberg, Joseph Schildkraut, Gusti Huber and Jack Gilford.

CHAPTER XXIX

QUALITY FROM ABROAD

WERE IT NOT for the witty, glowing, poetic contributions of the European playwrights, the American theatre in the fifties would have been in a much more parlous situation than it was. From Europe came drama that explored the nature of man and the contemporary world with originality, intellectual distinction and adult humor. Great Britain, France and Switzerland sent us inestimable gifts. We did not appreciate them all, nor did we make room for the best that other nations had to offer us.

We did offer increasing hospitality to complete companies from other lands. We had visits from Great Britain's uneven Old Vic with its notable *Troilus and Cressida* and cloying overstuffed pudding of *A Midsummer Night's Dream,* and the D'Oyly Carte Company in its traditional, still-ingratiating Gilbert and Sullivan. From France we had Louis Jouvet and company, the Jean-Louis Barrault–Madeleine Renaud troupe, the Comédie Française and the Théâtre National Populaire in their classics from Molière to Marivaux. The Greek National Theatre offered its choreographed classics. The Piccolo Theatro di Milano came with its enchantingly stylized production of Goldoni's *Servant of Two Masters,* a performance that made me understand better than ever the

[303]

sources of the Italian genius for opera buffa, for here was the basic form waiting for the composer to give it wings.

Of the older European figures whose plays reached New York the most venerable was Sean O'Casey, shouting defiance from his retreat on England's southwest coast. *Red Roses for Me* was finally produced. The lyricism was there, but the structure was looser than in the best plays, and naturalism clashed with flights from realism. *Cock-a-Doodle Dandy* was tried off Broadway, and *The Shadow of a Gunman* was revived on Broadway. The best of O'Casey, however, was to be savored in the many-volumed auto-biography.

T. S. Eliot was back in a playful mood in *The Confidential Clerk,* a farce rooted in Euripides' *Ion,* with such glittering play-ers as Ina Claire, Claude Rains and Aline McMahon. In *The Living Room,* a failure on Broadway, Graham Greene delved into the conflicting claims of blind faith and rationalism and found both wanting; in *The Potting Shed* he invoked the mystery form to examine questions of faith.

Christopher Fry's *The Lady's Not for Burning* made intoxicat-ing use of the English language, but I was bored and alienated before the evening was over, for the verbal ornamentation became tiresome. The play itself seemed to me little more than fancy posturing, though I admired the savor with which John Gielgud, Pamela Brown and the others read the lines. *Venus Observed,* which had the advantage of participation by Lilli Palmer and Rex Harrison, was another exercise in verbal opulence, but did not fare as well as its predecessor. *A Sleep of Prisoners,* soberer and loftier in intention, was performed in an Episcopal church. *The Dark Is Light Enough,* a somber comedy, failed despite Katharine Cornell and Tyrone Power, and so, despite Miss Cornell and An-thony Quayle, did *The Firstborn,* which dealt pretentiously and barrenly with a story of Moses.

A spirited work from Great Britain was *The Chalk Garden,* a high comedy with a flourish. Its shafts which impaled upper-class foibles came from the pen of Enid Bagnold, a woman in her six-ties, who had once written *The National Velvet* and another novel, *Serena Blandish,* under the *nom de plume* A Lady of Quality. Its performance by Siobhan McKenna, Gladys Cooper and others had the dry, effervescent quality of the dialogue. Written from the inside of an English aristocratic way of life, *The Chalk Garden* commented sharply on the processes of self-indulgence and decay without forfeiting its aplomb.

Compared with the point and sheen of *The Chalk Garden*, the works of Terence Rattigan, Noel Coward, Peter Ustinov and Benn W. Levy, for all their theatrical skill, were thin and glib. The showiest of Rattigan's contributions was *Separate Tables*, expert in development, smartly geared to be a tour de force for actors like Margaret Leighton and Eric Portman, and superficial in content. Coward worked his familiar vein of thin sophistication in *Quadrille*, which had the benefit of the Lunts as stars, and in *Nude With Violin*. Ustinov, more expansive and zestful in his humor and theatricality, introduced himself to us with *The Love of Four Colonels* and *Romanoff and Juliet*.

The English playwright who made the biggest noise was John Osborne with *Look Back in Anger*, the play responsible for the name inaccurately applied to all of Britain's new writers, "the angry young men." Osborne's Jimmy Porter, however, deserved to be called a "young angry." In his choleric rejection of everything in his environment he was amusing and provocative. It was good to have a drama with a temper and a sense of outrage, and Osborne could write, for Jimmy Porter's diatribes were not only eloquent but rooted in sound observation. But Jimmy was also a petulant brat, whose character was so self-centered, indeed narcissistic, that it diminished the force of his jeremiads.

In Tony Richardson's staging and with Kenneth Haigh as Jimmy and Mary Ure as his long-suffering wife, *Look Back in Anger* was a tonic, thanks to the sting of its vitriol and the exuberance of its style. I thought that Osborne's *Epitaph for George Dillon*, written earlier with Anthony Creighton, which reached New York later, was an acute study of a sleazy creature in a society that deserved no better.

In *The Entertainer*, which arrived hard on the heels of *Look Back in Anger*, Osborne skewered Archie Price, a spineless, squalid music-hall performer who had known better days. Though not so flamboyant as *Look Back in Anger,* this was a cool yet touching play, and it was brilliantly performed by Olivier, Joan Plowright and Brenda de Banzie. But it did not have anything like the commercial success of *Look Back in Anger.*

Another Broadway failure was Dylan Thomas's *Under Milk Wood.* Hardly a play at all, this robust and hushed tribute to the Welsh town in which Thomas grew up was bound to have trouble on a stage, for it was designed for radio. Overproduced on Broadway, it seemed affected. Produced without sets off Broadway at the Circle in the Square some years later, its lyricism, humor and tenderness had a winning effect.

A fresh, young writer from Britain was Peter Shaffer, whose *Five-Finger Exercise* was tightly constructed and sensitively written. It conveyed a sense of truth in describing the impact a young German had on a comfortable English home, although its use of a homosexual motif at the end gave it a fashionable, if honestly intended twist.

From France came plays by old and new writers of outstanding caliber. Jean Giraudoux, dead since 1944, was still being discovered by our theatre. Early in the decade we had *Ondine,* delicate and atmospheric but too shadowy for American tastes, even though Audrey Hepburn and Mel Ferrer brought magic to it. Late in the decade we had *Duel of Angels,* given elegance and beauty by Vivien Leigh and Mary Ure, but this last of Giraudoux's plays was weary in the refinement of its ironic style and the artificiality of its characters.

Giraudoux's distinction as a playwright was revealed most eloquently in mid-decade by *Tiger at the Gates,* Christopher Fry's translation of a play whose title could be translated literally as "The Trojan War Will Not Take Place." In this fresh look at the Trojan war, Giraudoux was saying ironically that the responsibility for fighting lay on the wise men who idealized war, not on the beauteous Helen or the warrior class represented by Hector. In dialogue gleaming with wit and wisdom, Giraudoux conveyed his tragic sense of the foolishness of man and the unavoidability of war. Written before the outbreak of World War II, this play was permeated by the pessimism of the prophet and by the sorrowing laughter of the philosopher. After the war, it seemed, in the performance staged by Harold Clurman and played by Michael Redgrave, Morris Carnovsky, Barbara Jeffords, Leueen McGrath and Diane Cilento, more sardonic than ever.

Anouilh, most prolific of French playwrights, cut a wide swath. There was *Ring Around the Moon,* which had wit and elegance. There was *Legend for Lovers,* a version of the Eurydice story. There were *Mlle. Colombe, Time Remembered* and *The Fighting Cock.* Most successful were *The Lark,* a treatment of the Joan of Arc story adapted by Lillian Hellman, and *The Waltz of the Toreadors,* translated by Lucienne Hill. *The Lark* offered a pragmatic, hard-bitten, peasant Joan, whose mystery was deepened rather than elucidated, with Julie Harris as the story creature and with Christopher Plummer as Warwick and Boris Karloff as Cauchon. *The Waltz of the Toreadors,* with Ralph Richardson as an old general and Mildred Natwick as his relentless wife, was a black comedy with farcical overtones, which gave romanticism a fierce going over.

Despite these two successes, Anouilh remained a problem for American audiences. The trouble was partly American restiveness in the presence of a French dramatic approach which tends to concern itself with verbal fireworks and philosophical explorations and which is not so worried as we are about consistency of action and about development of character. Another difficulty was Anouilh himself. Despite the brilliance of his dialogue and the astringency of his views, his plays were bravura displays rather than profound philosophical penetrations. His wit, in short, was often perverse, an end in itself. It shocked in its disillusionment, but it was also barren.

What about Samuel Beckett, who, though an Irishman, came to us by way of France? With *Waiting for Godot,* which arrived on Broadway in the 1955–56 season, the best of the decade—notable also for *A View from the Bridge, The Diary of Anne Frank, Tiger at the Gates, The Chalk Garden, The Matchmaker* and *My Fair Lady*—the most influential playwright of the postwar era made his first appearance on the American stage.

Let us give praise to Michael Myerberg, who had the courage to produce this enigmatic play, to Herbert Berghof's staging and to the performance by Bert Lahr and E. G. Marshall as the two tramps. But what about the play? Is it the masterpiece its admirers say it is?

Perhaps, though it does not affect me like one. I admire Beckett's gifts as a writer. There is no one quite like him in the precision and sensitivity of his dialogue, in the provocativeness of his symbolism, in the poetry of his imagery and the unexpected subtleties of his dark tragic-comic sensibility. I respect the distinction of Beckett's style. I can see that there are pain and tenderness and compassion in *Waiting for Godot*. But as he has pared away characters and setting in his succeeding plays, he has moved irrevocably toward a stripping away of all hope. He has every right to his view of the human condition, but I cannot follow him along the path of a pessimism that leads straight to nihilism. Being of a sanguine temperament, I feel out of place in his world, which has gone beyond shock into a kind of limitless weariness that, for all its beauty, whimpers helplessly of oblivion.

What about the theatre of the absurd, of which Beckett is supposed to be a founding father? I find the phrase, coined by Martin Esslin as a handy way to deal with a new school of writing, a mischievous portmanteau for too many diverse playwrights. Playwrights must be evaluated as individuals; indeed, each play by any writer deserves to be estimated on its own merits.

Beckett and a number of other writers may have in common a desire to turn away from realism and romanticism, and they may in their several ways invent characters, situations, and plots that are antidramatic, circuitous, symbolic, cryptic, allegorical and inhuman. Although their techniques have points of correspondence and their viewpoints are not far apart, they are individual writers working out their own creative destinies in the privacy of their own minds. They cannot be lumped together as a school and judged as an indiscriminate group or movement.

Thus, Friedrich Dürrenmatt seems to share the philosophy of the new writers, yet he is a writer of marked individuality. *The Visit* was one of the impressive works of the decade. Its pessimism was black, its disillusion pitiless. Staged by Peter Brook and played mordantly by Lynn Fontanne as the rich woman who came back to a small city determined to avenge herself on a man who had betrayed her and by Alfred Lunt as the helpless victim of an entire community she bribed with her wealth, *The Visit* was a horifying parable for our time—perhaps any time. For it tore the veil of pretense from the greed, indifference and egotism not too far below the surface in most men.

Although it responded with interest to works like *Tiger at the Gates, The Lark, Waiting for Godot,* and *The Visit,* the public on Broadway was indifferent to some of Europe's interesting writers. Ugo Betti, a questioning, subtle writer, failed with *The Gambler* and *Isle of Goats.* Camus's *Caligula,* a cool analysis of a monster in a place of power, written in 1938 when the subject was terrifyingly pertinent, got a production late in the 1959–60 season, but the reserved, intellectual style of the writing militated against its acceptance.

With its eye on the box office and the conventional merchandise most easily sold there, Broadway continued to be late in acknowleding the existence of new figures and dramas—or it abdicated entirely, leaving a large repertory of significance to the varying capabilities of Off Broadway. An influential playwright like Bert Brecht was hardly known to Broadway theatregoers. He had lived on the West Coast during the war years and had come East in 1945 for a few performances of one of his pieces at an Off-Broadway theatre, but hardly anyone in the mainstream of the commercial theatre paid him any mind.

The commercial theatre was equally indifferent, as it has been in our time, to the fact that the theatre has a history and a literature. It revived what it regarded as marketable, and more often than not the availability of a star dictated a revival. In the fifties there was a *Lear* to accommodate Louis Calhern. Olivier and Vivien Leigh brought their London pairing of Shakespeare and Shaw—*Antony and Cleopatra* and *Caesar and Cleopatra*—for the edification of Americans. Mary Martin flew through the air with the greatest of ease in *Peter Pan.* John Gielgud and Charles Laughton brought their Cambridge Drama Festival production of *Much Ado About Nothing* to a responsive New York. Katharine

Cornell appeared in Maugham's *The Constant Wife.* Tyrone Guthrie's version of *Tamburlaine,* swirling with theatrical invention, was imported from Stratford, Ontario. John Garfield had a fling at *Peer Gynt.* Smarting from the painful recollection that he did not play the title role in Odets's *Golden Boy* in the thirties, Garfield fulfilled that ambition for 55 performances in the early fifties, and then was suddenly dead. Bert Lahr appeared fleetingly in *Hotel Paradiso,* a modernized version of Feydeau. Julie Harris, Laurence Harvey and Pamela Brown disported themselves in a revival of *The Country Wife.*

Shaw got recurrent attention for the same reason—star interest. Katharine Hepburn had a whirl at *The Millionairess.* Uta Hagen brought eagerness to *Saint Joan.* Charles Laughton, Glynis Johns and Burgess Meredith tackled *Major Barbara.* Maurice Evans and Signe Hasso tangled with the wordy *The Apple Cart.* Margaret Webster and the Theatre Guild produced *Back to Methuselah,* reduced by Arnold Moss to an evening's length. Evans, Diana Wynward, Alan Webb, Sam Levene, Pamela Brown and Diane Cilento appeared in *Heartbreak House.*

For the lively revivals one could be grateful. But one could not forget that they came by chance and remained by unpredictable sufferance.

CHAPTER XXX

THE MUSICAL TRIUMPHANT

THE RECORD-BREAKING LONGEVITY and earning power of *My Fair Lady* did not establish the sovereign appeal of the musical. The trend had been in the making for years. If rising production and operating costs eroded the drama, why not musicals, whose expenses soared proportionately? The answer was that if a musical was a hit, its profits exceeded anything to be earned from any other theatrical endeavor.

New figures appeared in the musical theatre in the fifties but some of the old ones retained their gifts and cunning. Irving Berlin still had the touch in *Call Me Madam,* a good-humored lampoon of a female ambassador to a small foreign country, which Howard Lindsay and Russel Crouse put together as a takeoff on Perle Mesta, Truman's diplomatic representative in Luxembourg. Ethel Merman was a robust, extroverted Madam Minister, and with young Russell Nype she joined in a charming duet with two melodies in counterpoint, "You're Just in Love." Alert as ever to the political scene, Berlin also indited "They Like Ike," which turned out to be Eisenhower's campaign song.

Richard Rodgers and Oscar Hammerstein II could hardly do anything wrong commercially, though their work became increasingly sentimental. They were in good form in March 1951 when

The King and I appeared. In response to the urging of Gertrude Lawrence, they turned Margaret Landon's *Anna and the King of Siam,* a story of an Englishwoman who served as governess of the royal children of Siam, into a gay, romantic musical. With Miss Lawrence as the Governess and Yul Brynner as the King of Siam, this musical had charm, laughter and a delightful freshness. Songs like "A Puzzlement," "Getting to Know You," "Something Wonderful" and "Shall We Dance?" added appeal to a work and production full of imagination.

In their final collaboration Rodgers and Hammerstein shared in the writing in *The Sound of Music.* Based on the story of the Trapp Family Singers, this one had a slushy book by Lindsay and Crouse and equally sentimental songs. It was a sad reversion to a corny past that Rodgers and Hammerstein had fought to destroy. But success smiled on their effort. With Mary Martin in the lead, the musical ran for three years.

Cole Porter did only two new musicals in the fifties. *Can Can* had a book by Abe Burrows, recalling the Paris of Toulouse-Lautrec, with the French performer, Lilo, to give it Gallic esprit. Never happier than when in Paris, Porter turned out "Allez-Vous En," "I Love Paris" and "C'Est Magnifique." Michael Kidd's dance numbers had gusto, and a vivacious young dancer, Gwen Verdon, seized a small part to make a vivid impression. *Silk Stockings* was based on the film, *Ninotchka,* with a script by Burrows, George S. Kaufman and Leueen McGrath. This time the setting was modern Paris, but the sophisticated Porter touch was relatively subdued.

Harold Rome was involved in several successful musicals which added nothing to his reputation. This was increasingly the era of machine-made-musicals—with bulldozers kneading them into some sort of shape. *Wish You Were Here,* drawn by Joshua Logan and Arthur Kober from the latter's comedy of camp life in the Catskills, *Having Wonderful Time,* was a garish case in point. Logan, the Pooh-Bah of this effort, served as producer, director and choreographer as well as a librettist. His *pièce de résistance* on stage was a swimming pool that cost about $15,000. Since the pool could not be crated and shipped out of town for tryouts, the preparations had to be confined to New York. This practice became more commonplace in the sixties, but it was regarded as an oddity of show business in 1952. Although the reviews were not encouraging, Logan was undaunted. He kept rewriting the book, introduced new songs, brought in Jerome Robbins to revise the dances. Wonder of wonders, his faith in the show's marketability was vindicated; it ran for two years. Was it the swimming pool that pulled them in?

Leonard Bernstein was winning fame as a brilliant and versatile young musician with uncommon gifts as a conductor, composer and television performer who could make good music exciting to a vast multitude that knew little about its structure and language. Nevertheless, he found time for the theatre. His music helped Joseph Fields, Jerome Chodorov, Betty Comden and Adolph Green to convert *My Sister Eileen* into a robust valentine to New York of the thirties, *Wonderful Town*. Brought in late with Comden and Green, Bernstein turned out the score in five weeks. With George Abbott as the director and Rosalind Russell as an exuberant stage performer, *Wonderful Town* was fast, spirited, noisy and funny. Bernstein was uncommonly nimble in his application of music to the action. He had the musical know-how to construct a number like "Conversation Piece," which conveyed cleverly the awkward hesitations of five people at a party making casual, embarrassed conversation. His nicest tune, "Quiet Girl," was long-breathed in a way that was a shade unusual in the popular musical theatre.

Distinction of style marked his score for *Candide*. Lillian Hellman's book was not a comfortable stage treatment of Voltaire; probably his satire cannot be reduced to popular musical theatre. Bernstein's music, however, was a joy, abounding in parody of old forms and fresh melodic turns. For Barbara Cook, the Cunegonde, Bernstein composed "Glitter and Be Gay," a sardonic coloratura aria, which made fun and music out of the consolations a girl could find in sparkling jewels.

A huge success of the fifties was *West Side Story*, which made a tremendous impression abroad as well as in the United States. It dramatized the collision between scorned Puerto Ricans and longtime residents of New York's teeming neighborhoods—as a modern-day Romeo and Juliet tragedy. I admired the theatrical skill with which Jerome Robbins, who conceived the idea, staged the piece in taut, feverish, lyrical dance patterns. I enjoyed the vitality of the performance by Carol Lawrence, Larry Kert and Chita Rivera, and I found pleasant things in Bernstein's score. But I resented the romantic tragic style of *Romeo and Juliet* as imposed on a theme of contemporary urgency. To equate the conflict between races and nationalities with the romantic theme of a doomed love was to me a species of theatrical sentimentality. The problem was too serious for superficial and flamboyant parallels.

The partnership of Lerner and Loewe achieved its zenith in the fifties. On the basis of *Paint Your Wagon,* a heavy-handed tale of gold-mining days, only slightly redeemed by some of the songs and the performance of James Barton, who would have predicted *My Fair Lady?* But there it was—an unexpected and radiant creation. One must, of course, begin by giving a lion's share of the credit to the high comic style of Bernard Shaw. But many book writers were laying clumsy hands on the plays and novels of their betters, and it would have been easy for an untalented man to dissipate the wit and charm of *Pygmalion.* Lerner was reasonably faithful to Shaw in the book and caught his flavor in the lyrics. Loewe's music, except for the sticky "On the Street Where You Live," which would have turned Shaw's stomach, was bright and sophisticated. "Why Can't the English?" "Wouldn't It Be Loverly?" "With a Little Bit of Luck," "The Rain in Spain," "I Could Have Danced All Night," "Get Me to the Church on Time," and "I've Grown Accustomed to Your Face" were blooms in a fragrant bouquet, worthy of being preserved beside the best of Kern, Berlin, Gershwin, Rodgers and Porter. Moss Hart's staging, Oliver Smith's designs and the sparkling performances by Julie Andrews, Rex Harrison, Stanley Holloway and the others brought together under the management of Herman Levin, the producer, turned what Lerner and Loewe had made out of Shaw into enchantment for highbrow, lowbrow and middlebrow.

The saga of *My Fair Lady* is not yet completely told, for it continues to appear in unexpected places, like Iceland and Japan, and to reappear where it has had long runs in years gone by. The details of its unparalleled success are so familiar that only a few high points need be mentioned—the 3,000-plus performances of its first run in New York, the more than five years of its London incarnation, the more than $50,000,000 it took in at box offices, the millions of records it sold, the more than $5,000,000 paid for its movie rights. It marked the decisive entrance of broadcasting companies through their subsidiary record companies into the financing of musicals. Columbia Broadcasting through Columbia Records put up all the money and reaped a harvest. It is a rare musical today that is produced without a record company tie-in. In every way *My Fair Lady* was that wonder of the theatre about which producers dream—a dream that leads them down the primrose path to disaster with other ventures—a work that pleased nearly everyone.

Not far behind in quality, although its style was in the tough-cum-heart-of-gold manner made popular by Damon Runyon, was *Guys and Dolls*. Produced by a shrewd new team, Cy Feuer and Ernest Martin, who had started with a conventional musical success several years earlier based on *Charley's Aunt*, it had a brash, ebullient score by Frank Loesser, the man who had written the words and lyrics for *Where's Charley?* in the forties. The revision of the book by Abe Burrows, the last of a fistful of revisers, was rowdy and comical, and Loesser matched it with a boisterous, sentimental score that included "Fugue for Tinhorns," "The Oldest Established," "I'll Know," "A Bushel and a Peck," "Guys and Dolls," "Adelaide's Lament," "If I Were a Bell," "My Time of Day," "Take Back Your Mink," "More I Cannot Wish You," "Luck Be a Lady," "Sue Me," "Marry the Man Today," and that bouncing git-up-and-testify revival number, "Sit Down, You're Rockin' the Boat." A happy cast with Robert Alda, Vivian Blaine, Sam Levene, Isabel Bigley, Pat Rooney, B. S. Pully and Stubby Kaye helped to make it one of the joyous musicals of the epoch.

Loesser ventured forth on his own in *The Most Happy Fella*, his adaptation of Sidney Howard's *They Knew What They Wanted*. He aimed high, seeking operatic fullness of emotion, but kept looking back over his shoulder at the Broadway idiom, and his work was an uneasy amalgamation of both styles. Yet there were nice things in his score—"Standing on the Corner" and "Big D" in a popular vein, "Abbondanza" a laughing takeoff of the highflown operatic style, and the forthright lyricism of "Happy to Make Your Acquaintance," a duet for Robert Weede and Jo Sullivan, and "How Beautiful the Days," an attractive quartet. The work was shot through with music—it had recitatives, arias like "Rosabella" and "My Heart Is Full of You" and a variety of concerted numbers. It was not conventional musical comedy and not opera—and not a satisfactory form with a profile of its own.

New faces were beginning to appear in the fifties. Richard Adler and Jerry Ross—the latter died much too young—joined a team headed by George Abbott as director and Frederick Brisson, Robert E. Griffith and Harold S. Prince as producers to create *The Pajama Game* and *Damn Yankees*. For the former Abbott collaborated with Richard Bissell in converting his novel, *7½ Cents*, into a book about a strike in a pajama factory, and he had Jerome Robbins to help on the direction. For the latter Abbott guided Douglass Wallop in drawing a book out of his droll novel, *The Year the Yankees Lost the Pennant*. Each bore the Abbott trademark of speed and vitality, and the Adler-Ross songs lent themselves neatly to the snappy, professional gloss. One recalls the sultriness of "Steam Heat" and the beat of "Hernando's Hideaway" in *The Pajama Game*, with Carol Haney as a vibrant dancer, and one remembers especially the seductiveness of Gwen Verdon in "Whatever Lola Wants" in *Damn Yankees*. Although neither of these musicals marked an advance in form or style, each was in the Broadway groove.

Bissell parlayed his experience with *The Pajama Game* into further book and stage expressions. He wrote a novel, *Say, Darling*, based on his adventures in getting a musical to the stage, then helped to convert this new novel into another musical called *Say, Darling*, this time with the help of his wife, Abe Burrows, Betty Comden, Adolph Green and Jule Styne.

The life and person of Fiorello H. La Guardia were diluted in *Fiorello!* but this work had a certain exuberance that matched its protagonist's history, a score by Jerry Bock and Sheldon Harnick with some vivid numbers, including a lively, sardonic one, "Little Tin Box," and Tom Bosley, whose resemblance to La Guardia was uncanny, in the title role.

Meredith Willson was not afraid to be homespun in *The Music Man*, and his book and songs recalled affectionately the charms and sentimentality of small-town life. Not a brilliant melodist, Willson brought the skills of a trained musician and a relish for marching rhythms to his work. With Morton De Costa in charge of the staging and Robert Preston to give irresistible warmth to a glib conniving salesman of band instruments, this musical ran for three years, a choice example of a family show—wholesome, folksy, suitable for Grandpa and Grandma as well as the kids.

A young team, Charles Strouse and Lee Adams, joined a young writer, Michael Stewart, to fashion *Bye Bye Birdie*, which came along late in the 1959–60 season, and which was spirited in its treatment of teen-agers who were delirious about a new pop singer not unlike Elvis Presley. I thought Gower Champion's staging was fresh and imaginative, and the number that showed a jabber of teen-agers on the telephone was imaginative. I also relished Kay Medford's acidulous portrait of a mother who was determined to cling to her rich meal-ticket of a son.

Although the revue was seldom tried, it did well on occasion. *New Faces of 1952* was noteworthy for unearthing talent like Eartha Kitt, Carol Lawrence, Robert Clary, Alice Ghostly and Ronny Graham. The last John Murray Anderson *Almanac* introduced Harry Belafonte and Orson Bean. *The Boy Friend*, imported from London, caught the mannered customs and nostalgically curious costumes of the twenties in songs and sketches, but in the transplantation to New York there was so much stress and strain that the author, Sandy Wilson, was locked out of rehearsals. Robert Dhery's *La Plume de Ma Tante* from France proved to be a winner, and deserved to be. The first-act finale with four monks tugging at the ropes to ring the church bells and becoming wildly airborne to the tune of "Frère Jacques" was inspired nonsense. In a more reserved but equally individual and shrewd theatrical manner, Michael Flanders and Donald Swan turned original songs and genial, understated patter into an evening of low-pressure charm.

New musicals even began to appear off Broadway. The most successful were *Little Mary Sunshine,* in which Rick Besoyan spoofed the Indian sagas of long ago in his book and songs, and *The Fantasticks,* a light-footed work by Tom Jones and Harvey Schmidt. Marc Blitzstein's English version of the Brecht-Weill *The Threepenny Opera* ran for more than five years at the Theatre de Lys on Bleecker Street. For a blend of gusto and irony no musical work in New York could match it, but the New York production, when compared with the slashing version of the Berliner Ensemble, Brecht's East Berlin theatre, was merely genial caricature, not cutting satire.

CHAPTER XXXI

THE RISE OF OFF BROADWAY

THE IMPORTANCE OF OFF BROADWAY was in the drama. In the fifties this offshoot of the New York theatre became not merely a frayed fringe of a shrinking professional Broadway but a many-faceted and indispensable complement and counterpoise to a theatre that took fewer and fewer chances.

Broadway's neglect of the theatre's history and literature, of controversial playwrights abroad, of new and difficult ones in our own country, of experimental ideas and of young talent created a series of vacuums. Off Broadway almost inevitably had to be invented to fill them—no matter how awkwardly it sometimes did the job. In the forties the Off-Broadway movement had been a scattering of faltering, amateur, semiprofessional and occasional professional gestures, but in the fifties it became a professional movement of great diversity. Churches, meeting halls, old movie houses, dance halls, cellars, were converted to theatrical use. Greenwich Village was the favorite venue, but the theatres sprang up on the East Side, West Side, all over town. A few were well equipped for players and crew and comfortable for the audience, while others had cramped, inadequate stages and drafty, claustrophobic cells for auditoriums.

The ambitions of the producers and players often outran their competence and means. As a few works flourished and made money and new gladiators strode into this arena, the economics of Off Broadway became increasingly difficult. In a few years, production costs rose from $500 to $7,500 and went as high as $15,000 by the decade's end. The break-even point had been as low as 30 percent of capacity in the early days; it soon became 50 percent and pushed irresistibly upward. Rentals, which had been as low as $125 a week, shot up beyond $500. Production became the concern of experienced men and women; they formed a League of Off-Broadway Producers.

If there were troubles, there also were rewards. Standards of professionalism rose, particularly in a few theatres and companies which refused to settle for shortcuts and apologies. Occasionally these modest enterprises surpassed the Big Time in intelligence, sensitivity and style. Staging and acting could be surprisingly good. Sets and costumes could be ingenious triumphs over narrow quarters and strained budgets. They could also be horrible. The number of Off-Broadway productions in a season rose to 100, and many, of course, were stillborn. Good ideas went wrong; masterpieces were abused; self-indulgent writers, directors, designers and actors with money of their own or with rich, complacent relatives and friends put on vanity productions that made one flee into the night in dismay. But the good work, though rare, was recurrent enough to justify the travail and to prove that Off Broadway was filling, at least partially, a desperate need.

The immense thrust of the Off-Broadway theatre can be measured by what happened at the consistently professional and intelligent Circle in the Square. In the 1951–52 season this company sparked by José Quintero, a young director, Theodore Mann, a lawyer turned producer, and Leigh Connell produced Giraudoux's *The Enchanted,* which had been violated in its Broadway version, and then scored a thumping success with Tennessee Williams's *Summer and Smoke,* with the exciting young Geraldine Page in the principal role. If any production may be called a turning point in Off-Broadway fortunes, *Summer and Smoke* was it. The acclaim and the audiences it won encouraged others with talent and ideas to venture off Broadway.

By the end of the decade the Circle in the Square was producing Jean Genêt's *The Balcony,* a difficult, challenging work of bitter despair and savage, almost neurotic intensity. I was impressed by the fervor and tension of this open-stage, arena-style production. In Paris some months later I saw Marie Bell and a company of leading French actors in a subtle, silken production staged by Peter Brook, and I realized that New York's Off-Broadway production, despite its modest means, had coherence and integrity and compared respectably with the refinements of the Paris theatre at its suavest and most professional.

In those years the Circle in the Square made itself an impressive interpreter of O'Neill. It found several worthwhile contemporary plays, like Alfred Hayes's tender, if flawed, *The Girl on the Via Flaminia,* which moved up to Broadway, and Brendan Behan's angry and vital *The Quare Fellow.* It attempted a diversity of revivals like *The Cradle Song, Our Town* and Edwin Justus Mayer's *Children of Darkness.* It became an ornament of New York's cultural life.

The Phoenix Theatre was located off Broadway when it began its career in a large house on Second Avenue, in 1953, but its goal was a permanent enterprise of professional standards that could compare with Broadway's best. Founded by T. Edward Hambleton and Norris Houghton, it was an effort to rededicate the stage to high purpose, and it assumed that nothing old or new of quality was alien to its scope. It was often newsworthy and occasionally artistic. But it did not establish itself firmly either as a theatre with a special viewpoint or as an acting company with a particular style. Its approach kept changing, and its choice of productions was uneven, reflecting a need to adapt itself to stars, directors or works that might be available rather than an uncompromising adherence to a consistent artistic policy. Determined to avoid the devastating hit-or-flop psychology of the commercial theatre, the Phoenix found that it could not escape the joys and tribulations of the unexpected success and the ruinous failure.

The opening production was Sidney Howard's posthumous *Madame, Will You Walk?* Hume Cronyn and Jessica Tandy were in the cast. The opening occurred in the midst of the first of the strikes that shut down the principal New York newspapers. It was a comparatively brief shutdown, but it did not help the Phoenix debut. That first season included Shakespeare's *Coriolanus*, staged by John Houseman; an experimental musical by the John Latouche and Jerome Moross, *The Golden Apple*; and *The Sea Gull*, staged by Houghton, with Montgomery Clift, Judith Evelyn, Kevin McCarthy, Maureen Stapleton and George Voskovec.

The Phoenix record for the rest of the decade underlines how devotedly it sought to live up to its ideals. There were new and recent works like Robert Ardrey's *Sing Me No Lullabies, Sandhog* by Earl Robinson and Waldo Salt, *The Carefree Tree* by Aldyth Morris, *The Littlest Revue* by Vernon Duke and Ogden Nash, *The Terrible Swift Sword* by Arthur Steuer, *Queen After Death* by Montherlant, *The Chairs* and *The Lesson* by Ionesco, *The Infernal Machine* by Cocteau, *The Family Reunion* by T. S. Eliot, *The Power and The Glory*, based on Graham Greene's novel, by Denis Cannan and Pierre Bost. There were productions, ranging from attractive and mettlesome to disheveled and lackluster, of Shaw, Shakespeare, Ibsen, Pirandello, Strindberg, Turgenev, O'Neill, Otway, Rice, Ostrovsky, Brecht, Webster, Schiller, Capek, Kleist, Molière, Farquhar and Aristophanes.

Despite its ideals and goodwill, the Phoenix did not win the secure suffrage of the New York public. Yet Hambleton and Houghton were not dismayed. Somehow they found the money and the energy to go forward.

The Living Theatre was another creation of the fifties and one of the most individual and admirable. Founded by Julian Beck and his wife Judith Malina, it succeeded in developing a style and a philosophy of its own. It was not interested in commercial procedures. Built with the sweat, toil, tears and ecstasy of its founders and the enthusiasm of the actors allied to them in forging a genuine repertory company, it was able to give cohesive performance of works as varied as William Carlos Williams's *Many Loves*, Pirandello's *Tonight We Improvise* and the sleazily realistic play about drug addiction and the desperate isolation of modern man, Jack Gelber's *The Connection*.

The energy of Off Broadway manifested itself in an outpouring of revivals. The Shakespearewrights put on modest, attractive versions of works by the man whose name they took. There was an abundance of Chekhov, presided over largely by David Ross. Ibsen, Strindberg and a host of others were not forgotten, if not always flattered. There were numerous revivals of works that had failed or succeeded on Broadway, and many were not worth the candle or the expense, not even as a means of giving young performers a forum.

Off Broadway was most useful when it turned to material neglected on Broadway that was not beyond its limited purse. *The World of Sholom Aleichem,* a delightfully warm production with a performance of inimitable grace by Zero Mostel, ran for a season. A stage version of part of Joyce's *Ulysses,* with Mostel and Valerie Bettis, proved to be another unexpected delight.

Toward the end of the decade, Off Broadway was endorsed by Tennessee Williams, who consigned his double bill, *Garden District,* to one of its theatres, and the sensational second half, *Suddenly Last Summer,* propelled it into a long run. Maxwell Anderson's swan song, *The Golden Six,* a pallid piece on Roman history, had an off-Broadway première. Samuel Beckett's *Endgame,* one of the seminal plays of the second half of the twentieth century, despite its unrelieved despair, was first presented off Broadway, and so was his one-acter, *Krapp's Last Tape.* Jean Genêt's *Deathwatch,* preceding *The Balcony,* introduced this fierce and febrile Frenchman to America. Plays by Betti, Diego Fabbri, Ionesco, Montherlant, Mauriac, Arrabal, Bernard Kops, James Forsyth, made their first appearance off Broadway, not always to the advantage of the author and sometimes to the disadvantage of the audience. But no matter. The job needed doing.

First signs of new American playwriting talent that might take a prominent role in our theatre appeared off Broadway. Besides Gelber there were Jack Richardson with *The Prodigal,* a fresh view of a classic theme, and Edward Albee with *The Zoo Story,* in a tightly wrought, lurid and smoldering play.

While the Broadway theatre was growing narrower, more strident, more removed from life and art, more frantically commercial and less committed to standards of taste, style and intelligence, valiant spirits off Broadway and across the land were seeking to take up the artistic slack. A man of fierce determination like Joseph Papp remembered that audiences had to be served and cultivated in places where they had been neglected, and he forced through, over the objections of the powerful Park Commissioner, Robert Moses, his admirable seasons of free Shakespeare in Central Park.

New, eager young spirits were fighting to establish independent permanent theatres in cities throughout the nation. At the decade's end, when the Broadway situation was grim, artistically, financially and psychologically, new forces were appearing. It was possible that the theatre would not live or die by what happened in the narrow area around Times Square, and that these new energies might even inject fresh red corpuscles into Broadway's hectic, tired blood.

CHAPTER XXXII

DISARRAY IN THE SIXTIES

As if to illustrate the nadir reached by the commercial theatre, Broadway was shut down for twelve days in June 1960. Actors Equity struck one production, *The Tenth Man,* whereupon all the others were closed. Other business interests like restaurants, hotels, transportation and shops suffered from the blackout, and a cloud hung over the city. For the Broadway theatre, whatever its limitations, is the centerpiece of New York's entertainments and arts. Without them the city would be an unimaginably vast anthill of glass and steel, brick and mortar—another, larger marketplace, workshop and dormitory. New York suddenly realized, as it did during the 1919 Equity strike, that its stages had been, for better or worse, the soul of the American theatre for two centuries.

After the usual recriminations, charges and countercharges, the strike was settled. The actors won improvements in salary and fringe benefits, which they were entitled to. For of all the workers in the theatre the actors, not counting the glamorous stars, whose weekly earnings are in the thousands, are rewarded with the least generosity. It is either feast or famine for the performer. What tenacity or devotion keeps actors in the theatre in the face of its monstrous insecurities, I shall never know.

The settlement of the strike and the return of the welcome lights to marquees of the Broadway theatres did nothing to solve a host of corrosive problems. After the disappointing record of the late fifties, the first seasons of the sixties were, if anything, a further deterioration. There were hardly any plays approaching distinction by American writers.

The desperate situation was summed up by the blight that befell nearly all of our dependable writers, new or old, in the 1962–63 season. Has there ever been a twelvemonth in which so many established playwrights fared so poorly? Sidney Kingsley with *Night Life,* S. N. Behrman with *Lord Pengo,* Tennessee Williams with *The Milk Train Doesn't Stop Here Anymore,* William Inge with *Natural Affection,* Lillian Hellman with *My Mother, My Father and Me* and Irwin Shaw with *Children from Their Games* had failures or near failures. The greatly promising Jack Richardson entered the Broadway area for the first time with *Lorenzo,* a failure too. Nor was any of this a miscarriage of justice. The writing was tired or repetitious, unresolved or superficial, windy or pretentious, and, in a couple of cases, so sick and vindictive as to demean itself rather than reveal and comment on the ailments of our society.

Costs kept mounting—both the initial outlay to bring in a show and the operating expenses to keep it going. The result was an intensified, almost compulsive drive to secure the unsecurable. Among the feverish recourses were a stress on film and TV reputations supposed to be irresistible box-office and production excesses emphasizing the razzle-dazzle of flashy scenic effects, speed, stridency and hokum as camouflages for shoddy plots, character and ideas.

It serves no purpose to recall the horrifying empty pastiches brought into Broadway theatres at costs ranging from $100,000 and more for a play to $450,000 and more for a musical not fit to entertain even the undemanding audience that sits vacuously night after night before the emptiest and dreariest stuff on the home screens. Especially dispiriting was the way in which works with potentialities were distorted and debased.

On a modest level there was the case of *Midgie Purvis,* by Mary

Chase, author of *Harvey, Mrs. McThing* and *Bernardine*. Not a distinguished writer, Mrs. Chase had proved, however, that she could use fantasy with humor and affection. In *Midgie Purvis* she was manifestly saying that parents, their capacities for wonder atrophied, do not appreciate the imaginative world of their children. But somewhere on the path to the Broadway opening nearly everything went wrong. Was the author inflexible about her script? Was the casting of Tallulah Bankhead, whose natural style is hard and unlovable, a blunder? Did the director accentuate the wrong values? One thing is certain: what came into New York was confused, messy and unlovely.

Lillian Hellman's *My Mother, My Father and Me* went down the drain quickly even though it contained good stuff; another victim, I suspect, of wrong-mindedness and cross-purposes in the course of production. Mistakes in judgment about the nature of the piece and the way it should be done probably were made early in the game. So great are the pressures once a production has been set in motion that it is almost impossible to make drastic changes en route to the New York opening, and there never is time for writer, director or producer to achieve a desperately needed perspective.

A production of Brecht's *Mother Courage* staged by Jerome Robbins collapsed after a short run early in 1963 because, among other reasons, it had not been fused into a tight-knit whole. Miss Bancroft, a gifted actress, did not have time to grow into the title role. Robbins realized that his first approach needed reorientation, and he undertook to change it, but he did not have as much time as the work required. When one compares the urgencies of preparation for Broadway with the leisurely schedule of the Berliner Ensemble, one realizes the built-in hazards of a Broadway production of Brecht or any other difficult and challenging work. Brecht, after all, is the Berliner Ensemble's main business; the company is Brecht's creation and is run by his artistic heirs. Yet this East Berlin company takes months to study and mount a piece. For the New York production of *Mother Courage* a group of actors was assembled from scratch, most with no experience of Brecht. How can something probing and fructifying emerge?

The 1963 production of *Arturo Ui* proved that hard-hitting flashy techniques, so comfortably within Broadway's grasp, could also distort Brecht. This treatment was all jazzy garishness. In place of a savagely sardonic style there was a stagy cuteness. *Arturo Ui* is one of Brecht's weakest, most obvious pieces, but gaudy, show-business techniques are not the answer to its problems.

If the feverish way of Broadway life in the sixties undermined much of what it touched by underpreparation, overproduction and flamboyance, there was another serious deficiency—nonproduction of plays that belonged in a mature, well-balanced dramatic culture. Who was to blame? The producers? No doubt that taste, conviction and a viewpoint were in short supply. No doubt that the theatre's gamble and scramble attracted all sorts of incompetents from impecunious, fast-talking, tasteless promoters to well-heeled, innocent amateurs blinded by stardust. But among the producers were some who had learned the intricacies of an exacting career the hard way, and they were not the enemies of challenging, unusual, experimental drama. A few kept trying, though the chances of success were shrinking. Their lot was not made easier by the increasingly stony path to be traversed by plays of serious content.

I do not think that Tad Mosel's dramatization of James Agee's tremulously tender novel, *A Death in the Family,* was a complete success as a play. After the death of the young father at the end of the first act, the drama had little to say or do. Nevertheless, *All the Way Home* had touching moments and fresh insights. Compared with trivialities that flourished, it deserved to be seen. And it was kept alive through the entire season, even though it was announced to close several days after its opening. Sacrifices by the company and the author and concessions by the theatre owner enabled it to stay in business until the spring when it captured the New York Drama Critics Circle Award and the Pulitzer Prize. Despite the run and the kudos, the producers and backers took a loss.

It looked in the early sixties as if Broadway could hope for only one big success a season in the category of serious plays. The triumph of 1961–62 was Robert Bolt's *A Man for All Seasons.* The money-maker of 1962–63 was Edward Albee's *Who's Afraid of Virginia Woolf?* To attempt expensive productions even of proved material required courage and the insurance of dazzling stars. Anouilh's *Becket* earned its costs and a profit because it had Laurence Olivier and Anthony Quinn as stars. The same author's *The Rehearsal*, less pretentious, wittier and sharper, had a modest run and incurred a loss, even though Alan Badel illuminated it with a brilliant high-comedy performance. John Osborne's theatrical, often provocative *Luther* drew impressively in the months when Albert Finney played the title role, and then it faded away. A highly publicized star like Richard Burton made a success of *Hamlet.*

It was obvious that the principal commercial theatres of New York were not reflecting the best of the drama, present or past, American or foreign. Apportion the blame however you will—on the high cost of tickets, on the necessity to be a hit quickly or to fail miserably, on the reluctance of many theatregoers to use their own judgment rather than to wait until they heard about a unanimously approved production. The fact remained that there was justification for Edward Albee's accusation—that Off Broadway was doing the works that should have been the concern of the major theatrical channels while Broadway was preoccupied largely with trifles that might be the proper business of subsidiary stages.

How could one argue in the face of profits and losses? It was a fact that the enduring dramas rarely paid off as a commercial investment as the Burton *Hamlet* did. The tendency to leave them to Off Broadway, where the costs were not so onerous, was understandable. But the trouble there was that the talent and financial resources seldom measured up. It was most exceptional to get a production like the Circle in the Square's eloquent *The Trojan Women*. Here were a fine cast and incandescent staging by a young Greek, Michael Cacoyannis. The result—Euripides' scathing denunciation of war and the human folly that begets it was as overwhelming in Edith Hamilton's sensitive, forthright English version in the 1960s as it must have been in 416 B.C. in Athens when the play was new.

Off Broadway gamely tried to provide productions of Calderón,

Ibsen, Strindberg, Brecht, Betti, Pirandello, Chekhov, Gorki and other vital dramas of the past, but more often than not, the audience had to settle for half-baked work. Casts were rarely equal in strength; direction was variable; stages were not suitable for the scope and resonance of certain works; music, lighting and designs were skimpy.

Nevertheless, it fell increasingly to Off Broadway to be the proving ground of new playwrights. In some cases producers and playwrights turned to London for trial runs, since the expenses of mounting a play there remained far below those in New York. But the responsibility for newcomers devolved largely on Off Broadway, which also operated according to the laws of free enterprise and which also was largely a helter-skelter, anarchic, hit-or-miss forum.

Yet in the early sixties Off Broadway undertook any number of projects that a self-respecting theatre must concern itself with. Among the arresting plays from abroad it offered Genêt's *The Blacks,* a scorching prose poem of the ritual slaughter of the whites; Samuel Beckett's *Happy Days,* a beautifully written, aching examination of disintegration and despair that left one feeling, despite the tenderness of its emotion, that there was nothing left in this life save to end it quickly; Brecht's *In the Jungle of Cities,* done with striking theatricality and passion by the Living Theatre, and his *A Man's a Man,* produced simultaneously by the Living Theatre and by another group in a regrettable duplication of effort; Arnold Wesker's *Roots,* a more touching play in London with Joan Plowright in the lead than off Broadway with a much less gifted cast; Harold Pinter's *The Collection,* with its ominously enigmatic relationships; and Athol Fugard's *The Blood Knot,* a penetrating evocation of the needs and hatreds that drew together and pulled apart half brothers of white and dark skin in South Africa.

Young American writers were not neglected off Broadway. Jack Richardson was represented by a sardonic pair of one-acters, *Gallows Humor.* Jack Gelber came up with *The Apple,* a disappointment despite the best of efforts of the Living Theatre's production. Arthur Kopit emerged as a spirited newcomer with *Oh*

*Dad, Poor Dad, Mama's Hung You in the Closet and I'm Feelin'
So Sad,* a glinting, macabre spoof on Freud-oriented drama. This
work, a happy enterprise of the Phoenix Theatre after it moved
from its huge Second Avenue house to a small theatre on East 74th
Street, was staged brilliantly by Jerome Robbins, and played with
mad, yet innocent expansiveness by Jo Van Fleet and young Barbara Harris.

Among other new writers who gave encouragement for the
future were Frank Gilroy (*Who'll Save the Plowboy?*), William
Snyder (*The Days and Nights of Beebee Fenstermaker*), David
Rayfiel (*P. S. 193*), Murray Schisgal (*The Tiger* and *The Typists*),
Oliver Hailey (*Hey, You, Light Man!*), William Hanley (*Whisper
Into My Good Ear* and *Mrs. Dally Has a Lover*), Lewis John Car-
lino (*Cages* and *Telemachus Clay*) and John Donovan (*Riverside
Drive*). In 1964 Gilroy, Schisgal and Hanley made it to Broadway.
In *The Subject Was Roses* Gilroy wrote sensitively and precisely
about a young man returned from the war and his relations with
his parents. In *Luv* Schisgal, writing in a broad, mocking style,
ridiculed the pretensions of love and marriage, and Anne Jackson, Eli Wallach and Alan Arkin performed brilliantly under Mike
Nichols' direction. In *Slow Dance on the Killing Ground* Hanley
wrote with imagination and intensity about three isolated persons, and if his manner was too luxuriant, it was a venial sin of
a talented young playwright.

The Phoenix Theatre had the admirable idea of developing a
special series of productions geared for schoolchildren, and the
first productions of *Abe Lincoln in Illinois* and *The Taming of
the Shrew* had merit. But the venture was unlucky. It began during the four-month New York newspaper blackout, and was defeated by the failure of communication so urgently required by
a new enterprise.

The Circle in the Square, which occupied itself with Thornton
Wilder's adventure in one-act cycles and interesting revivals of
Under Milk Wood and *Desire Under the Elms,* achieved its finest
hour with *The Trojan Women.* The success of this production reflected the community's hunger for drama of passion and dimen-
sion.

CHAPTER XXXIII

MANY VALLEYS, FEW PEAKS

THE JUMP FROM OFF BROADWAY to Broadway remained, symbolically and practically, as important as moving from the minors to a major league baseball club. Even Edward Albee, whose fierce loyalty to Off Broadway was unswerving, could not deny that basic truth, however much he insisted—and rightly—that art and talent were where you found them.

The American Dream, a satirical allegory on our debased values, and *The Death of Bessie Smith,* a glimpse at the sources of a white girl's hysterical hatred of the Negro, were done off Broadway, but with *Who's Afraid of Virginia Woolf?* he moved resoundingly onto Broadway.

The raging disagreements over *Who's Afraid of Virginia Woolf?* matched the fury that informed the play. As staged by Alan Schneider and played by Uta Hagen, Arthur Hill, George Grizzard and Melinda Dillon, this drama had the ferocity of Strindberg's *Dance of Death.* While I did not swallow whole Albee's combatants in the almost mortal domestic duel, I felt that they were compelling, that there was enough underlying anguish to make clear that these were human beings and not monsters and that the work and its performance had a dramatic power all too rare in our polite and placid theatre. I recognized that there were unhealthy viruses at large in the drama, and they made me uncomfortable. I do not think for a moment that *Who's Afraid of Virginia Woolf?* is a masterpiece. But not to recognize that here was a playwright with passion and intensity was to be insensate and perverse.

In his dramatization of Carson McCullers's *The Ballad of the Sad Café*, Albee did a skillful job but could not make fully dramatic a novelistic subject. However, he created a mood, and Schneider's staging as well as the performance by Colleen Dewhurst and Michael Dunn as the dwarf achieved atmosphere and moments of haunting emotion. Again Albee returned to a preoccupation with abnormality of the passions. In *The Zoo Story* there was an open concern with homosexuality; in *The American Dream* it was implicit. Many detected mysterious hints of it in *Who's Afraid of Virginia Woolf?* There were intimations of it in *Tiny Alice,* in which Albee, using ideas from the New Testament and a multitude of symbols, dealt enigmatically with the possibilities and values of faith in a world where it was increasingly difficult. John Gielgud, Irene Worth, William Hutt and John Heffernan played with distinction in a play that was a conversation piece of the season.

There is no doubt that a preoccupation with homosexuality has colored many modern plays. Like any other human manifestation, it is a valid theme. Homosexuality is a fact of life, and has been for millennia. I have inveighed against its use only when it falsified and distorted. I have grown weary of plays in which females are baneful or pitiful but never women with a recognizable balance or confusion of strength and weakness. I have tired of men as symbols of the irresistibly priapic or of the shiningly remote and neutral. I do not question the right of playwrights to pursue their visions of the world as they know it or wish it to be, no matter how psychologically and emotionally maimed the characters and visions may be. But I rebel when a play about a homosexual relationship is masked by a false heterosexual façade. I am fed up particularly with fashionable or self-indulgent intrusions of homosexual motifs.

Odd how the theme of homosexuality infiltrated the plays of the fifties and sixties—American or foreign, on or off Broadway. It is simpler to mention the playwrights who have invoked it in one way or another, openly or furtively, than to mention all the plays —Tennessee Williams, William Inge, Robert Anderson, Arthur Laurents, Edward Albee, Arthur Kopit, James Costigan, Jean Genêt, Harold Pinter, Shelagh Delaney, Terence Rattigan, Brendan Behan (who hooted at it in *The Hostage*), Lewis John Carlino, Gore Vidal, Hugh Wheeler, Anouilh, Peter S. Feibleman, Sidney Kingsley—and so on and so forth.

The enormous financial success of *Who's Afraid of Virginia Woolf?* enabled Albee, a man of admirable generosity, and his producers, Clinton Wilder and Richard Barr, to make a contribution to the development of new American playwrights. They allocated a portion of their profits to the establishment of a workshop. In an off-Broadway theatre they gave new writers a chance to see their work staged and performed. Fully aware of the frightening and possibly devastating impact of a Broadway premiere, Albee and his associates sought to give young writers a chance to acclimatize themselves gradually to the theatre's uncertainties. In its first year the workshop presented in professional off-Broadway settings such new writers as Adrienne Kennedy and LeRoi Jones, young Negroes with a scorching report on the agony of being a Negro and an alien in one's own land.

Miss Kennedy's *Funnyhouse of a Negro* was the surrealistic nightmare of a Negro girl. Jones's *Dutchman* surged with violence and hatred for the provocateur in the white man, who even in his liberal aspect grants the Negro certain privileges only so long as he is tame enough to satisfy the liberal's notion of the decencies of behavior. In *The Toilet* and *The Slave*, however, Jones had become something of a provocateur himself. There was validity in his theme that love between Negro and white had become almost impossible, but the brutality and obscenities of his style seemed to be designed chiefly to shock.

James Baldwin in *Blues for Mister Charlie* was another who articulated the Negro's desperation and irreversible determination in explosive theatrical terms. As a call to arms this play resembled Odets's *Waiting for Lefty* of the thirties. Not well made or satisfying as a dramatic work, it was the voice of the Negro speaking for himself with bitterness and anger, tears and resolution. Staged by Burgess Meredith with fluidity and intensity and played searingly by a company of white and Negro players under the aegis of the Actors Studio Theatre, it was another step along the path toward full Negro citizenship in the theatre.

Among the members of his own profession the Negro had long since won full equality. Actors Equity for years had been a leader in the fight against segregation, and in 1964 it chose a Negro, Frederick O'Neal, to be its president. The theatre was less inhibited than the films and television, which were fearful of southern audiences. Thus Negroes had a modest shot at jobs in the drama. By the sixties it became a commonplace to find at least a few Negroes in the choral and dance ensembles of musicals. The casting of Negroes in principal roles depended, in a largely naturalistic theatre, on plays that called for them. Yet progress was being made. It was no longer a matter for excitement if a Negro got a role hitherto assumed to be a white player's, as Diana Sands did in *The Owl and the Pussycat*. A pioneer in this breakthrough was the Metropolitan Opera under Rudolf Bing, who in the fifties had the audacity to present not only a world-famous artist like Marian Anderson but a Gloria Davy as Pamina in *The Magic Flute* and a Leontyne Price in *Trovatore*. Samuel Chotzinoff, as producer of N.B.C.'s Opera Company, also had the temerity to present Leontyne Price as Tosca. Aïda was no longer the only part available to a Negro soprano.

In the theatre the day had passed when parts like the Emperor Jones and Othello or the menial servant bits were all a Negro might hope for.

The Negro discovered that he could, if he chose, write for the stage in terms of fantasy, satire or burlesque. Ossie Davis, himself an actor, contributed *Purlie Victorious*, which mocked the South's ancient clichés of white paternalism and superiority and Negro inferiority and servility. Davis was as intense in his convictions as Lorraine Hansberry and James Baldwin. But it was a sign of the changing order that the Negro could use laughter as a weapon.

The established writers produced little of moment. Tennessee

Williams's *The Night of the Iguana,* badly flawed, had some affecting moments. His so-called serious comedy, *Period of Adjustment,* was neither serious nor comic. Arthur Laurents in *Invitation to the March,* another tepid homily on the virtues of nonconformity, Sidney Kingsley's realistic and empty *Night Life,* William Inge's garish and sensational *Natural Affection,* were disappointments. Paddy Chayefsky's dangerous tendency to be fancy and sententious did not get out of hand in *Gideon,* his fantasy about God and his chosen warrior, Gideon, but it slopped over forbiddingly in the misguided attempt to deal with Stalin, Lenin and Russian history in *The Passion of Josef D.* Among the new writers on Broadway Peter S. Feibleman (*Tiger Tiger Burning Bright*) and Hugh Wheeler (*Big Fish, Little Fish*) had suggestions of quality.

As usual the market for light comedy was larger than for any theatre product except musicals. Here, too, there were some new writers. The best were Neil Simon and Muriel Resnik. Simon's comic muse followed conventional patterns in *Come Blow Your Horn,* though his knack for a fresh, droll line was evident in the hackneyed plot. He achieved a liberated lightness of plot and characterization in *Barefoot in the Park* and an easy, chuckling humor in the transparently simple *The Odd Couple.* Miss Resnik appeared out of nowhere with *Any Wednesday,* which had its elements of formula plotting but which was redeemed by its unexpected drollery. Jean Kerr's *Mary, Mary* was a long-running specimen of a popular, superficial genre.

Two comic works with a little more substance were S. J. Perelman's *The Beauty Part* and Ronald Alexander's *Nobody Loves an Albatross. The Beauty Part,* a mad lampoon of a materialistic world, was not perfectly suited to the stage; only part of the time was it expressed in dramatic terms. Yet Bert Lahr's performance in a variety of roles from a Hollywood producer named Harry Hubris to an irascible old millionaire owner of a chain of stores made it a comic enterprise to remember. More than most productions, *The Beauty Part* was victimized by the blackout of the major New York newspapers in 1962–63.

Nobody Loves an Albatross was an unexpected boon. Once an

actor, the author had labored in Hollywood and in the fifties had reached Broadway briefly with *The Grand Prize* and *Holiday for Lovers*. In *Albatross* he applied a light-footed farcical style to the Hollywood mills that grind out fodder for the TV multitude. His play about a writer who can't write but is a power as a producer was not only funny but pointed, and Robert Preston played his "hero" with a fraudulent innocence.

There was not even a great deal to cheer among the musicals. Lerner and Loewe, with Moss Hart on his last directorial job, produced *Camelot*, spotty in content but magnificent in looks, with Julie Andrews, Richard Burton and Robert Goulet to enliven an overelaborate and overearnest book. Thanks to the clouds of glory trailing *My Fair Lady*, the advance was so huge that Richard Maney, the puckish press agent, could shrug off the unfavorable reviews with the remark that *Camelot* would be "a two-year flop." Meredith Willson could not recapture the first, fine corny laughter of *The Music Man* either in *The Unsinkable Molly Brown* or *Here's Love*. Richard Rodgers, bereft of his friend and collaborator, Oscar Hammerstein II, added lyric writing to composing for *No Strings*, and his score as well as an inventive production animated Samuel Taylor's book about a romance between a white man and a Negro model in Paris. The handling of this relationship was sensitive, but the essential story was thoroughly conventional. Rodgers next turned to Arthur Laurents and his play *The Time of the Cuckoo* and to Stephen Sondheim, lyricist, as collaborators on *Do I Hear a Waltz?*—a musical that somehow lacked a true spark of inspiration.

The secrets of success vary from musical to musical. *How to Succeed in Business Without Really Trying* prospered because it had unity of viewpoint and style. The book by Jack Weinstock, Willie Gilbert and Abe Burrows adopted a broad, satiric view toward the machinations of a young heel on the make in the business world; the songs by Frank Loesser, though not the kind you could whistle, suited the action and the characters, the direction by Burrows was shrewd and snappy, and the performance by Robert Morse and Rudy Vallee was spirited. All the elements admirably fitted a coherent, broadly cynical pattern.

A Funny Thing Happened on the Way to the Forum thrived because of its rowdiness and ribaldry. Burt Shevelove and Larry Gelbart managed to convert material from the Latin comedies of Plautus to boisterous modern use, and Stephen Sondheim's songs were in the vein. George Abbott's staging was fast and loud. But it was the high skill of comedians practiced in the hard schools of farce, burlesque and night clubs like Zero Mostel, David Burns and Jack Gilford that gave this uninhibited romp its zestful style. Best of all was Mostel, whose comic style approached a Chaplinesque subtlety and variety of movement, gesture and fancy.

Hello, Dolly! was a success because it remained faithful, at least part of the time, to the spirit of Thornton Wilder's *The Matchmaker*, which, as a play, resounded with implicit melodies. Michael Stewart's book retained the outlines of the story, Jerry Herman's songs were sprightly, Gower Champion filled the spaces between the words and notes with acting and choreography full of color and comment, and Carol Channing brought her flushed radiance and David Burns his W. C. Fields-like querulousness to the performance.

The names of the craftsmen of musicals recur. Thus Bob Merrill, who composed the songs for Michael Stewart's book for *Carnival!*, a sentimental affair about a waif with a traveling show, wrote the lyrics for songwriter Jule Styne and *Funny Girl* in 1964. This work, based on the life of Fanny Brice, recaptured something of the spirit of the musical theatre of five decades earlier, and young Barbra Streisand, who had made a marked impression in a small role in *I Can Get It for You Wholesale*, achieved stardom in a brash, comic performance as Fanny Brice.

With *Fiddler on the Roof* the musical theatre turned to Sholom Aleichem and his world of poor Jews in the Russian villages of the turn of the century. An unusually meaningful story and an unforgettable character highlighted this musical by Joseph Stein, Sheldon Harnaick and Jerry Bock. Zero Mostel gave one of the great performances of our musical theatre as Tevye, the dairyman, who knew how to endure a difficult life with dignity, simplicity and humor. If touches of show business marred Jerome Robbins' production, the musical as a whole deserved its smash-hit status.

Of the imported musicals, *Irma La Douce*, which came to New York from Paris by way of London, had the most individuality. Although its story of the *poule* and her *mec* was worn Gallic theatrical goods, it was displayed with vivacity.

If the American musical theatre in the sixties could use grants in aid from abroad, think of the state of the drama on Broadway. What distinction the theatre had in those troubled years stemmed largely from Europe.

The 1960–61 season was improved for having Shelagh Delaney's *A Taste of Honey*, Brendan Behan's *The Hostage*, Ionesco's *The Rhinoceros* and Anouilh's *Becket*.

A remarkable first effort by a girl of nineteen, *A Taste of Honey* recounted in touching, bittersweet terms the story of a lonely, rejected little girl, and Joan Plowright played her with heartbreaking gallantry. In *The Hostage* Behan used the theatre with hilarious irreverence and annoying indiscipline, and Joan Littlewood's free, improvisational staging almost redeemed its ease and looseness. *The Rhinoceros*, regarded by some proponents of the avant-garde as a comedown for Ionesco because its point was not only explicit but obvious, was done here in a broad style conceived by Joseph Anthony. Although it backtracked and marked time, it had spirit, and Zero Mostel, Eli Wallach and Anne Jackson led a notable performance.

Despite the sumptuousness of its appearance, *Becket* struck me as a wordy, pretentious affair, amusing at times in the irony and pith of its dialogue but barren of fresh insights into Thomas à Becket and his sovereign, the childish and wise Henry II. Laurence Olivier, however, gave further proof of his right to be considered one of the great actors of our generation by playing Becket with silken elegance and dignity and then turning around at the end of the run and doing the coarse, childish, petulant Henry with equal brilliance.

In the 1961–62 season we got two outstanding plays from England—Harold Pinter's *The Caretaker* and Robert Bolt's *A Man for All Seasons*. In the former, Pinter, most talented of England's young writers, adopted some of the techniques of Samuel Beckett and transformed them into a style of his own. Overtones of peril, humor and compassion sounded through this subtly and tersely written story of an old derelict who temporarily finds shelter in an abandoned house with two brothers, one imperviously sealed from the world and the other equally remote despite his use of the jargon and manners of the fast-talking man of affairs. Donald Pleasence was superb as the ragged, sniveling, scrofulous old tramp, and Robert Shaw and Alan Bates were not far behind as the brothers.

Paul Scofield's nuanced performance of Thomas More in *A Man for All Seasons* was worthy of the play it graced. Using a Brechtian technique, Bolt told in terms meaningful for our day of the martyrdom of a man who would not compromise on an issue of conscience. The Common Man, played with enormous relish and humor by George Rose, was the playwright's detached voice for comment of contemporary pungency.

Among the most agreeable imports were *Beyond the Fringe* and *The Hollow Crown*. The former poked very English, yet universal, fun at English foibles and institutions, from Shakespeare to Prime Minister Macmillan. The latter sketched the history and personality of Britain's monarchs with savor and gusto, and introduced us to the enormously gifted Dorothy Tutin, who lit up the stage with her magnetism and her range as an actress.

The 1963–64 season brought a deluge of foreign plays. In addition to Osborne's look at *Luther,* there were *Chips With Everything,* an attack on Britain's caste system and antagonisms, which was evidence of Arnold Wesker's growth as a playwright, and Peter Shaffer's *The Private Ear* and *The Public Eye.* The latter, a tale of a fey private detective who repairs a breaking marriage, was high comedy of charm and elegance. Enid Bagnold introduced *The Chinese Prime Minister* to New York rather than London, and despite weaknesses of structure, this play about an actress who at seventy decides to cultivate her freedom and individuality had unusual independence of mind.

There are times when a theme is so large that it transcends defects in treatment. Rolf Hochhuth's *The Deputy* was such a work. It arrived in New York embattled in controversy, which the production here intensified. The impossibly long play was cut for

Broadway to drive home more sharply its thesis that Pope Pius XII failed in his obligation to speak out against the Nazi persecution of the Jews. The character of the Pope was childishly conceived, but this glaring shortcoming did not vitiate the thrust of Hochhuth's polemic.

Two of Europe's best postwar plays were slow to reach New York. One of these, John Whiting's *The Devils,* based on Aldous Huxley's *The Devils at Loudun,* was performed with symphonic fluidity at the Arena Stage in Washington under Zelda Fichandler's direction. A highly literate play, which wove many strands into a vivid and poignant tapestry about superstition and conscience, *The Devils* finally was scheduled for New York production late in 1965.

Jean-Paul Sartre's *The Condemned of Altona,* which I saw in Paris in 1960 and later read in an English translation, seemed to me another significant play. A story about the struggle for the German soul as revealed by the conflicts of an incestuous postwar German family, this drama was a remorseless commentary on the bitter fighting in Algeria and on new wounds left by nationalism and colonialism on a tormented world. The New York theatre was not to blame for losing the chance to do this play, for the film rights were sold to a movie man who got a contract forbidding an American performance. Yet it is hard not to believe that if commercial considerations were not all-important the play would have been done in the United States. In view of the mayhem inflicted on the play by the film, the loss to the American theatre was all the greater.

The traffic in full companies from abroad quickened. With high-speed jets, it became easy, once the inevitable budget was met by private entrepreneurs, often with the help of the companies' own governments, to arrange transoceanic tours. From France we had the Comédie Française, highlighted by the precision and vitality of Robert Hirsch's acting, particularly in Molière's *Scapin;* Marie Bell and her company in Racine's *Phèdre* and *Bérénice,* and the Renaud-Barrault company in a dazzling exhibition of group versatility ranging through Beaumarchais, Molière, Racine, Ionesco and Offenbach. From Great Britain we had the Old Vic and the ever-popular, ever-traditional Gilbert and Sullivan by the D'Oyly Carte Company. The Old Vic's *Romeo and Juliet* staged by Franco Zeffirelli in earthy, fervent neorealistic style was impressive and exciting, in violent contrast to this director's staging of *The Lady of the Camellias* in another season, which was disastrous in its ugliness and distastefulness. From Canada came a couple of productions of Gilbert and Sullivan that had been staged at Stratford, Ontario. From Germany there was a *Faust* by a Hamburg troupe led by Gustaf Gründgens. From Greece came the Greek Tragedy Theatre in its choreographed and choral *Electra* and *Medea*. From Stockholm came the Royal Dramatic Theatre playing Strindberg with ensemble integrity and O'Neill with respect. From Israel, Habimah in a traditional *Dybbuk* and contemporary Israeli plays. From Taiwan, the Foo Hsing Theatre in Chinese drama full of old, naïve wonders. From the Soviet Union, the Obraztsov Puppets, more disciplined and imaginative than a lot of human actors, and the Moscow Art Theatre, incandescently comic and heartbreaking in Chekhov's *The Cherry Orchard* and *The Three Sisters*.

Eddie Fisher, Jack Benny and Danny Kaye were among the Americans who took over theatres for what amounted to evenings of variety centering around a greatly popular entertainer. Benny's sense of timing remained unexceptionable as well as comic. Kaye's versatility as a performer was beguiling. Elaine May and Mike Nichols held the stage at the Golden Theatre for an entire season with their shrewdly observed comic and occasionally poignant sketches.

Anthologies had a vogue. Bette Davis and several colleagues sought to weave an entertainment out of *The World of Carl Sandburg*, and some of this material was touching and diverting. George Tabori fashioned a program of *Brecht on Brecht*, which captured something of the pungency and astringency of that playwright's thought about the theatre and the world and became an off-Broadway success. When there are no new plays, the theatre scratches in odd corners for sustenance—and sometimes returns nourished.

CHAPTER XXXIV

OF ACTING, DIRECTING
AND DESIGNING

Iт would be pleasant to believe that the passage of time brings progress. In the early decades of the twentieth century there was, in fact, an improvement in American acting, which evidently had, for the most part, nowhere to go but up. Our theatre was slow to be affected by the teachings of Stanislavsky and other revolutionaries. Indeed, in some cases it over-reacted to the Stanislavsky influence by applying his ideas dogmatically and ponderously until they were distorted into a foolish and misleading fetish. But gradually and inevitably, despite misguided schools and doctrinaire systems, our acting responded to new demands for naturalness, integrity and penetration of character.

The response, of course, was variable, depending on the talents and intelligence of the actor—and the influence, magnetism and perception of the director. But no one, not the most gifted actor or the most responsible director, functions in a vacuum. The theatre takes its tone and color from the nature and quality of its time. In submission or rebellion it inescapably mirrors the world around it, and when it is sensitive and vigorous, it can even play a part in modifying its environment.

The surge of individuality and the new sense of power that marked our theatre in the 1920's conditioned acting styles. The superficial elegancies of the drawing room in imitation of the refinements of English stage manners, the genial simplicities that were supposed to reflect the native democratic tradition, the innocent lavishness of an undemanding musical theatre, were carried over from the century's first two decades. But fresh energies, urgencies and awarenesses were at large. Actors learned to adjust to new needs. For the rowdy farces they found—perhaps rediscovered, for it is an old American affinity—the note of ebullience which could shade in and out of a dry, deadpan manner, thereby achieving contrast and additional fun. The American drawing-room comedy could not suppress its vigor and brashness even to be sophisticated and thus became a native, occasionally bracing blend of smartness and dash. For the new dramatic requirements, ranging from realism to fantasy, actors summoned up emotional resources expressed at times in subtlety and reserve and more often in bold, splashy devices that could easily tumble over into excess. For the melodramas, whodunits and costume romances not much in the way of change was necessary, except perhaps a slight subduing of broad gesture, flashy gallantry and obvious histrionics. Exaggeration and flummery were still in evidence in the twenties, but compared with what was visible on the silent films, the acting on the stage often looked natural and credible. After the films began to talk, the theatre became more self-critical, for it realized that the screen had taken over and magnified stock attitudes of ham acting and was welcome to them.

Although theatrical activity in the twenties boomed and embraced a wide variety of plays and musicals, American acting did not become a rationalized, cultivated craft. Nor has it become one since. Some schools in the United States teach acting at the college or graduate level, though how well is open to argument. Once the schooling is completed, the rest is up to the individual and chance. To experience the equivalent of a young physician's internship is difficult, if not impossible. The young actor has few places where he can learn and grow. The wonder is that so many cling to a profession that scarcely troubles itself with the coming generation and gives its best and maturest performers so precarious a career and livelihood.

The result is that as we move into the final third of the twentieth century our acting standards have not advanced measurably. We have a substantial body of players who can do a few things well. Our actors are still expert at boisterous farce. They can manage realistic slices of life capably. They have the cheerful resilience for fast-moving, earthy comedy of contemporary vintage. They can convey the glow and geniality so much of our musical theatre requires. But the range of the majority is limited. Too many of our players are victimized by type casting. Too many have been doomed to play variations of one character, usually the actor's own.

A villain of the piece is the star system. A young actor gets a role that suits him perfectly and is hailed as a new messiah of our stage. His play becomes a hit and he leaps into international fame. If he remains in the theatre, his next role is tailored to match the one that catapulted him to glory and riches. If he refuses to be typed and insists on something entirely different, he runs the risk that he is not far enough along as an artist to encompass a role markedly divergent from himself. The greatest likelihood is that he will gravitate to the big money in films and television, where his chances of growing will rarely be enhanced.

I am not speaking theoretically. Consider the case of Marlon Brando, who could be our most brilliant and versatile actor. It has been contended that with Kowalski in *A Streetcar Named Desire,* he did what came naturally—that the T-shirted, sensual, brutish male who grunted and growled and mouthed his words explosively was less a feat of acting than self-revelation. I have seen Brando in other roles in the films and am certain that his gifts far transcend the cliché that the crude, virile roughneck tended to become in his career and the work of a host of admirers. Brando is not to blame for his imitators on stage and screen, but it is unfortunate that he has allowed himself to be limited. It is saddening that a man who could attain the stature of the great figures of the English and French stage finds it more rewarding to remain in the films, which have not stretched his potentialities to their fullest.

Consider, on the other hand, the career of Laurence Olivier, Britain's finest actor and the best of our time on the English-speaking stage. He has done his share of films, but the stage has always been the core of his activity. Because his base has been London, he has been able to function in the diverse, modern world without sacrificing his fundamental concentration on the stage or his chances to share in the huge earnings available on the screen.

London is the center of Britain's arts and entertainments. The film and television studios are in the city or easily accessible. An actor can work on the stage and be within easy reach of movie and TV opportunities. Young Peter O'Toole found time for a taut, passionate Shylock at Stratford-on-Avon and for a Hamlet at the National Theatre between remunerative film jobs. In the United States a continent separates New York and Hollywood, and though distances have shrunk, they have not been eliminated. An actor in New York, no matter how clever, cannot appear regularly on Broadway and simultaneously make films on the West Coast.

To an Olivier the theatre is an endless challenge. He never has ceased to enlarge his range. He recalls that when he started in the theatre he appeared in more than ten flops in succession. He regards these failures as a matter of great good luck, for they saved him from being typed. They gave him an awareness of the possibilities open to an actor. For today's beginners the privilege to learn from failure has narrowed. In New York a young Olivier probably would be destroyed by a run of fiascos.

The problems of American acting have their roots in haphazard training. Of the abundance of natural talent in the United States there is no doubt. Its nurture, however, is another thing, a matter of chance and caprice. Our technical schools and studios vary wildly in the quality of their training. Some have highly competent teachers of another generation and are preparing actors for approaches that are now old-fashioned and unsuitable for plays, theatres and styles reflecting our world. Other teachers resort to idiosyncratic, limited techniques that constrict rather than liberate a young actor's gifts. Worst of all, too many teachers neglect the fundamentals of the actor's craft.

Sitting in the theatre night after night, on Broadway and off and in repertory houses across the land, I have been appalled by the inadequacy of so many young actors in their handling of the indispensable tools of their trade. They do not know how to produce and project their voices; when they have to work in a theatre without amplification they cannot be heard beyond the first few rows. They do not know how to speak their own language, and the depressing thing is that they do not hear themselves. Neither do many of the directors, and if they do, they often are unaware of what is wrong. Many actors have not learned to be in full control of their bodies, which with the voice are the vehicle of their performance. They have not learned to move properly and even less to remain in repose, to listen and to react so as to be an integral element of a scene and not a conspicuously loose end. The real actor is fully engaged even when he is not speaking. By his responses he can create mood and tension. I remember watching Sybil Thorndike in a mediocre English play dominate a London stage that also held Edith Evans and Wendy Hiller by the sheer concentration of a long, intense, mesmeric silence.

It has been wisely observed that an actor trained for the classic stage can easily adapt himself to the demands of modern drama, for he has all the basic equipment. There is a large measure of truth in this dictum, though I am not sure that even the most thoroughly grounded actor would be comfortable in every sort of role. The trouble in the United States is that so few of our actors have a thorough grounding. Those who have grown up entirely on contemporary plays tend to be lost in the classics. They have no idea of how to read verse, no notion of the stylish swagger of comedy or the grand thunder of tragedy, little feeling for anything but a narrow realistic theatre.

There are Americans who have found the guidance they needed and have prepared themselves conscientiously for a broad, versatile career. They have good voices, speak English clearly and well, can move and remain in repose and can adapt themselves to diverse styles. But we do not have so many as the English stage, and we certainly do not have anywhere near so many of star eminence. Besides Olivier there are Paul Scofield, John Gielgud, Richard Burton, Michael Redgrave, Alec Guinness, Emlyn Williams, Alan

Badel, Rex Harrison, as well as younger ones like Albert Finney and O'Toole.

I do not wish to exaggerate British virtues and American short-comings. Plenty of British actors are limited in talent, training and experience to playing themselves. Many British actors swallow their words, speak through their noses and abuse the Queen's English. There are many Johnny-one-notes in the London theatre. But the atmosphere in London is somewhat more propitious for an actor's growth. The training is likely to be more orderly and is often followed by several years with a provincial repertory company. There are two first-rate, nationally scaled repertory companies—the National and Royal Shakespeare Theatres—to which an actor may be called and in which he can expand his techniques and horizons as he works with outstanding artists. If he decides to move on to the West End, Broadway or the films, he does not necessarily abandon the repertory company forever. The best British actors return for a season or two to play roles they would not do otherwise and thus they refine and deepen their skills and perceptions.

What is true of the British actors holds true for the actresses. The stars do not hesitate to ally themselves with a permanent company. Peggy Ashcroft has devoted years to the Royal Shakespeare Theatre. So has Dorothy Tutin, one of the young luminaries. Joan Plowright and Maggie Smith, bright young talents, have been members of the National Theatre. Grant that these women have personality and natural gifts. But they also have a command of the essential techniques, and they play roles, not themselves. I have seen Miss Tutin as Portia, Viola, Antigone and in bits as Elizabeth I and Victoria; the characters were foremost, not the quirks of an actress. I have seen Miss Plowright in Wesker's *Roots,* Delaney's *A Taste of Honey* and Chekhov's *Uncle Vanya* and each role was perceptively and touchingly individualized.

I do not mean to suggest that the American stage is bereft of actors worthy to stand with the finest in other lands. The Lunts have been refulgent ornaments of our stage for more than four decades. From their first joint appearance in *The Guardsman* in 1924, Lynn Fontanne and Alfred Lunt have been a sparkling team. She was born and began her training in England, but her career has been largely American. Although they did not cover the full range of the classics on Broadway and did not devote much time to tragedy, there was hardly anything they touched that they did not grace. One thinks of their distinction in the brooding visions of O'Neill and the black satire of Dürrenmatt, and one remembers their glinting wit and exhilarating comedy in Shaw and Sherwood. They played together and against each other with the gleam and thrust of flashing sabers. They knew their craft, yet never ceased to refine their techniques. In the midst of a long run, they saw to it that neither they nor their colleagues took a performance for granted. On the closing night of a New York success they might still be improving a minute detail. They scrupulously followed the dictates of artistic conscience, but they could also laugh at themselves.

I remember when Lunt was staging *Così Fan Tutte* at the Metropolitan Opera in the 1951–52 season and was achieving, even with several opera singers whose acting gamut was almost nonexistent, a dazzling, laughing production that perfectly suited Mozart's opera. Although he established a style so like his own in artificial comedy, formal elegance in an antic mood, he did not forget that underneath the story's artifices Mozart had remembered the heart. He made sure that in her big second-act aria Fiordiligi ceased to be a charming puppet and became a vulnerable woman. No meaningless action was allowed to obtrude on the aria. With the uncommon sensitivity of an artist he knew that this moment of truth must be conveyed purely and simply through Mozart's genius and the singer's voice.

During the preparation of *Così*, which I watched from time to time, Lunt fussed and fretted and gloomily predicted that he would prove that the opera house was not his métier, and I wrote a piece poking fun at his fears and lamentations. Was he affronted? Of course not. And when he introduced me to Miss Fontanne at a dress rehearsal, she smiled quizzically. "So you're the one who wrote that mischievous piece about Alfred," she said, and her amused tone gave a hint of the sources of the dancing, malicious, probing spirit that informed their high comic style.

Although Alla Nazimova was not born in the United States, she looms in my memory as the finest actress I have seen on our stages. Is it distance that lends enchantment? In any event, I can still call up in my mind's eye her Ranevskaya in *The Cherry Orchard*. It did not—and does not now in retrospect—seem like acting. This was a human being—impulsive, wistful, foolish, generous and gallant. One could not imagine that Chekhov had invented her or that Nazimova was reading an author's lines. Through a miracle a heartwarming woman out of another time and place materialized on the stage and, though her words were spoken in accented English, she was specifically old-world Russian and at the same time endearingly, credibly true here and everywhere.

My admiration for great ladies like Helen Hayes and Katharine Cornell is not unreserved. Miss Hayes taught herself to be a superb technician. Her enormous skill was impressively illustrated in the metamorphoses of appearance, movement and speech as she lived through a long, royal life in Laurence Housman's *Victoria Regina*. To her instinct for the stage she added a relentless concentration on detail, and she had the knack of digging for hidden facets of a role. What I found lacking at times was a sense of deeper truth, a sense of an animating spirit to irradiate a handsomely composed portrait.

Miss Cornell was always guided by the strength of her will and intelligence. Candida and Elizabeth Barrett were ideal for her gifts. She knew how to bring to life women with independence of mind and character, how to make irresistible their pride, how to convey a sense of fundamental wisdom and unostentatious wit. She also had an uncommon affinity for stateliness and grandeur. What I found wanting in some of her roles was passion. When she attempted Shakespeare's Juliet and Cleopatra, she gave us simulations of their consuming emotions.

Miss Hayes and Miss Cornell, like the Lunts, spent a lifetime dedicated to the American stage. They did not rush off to Hollywood when tempted with huge fees. It may be that they were worshiped excessively for themselves, but as conscientious leaders they deserved admiration. They tried to keep their standards high; they tried to make creative use of a theatre that was not always an art. They gave pleasure and occasionally a sense of adventure and excitement to several generations of theatregoers.

Because of their eminence, actresses like Miss Hayes and Miss Cornell could forge opportunities for themselves. Others, less fortunate, could not do so with similar consistency. However, I have fond memories of the special gifts of others. Tallulah Bankhead could draw fire like flint on stone from a unique toughness, as she did with Regina, the craftiest of the "Little Foxes." Katharine Hepburn could communicate, with her flat Main Line accent and a charming, gawky manner, the brightness of sophistication and the feel of its emptiness, as she did in *The Philadelphia Story*, but, oh my, was she miscast as Shakespeare's Cleopatra! Ruth Gordon knew how to be warm and credible under a mannered, comic façade, as she was in *The Matchmaker*. Judith Anderson, Australian-born but long of our theatre, had the voice, endurance and passionate abandon to encompass Medea. Julie Harris harks back to the concentration of the older generation in her determination not to be confined to a single style or commercially attractive image. She attempts comedy, farce and tragedy; her achievements have encompassed the affecting and funny pre-adolescent in *The Member of the Wedding*, an earthy, intelligent Joan in *The Lark* and an ardent Juliet, for which she gladly spent a season at Canada's Stratford. Rosemary Harris, English by birth and training, has allied herself with our stage and has become, in her technical resource and personal glow, one of our ablest performers. Kim Stanley has an impressive personal intensity, which reached its finest moment as Masha in a revival of *The Three Sisters*. Geraldine Page has a gift for a kind of tremulous strength, as was evidenced in her Nina in a revival of *Strange Interlude*. Potentially one of the commanding actresses of our generation is Maureen Stapleton, but she has absented herself from the stage for long periods. Diana Sands in her temperament, intensity and eagerness to broaden her range is a talent in her own right and represents the new freedom of a Negro to be an actress in any style and not to be held down by the color of her skin.

In the musical theatre I have fond recollections of four women —Ethel Merman, Mary Martin, Carol Channing and Beatrice Lillie. Miss Merman's trumpetlike geniality, her sure knowledge of how to make every move and inflection count, have filled our musical theatre with a refreshing earthiness. Miss Martin has exuded a personal radiance that irradiates us all; yet when she sings, in that astonishingly full, low voice, which gives the joyous lie to her lady-like appearance, she seems to be singing to you alone. Miss Channing acts and sings with a kind of childlike knowingness. The high color in her cheeks, the gleam in her eye and the scratchy lilt in her voice proclaim her pleasure at spreading pleasure. Miss Lillie transcends discipline and split-second timing inevitable on the stage to remain a free spirit. This is not to say that she is anything but professional in her scrupulous attention to script and score. But her comic afflatus cannot be suppressed. I like the way it expressed itself on the opening night of a merely passable musical, *High Spirits*. Playing a raffish medium, she sat in her boudoir in nightgown, nightcap and slippers adorned with bunnies and sang a song of rapt self-approval. When she finished, the audience roared its delight. It would not let the show go on, and Miss Lillie thought that it would be nice to show her gratitude. She improvised a travesty of a ballerina doing arabesques and the like—a complete, hilarious vignette. Again thunderous applause—again the show stopped. What to do now? Miss Lillie went through a series of mock curtsies of a *prima ballerina assoluta* thanking her devoted public. Spontaneously she had enriched the show, and the additions stayed in for the rest of the run.

In the musical theatre, which is our distinctive métier, we still produce new artists of stature. However, the old school of comedians who gladdened so many musical comedies in the early decades of the century has faded, and the reason is not far to seek. There are fewer places for comedians to develop except in front of mikes —in nightclubs, on radio and television—and a man chained to a mechanical gadget is not likely to become a resourceful actor. Performers like Jack Benny and Bob Hope have mastered the art of communicating personality even when they fire a volley of gags from a fixed position in front of a mike, but their early experience on the stage has been a source of strength. Bert Lahr is one of the rare, delightful leftovers from a day of mobile comedians who knew how to combine movement, facial expression, timing and the spaces of the entire stage; even in a shabby musical he can create fun and he has the skill to move over into the world of Beckett and play *Waiting for Godot* with poignant lunacy. Danny Kaye, immensely adaptable, can compete with the best of the new crop of stand-up comedians in front of a mike, but he has retained the skills that make him at home on any stage. Have you ever caught his mad routine as a maestro when he undertakes to conduct a major orchestra? He once made a benefit appearance as guest conductor of the New York Philharmonic and did a marvelous comic job. Afterward he told me with immense relish how he had thrown the musicians an unexpected curve. He had prepared himself by listening to a recording of a piece he was to conduct and, thanks to his keen ear, had memorized it in considerable detail. On the podium he stopped the instrumentalists midway to make a point. A joke, they thought; but he knew what he was talking about. Do you recall what he could do with a scat song in *Lady in the Dark* (remember the tongue-twisting "Tchaikovsky"?) and *Let's Face It* (remember "Farming")? Zero Mostel is another complete comedian who took years to polish his craft. Despite his girth and size, he can move like a ballet dancer and make a comic point with the delicacy of a Chaplin. Like Lahr, he can shift to the theatre without music and enrich it with his taste and personality.

The American theatre is weakest in the classics. Our Shakespeareans are often tentative and pallid. There is, of course, a magnificent exception like Morris Carnovsky's Lear. Building on years of wide experience and approaching the role from a backlog of other Shakespearean parts, he tackled Lear with the boldness of a veteran willing to risk everything on a big conception. In his first try at Stratford, Connecticut, he had an impressive grip on the tragic bitterness and ultimate humility of the role. He then worked on it further in Chicago, Los Angeles and Stratford, Connecticut, seeking answers to questions that had eluded him and finding new heartrending depths.

Despite the chaotic pattern of our theatre, young men manage to find an outlet for their desire to grow as artists. George Griz-

zard went to Minneapolis to play Hamlet and Richard II and discovered that he had exceptional gifts for character parts with a
remarkable performance of the Dauphin in *Saint Joan*. Michael
O'Sullivan got a perhaps premature shot at Lear in San Francisco
but was ready for a fine off-Broadway achievement as the director
in *Six Characters in Search of an Author* and for a splendid Tartuffe at the Lincoln Center Repertory Theatre. James Earl Jones,
who has worked a great deal off Broadway largely in Negro roles,
showed how much passion and size he could bring to Othello in
Central Park and in an off-Broadway run. Sidney Poitier is another Negro who could become an important actor if he could
afford to take a sabbatical from films and could find the stage opportunities worthy of his potentialities.

One cannot speak of acting at this point in the American theatre's history without recognition of the dominance of the director,
for good or evil. It has not been uncommon in recent decades
for directors like Elia Kazan, Mike Nichols, Tony Richardson,
Tyrone Guthrie, Gower Champion and Jerome Robbins to receive a larger percentage of a show's gross than the star. Indeed, a
director like Kazan has influenced the reshaping of plays until
they were reflections of his vision as much as the author's. Miller,
Williams, Wilder and MacLeish are among those who can bear
witness to the power of his drive and imagination. When his imprint with its sharpness of outline, insistence of tension, eye for
the vivid, even savage detail of naked action is right for a character, scene or play, it can make for snap, precision, eye-catching and
breathtaking theatricalism. It can, however, be disturbing to a
play's integrity, and it can be downright disastrous in a case like
The Changeling, a seventeenth-century classic. Kazan's instinct
for what is right for him rarely betrayed him, and for years he was
a commanding figure in the commercial theatre. He could do
whatever he wished, choosing plays and players virtually at his
discretion, demanding rewrites to meet his conceptions, compelling actors to perform with an intensity almost beyond their
powers and obliging others to adopt mannerisms of style that
eventually hampered them.

As much as any man, Kazan has been responsible for the evolution of what became known as the director's theatre. The seeds for this development were sprouting in the 1920's when Kaufman and Abbott proved that a strong controlling hand guided by a shrewd instinct for the stage could pay off. Other American directors who have become a species of star are Joshua Logan, Harold Clurman, Alan Schneider, José Quintero, Joseph Anthony, Mike Nichols, Abe Burrows, Gower Champion and Jerome Robbins. Among the British directors who have played significant roles in our theatre the most notable have been Guthrie, Peter Brook and Tony Richardson.

Guthrie, like Kazan, is a man whose personality and viewpoint have colored everything he has done on the stage. His productions have been in many ways re-creations, like the interpretations of some conductors who take a familiar symphony or opera and reshape it to their own taste. One thinks of Leopold Stokowski, master technician of orchestral sound and discipline, as a comparison, for the conductor had a similar gift for control, flamboyance and personal expression. Guthrie's imagination is always alive, and his invention is unflagging. He cheerfully expriments with the classics, moving them forward centuries in setting and costume. His *Hamlet* for the inauguration of the Guthrie Theatre in Minneapolis was an example of his personal touch; it was ludicrous and infuriating, provocative and illuminating, but never boring. He set the tragedy in a twentieth-century principality and invested it with a host of modernisms. Some were totally ridiculous: Laertes wearing a trench coat with a holster and pistol over it like a comic secret agent of films or TV; Laertes thrusting the pistol into Claudius's ribs, Ophelia in outdoor whites with a brace of tennis racquets under her arm seeing Laertes off; spotlights on the fringes of the open stage to light the play within the play, which were also turned to rake the audience; the cry in a juicy British accent of a courtier during the swordplay between Hamlet and Laertes, "Most irregulah!" One could argue that for a public with little or no experience of *Hamlet,* this freedom of style robbed the tragedy of its stride and grandeur and that the clever modernisms were a director's amused, self-indulgent emendations that did not give the play the immediacy he sought. True, but there were things in this *Hamlet* that had freshness. The nature of the politicking in a small state came through with special sharpness. One felt a heightened sympathy for a Hamlet faced with an overwhelming problem of conscience in a court redolent of intrigue.

Each director has his own way of working. Some are cool and businesslike, some patient and laconic, some flamboyant like a swashbuckler in a melodrama, some Svengali-like with young actresses whom they treat like Trilby, some endlessly garrulous and some frenetic. There is the anecdote of a director who staged a great musical success in the fifties with so many frantic changes of mind and direction that when it was over one of the authors said, "If I ever have to work again with that fellow, I'll cut my throat first."

I have the feeling that while the importance of the director will not diminish—note well how several successes by Mike Nichols caused every producer to camp at his doorstep—a subtle shift has begun. A new group of directors is coming to prominence. Among them are strong personalities with clear minds and firm viewpoints, but they have no desire, expressed or inarticulate, to remake every play in their own images. They have a grasp of the literature of the drama, they have imagination, they think of theatre in larger terms than its commercial possibilities. They look upon their labors with a play as an effort and a duty to let the play speak for itself. They abjure the temptation to wrench it out of shape and to torture it into their mouthpiece, rather than the author's. Alan Schneider and Ulu Grosbard are typical of this new breed.

The new school of directors naturally has been conditioned by new ideas in staging. The increasing adoption of thrust or open stages, which offer exciting opportunities for the production of classics, has stimulated the development of flexibility. Some plays, directors and players are lost without the support of the familiar box stage and its delimiting proscenium, and there have been egregious miscalculations in what has been attempted on thrust or arena stages. But the willingness to try fresh approaches or, in essence, to find new validity in old ones—the open stage, after all, goes back to Periclean Athens and Elizabethan London—has been an exhilarating instrument for directors, actors and playwrights who have sought to break out of the naturalism that dominated and often confined the American theatre in the middle decades of the twentieth century.

These changes in orientation have been accompanied by new freedom and flexibility in stage design. For many years a set was an exercise in meticulous imitation. Even now there are endless plays on Broadway in which living rooms look so real you could move in and begin housekeeping. Were it not for union regulations, you could use one set interchangeably for a score of plays, saving money on salaries, furniture and props.

The open stage has required a new attitude toward design, also noticeable in proscenium theatres, which need not inhibit fresh ideas. Writers and directors are rediscovering the ancient truth that it is best to release the audience's imagination and to involve it in the creative process. Sets have been simplified to stress allusiveness rather than literalism. Lighting is being used creatively. The proliferation of electronic equipment backstage has given the scenery wings. On proscenium as well as open stages it is not uncommon for sets to be changed in full view, often with the swiftness and agility of a magician pulling rabbits out of a hat.

Sets in themselves cannot make a play or a musical. Imaginative designers, whether veterans like Jo Mielziner, Donald Oenslager, Boris Aronson and Oliver Smith or the newer school like Tanya Moiseiwitsch, Will Steven Armstrong, William and Jean Eckart and William Ritman, know that their business is to provide an evocative background that expresses the play's mood and meaning.

But if the new ideas and equipment have liberated stage design and the audience's imagination, they also have provided directors and producers with tempting new gimmicks. There are Broadway productions that, like a small boy with a new toy, show off the trickiness of the sets as if they were the center of attraction. They invoke speed, color, all the razzle-dazzle of staging and electronic know-how to awe the naïve. The more bloodless and infirm a piece the more likely that the sets will perform capers. Even interesting moments in plays and musicals are distorted because a designer, director or producer tricks them out in visual effects made possible by the latest electronic marvels. If we are not careful, we shall go from the exaggerations and constrictions of the director's theatre into the tyranny of a gadgeted one.

◆((

CHAPTER XXXV

NEW FORCES AND NEW HOPE

Rꜰᴘᴇᴀᴛᴇᴅʟʏ ɪɴ ᴄʀɪsɪs and often on the brink of the abyss, the American theatre recurrently falls into such disarray and despair that its prospects of survival look bleak. How many times in two centuries have sober judges pronounced our stage so trifling that its continuance was a matter of supreme indifference? How many times has the American theatre plumbed what looked like new lows?

And they were, you may be sure, lows. But were they as depressed as the nadir reached in the early 1960's? Yes, and lower. Not that I wish to minimize the shoddiness of the preponderance of what the commercial theatre offered in the sixties. The cost of mounting trash reached new peaks. Although the losses in time and money were prodigious, the injury to human pride and dignity was severer. But even as standards deteriorated—probably because things were going from bad to worse—new forces began to coalesce and new signs of hope could be discerned.

Producers in the commercial theatre might continue on their nervous competitive way, hoping that the next throw of the dice would be the unimaginably lucky one. But they were also taking stock. Led by the energetic and successful Harold Prince, they attempted to revitalize their League of New York Theatres and undertook a study, chaired by John F. Wharton, lawyer and longtime friend of the theatre, that they hoped would lead to more comfortable and attractive, if not cheaper, theatregoing. They were aware that they had a responsibility to do something beyond musicals and light comedies that might make a killing. They realized that patrons with adult concerns had been alienated by unending piffle and had deserted the living theatre for the more venturesome cinema, particularly the best foreign films.

One may think what one likes of the methods and personality of David Merrick, and his fellow producers and other theatrical people regard him with something less than modified rapture. But one must evaluate objectively what appears on the stage under his imprimatur without regard to the pyrotechnics of comment and display that mark his operations. In his competitive zest he often outbids rivals for choice foreign and native works; he is not above raising the established ante on royalties and percentages to sign writers, directors or actors in great demand. When business at *Look Back in Anger,* a play well worth supporting, fell off, a woman unexpectedly rushed one night from the audience onto the stage and slapped the face of the actor playing the irascible, offensive Jimmie Porter. The result was a coup in publicity—front-page stories. Was the public amused? Did it feel gulled when the truth leaked out? And what about the idea of hiring a sandwich man to march in front of a theatre with another producer's *Flower Drum Song* to hail Merrick's *The World of Suzie Wong* as "the only truly authentic Chinese play in New York"? Was that a divertingly impudent stunt or just dirty pool?

Merrick has declared that he will do anything to stimulate patronage. He has also indicated that some of the outlandish things he says and does are said and done in a spirit of good, clean fun—to amuse himself and the public. Are you amused or repelled? No matter. What does matter is his record. He has produced trivial and trashy things—and turned some into money-makers. But he has also committed himself to theatre of ideas and quality. Like Roger L. Stevens, who has also produced or shared in producing a large number of works season after season, Merrick has presented plays that deserved to be put on—the plays of Anouilh,

Osborne, Shelagh Delaney, and a pungent revue like *Oh What a Lovely War*. Lately he has set up his own foundation with profits from other productions to present plays difficult to finance and mount under a profit system.

While one respects the desire of the commercial producers to serve a mature theatre when they can, one cannot count on them to establish institutions with continuity and high purpose. The days when free enterprise could do so are long since gone. One can no longer expect the reincarnation of a substantial private enterprise like Wallack's Theatre in the decades before and after the Civil War with its accent on English plays, classic and modern, and its accomplished, well-balanced acting company. New institutions are needed. The promise of the sixties was that they might prove to be the turning point in our theatrical history, that they might stimulate the creation of such institutions and that they might provide the encouragement and assistance to those struggling to stay alive.

The Lincoln Center of the Performing Arts has committed itself to a permanent repertory theatre, and even if the first years have been difficult and strife-torn, the commitment stands. The Actors Studio has founded a production arm in the Actors Studio Theatre. The Phoenix Theatre has arranged an alliance with the Association of Producing Artists, a cooperative of theatre people who decided to work out their own destinies away from the long, empty wastes that lay before them in the commercial theatre. The American Place Theatre was established in a church to foster literate drama. Outside New York new professional, permanent companies have sprung up. And the foundations, notably the Ford and Rockefeller, have made large grants designed to encourage a progressive, living dramatic culture.

The story of the Lincoln Center Repertory Theatre is in its earliest chapters but has had its share of crisis, bloodletting and suspense. Before the second season was over, the original co-directors, Robert Whitehead and Elia Kazan, were gone, and the last of four promised productions was canceled and refunds had to be made to subscribers. Nevertheless, despite conflicts, anxieties and disappointments, a start had been made. Despite rough going, the project would continue.

The company was formed several years before its permanent home, the Vivian Beaumont Theatre, was completed. The first co-directors had as little personal experience of repertory theatre as the board of directors which chose them. Whitehead and Kazan were aware of what they had to learn and thought that it would be useful to have a shakedown cruise of several seasons before berthing at the Beaumont. Their first notion was to preempt a vacant lot on Lincoln Center land and put up a temporary structure. They estimated that the cost of such a theatre would not exceed the two-year rental of a Broadway house. Their plan was opposed by powerful members of the board, and they came up with an alternative—a temporary theatre on a site off Washington Square lent by New York University. Again there was opposition by board members. When Whitehead personally persuaded the board of ANTA to finance such a theatre, his board went along.

Built on simple architectural and engineering principles, the ANTA Washington Square Theatre with its auditorium raked steeply like a classic amphitheatre and with its huge open playing space was ready in a matter of months. It was as if New York had reverted to the happy days of 150 years earlier—though working hours were now stringently regulated by union rules and costs were affected by stiff overtime charges. There was the inevitable scramble to prepare the theatre for the first preview audience of the opening production—Arthur Miller's *After the Fall*. On the night before this preview the seats still had to be fastened into place, and among those who plied hammers and screwdrivers into the early hours of the morning were Whitehead, Kazan and Miller.

The first season generated fierce controversy. The commercial theatre sniped at the impertinent infant because it was presenting new plays, which Broadway considered its province and thought it could do as well, if not better. The intransigent advocates of instant perfection savaged the company because it did not at once meet their pet specifications. One wonders how much irritation and envy were mixed into the fury at a newcomer which began life with an advance of 47,000 subscribers.

The company made mistakes, as it was bound to do. It is even probable that Whitehead and Kazan were not ideal choices to preside over its destinies. Their decision to float their initial season on two new American plays and *Marco Millions,* lesser O'Neill, was unwise. The first production of the second season, Kazan's misguided and vulgar version of the seventeenth-century *The Changeling,* was a disaster, but the next two, Miller's *Incident at Vichy* and a revival of Molière's *Tartuffe,* were anything but a disgrace.

Controversy in the theatre is not only inevitable but healthy. It is a symptom of good circulation in a vital organism. *After the Fall* was reviled by some as a shameless, self-pitying author's *apologia pro vita sua* and by others as a cheap example of kissing and telling. As one who thought well of the play, I was not outraged by its autobiographical content, nor was I upset because it unmistakably and ungallantly described Marilyn Monroe, the author's deceased, unhappy second wife. I felt that there was merit in the honesty with which its protagonist looked at himself and his world. I did not regard the play as a great work of art, but it had maturity because in the end the protagonist assumed responsibility for his acts and fate. The victim of his own emotional flaws, he was at last prepared to face the truth of his nature. I thought that *Incident at Vichy,* with its inquest into the roots of evil that could unleash a monstrous horror like Nazism, was larger in size and deeper in content. In both plays Miller retained, even intensified, his command of the stage. Scenes were built with power and urgency; character had the resonance of life.

Behrman's *But for Whom Charlie,* presented in the first season, reflected the author's wry awareness of our world's pretensions, but it was weary as well as disenchanted. What was worse, it was poorly directed by Kazan and ill at ease on the open stage. But even in the first two seasons there were indications that actors like Jason Robards Jr., David Wayne and Joseph Wiseman could enlarge and be enlarged by a repertory theatre.

The troubles of the Whitehead-Kazan stewardship boiled over

early in the second season. Kazan in fact had quietly shed his co-directorship before *The Changeling* opened. The Repertory Theatre board and some Lincoln Center officials said privately that they were dissatisfied with Whitehead's artistic and business leadership, and they were well within their province to conclude that he must be replaced. But the manner in which they went about negotiating for a replacement was clumsy and tactless, and Whitehead pulled out indignantly. After weeks of conscientious investigation, the board chose Herbert Blau and Jules Irving, founders and directors of the Actors Workshop in San Francisco, and they took over the assignment of reorganizing the company and preparing for the entry into the Vivian Beaumont Theatre.

For Blau and Irving, who had created the Actors Workshop out of their own remitting toil and sacrifices, the new job was both recognition and challenge. In their first San Francisco season they had been only a few dollars from collapse. In their final Workshop season, though their operations now encompassed two theatres, tours, training activities and a budget of $350,000, they were still functioning precariously. The Workshop had won the loyal support of an intelligent public, but it still lacked the wide backing in patronage and money that it deserved.

On the basis of what they had done in San Francisco, one might hope Blau and Irving would infuse the Lincoln Center Repertory Theatre with ideas and vision. The expectation that a permanent theatre of provocative and mature content could be built in New York was renewed. The hope that Lincoln Center might do its part in recalling the greatness of the drama's past and exploring the ideas of stimulating contemporaries could be rekindled.

The Actors Studio also appeared at last to be on the march. In its years as a professional corner where theatre people could study and work and, with luck, expand technique and deepen perceptions, it had become, no matter what one thought of the "Method" associated with it, a force for morale and growth. Its influence was wide and penetrating, if not always beneficent. Its leaders no doubt expected to be part of Lincoln Center and were hurt that the Studio was not invited to move in as a unit. In any case, the decision to activate a producing program bore a high potential, though in practice the operation at the outset was erratic.

The revival of *Strange Interlude* as the opening production had some justification since it provided a chance to revisit a great success of the late twenties and offered challenging parts to a number of actors. But there was little artistic reason to produce June Havoc's *Marathon '33*, an unleavened recollection of a mindless, depression-time phenomenon, or an arty piece like James Costigan's *Baby Want a Kiss*, even if it brought two movie stars, Joanne Woodward and Paul Newman, back to the stage. Baldwin's *Blues for Mister Charlie*, though rhetorical in style and hysterical in tone, was more like what one had a right to expect from a serious venture, and the revival of *The Three Sisters*, staged by Lee Strasberg, the Studio's reigning divinity, was proof that the venture could be significant.

Like the Lincoln Center Repertory Theatre, the Actors Studio Theatre had a right to make mistakes. It was entitled to time and indulgence as it sought to hammer out a fruitful course. In the 1964–65 season it paused to evaluate and plan for what it hoped would be a sustained and vigorous program in the years to come.

As private enterprise in the theatre grew more cautious, it was imperative to find as many ways as possible to organize companies and theatres on some sort of noncapricious basis. Decades earlier the youthful, vigorous Theatre Guild had made itself the medium for powerful intellectual forces and a rallying place for all sorts of talent; in the sixties it had become another commercial management. A cooperative like the A.P.A. now was one way to cope with the acute pressures and to fill some of the gaping voids in our theatre. Actors, directors and designers led by Ellis Rabb formed a cooperative determined to employ its members's energies and talents. The A.P.A. appeared in seasons on college campuses— Princeton and Michigan—and undertook some touring. It made an independent visit to New York, then joined the Phoenix, offering a spirited repertory of Pirandello, Gorki, Molière and Cohan in the first joint season and an even livelier one of Shaw, Tolstoi and Giraudoux in the second. Although it had no subsidy, the

A.P.A. was hell-bent on retaining its integrity and independence and against returning to the rat race of the commercial theatre.

The American Place Theatre, sparked by an energetic and idealistic clergyman, Sidney Lanier, undertook, at first as a kind of private workshop, to encourage established and new writers of quality to try their hand at the stage. To this end it provided them with readings of works in progress. In the autumn of 1964, it expanded into the public arena. A church on West 46th Street in New York was lent by the Protestant Episcopal Diocese and its sanctuary turned into a well-equipped stage. Here the first offering open to the public on a membership basis was two parts of *The Old Glory*, a three-part play by one of America's leading poets, Robert Lowell. The last and longest section, *Benito Cereno*, based on Melville's story, achieved tragic size. It was an impressive beginning of what might become a new intellectual agency in the theatre. It gave actors like Lester Rawlins and Roscoe Lee Browne a chance to shine in a highly literate and dramatic style and Jonathan Miller, once of *Beyond the Fringe*, an opportunity to reveal his mettle as a director.

The time had come for decentralization. New York would inevitably be the center of our theatre for a long time to come, but other cities across the nation were arising from a long somnolence. Zelda Fichandler in Washington, Nina Vance in Houston and Blau and Irving in San Francisco had established intelligent, struggling, dedicated companies in the fifties even as had Margo Jones in Dallas in the forties. I saw for myself in Houston in 1961 that wealthy citizens ignored the valiant company in their midst while they dissipated huge sums backing vulgar productions in New York. When the Ford Foundation offered partial underwriting for a nucleus of skilled actors, San Francisco and Houston were painfully laggard in raising matching funds.

Despite endless difficulties, the young regional companies endured and inspired the founding of other troupes. Tyrone Guthrie lent his prestige and imagination to the creation of an exciting theatre and company, dedicated primarily to Shakespeare, in Ontario's Stratford, and then to a repertory company in a new home, named gratefully the Tyrone Guthrie Theatre, in Minneapolis.

Seattle took advantage of its 1962 Fair to prepare the site, buildings and atmosphere for an arts center and imported Stuart Vaughan to organize and direct a permanent repertory company. In Oklahoma City a young enthusiast, Mark Scism, for some seasons fought indifference to build a company and was generously embraced when the community discovered that a theatre could be useful in showing badly wanted scientific talent that the city could offer something beyond creature comforts.

The Ford Foundation, which had been making modest grants in the drama, decided in 1962 to donate more than $6,000,000. The new grants were designed to help Houston and Oklahoma City build new homes for its permanent companies, to contribute toward wiping out a mortgage on the new Arena Stage in Washington, to encourage advances in San Francisco and Los Angeles, to provide the means to Connecticut's Stratford to set up a training program in classic acting, and to aid the Actors Studio in the formation of its producing arm. Several years later the Rockefeller Foundation elected to increase its support of cultural activities, including the theatre. A typical grant provided funds to the Seattle Repertory Theatre to keep a company intact for study and training in the off months.

In the 1960's there were signs of a new association between the campus and the professional theatre. For decades college and university drama departments had functioned according to their varying aims and talents. In a few places valuable creative work was done; in others apearances were more impressive than the reality of accomplishment. American confidence in imposing and expensive buildings rather than in people and ideas was visible in campuses across the land. On a western campus I saw in a new arts building two magnificent theatres—one of medium size and the other small—with excellent backstage facilities and the most modern equipment. I thought of the strange irony of a nation that gave money unstintingly to furnish superb plants for youngsters who were just learning and who often had no gift or desire for theatre as a career while men and women who could act, direct and design were obliged to work in shabby, ill-equipped plants.

Was the answer going to be collaboration between professionals and campus? Princeton, Michigan, the University of California in Los Angeles and Stanford thought so. The first two brought in professional units for extended visits. At U.C.L.A. the Theatre Group was organized and supported by University Extension; with Ford Foundation help, it looked forward to its own building and a permanent professional company. Stanford set up a repertory company on a professional basis on its own campus.

Colleges and universities were following the fashion by establishing their own arts centers. At Dartmouth the Hopkins Art Center had two theatres, and in the summers it offered seasons built around professional troupes. Brandeis used an outdoor auditorium as the forum for a summer season of professional theatre oriented to the community at large. Wherever you turned, new arts centers were being built and dedicated on campuses.

Had the American stage found a panacea for the ills that plagued it? No one could say. Some of the plans and activities looked unhappily to be like an imitative preoccupation with bricks and mortar. But there was no question that new forces were in ferment and might make a difference.

Great Britain's example could not be ignored. After a century of talk, Britain founded its National Theatre and placed Laurence Olivier in artistic command. Starting in the autumn of 1963, it quickly affirmed its validity. The Royal Shakespeare Theatre, whose government grants were increased steadily and deservedly, became a vital, progressive, adventurous force in the sixties, under the visionary leadership of Peter Hall in association with Peter Brook and Michel Saint-Denis. Playing in London's Aldwych Theatre as well as in Stratford-on-Avon, this reinvigorated company brought new ideas to the performance of Shakespeare and plunged into a vivid, controversial repertory of old and new works in its London home. By using its permanent company interchangeably, it enriched the players and the British theatre, and as if to spread its largess of boldness and imagination, it sent sections of its company on world tours, notably a bitterly modern, existentialist *Lear* with Scofield in the title role.

There was the example of France, which under the guidance of André Malraux, Minister of Culture in De Gaulle's Fifth Republic, revitalized its old national stages and increased its support of other Parisian and regional theatres. The Comédie Française as well as the Théâtre National Populaire and the Renaud-Barrault company at the Odéon received generous subsidies, and provocative experimenters like Roger Planchon in Lyons were granted the opportunity to function daringly.

The United States Government, traditionally averse to subsidizing the arts though it has long been generous with its assistance to one industry or another, was approaching the day when it must act. President Kennedy had tiptoed carefully in this direction, and the pressure on President Johnson was growing. In the summer of 1964, Congress, after years of hesitation, finally passed a bill to set up a national advisory council on the arts. It was a timid, narrow gesture, unsupported by an appropriation of any size, and it was months before President Johnson got around to naming the council. Nevertheless, it was a step toward acknowledgment of national responsibility.

Meanwhile, states and municipalities were taking bolder steps toward becoming patrons of the arts. New York under Governor Nelson A. Rockefeller set up an Arts Council, and so did California under Governor Edmund E. Brown. By 1965 half of the states and scores of cities and countries were establishing their own arts councils. When guided by men and women of taste and imagination, these councils could be useful agents in the spread and cultivation of the arts. But in too many cases the councils were superficial, an effort to be in fashion. So, it seemed, was the widespread vogue for arts centers. Too often there was more concern for buildings than for what would go on in them. Would they become the latest thing in halls and stages for touring attractions or would they be used creatively to develop vigorous institutions with character of their own?

In its two centuries the American theatre has never had long-range solidity. It never has anywhere—not even in a monolithic state like the Soviet Union, which has always understood the value, if not the scope and power, of the arts. For if the Soviet Union gives its actors and directors security by providing them with subsidized, year-round theatres in Moscow, Leningrad and hundreds of cities throughout the vast land, it stands, like Big Brother, over the writers and managing directors, making sure that nothing subversive or even perturbing will be enacted. Early in 1965 the new masters of the Kremlin let it be known that the arts were to have more freedom and that conflicting viewpoints were to receive hearings, but—and what a but!—always within the confines of socialist realism.

In the United States the theatre has been through transitions from the adventurous, pioneering actor-managers and players of colonial times through companies dependent on actor-managers to star-oriented theatres and, in our own era, theatres dominated by directors and producers. What the country needed to strive for— and perhaps was beginning to—was permanent companies with an awareness of the joyous, transfiguring, searching place the theatre could have in our society. The challenge was to lift up our sights, to go beyond the ambition to be a magic carpet of escape and to let the drama speak questioningly, bluntly and possibly truly about the nature of our civilization as it is and as it might be.

A theatre of this order cannot be expected in the feverish pursuit of the isolated productions and hit-or-flop psychology of the commercial theatre. Distinctive ensemble styles cannot be forged in *ad hoc* companies, which at best repeat a work week in and week out, year in and year out, until it becomes a livelihood and possibly a shriveling grind.

In several visits to East Berlin I have sat for long hours in conversation with Helene Weigel, widow of Brecht and head of the Berliner Ensemble he founded, and members of the company. As they talked of the months they required to prepare a production, of the long rehearsals and the mutual analysis of progress, I understood why the performances were remarkable. One could see on the stage that no role or detail was too insignificant for the most scrupulous concern. One sat absorbed by the thrust and cohesion of the Brecht plays, and even in a new, transparently propagandistic East German play, there was a breathtaking ensemble style.

Watching the Moscow Art Theatre during its 1965 visit to New York, one was struck by the astonishing balance of the company —veterans and young players—in works of Chekhov, Gogol and

Pogodin. Penetrating performances of this order do not stem
merely from government subsidies and permanent personnel.
They are the product of a community of effort, imagination and
integrity in casting and performance. The Moscow Art did not
think that the tipsy beggar in the second act of *The Cherry Orchard* was a part for a walk-on. The role was played by an actor
of long standing and high honors. In the brief time required to
walk from one side of the stage to the other, as he asked directions
and a handout and received gold instead of a silver piece from the
impulsively generous Ranevskaya, the actor created an unforgettable image of truth.

I remember years ago in a visit to Moscow talking with Nikolai
Okhlopkov, outstanding director and chief of the Mayakovsky
Theatre. I was about to see his production of *Hamlet*. Indeed, I
saw it on a Sunday morning in an audience full of youngsters
whose responsiveness heightened my pleasure in a performance of
classic breadth and intensity. Okhlopkov was modest about this
Hamlet, and I discounted his diffidence as natural in a man who
did not wish to puff himself. "After all," he said earnestly, "I had
only three months of rehearsals."

Three months may not help some directors and actors, but how
our directors and actors would love them! What such working
conditions would mean is beyond conjecture. No one looked for
such consummations even amid the new hopes and energies of the
sixties. But the pressure of onrushing events, new ideas and changing and fresh institutions made clearer than ever that a vital
theatre depended on an indivisible trinity: the writers, the inter-
preters and an eager, enlightened audience.

It was possible to hope that the contribution of the sixties would
be a closer interrelation of all three. It was possible to believe that
with private, foundation and government support permanent
companies would increase and become firmly established and
would provide the indispensable, continuous forum of great
drama of past and present. The commercial theatre, for two centuries the delight, irritation and conscience of the nation's dramatic culture as well as so much of its entertainment, could still
amuse, entertain and charm. Occasionally it might still muster the

courage, imagination and money to produce dramas that confronted the large, insistent themes of a world adapting itself to unimaginably destructive weapons, incalculably promising scientific frontiers and turbulent rearrangements of social structures, a world that despite its unimaginable advances of knowledge had to cope with the same old obstinate, capricious, selfish, selfless human nature. But whoever produced them, those dramas would be written and heard. For the theatre remained one of the boldest and freest places for the examination of man's relation to man, his world and his beliefs. In the theatre a people could still look at themselves, criticize, rejoice, reflect, dream, mourn and celebrate. Whatever its ailments and miseries, the theatre somehow would always function. One might hope that in America its past was merely prologue and the best was yet to be.

INDEX

[373]

AMERICAN POLITICAL SCANDALS
PAST AND PRESENT

AMERICAN POLITICAL SCANDALS

PAST AND PRESENT

BARBARA SILBERDICK FEINBERG

Franklin Watts
New York   Chicago   London   Toronto   Sydney

Photographs copyright ©: The Bettmann Archive: pp. 1, 2, 3, 6, 7, 9 top & center; Wide World Photos: pp. 4, 12 bottom, 14, 16: UPI/ Bettmann Newsphotos: pp. 5, 8, 9 bottom, 10 bottom, 11, 12 top, 13, 15; Archive Photos: p. 10 top.

Library of Congress Cataloging-in-Publication Data

Feinberg, Barbara Silberdick.
American political scandals past and present / Barbara Silberdick Feinberg.
p. cm.
Includes bibliographical references and index.
Summary: A survey of American political scandals from the earliest days of the republic to the present.
ISBN 0-531-11126-1
1. Political corruption—United States—History—Juvenile literature. [1. Political corruption. 2. United States—Politics and government.] I. Title.
JK2249.F42   1992
320.973—DC20   92-25485 CIP AC

AMERICAN POLITICAL SCANDALS
PAST AND PRESENT

TO A. M. S. WITH GRATITUDE

CONTENTS

ACKNOWLEDGMENTS

I wish to thank Victoria Mathews, Senior Editor at Franklin Watts, Inc., for proposing the topic to me.

The following institutions and individuals helped me to obtain some of the research materials needed to prepare this book. For their assistance, I am especially grateful to:

The Historical Office of the Senate and the Historical Office of the House of Representatives

Marilyn Bunshaft, Community Affairs Officer, East Meadow Public Library, East Meadow, New York

Gerald Feinberg, my husband and professor of physics, Columbia University

Suzanne Freedman, freelance researcher

Sara Lippincott, editor at *The New Yorker*

Pat Milone, secretary at the District of Columbia Court of Appeals

Michael Neft, Class of 1993, Connecticut College, New London, Connecticut

Ethel Scheldon, aunt and retired educator

Jeanie Smart, neighbor and friend

Several people have given me the benefit of their comments and criticisms. Their suggestions have made the manuscript far more readable and lively. I value the discussions I have had with:

Doug Feinberg, Class of 1994, Columbia University

Gina Cane, teacher, Mamaroneck School District

Harrison Roth, senior options strategist, Cowen and Company, New York

CHRONOLOGY

1791 Andrew and Rachel Jackson's unintentionally bigamous marriage
1804 Aaron Burr–Alexander Hamilton duel
1824 John Quincy Adams–Henry Clay "Corrupt Bargain"
1829–1831 Peggy Eaton affair
1836 Furor over vice-presidential candidate Richard Johnson's interracial liaisons
1856 Representative Preston S. Brooks's attack on Senator Charles Sumner
1866 Representative Lovell Rousseau's assault on Representative Josiah Grinnell
1872 Crédit Mobilier scandal
1875 Whiskey Ring exposed
1876 Secretary of War William Belknap's kickback scheme revealed
1876 Disputed results of Rutherford Hayes–Samuel Tilden presidential election
1876 Publication of "Mulligan Letters" disclosing Representative James Blaine's shady deals
1884 Grover Cleveland's bachelor fatherhood revealed
1902 Fight between Senators Ben Tillman and John McLaurin
1905 Warren Harding's affair with Mrs. Carrie Philips
1915 Warren Harding's liaison with Nan Britton
1918 Eleanor Roosevelt first learns of her husband's affair with Lucy Mercer
1921–1923 "Ohio Gang" operations
1922 Director Charles Forbes's sale of Veterans Bureau supplies exposed
1923 Teapot Dome scandal uncovered
1948 Lyndon Johnson–Coke Stevenson primary controversy

1949 General Harry Vaughan had deep freezers sent to President Truman and members of his administration
1951 The wife of former federal loan administrator E. Merl Young received a mink coat from a lawyer representing a loan applicant
1952 Richard Nixon accused of having a slush fund
1958 Gifts to Sherman Adams disclosed in influence-peddling investigation
1960 John Kennedy–Richard Nixon election irregularities
1961 President John Kennedy's involvement with Judith Campbell Exner
1964 Creation of Senate Ethics Committee as result of Bobby Baker disclosures
1967 Adam Clayton Powell, Jr., expelled from the House of Representatives; creation of House Ethics Committee
1969 Abe Fortas's resignation after revelation of ties to Wolfson Foundation
1969 Senator Ted Kennedy's automobile accident at Chappaquiddick
1972 Vice-presidential candidate Thomas Eagleton dropped from Democratic ticket because of treatments for mental depression
1972–1974 Watergate scandal
1973 Vice President Spiro Agnew resigns in disgrace
1974 Ouster of Wilbur Mills from House Ways and Means Committee chairmanship because of alcoholism
1976 Congressional inquiry into Tongsun Park's gifts to representatives
1977 Resignation of Budget Director Bert Lance as a result of congressional probe
1978–1980 Abscam investigation
1980 Senate probe of Billy Carter's ties to the Libyan government
1983 Environmental Protection Agency administrator Anne Burford's resignation under fire
1983 Rita Lavelle of the Environmental Protection Agency found guilty of lying to Congress

1983 Secretary of the Interior James Watt fired for insensitive remarks
1984–1987 Iran-Contra scandal
1984–1986 Wedtech scandal
1984 Investigation of Democratic vice-presidential candidate Geraldine Ferraro on conflict-of-interest charges
1985 Frank McCloskey–Richard McIntyre disputed congressional race
1987 Douglas Ginsburg's withdrawal as Supreme Court nominee because of earlier marijuana use
1987 Senator Joseph Biden accused of plagiarism during bid for Democratic presidential nomination
1988 Presidential candidate Gary Hart's relationship with Donna Rice revealed
1989 Senate rejects John Tower as secretary of defense; his earlier history of excessive drinking is blamed
1989 Housing and Urban Development agent Marilyn Harrell accused of misappropriating department funds
1989 Federal judges Alcee Hastings and Walter Nixon impeached
1990 Senate investigation of the "Keating Five"
1991 Former Silverado Savings and Loan director Neil Bush penalized for conflicts of interest

1
SOME THOUGHTS ABOUT SCANDALS

What is a political scandal? One broad definition is: anything in a public official's professional or personal life that defies the code of conduct Americans set for themselves. Of course, times change, so one generation's code of conduct may not suit the next. For example, American politicians could fight private duels without attracting much attention until 1804, when a vice president killed a former secretary of the treasury. This caused such a public furor that government officials soon had to find less deadly ways to settle their differences. In 1825, a defeated presidential candidate accused the Speaker of the House of Representatives and the secretary of state of striking a "corrupt bargain" because the Speaker, in exchange for a cabinet post, helped the secretary become president of the United States. At the time, this political deal was considered a scandal. Today such arrangements are regarded as "politics as usual."

Codes of conduct affecting the private lives of public officials also reflect shifts in popular attitudes. Until the latter part of the twentieth century, most politicians believed that the public would reject a presidential candidate who had been divorced. With the 1952 nomination of Democrat Adlai E. Stevenson and the 1980 election of Republican Ronald W. Reagan, presidential hopefuls with failed first marriages were no longer written off as lost causes.

Not only have codes of conduct changed with time, but so has publicity about the people who violate the codes. The romantic entanglements of two founders of the American republic, Benjamin Franklin and Thomas Jefferson, made headlines in the newspapers of their day. As a matter of fact, the press declared open season on the seamier side of politicians' private lives throughout the nineteenth century. Only in the twentieth century were such stories no longer newsworthy. By this time, the Washington community and the press corps had begun to treat marital misadventures as "insider information" not to be aired in public. Even politicians refused to take advantage of their opponents' personal failings. An informal blackout kept the public in the dark. Instead, officials' families were placed on a pedestal as examples of virtue and morality. That could explain why many twentieth-century Americans felt so terribly disillusioned when they finally discovered that some of their most respected presidents had been unfaithful husbands. Given these belated revelations, it was not surprising that public concern about politicians' private morality became an issue once again, especially during the 1988 presidential campaign. It is only fair to note that some effective American presidents led private lives that fed the scandal sheets of their day, while other very moral presidents were not very successful national leaders.

Codes of conduct for politicians may be inconsistent, too, leaving politicians with confusing guidelines. This can happen when citizens set a higher standard for their leaders than for themselves. Since the 1960s, people have been more permissive than ever before about the words used in books and the explicit behavior shown in movie theaters. Yet in 1974, when people read published transcripts of a president's private conversations, they were shocked by his vulgar language. In 1987, they found a married

presidential candidate's love affairs deplorable. What is a politician to do?

To uphold codes of conduct and expose wrongdoing, the public has relied on reporters and officeholders. Ever since this republic was founded, reporters have "dug up the dirt" about the nation's leaders. They have often done the country an enormous service by researching and writing articles or by broadcasting interviews and features that uncovered dishonesty in government. They have also turned up instances of personal misconduct. In return, they have been labeled as "muckrakers," summoning up images of cleaning out filthy stables, or "investigative reporters," bringing to mind trench-coated sleuths hiding in the shadows, watching suspects and looking for clues. Collectively, these private individuals have earned their reputation as the "fourth branch of government."

The three traditional branches of government have not let journalists claim all of the glory for exposing the political corruption or private failings of public officials. Because of the constitutional doctrine of checks and balances, the presidency, Congress, and the courts must interfere in each other's business. As a result, quite a number of political scandals have come to light. Exercising their shared responsibilities for making, carrying out, and interpreting laws, each branch of government has pried into and spied on the others, calling upon officeholders to defend their policies, performances, and occasionally their personal life-styles. Party politics have also encouraged politicians to examine their opponents' positions and publicize any government wrongdoing, especially around election time.

The executive branch has relied on its departments and agencies to carry out checking and balancing responsibilities. The Department of Justice has uncovered scandals through its law enforcement arm, the Federal Bureau of Investigation (FBI) and its

prosecutors, who have gathered evidence of crimes to present in court. The Treasury Department's Internal Revenue Service (IRS) has exposed the operations of greedy politicians and their associates. Presidents themselves have named special commissions to look into the behavior of officials who abused their powers.

For many generations, Congress has served as the government's watchdog, sniffing out scandals within its own membership and among other officeholders. A number of congressional committees have held public hearings to look into charges of misconduct. Since the 1950s, watching the more sensational hearings on television has become a popular public pastime, rivaling the devotion of soap opera fans for their heroes and heroines. House and Senate codes of ethics also keep legislators on their toes. As its ultimate weapon, Congress can use its impeachment powers to remove offenders from office. The federal courts have also played an important role. Not only have judges tried officials accused of corruption, they have even helped to uncover scandals. For example, judges have issued orders forcing the government to release information that has ruined more than one political career. Bridging the public and private sectors are the fearless "whistle blowers," those concerned citizens who have risked their jobs and reputations to bring evidence of wrong-doing to light.

The public has thrived on tales of misdeeds in high places, whether true or false. No wonder tabloids are supermarket best-sellers and exposé television shows have high ratings. Nor is it any surprise that public opinion polls constantly rate politicians quite low on scales of professions people regard as having high standards of honesty and ethical conduct. While this nation has come to expect the worst from its leaders, such expectations fortunately fall short of reality. Most politicians do deserve the public's respect and trust.

To be a politician is to live in a goldfish bowl—to be stared at, studied, and investigated. Of course, there are many honorable officeholders who willingly submit to public scrutiny to keep themselves accountable to the people they serve. With nothing to hide, they do not shy away from the spotlight of publicity. Publicity is one of the duties they accept and one of the rewards they receive for the demanding and sometimes impossible job they do—governing the nation. All of them shouldn't be condemned because some officials go astray, or as the old saying goes, "Don't throw the baby out with the bath water!" Of course, it is the "dirty" politicians, the ones who most need the bath water, who should be removed from office.

American Political Scandals Past and Present surveys the country's most colorful and intriguing political scandals. It also includes other, less familiar incidents that either made an impact on the politics of their day or offer fascinating human interest stories. It would take several volumes to cover all of the misdeeds and misjudgments that have shocked generations of Americans. Because of this, events resulting from politics (such as the impeachment of President Andrew Johnson) that did not involve questions of political or personal morality are not discussed here. Consult an American history textbook instead. Also missing are charges, countercharges, and accusations that could not be verified as fact at the time this book was written. Thus, there is no mention of the sexual harassment hearings involving Professor Anita Hill and Supreme Court nominee, now Justice, Clarence Thomas, nor the Senate Foreign Relations Committee inquiry into claims that the election of 1980 was stolen from President Carter through a deal to delay the release of American hostages held in the United States embassy in Iran. State or local scandals are mentioned only in passing. For those of you who are curious about them,

look up Lincoln Steffens's 1904 classic, *The Shame of Cities*, and go on from there.

For the most part, women and minorities play only supporting roles in these pages because for most of American history, government has been the preserve of white males. One sign of the increasing democratization of American politics is that these formerly neglected groups have increasingly been in the spotlight. If past history is indeed a guide to the future, they will make their presence known more and more on the national political scene, raising eyebrows and causing public outrage. Indeed, in this book, women and minorities have already been cast as featured players in several bribery, graft, and corruption scandals.

The chapters are organized chronologically around the topics indicated in the Contents. Each scandal has been documented by eyewitnesses, reporters, or historians. As you will soon discover, truth is indeed stranger than fiction—and far more interesting. If you want to learn more about a particular person or event, turn to the Bibliography. It will tell you where you can find additional information. Some political terms may not be familiar to you. If you are uncertain about their meaning, consult the definitions in the Glossary. Now that you have been properly introduced to the subject matter of this book, read it and enjoy it.

2

VIOLENT POLITICAL QUARRELS

In the woody bluffs of Weehawken, New Jersey, a vice president of the United States and a former secretary of the treasury stood ten paces apart, their dueling pistols sparkling in the early morning sun. One of the two men raised his arm as if ready to shoot, but then lowered it, reached in his pocket, and pulled out a pair of eyeglasses, which he promptly put on. "I beg your pardon for delaying you, but the direction of the light sometimes renders glasses necessary," he apologized to his adversary.[1] After this interruption, both men heard a voice call out, "Present." Within seconds, a shot was fired, causing the bespectacled duelist to fall forward, face down on the ground, his pistol going off into the air. The victor hurried away while the loser, with a bullet lodged in his spine, was carried to the banks of the Hudson River and rowed back to New York City. He died the following day. It was only a few minutes after seven A.M. on July 11, 1804, when Aaron Burr shot Alexander Hamilton, causing a scandal that ruined Burr's political career.

Perhaps Burr and Hamilton were destined to be political opponents. Both were very ambitious men from different backgrounds whose lives collided with disastrous consequences. Alexander Hamilton, born in Nevis in the West Indies, was an illegitimate child. Abandoned by his father, he was sent to school in New

Jersey and eventually attended King's College (now Columbia University). In contrast to Hamilton, Aaron Burr came from a privileged New Jersey family. Born in Newark, he was the grandson of the famous New England preacher, Jonathan Edwards. Both his father and his grandfather were presidents of The College of New Jersey (now Princeton University), where he eventually became a student.

After serving in the American revolutionary army, both men settled in New York, where they became successful lawyers and were quickly drawn to politics. Burr was elected to the New York State Assembly and then became state attorney general. Hamilton's talents were displayed in a larger arena. In 1787, he went to Philadelphia, where he took part in the discussions that produced the Constitution of the United States. Back in New York, he coauthored the *Federalist Papers*, a series of brilliant essays explaining why the new national government was necessary and how it would work. Under President Washington, Hamilton served as the country's first secretary of the treasury. He proposed measures favorable to commercial rather than agricultural interests, placing himself in opposition to the policies of Virginian Thomas Jefferson, Washington's secretary of state.

Since the nation's first capital was located in New York, Burr and Hamilton often visited each other's homes. This public display of friendship concealed a bitter rivalry. As lawyers, they had competed for cases; as politicians, each wanted to control New York state politics. Burr first antagonized Hamilton by forming a political coalition against Hamilton's father-in-law, Philip Schuyler, in order to win a seat in the United States Senate. The tables were turned in the presidential election of 1800 when Vice President Thomas Jefferson, leader of the Democratic-Republican party, chose to run against Federalist president John Adams.

Burr became his running mate. The unexpected outcome of that election gave Hamilton a chance to get even with Burr.

Until the Twelfth Amendment to the Constitution was passed in 1804, the electoral college, which formally elects the president of the United States, did not hold separate elections for president and vice president. Instead, the candidate with a majority of votes became president; the runner-up, vice president.* Electors from each state voted for two candidates from the same political party without being able to indicate their presidential preference. To elect one of the candidates president, plans had to be made to discard votes for the party's other candidate. When the electoral votes were counted in the election of 1800, both Jefferson and Burr received seventy-three votes, the only tie for president in American history. This happened because the New York electors had assumed that the Virginia electors would throw away a vote so that Jefferson could win. The Virginians thought the New Yorkers would do it, and so nothing was done. With the advantage of hindsight, Jefferson shrewdly commented: "It was badly managed not to have arranged with certainty what seems to have been left to hazard."[2]

Because of the tie, the election was thrown into the House of Representatives, with each state casting one vote. To complicate matters, Burr decided to seek the presidency for himself and actively tried to put together the nine-state majority he needed to win. Preferring Jefferson as the lesser of two evils, Hamilton sought to thwart Burr's ambitions. He wrote to his friends in Congress, "For heaven's sake, let not the federal party be responsible for the elevation of this

* See Chapter 3, p. 36 for a more detailed discussion of the electoral college system.

man."[3] The House voted thirty-five times, unable to give a majority to either candidate. After six days of voting, neither candidate had won, although more states supported Jefferson than Burr. Then on the thirty-sixth ballot, Federalist James Bayard of Delaware abstained from voting, giving Jefferson the presidency. Vice President Burr could blame Hamilton for contributing to his defeat.

The two men clashed again when Hamilton masterminded Burr's defeat in the 1804 race for governor in New York. Matters came to a head when Burr read a newspaper article in which Hamilton was quoted as saying that Burr was "a dangerous man and one who could not be trusted with the reins of government."[4] The writer went on to tease his readers, saying, "I could detail to you a still more despicable opinion which General Hamilton has expressed of Mr. Burr."[5] Over the years, friends had constantly given Burr exaggerated reports of the unkind things Hamilton had to say about him. This time, Burr had something in print, something concrete he could use to avenge his honor. Burr wrote a series of polite but angry letters to his antagonist and wound up challenging him to a duel. Hamilton was reluctant to accept. His son Philip had died in a duel just three years earlier. However, he finally agreed to meet Burr at Weehawken.

A number of prominent New York politicians, including a mayor, a district attorney, and a judge, had fought duels and hardly caused a stir. However, antagonists were expected to wound, not to kill, one another. Burr defied that custom when he shot Hamilton. A vice president had caused the death of a founder of the American republic and former secretary of the treasury. So great was the popular outcry that two states issued warrants for Burr's arrest, accusing him of murder. These were never served and were later dismissed.

In the aftermath of that fatal July morning, Alex-

ander Hamilton's reputation continued to glow while Burr's political star went into decline. Burr fled to Pennsylvania; then he left for the South, seeking refuge first in Georgia, then in South Carolina. By January, he was back presiding over the Senate, serving the remainder of his term as vice president as if nothing had happened. He was safe from arrest in Washington since the states had no jurisdiction in the nation's capital. He did not leave office until March. (The government year started in March until 1933, when the Twentieth Amendment to the Constitution changed it to January.) Jefferson, elected to a second term as president, had already replaced him with another running mate, George Clinton of New York.

Then Burr embarked on a curious plot, hatched while he had sought refuge in Pennsylvania. Along with U.S. Army officer, General James Wilkinson, and another associate, he planned an invasion of Mexico, a Spanish possession, to set up an independent government and possibly to carve out an empire in the Southwest. A worried Wilkinson eventually betrayed Burr to President Jefferson. Burr was captured while trying to escape into Spanish territory. He was tried for treason and acquitted on a technicality in 1807. His reputation in tatters, Burr lived abroad for four years and then returned to New York where he practiced law until he died in 1836, a lonely and forgotten man.

A political quarrel had cost one man his life and another his political career. Yet quarrels and disagreements are part of the give-and-take of the American political process. The practice of attributing negative qualities to rivals is as old as the American republic. In the heat of a campaign, politicians are expected to block, frustrate, and discredit their opponents' efforts. Of course, once elected, they are also expected to negotiate and compromise their differences. The Burr–Hamilton duel is perhaps a tragic example of a politi-

cian's failure to heed the old saying "If you can't take the heat, get out of the kitchen." Burr had turned a series of political disagreements into a disastrous personal vendetta.

The Burr–Hamilton duel was not the only outburst of violence to result from political differences. Others took place in Congress during the second half of the nineteenth century and the beginning of the twentieth century. Custom required lawmakers to treat each other with courtesy and respect and to always refer to each other in such polite, if insincere, terms as "the honorable gentleman" on the floor of each chamber. However, some representatives and senators got carried away. During debates over slavery and, later, over the inferior position of blacks in American society, southern lawmakers and their supporters resorted to brawls, scuffles, and even deliberately planned assaults to defend their views. Because of intense feelings, these passionate lawmakers sometimes inflicted serious injuries on their northern and midwestern opponents.

For example, Representative Preston S. Brooks of South Carolina attacked and severely wounded Senator Charles Sumner of Massachusetts at his Senate desk. This assault took place during the 1850s, when fiery debates over slavery roused legislators' emotions and divided the nation. The focus of North-South antagonism was Kansas, a territory preparing to enter the Union. Extremists were pouring into the state; there were groups determined to prevent the further spread of slavery and others intent on extending it to Kansas. Roving proslavery bands terrorized antislavery groups by burning their strongholds. Each of their raids was met by a counterattack. "Bleeding Kansas" became a popular phrase, aptly describing the rapidly deteriorating situation.

In response to the growing strife and lawlessness,

Senator Sumner, a tall, arrogant, and tactless man, delivered his "Crime Against Kansas" speech on May 19, 1856. In no uncertain terms, he blamed the South for all of the violence in Kansas and spoke out against efforts to make the territory a slave state. Unfortunately, many of the senator's comments were directed against a sixty-year-old Democrat, Senator Andrew Pickens Butler of South Carolina, who wanted Kansans to decide for themselves what course to take. Sumner claimed that Butler had a mistress, "the harlot, Slavery." Sumner also had the bad taste to make a pointed remark about Butler's speech impediment, caused by a recent stroke. "With incoherent phrases, discharged the loose expectoration of his speech . . . with error, sometimes of principle, sometimes of fact . . . [H]e cannot ope his mouth but out flies a blunder."[6] Exaggeration in the heat of the moment is perfectly acceptable on the floor of the Senate, but references to personal defects are not.

Butler was absent from the Senate that day, but his nephew, Representative Preston Brooks, was there and heard every word. Quick to take offense at Sumner's reckless remarks, Brooks carefully plotted his revenge. On May 22, at 12:45 P.M., just after the Senate had adjourned for the day, he approached Sumner, who was seated at his desk in the Senate chamber. The representative stated: "I have come over from the House to chastize [*sic*] you for the remarks that you made against my relation, Senator Butler. I have read your speech and it is a libel on South Carolina."[7] Brooks raised his cane and brought it down on Sumner's head. Sumner tried to protect himself, but his long legs were twisted under his desk so that he could not get up. Brooks continued to hit him until the cane fell apart. Savagely beaten, the senator lay on the floor covered with blood.

Senator John Jordan Crittenden of Kentucky had

tried to break up the fight, but another South Carolina representative, Lawrence Keitt, who had accompanied Brooks, lifted his cane to strike the elderly lawmaker. Georgia senator Robert Augustus Toombs rushed to Crittenden's side to deflect the blow. However, few senators seemed eager to help the stricken Sumner. Aided by a Senate employee, he eventually made his way to the cloakroom where he lay on a sofa while a doctor examined him. Then, despite serious head wounds, he slowly walked down the Capitol steps into a waiting carriage and was driven away. Sumner's injuries left him almost blind in one eye. He did not return to work for three years.

Reports from "Bleeding Kansas," followed by news of "Bloody" Sumner, inflamed public passions. Outraged Northerners grabbed up copies of Sumner's speech, while Southerners treated Brooks as a hero, showering him with canes and other gifts. The Bill of Rights gives American citizens and politicians alike the freedom to express their opinions in public. The Constitution specifically protects congressional speeches and debates by granting members of Congress immunity from penalties for statements they make in the legislature. In a fit of anger, Preston Brooks had ignored both provisions and had taken matters into his own hands. What made the Preston Brooks episode notorious was the fact that it was calculated and premeditated. The fact that it occurred during a period when the nation's passions were inflamed also contributed to the scandal.

Within days, the Senate investigated the incident. Sumner made a dramatic appearance, wrapped in bandages, to testify about the attack. However, the Senate decided that it was the responsibility of the House of Representatives to reprimand its members. A House Select Committee (a temporary committee created for a special purpose) soon held hearings on the assault.

On June 2, 1856, it issued a majority report that found Brooks guilty of violating congressional rules and recommended that he be expelled from Congress. Northerners and Southerners spent the rest of the month debating the report, inflaming the public with their fiery speeches. It was no wonder that the House was unable to muster the necessary votes to oust Brooks or to conduct any other business.

Justice was finally served, but not quite as the lawmakers had intended. The House did manage to censure Lawrence Keitt for his role in the attack. Disgraced before his colleagues, he had to stand in their presence and listen as the charges against him were read aloud. The day before, July 14, Brooks had surprised his colleagues by deciding to resign. After giving up his seat, the representative immediately ran for office again and was returned to Congress in August. However, no one could have guessed that within five months he would die from a liver disease. His foe, Charles Sumner, went on to have an impressive career in the Senate, where he served as chairman of the Committee on Foreign Relations for ten years. He died of a heart attack in 1874. As for Kansas, its status was not resolved until after the outbreak of the Civil War in 1861, when it entered the Union as a free state.

Another violent outburst took place in Congress in 1866, during the Reconstruction era, only a decade after the attack on Senator Sumner. The North was imposing penalties on the defeated South, but not all members of Congress were in agreement about what should be done. During the heated debates, misunderstandings and differences of opinion led one representative, Lovell H. Rousseau of Kentucky, to strike another, Iowa representative Josiah B. Grinnell. Both members of the Thirty-ninth Congress were Republicans with distinguished careers. Lovell Rousseau had

fought in the 1840 Mexican War, receiving special mention for gallantry at the Battle of Buena Vista. He was credited with single-handedly keeping Kentucky on the Union side during the Civil War, and he served as a Union brigadier general at the battles of Shiloh and Perryville. His antagonist, Josiah Grinnell, a Vermont-born clergyman, is said to have been the subject of newspaper editor Horace Greeley's famous remark, "Go West, young man, and grow up with the country." He did. In 1854, he founded Grinnell College in Iowa, where he was a trustee until 1884.

A misunderstanding led Rousseau to attack Grinnell. Rousseau had objected to some remarks Grinnell had made during a debate on the Freedman's Bureau. This Reconstruction agency had been set up to help former slaves adjust to life as free people after the Civil War. Grinnell supported the position that southern white families who had been accused by a former slave could be arrested and held for an indefinite period before trial, a position Rousseau found offensive. "If you intend to arrest white people on the *ex parte* [uncontested] statement of negroes, and hold them to suit your conveniences for trial, and fine and imprison them, then I say I oppose you; and if you should so arrest and punish me, I would kill you when you set me at liberty."[8] Like many others at the time, Rousseau did not have much respect for the former slaves, nor did he necessarily agree with every Reconstruction policy adopted to help them.

The Kentuckian grew even angrier when Grinnell replied, "History repeated itself. I care not whether the gentleman was four years in the war on the Union side or four years on the other side; but I say that he degraded his State and uttered a sentiment I thought unworthy of an American officer when he said he would do such an act on complaint of a negro against him."[9] Rousseau felt that Grinnell had insulted his war

record and his personal honor. Perhaps it was the need to restore his reputation that led Rousseau to act. Accompanied by a friend, he sought out Grinnell on the eastern portico of the Capitol and struck him several times with his cane. He was censured by the House for this premeditated attack. Grinnell soon recovered from the beating. He went on to serve as the president of the Central Railroad of Iowa and died in 1891. In 1867, Rousseau was promoted to major general in the United States Army and was placed in charge of the Department of Louisiana, which was then under martial law. He died the following year.

The House of Representatives did not have a monopoly on violence. In 1902, the Senate censured two South Carolina senators, Democrats Benjamin Ryan Tillman and John L. McLaurin, for having a fistfight on the Senate floor. The incident was the outgrowth of a personal rivalry, intensified by political differences. An extreme racist, "Pitchfork Ben" Tillman was a conservative Democratic spokesman for southern white farmers. As the leading South Carolina politician of his day, he had used his considerable influence to advance the political career of his friend and henchman John McLaurin, securing for him the posts of attorney-general, congressman, and senator.[10] (State legislators, not the public, elected United States senators until the passage of the Seventeenth Amendment to the Constitution.)

In exchange for these favors, Tillman expected his protégé to be loyal and obedient. McLaurin, a weak and opportunistic man, found the price too high. He decided to strike out on his own. Both senators had been attempting to get Republican president William McKinley to appoint their supporters to federal jobs such as judgeships and postmasterships in South Carolina. McLaurin eventually got his hands on these jobs because he was willing to vote with the Republicans on

many issues in the Senate. This was something that Tillman, a staunch Democrat, could never do. As a result, the two senators drifted apart.

The annexation of the Philippines drove them further apart. The American people and their politicians found themselves divided over the fate of the Philippines, one of the overseas territories turned over to the United States as a result of the 1898 Spanish-American War. While most Republicans favored annexation, Democrats McLaurin and Tillman originally voted against it. Like many southern senators representing farming interests, they feared competition from Philippine agriculture. As white supremacists, they did not welcome dark-skinned peoples into the budding American empire. Then, without warning, to please President McKinley, McLaurin suddenly changed his mind and voted with the Republicans in favor of taking over the Philippines. Tillman was furious.

What provoked the actual fight was a debate on a Philippine revenue bill. Northern Republican senators had been taunting Tillman about lynchings and segregation laws in the South. The frustrated senator, known for his bad manners and hair-trigger temper, hurled bitter accusations against his absent colleague from South Carolina, denouncing his ties to these Republicans. He charged that "improper influences" had led McLaurin to change his vote on the treaty to end the Spanish-American War. As soon as McLaurin heard about Tillman's outburst, he returned to the floor of the Senate and issued a denial. "I now say that the statement is a willful, malicious, and deliberate lie."[11] Tillman leaped from his desk and hit McLaurin in the face. They continued to exchange blows until an assistant doorkeeper and several senators separated them. Personal and political differences had built up and exploded into a violent confrontation. Both men were

censured by the Senate. They could no longer be called on to address their colleagues or be counted as present in the chamber. After they offered a formal apology to the Senate, their privileges were restored. Tillman served in the Senate for a total of twenty-four years, dying in 1918 just before he completed his fourth term in office. McLaurin left the Senate in 1913 and became a member of the South Carolina state senate from 1914 to 1917. A cotton planter since 1903, when he retired from politics, he returned to his former occupation. He died in 1934.

A common thread winds through all of these incidents: Each antagonist sought vengeance for a real or imagined insult and turned a political dispute into a physical conflict, sometimes with tragic results. Sectional differences as well as disagreements over slavery, and later the status of freed blacks, triggered all but one of these violent outbursts. The political adversaries can be seen as victims of the extremist passions that divided the nation in their day. However, neither the public nor Congress was prepared to excuse their conduct. Whatever the motive, political violence was viewed as outside the mainstream of American politics.

3
CONTROVERSIAL ELECTION RETURNS

According to family tradition, he was supposed to wait until the public asked him to serve; he was not expected to actively campaign for the highest office in the land. Yet the wait was frustrating. This well-qualified candidate felt he was destined for the presidency. In his early teens, he was a secretary-translator for the American minister to Russia. Later, he represented the United States in Europe, serving at one time or another as minister to Russia, the Netherlands, Prussia, and Great Britain. He helped to negotiate the terms that ended the War of 1812, and as secretary of state, in 1823 he worked on the famous Monroe Doctrine that kept Britain and other foreign powers from interfering in the Western Hemisphere. His credentials seemed so much more impressive than those of his political rivals: Secretary of the Treasury William Crawford, Speaker of the House of Representatives Henry Clay of Kentucky, and Senator Andrew Jackson of Tennessee, hero of the Battle of New Orleans. Like them, John Quincy Adams was eager to win the election of 1824. He wanted to have the chance to follow in his father's footsteps and become president of the United States.

Earlier in the year, the congressional caucus, a group of lawmakers who belonged to the same political party, had gathered as usual to nominate a presidential candidate. These heirs of Jefferson's Democratic-

Republicans picked William Crawford, a southern planter. This time, because of widespread dissatisfaction with the undemocratic caucus system, state legislatures and mass rallies chose their own nominees. As a result, Clay, Jackson, and Adams were encouraged to compete for the presidency as the party's "unofficial" candidates. Perhaps John Quincy Adams would have a chance to make his dream come true.

After the election, when the popular vote was finally tallied, Andrew Jackson led with a plurality of 153,544 votes; John Quincy Adams came in second with 108,740; Clay received 47,136; and Crawford, 46,168.[1] Although disappointed, John Quincy Adams quickly realized that Andrew Jackson wasn't president yet. Because of the complicated procedure the Constitution required for presidential elections, Jackson also had to win a majority of electoral votes to become the victor. Within each state, the candidate with the highest popular vote was supposed to receive all of the state's electoral votes. The number of electoral votes at a state's disposal was determined by the number of senators and representatives in the state's congressional delegation, that number being based on the state's population.

Jackson won ninety-nine electoral votes; Adams had eighty-four; Crawford had forty-one; and Clay, thirty-seven. However, Jackson still didn't become president; he lacked a majority of electoral votes. Under these circumstances, the Constitution provided that the House of Representatives should decide who the next president would be, with each state casting one vote. The Twelfth Amendment limited the choice to the three candidates with the greatest number of electoral votes. With four more electoral votes than Clay, Crawford knocked him out of the race. However, a disabling stroke turned Crawford into an invalid and ended his presidential bid. The legislators would have

to pick either Andrew Jackson, who had won the most popular votes, or runner-up John Quincy Adams.

John Quincy Adams faced a tricky situation. He knew that whether he or Andrew Jackson became president would now depend on what Henry Clay decided to do. As Speaker of the House, Clay was a man of enormous influence. In his own presidential bid, he had carried Missouri, Kentucky, and Ohio. If Adams could add those three states to his New England total, he would win. In the past, he and Clay had supported a program of internal improvements to strengthen national trade and transportation. Both men shared a common interest in the new western territories, and neither one thought Jackson would make a capable president.

Henry Clay was a visitor at the Adams's home on January 8, 1825. Historians have no record of what actually went on at that meeting, but from that point on, the two men worked together to ensure Adams's victory. On February 9, 1825, when the House held the presidential election, Adams defeated Jackson by a vote of thirteen to seven; four votes went to the ailing Crawford. With a majority of the House supporting him, Adams had become president. Shortly afterward, he appointed Henry Clay secretary of state, at that time the traditional path to the presidency.

Since Andrew Jackson had received the most popular and electoral votes, he and his supporters cried foul. They charged Adams with stealing the presidential election by making a "Corrupt Bargain" with Clay and ignoring the results of the popular vote. Despite the growing scandal, Adams took the oath of office. So widespread was the belief that Adams and Clay had conspired to deny Jackson his due, that during the next four years, Congress blocked most of the measures Adams sponsored. He was unable to live down the questionable circumstances surrounding his election.

In the end, Jackson had his revenge. In 1828, he overwhelmed Adams with an electoral vote of 178 to 83 and became president. Adams went on to become the only former president to serve in the House of Representatives, where he opposed the spread of slavery. Clay made two more unsuccessful attempts to become president. He ultimately won the nation's respect as the author of the Compromise of 1850, which tried to balance the admission of free states and slave states into the Union.

While the "Corrupt Bargain" was viewed as a scandal at the time, with the passage of years it came to be regarded as "politics as usual." Standards of acceptable political conduct gradually changed. Would-be presidential candidates began to promise important government posts or ambassadorships to their competitors to get them to withdraw from the race. Whether or not Adams had "stolen" the election from Jackson, he had been duly elected by proper constitutional procedures. He could not be faulted for that.

Rutherford B. Hayes, on the other hand, came to the presidency by a far more questionable route. His opponent, Samuel J. Tilden, had every reason to claim that the election was stolen from him. Instead, he commented: "I can retire to private life with the consciousness that I shall receive from posterity the credit of having been elected to the highest position in the gift of the people, without any of the cares and responsibilities of the office."[2] How this came about made the election of 1876 one of the most disreputable episodes in American history.

The Democratic party's prospects for the presidency had looked promising. They controlled the House of Representatives for the first time since the Civil War, and popular discontent with Republican government had been mounting. The economic depression that started in 1873 was growing worse. The

country was sick of the punitive Reconstruction policies that had turned the defeated South into an occupied territory. People were disgusted with all of the charges of bribery and corruption that were surfacing as President Grant's administration drew to a close.* It took seven ballots before a badly divided Republican party finally nominated Rutherford B. Hayes as their candidate. Although he was not an especially distinguished leader, he had sponsored some civil service reforms during his three terms as governor of Ohio. Unlike most of his rivals for the nomination, he had made no political enemies and had an unblemished reputation for honesty. But he was virtually unknown nationally.

The Democrats chose Governor Samuel J. Tilden of New York to be their presidential candidate. As a lawyer representing railroads and corporations, he had amassed a personal fortune. Then he entered politics and played a major role in ridding the state of a number of corrupt judges and in bringing down New York City's notorious Tweed Ring. This political machine was a self-perpetuating organization of politicians who ran local government for their own personal profit. Like other political machines of the era, members of the Ring arranged to have ballot boxes stuffed with false votes to stay in power, found cushy jobs for political cronies, and received bribes and payoffs in exchange for city contracts. The Ring cheated the city out of anywhere from $30 million to $200 million; estimates varied. In 1874, as a reform governor, Tilden cleaned up the remnants of the Tweed organization and took on the Canal Ring, an upstate circle of corrupt politicians. A tight-lipped, cautious, and secretive man, Tilden had a flawless record with which to challenge the heir to the scandal-ridden Grant administration.

* See Chapter 5, pp. 65–71.

When all the shouting was over, 4,285,992 voters had cast their ballots for Tilden, while Hayes received 4,033,768 votes. By November 10, Tilden had 184 electoral votes to Hayes's 166, but 19 electoral votes remained in doubt, those of South Carolina, Louisiana, and Florida. Tilden needed twenty more votes to win the required constitutional majority in the electoral college. This prompted Hayes to announce, "I think we are defeated in spite of recent good news. I am of the opinion that the Democrats have carried the country and elected Tilden."[3] However, his supporters refused to concede the election. James C. Reid, editor of the *New York Times*, and a dedicated Republican, schemed with key party leaders to put the three remaining states in the Hayes column—even though the solid South had not voted for a Republican presidential candidate since the Civil War.

In the three southern states, both political parties busily "adjusted" and "corrected" the voting totals. They demanded recounts and offered their own set of election returns as the official results. As the recounts dragged on, Congress was asked to choose between the two sets of election returns in each of the three disputed states. It was a unique situation, and the Constitution offered no guidance. So the legislators made up the rules as they went along. Both the Republican-controlled Senate and the Democratic-led House of Representatives claimed the right to decide which set of votes was valid. As a compromise, the two chambers agreed to appoint a commission. Tilden objected to this extralegal procedure, preferring to leave the decision up to the House. As bitter feelings intensified in the South, he finally agreed to accept the compromise solution.

Congress set up a fifteen-member commission made up of ten senators and representatives and five justices of the Supreme Court, evenly divided between

Republicans and Democrats. Justice David Davis, an independent, was expected to hold the balance of power, but at the last minute, he accepted the post of senator from Illinois and resigned from the bench. Republican Joseph P. Bradley replaced him. The night before Bradley was to cast the deciding vote, supporters from each side visited his home in a last-ditch effort to influence him. However, the Republicans outstayed the Democrats. The next morning, the commission announced that Hayes had won, their vote following straight party lines, 8–7. Hayes was given 185 electoral votes to Tilden's 184.

So great was the Democrats' outrage that they threatened a filibuster (a nonstop speech-making marathon) in the Senate that would hold up the election and all other government business. During the remaining three weeks before the inauguration, moderates from both sides hammered out a series of compromises to give Hayes the presidency while gaining concessions for the South. The concessions included the appointment of a southern Democrat to the Hayes administration, railroad construction and internal improvements, and most important the withdrawal of federal troops from the South. Fearful that further delays would cause another civil war over the election, Congress accepted these terms. As a result, the South regained control of its own political affairs, the region's Republicans were swept from office, and freed blacks were left to an uncertain fate.

Hayes entered office under a cloud of suspicion. His name would be forever linked with the infamous election of 1876. Yet he went on to become a reform-minded president, breaking up state political machines and appointing officials on the basis of their competence rather than their political loyalties. Hayes's wife gave a high moral tone to the White House, earning the nickname "Lemonade Lucy" for refusing to serve alco-

holic beverages to visitors. Fulfilling a promise he had made when he became president, Hayes served only one term. In retirement, he promoted humanitarian causes. Within ten years of Tilden's defeat, he was dead, having served as a senior adviser to his party in the time that remained to him.

Despite the huge public outcry over the election of 1876, the Hayes–Tilden scandal did not put an end to vote stealing. To control election returns, state and local political machines continued to employ repeaters, people paid to vote in more than one polling place on Election Day, and ghosts, people paid to vote under the names of deceased citizens whose names were kept on the registration lists. Poll watchers, whose job it was to keep elections honest, and certifying boards, who tabulated the results, were still bribed or threatened to produce victories for the political machines' candidates. As long as political machines remained in power, these practices continued.

To break the grip of political machines on American politics, reformers had exposed their corruption and brought officials to trial, but they could not overcome widespread voter ignorance and indifference. In the early 1900s, they went a step further. They tinkered with election laws and came up with the primary election to return control over party nominations to the voters. Finally, the public, rather than professional politicians, would have the opportunity to select a party's candidates for office. However, political machines soon learned how to manipulate the new system and managed to keep their candidates in power.

This explains why, fifty years later, Congressman Lyndon Johnson could still rely on help from a political machine in his bid for the 1948 Democratic senatorial nomination in Texas.[4] His opponent was former governor Coke Stevenson. In those days, the Texas Democratic party's grip on state politics was so tight that

winning a primary virtually guaranteed election. There simply weren't enough Republican voters to defeat the Democratic candidates. Democratic primary contests attracted a number of ambitious politicians. They were eager to be chosen as the party's nominee for national or local office. With so many candidates on the ballot, it was often difficult for anyone to achieve the majority vote required to win. So a runoff primary would be held among the top contenders. That is why Stevenson and Johnson found themselves facing a second primary election in their bid to secure the senatorial nomination.

In Texas, county voting returns were often "corrected," adjusted to benefit one candidate or another, within a day or so after the election. During that time, political machines commonly bought, changed, and manufactured votes as needed. In several southwestern Texas counties, George B. Parr's political organization sold votes to the highest bidder. In the 1948 senatorial runoff primary, that bidder proved to be Lyndon Johnson. As the votes were tallied, Johnson was running behind Stevenson. However, six days after the primary, an unheard of amount of time even in Texas, Precinct 13, in Jim Wells County, phoned in more changes. This southwestern Texas election district gave Lyndon Johnson an 87-vote advantage over Stevenson. The final count stood at 494,191 for the congressman and 494,104 for the former governor.

Coke Stevenson, a legendary figure in Texas politics, was an old-fashioned conservative who believed in the processes of law and justice. He sent his lawyers to Jim Wells County to investigate the election results in Precinct 13. With some difficulty, his lawyers were able to glance at the list of voters. They suspected that two hundred names had been added after the election because a different-color ink was used. The lawyers even managed to find a few of these alleged voters and took

sworn statements from them that they had not voted in the runoff primary. In view of the evidence, Stevenson urged the local Democratic executive committee, made up of reformers, to throw out the questionable returns from Precinct 13.

Lyndon Johnson was able to stop Coke Stevenson from proving what everyone suspected—that the returns from Precinct 13 were indeed fraudulent. He arranged for a sympathetic judge, a friend of George Parr's to issue a restraining order. It prevented the local reform committee from doing anything about the disputed returns until the courts could rule on the matter. Johnson had bought time so that he could persuade the Democratic State Executive Committee, the party's ruling organization, to recommend that he be made the party's senatorial candidate. Despite Stevenson's claims of election irregularities, the state committee endorsed Johnson by a margin of one vote. The state party convention, a meeting of delegates from local party organizations, confirmed this decision. To win the nomination, Johnson had made a deal with the leaders of the state party organization. They needed his backing to keep a rival group from being recognized as the official Texas delegation at the upcoming Democratic National Convention, which would nominate the party's candidates for president and vice president.

When the local and state political organizations failed him, Coke Stevenson did not give up. He sued in the United States District Court, claiming that he had been denied his civil right to have the votes cast for him counted honestly. Johnson's attorneys argued that the court lacked jurisdiction over the case because it was a local matter. Judge T. Whitfield Davidson offered a compromise. He suggested that both men's names be placed on the ballot. Texas voters would decide. Uncertain that he would win, Johnson rejected this plan.

So Judge Davidson went ahead with the trial. Witness after witness boldly lied on Johnson's behalf. However, Stevenson's lawyers produced citizens from Jim Wells County who had sworn that they did not vote in the runoff primary even though their names were listed on the Precinct 13 voting list. After listening to their testimony, Judge Davidson ruled that Johnson's name would be kept off the ballot until the issue of voting fraud was resolved. He ordered court officers to examine the ballot boxes in question. The boxes contained the actual votes and voting lists. Although copies of the Precinct 13 list had "mysteriously" disappeared, rumors circulated that one copy had survived. If it turned up in the ballot boxes, Johnson could be in serious trouble. His lawyers stalled for time, hoping their legal maneuvers in the federal appeals courts would end the trial before the damaging evidence could be found.

Johnson and his lawyers sent a hurried appeal to the circuit court judge most likely to reject their case. As they had anticipated, when they asked him to overrule Judge Davidson and let Johnson's name appear on the ballot, they were turned down. Once they lost their case, they were entitled to present an appeal directly to a justice of the United States Supreme Court. They asked Justice Hugo L. Black to overturn the circuit judge's decision. Black was known to prefer that judges not interfere in state politics. As Johnson's lawyers predicted, Black restored Johnson's name to the ballot, reasoning that the Senate could best judge the qualifications of its members. He also postponed the district court trial until the Supreme Court could consider the matter. The Supreme Court later denied Stevenson's petition to continue the trial.

Black's ruling came just in time to prevent court examiners from opening the ballot box for Precinct 13. The rest was history. Lyndon Johnson went on to the

Senate, where he eventually became Senate majority leader. He later served as vice president and then president of the United States. After his defeat, Coke Stevenson retired to his ranch, where he lived in contentment for another twenty-seven years.

Johnson's case was classic but far from unique. In 1948, Oklahoma senator Robert S. Kerr's victory was also tainted with charges of irregularities. One of the most perplexing questions in politics is why the American people look the other way when bribery and corruption devalue their vote. There are local laws to prevent such crimes, but enforcement is haphazard and proof is difficult to obtain. What's more, unlike Coke Stevenson, not every losing candidate tries to fight back.

Such was the case in the 1960 presidential campaign, when Democrat John F. Kennedy defeated Republican Richard M. Nixon by a margin of less than two-tenths of 1 percent. The popular vote was split 34,227,096 to 34,108,546. However, the electoral college gave Kennedy 303 votes to Nixon's 219. Both parties were guilty of election irregularities, but the most blatant example of fraudulent vote counting occurred in Cook County, Illinois, the base of a powerful political machine run by a Kennedy ally, Democratic mayor Richard J. Daley of Chicago. Suspicious returns were also reported from counties in southwestern Texas, loyal to Kennedy's running mate, Lyndon Johnson. At the time, Illinois had twenty-seven electoral votes and Texas had twenty-four votes, enough to have made Nixon president instead of Kennedy.

However, Nixon decided not to contest the election outcome. To demand individual county recounts would have been a long and laborious process because there was no federal election law to cover such problems. Moreover, Nixon did not want to divide the country in another Hayes–Tilden dispute. He believed that the

United States could ill-afford a contested election at a time when its foreign policy demanded strong leadership. However, the lesson of the 1960 election was not lost on him. In Nixon's subsequent campaigns, he allowed his supporters to use any means, fair or foul, to ensure him a wide margin of victory.*

Since 1960, other disputed elections have made headlines. For example, in 1985, the House of Representatives took up a controversial Indiana congressional race between incumbent Democrat Francis X. McCloskey and his challenger, Republican Richard McIntyre. Indiana officials had certified McIntyre as the winner, 116,490 to 116,456, but the Democratic majority in the House rejected their decision. Article 1, Section 5, of the Constitution gives the legislature the right to decide on the "elections, returns, and qualifications" of its members, so the House ordered a recount. It was conducted by auditors from the General Accounting Office under the direction of a three-member task force of the House Administration Committee. This panel, made up of two Democrats and one Republican, focused on returns from absentee ballots claimed by both sides. On April 18, five months after the election, the panel declared McCloskey the winner by 4 votes out of the 234,000 total. Angry Republicans decided to disrupt the business of the House. On April 30, the Democrats voted down a Republican proposal to declare the seat vacant; this would have required another election. On May 1, the House voted 236–190 to seat McCloskey, and the Republicans briefly walked out in protest.

Over the long run, American elections have produced highly qualified leaders, even though some of them have won office by making private deals and encouraging voting irregularities. Of course, the legis-

* See Chapter 8, pp. 109–117.

lature can always investigate disputed elections as it did in the 1985 McCloskey race. Defeated candidates can still bring suits in court, as Coke Stevenson did in 1948. Perhaps there should also be a federal election law to provide remedies for fraudulent vote counts in presidential elections, such as those that took place in 1876 and 1960. However, prevention is preferable to cures. Alert and vigilant citizens can insist on having their votes counted accurately and can volunteer as poll watchers and members of certifying boards to ensure that elections are honest.

an increasingly difficult situation. Rachel
years of marriage, she
continued to harass Rachel
drew Jackson, wh
went off to
had

On March 4, 1829, the
cloudy skies over the Cap
man addressed the assemb   a
somber suit with a black armba   , he
had just become the seventh presio   United
States. He wished his wife could have   essed his
moment of triumph, but she had died only nine weeks
before his inauguration. How the opposition had slan-
dered her when he ran for Congress. They had accused
her of adultery and bigamy. Back in his failed 1824
presidential campaign, one political pamphlet had
even asked, "Ought a convicted adulteress and her
paramour husband to be placed in the highest offices
of this free and Christian land?"[1] He was certain that
the incessant name-calling and gossip that plagued
this election campaign had shortened her life, had
brought on her fatal heart attack. She could not share
the greatest day of his life, but Andrew Jackson would
never forget his wife, Rachel.

As a young lawyer, Andrew Jackson had boarded
with Rachel Donelson's family. Rachel had married a
very possessive and jealous man, Captain Lewis Robards. If she paid the slightest attention to another
man, Robards instantly suspected her of being unfaithful to him. When he pointed an accusing finger at
Andrew Jackson, the lawyer moved out, hoping to ease

wever, Robards
 ter five tumultuous
 ed her family for help. An-
 had long admired her from afar,
 tch her from Kentucky, where the couple
 oved, and returned her to the Donelson home.
When Robards threatened to take her back to Kentucky with him, the Donelsons arranged for Rachel to stay with their friends in Natchez, Mississippi. Andrew Jackson escorted her on the 200-mile (320-km) trip to their plantation. Back in Tennessee, Jackson learned that Virginia authorities had granted Robards a divorce from Rachel. His law partner had assured him that she was free to wed. So in 1791, Jackson married his beloved backwoods bride in Natchez and brought her to Nashville, Tennessee, where he resumed his law practice. It was not until two years later that he found out he had been misinformed: Robards had not divorced Rachel until 1793. The couple remarried in 1794, but the damage was done. They had unintentionally violated society's rules, and Andrew Jackson's political opponents would never let them live it down. Respectable women refused to invite Rachel to their social gatherings, and Jackson took plenty of political abuse. Over their thirty-seven-year marriage, the scandal kept gossipmongers busy.

Rachel Jackson had suffered personal penalties for breaking the accepted social code. Perhaps that was why President Jackson was so anxious to save others from a similar fate. Even as he took the oath of office, he was aware that a scandal was brewing within his cabinet, the group of officials who headed government departments. Their wives, self-appointed leaders of Washington society, had refused to acknowledge Secretary of War John H. Eaton's beautiful new bride, Peggy, at the inauguration ceremonies and at the ball held later that night. These refined and proper ladies

treated Margaret (Peggy) O'Neale Timberlake Eaton, the widowed daughter of a Washington tavernkeeper, as their social inferior.

At the age of sixteen, Peggy had married John B. Timberlake, a navy purser with the rank of lieutenant. Because of her background, the beautiful, dark-haired young woman was excluded from many social gatherings that her husband's position entitled her to attend. At the time, two senators from the frontier state of Tennessee, John H. Eaton and Andrew Jackson, were boarders at her father's tavern. Jackson provided this glimpse of her in a letter written in 1823: "Mrs. Timberlake, the married daughter whose husband belongs to our Navy, plays on the Piano delightfully, and every Sunday evening entertains her pious mother with sacred music to which we are invited."[2] Peggy set tongues wagging about her supposedly loose morals because she was often seen in the company of widower John Eaton when Timberlake was away at sea. Of course, the genteel ladies of Washington may have been jealous of her good looks and her ability to put men at ease. Upon Timberlake's death in 1829, President Jackson advised Eaton, now secretary of war, to marry Peggy in the hope of silencing the gossips. Neither man realized that the ladies of Washington would still refuse to welcome her into their social circles. Jackson and Eaton had much to learn about the role of "petticoat politics" in Washington.

The cabinet wives' persistent refusal to accept Peggy Eaton began to threaten the success of the new Jackson administration. A congressional delegation even advised Jackson to dismiss John Eaton from his post. He retorted: "I did not come here to make a Cabinet for the ladies of this place, but for the nation."[3] Instead, the president called a special meeting of his cabinet, excluding the secretary of war, to defend Mrs. Eaton's reputation. He demanded that the secretaries

take steps to end their wives' deplorable conduct. Then Jackson gave a formal dinner for the cabinet officials and their ladies. In a show of support for Mrs. Eaton, he arranged for her to be seated in a place of honor, next to him. This gesture further antagonized the cabinet wives. Later in the evening, when Peggy was asked to dance, they abruptly left the room. Jackson's intervention only increased their hostility to Peggy Eaton.

Then she made matters worse. Not able to win over the cabinet wives with kindness, she made a point of irritating them whenever they had to meet. Even the president's niece, his official hostess, refused to have anything further to do with her after they quarreled over a bottle of perfume and a fan. To avoid entertaining her uncle's tainted guest, she chose to leave the White House. President Jackson was so committed to Mrs. Eaton's cause that he was even willing to lose the companionship of his niece.

Within a short time, "petticoat politics" was transformed into "power politics." Members of the cabinet were divided over whether or not to snub Peggy Eaton. Vice President John C. Calhoun and his wife, Floride, led the anti-Peggy forces while Secretary of State Martin Van Buren, a widower, sponsored the Eatons. Both Calhoun and Van Buren were determined to succeed Andrew Jackson as president and used the Peggy Eaton affair as a springboard to power. Van Buren threw a lavish party for Peggy and encouraged his supporters to follow his example. But, the Calhouns would not receive her in their home and expected their camp to exclude her as well. Congressmen and diplomats were forced to join one side or the other, and government virtually came to a standstill.

In 1831, Martin Van Buren finally came up with a solution to the problem. He and John Eaton volunteered to withdraw from Jackson's administration. He

also suggested that the president ask other members of his cabinet to hand in their resignations. This allowed Jackson to appoint replacements and put an end to the controversy. Although Van Buren lost his post as secretary of state, he next became Jackson's adviser, then his vice president, when Jackson was reelected in 1832, and finally his successor in 1837. The Peggy Eaton affair drove a wedge between Jackson and Calhoun, but they became bitter opponents because they disagreed on national issues. John Eaton went on in 1834 to a successful career as governor of Florida and as ambassador to Spain in 1836. He died in 1856. Toward the end of her long life, Peggy Eaton created another furor when she married an Italian dancing master who defrauded her and ran off with her granddaughter. She died in 1879, alone and poverty-stricken.

The private lives of a president's wife and a cabinet officer's bride had become public knowledge. Social condemnation, as well as political accusations, played an important role in creating and perpetuating these scandals. In the Jacksonian era, the political world was no longer confined to the southern aristocrats and New England patricians of the Eastern Seaboard, but these pillars of society continued to turn up their blue-blooded noses at upstarts from the backwoods of Tennessee or tavernkeepers' daughters who rose above their humble origins. Pipe-smoking Rachel Jackson and flirtatious Peggy Eaton were not considered refined, upstanding members of the community, so their alleged disgraces could not be "swept under the rug."

Men as well as women could be forced to pay penalties for offending the existing social order. One nineteenth-century politician whose private life ultimately cost him his job was Richard M. Johnson, Van

Buren's first vice president. Johnson was lionized as the man who reputedly killed Indian leader Tecumseh during the War of 1812 (the truth of the claim was never established). He was a little-known Kentucky senator until William Emmons's heroic biography of his wartime feats catapulted him to fame. On this basis, he was chosen to be Van Buren's running mate in the 1836 presidential election. In those days, background checks were not a common feature of the nomination process, although Van Buren may have wished he had looked into Johnson's personal life more closely.

Not only did the opposition discredit Johnson's much publicized war record, they attacked him for having fathered two children with Julia Chinn, a black slave woman. When she died in 1833, Johnson took daughters Adaline and Imogene to live with him. As a proud father, he expected them to be accepted wherever they went. He frequently displayed them in public; for example, he took them for carriage rides in Washington, D.C. At the time, most Americans, not just Southerners, found his behavior offensive.

Using the most inflammatory language, newspaper articles and editorials made political as well as social capital out of Johnson's affection for his daughters. They accused him of defying the Constitution by supporting abolitionists in their attempt to end slavery and of upsetting the social order by seeking to "amalgamate" blacks and whites. Johnson's personal life quickly became the major issue of the 1836 election campaign. However, Van Buren stood by his vice-presidential nominee. Johnson's neighbor, a clergyman, wrote letters to the press attesting to the late Julia Chinn's fine character and homemaking abilities.

The voters easily elected Van Buren to the presidency. However, Johnson received 147 electoral votes, one short of the required majority. In accordance with Constitutional provisions, this election was turned over

to the Senate.* By a vote of 33–14, Johnson became the only vice president in American history to be elected to office by the Senate. To polite society in Washington, he remained a misfit and an outcast who would never gain acceptance.

He continued to outrage politicians and the public alike by living openly with a number of black and Native American women. In 1839, realizing that his personal relationships would prevent him from rising higher in the political world, Johnson took a leave of absence and went off to Virginia, where he managed a hotel he owned. During his lifetime, his attractive daughters married white men and received large tracts of land from their indulgent father. However, when he died at the age of seventy, it was recorded that he left "no widow, children, father or mother living."[4] According to prevailing social customs, the law failed to recognize that his daughters had ever existed.

In 1884, the revelation that another candidate for national office, Grover Cleveland, was a bachelor father gave rise to a scandal that nearly cost him the presidency. The Democratic party had made him its standard-bearer, planning to make the most of his reputation as a reformer. As mayor of Buffalo, New York, he had rid his native city of corruption before going on, as governor, to fight New York City's infamous political machine, Tammany Hall. His supporters had every reason to think he was a shoo-in. After all, most Americans believed that his Republican opponent, former Speaker of the House of Representatives James G. Blaine of Maine, was a crooked politician.

* The procedure is similar to that described in Chapter 3, pp. 36–37, for the election of a president in the event of a tie or a failure to achieve a majority of electoral college votes, but in the case of a vice president, the Senate, rather than the House, made the decision.

In Congress, Blaine had accumulated a fortune, accepting money to promote railroad and other business interests. Boston bookkeeper James Mulligan possessed a sheaf of letters documenting Blaine's illegal dealings. Once Blaine knew the Democrats were on his trail, he got hold of the incriminating "Mulligan Letters." In a dramatic but foolish gesture, he brandished these documents before his colleagues in the House and proceeded to read excerpts aloud, hoping to establish his innocence. However, once the letters were printed, his reputation was seriously damaged. It was no wonder that Cleveland's supporters expected a landslide victory.

Instead, their candidate had to fight for his political life in one of the dirtiest presidential campaigns in American history. On July 21, 1884, the *Buffalo Evening Telegraph* ran a story under the headline "A Terrible Tale." The newspaper revealed that bachelor Cleveland had fathered an illegitimate son. The article claimed that Cleveland recognized the child as his own, paid financial support to its mother, and then sent the child to an orphanage and the mother to an asylum. The Republicans were overjoyed. Soon a nasty little song made the rounds: "Ma! Ma, where's my pa? Gone to the White House, Ha! Ha! Ha!"[5]

Since the charges were made early in the campaign, Cleveland had time to deal with them. Known for his honesty and integrity, he instructed his campaign managers: "Whatever you say, tell the truth."[6] They told the public that Cleveland had indeed been involved with the widowed Maria Halpin in the early 1870s. In 1874 she had a son and, although she had been seeing several men at the time, she named Cleveland as the father. There was no proof of his paternity, but Cleveland accepted responsibility for the child because the other men in Maria's life were married. When Maria began drinking to excess, he placed her in

Date: _____

Time: _____

Day of Week: _____

Service: _____

Technician: _____

ian & company

INC.

Hairstyling

Tanning

Opposite NationsBank, Millhopper

2622 N.W. 43rd Street, Suite A-1 • Gainesville, FL 32606

(352) 373-5189

(352) 371-6898

an asylum and gave the child to a New York couple to raise.

While Cleveland was admitting to the sensational paternity charges, his Democratic supporters came up with new accusations against his opponent. They learned that Blaine's wife had given birth to a child just three months after her marriage. However, Cleveland would not let them publicize this nasty story. It leaked out anyway, and Blaine responded with a confused disclaimer. On Election Day, the troubled voters had to choose between a man with an impressive public record and a tarnished private life and a man whose public and private reputations were scandal-ridden. Understandably, the election was close. Cleveland received 4.9 million votes to Blaine's 4.8, but the Democrats triumphed over the Republicans, 219 electoral votes to 182.

Both politicians weathered the political storms their campaigns had stirred up. In 1886, President Cleveland, a forty-nine-year-old bachelor, married Frances Folsom, aged twenty-two. She became the youngest first lady in the nation's history. Blaine went on to serve as secretary of state under Benjamin Harrison. Harrison was defeated by Grover Cleveland in 1892, when Cleveland won a second, nonconsecutive term as president. Maria Halpin eventually remarried and moved to New Rochelle, New York, and her son grew up to become a doctor.

Nineteenth-century Americans expected public officials and their families to serve as pillars of the community. When politicians violated the commonly accepted code of conduct, journalists had a field day. Scandals were aired in public and were quickly turned into campaign fodder. Voters had the opportunity to reject candidates whose wrongdoing made headlines. For the most part they did not. If women had had the right to vote, perhaps the election results might have

been different. Given the double standard of the age, women were regarded as the custodians of family virtue while men were permitted the freedom to stray. That may be why men were more tolerant of other men's failings than their wives, daughters, or sisters were.

It is ironic that in the moralistic nineteenth century journalists were willing to publicize politicians' misdeeds, while in the more permissive twentieth century, modern reporters chose to keep the public in the dark about private affairs of the nation's leaders. One of the well-kept secrets of the "roaring" 1920s was the complicated romantic life of the nation's president, Warren G. Harding. This handsome Ohioan, the editor and co-owner of a hometown newspaper, married a local girl and entered politics. He made his way to the United States Senate in 1915, where he failed to introduce even one important piece of legislation. However, his utterly unimpressive record made him an attractive presidential candidate. The opposition would have little to hold against him.

The press had heard rumors about Harding's infidelities, but unlike their nineteenth-century predecessors, they did not print the stories. The same rumors reached the opposition, but they were too distracted by a flood of leaflets, mistakenly claiming that Harding had black ancestors, to pay attention to the other gossip. On the eve of the presidential nomination, Harding was asked whether there were any "skeletons in his closet." After thinking the matter over, the would-be candidate issued a denial because he had survived three previous elections without mention of his romantic entanglements. Upon receiving his party's endorsement, the poker-playing Harding exclaimed, "I feel like a man who goes in on a pair of eights and comes out with aces full."[7] His private life was forgotten in the storm of campaign debates over

whether the United States should join the League of Nations, a world organization established to preserve the hard-won gains of World War I. Harding won an overwhelming victory over the Democrats in 1920.

Harding's private life would certainly have kept the gossip columnists busy if they had only known what was going on. In 1905, he had begun an extramarital liaison with Carrie Phillips, the wife of a businessman friend. The Phillipses and the Hardings saw each other socially. The couples even went on a cruise to Europe together, so it was a great shock to Florence Harding to find out about her husband's infidelity. Threatened with divorce, Harding assured her that the affair was over. Nevertheless, he continued to see Mrs. Phillips. Later, during Harding's presidential campaign, the Republican National Committee even made payments to her, ensuring that she would not reveal her relationship with the candidate. In 1915, as a senator, Harding had also become involved with Nan Britton, an impressionable young woman. In 1919, she bore him a daughter whom he supported but never met. It wasn't until 1927, with the publication of Nan Britton's sensationalist book, *The President's Daughter*, that the public learned the intimate details of their affair. By that time, Harding had conveniently died.

Even more shocking were revelations that four-time president Franklin D. Roosevelt had been unfaithful to his devoted wife, Eleanor. During his lifetime, the press had carefully protected the president's privacy. They did not even photograph him in a wheelchair. The president, crippled by polio as a young adult, had achieved heroic stature by seeing the country through a devastating economic collapse and the perils of World War II. His activist wife had earned the nation's gratitude for her compassion toward the poor and disadvantaged. Until her death in 1962, Eleanor dedicated herself to public service, even representing her

country at the United Nations. So when the story of his infidelity finally broke, the public was astounded.

Most Americans knew that the elegant Franklin had married his fifth cousin, Teddy Roosevelt's niece Eleanor. The "ugly duckling" bride had blossomed into a caring wife and mother of five, despite the domination of Franklin's overbearing mother, Sara. What the public did not know was that Franklin had had an affair with Eleanor's social secretary, the charming and beautiful Lucy Mercer. She was hired in 1913, soon after Roosevelt became assistant secretary of the navy. Eleanor Roosevelt first learned about her husband's extramarital relationship in 1918. Helping him recover from pneumonia, she came across some love letters from Lucy while sorting out his mail. As she wrote to her biographer, Joseph Lash, many years later: "The bottom dropped out of my own particular world, and I faced myself, my surroundings, my world, honestly for the first time. I really grew up that year."[8] Eleanor and Franklin did not divorce. Such factors as the children's needs, his political aspirations to higher office, his mother's disapproval, and Lucy's Catholicism (she could not marry a divorced man) entered into their mutual decision. However, Franklin ended the affair, and Lucy soon married Winthrop Rutherfurd. The nature of the Roosevelt marriage changed from intimacy to companionship.

Later on, in 1941, during his third term as president, Lucy Mercer Rutherfurd began seeing Roosevelt again. As a recent widow, she visited him at the White House when Eleanor was out of town. She was even at his side in Warm Springs, Georgia, when he died of a cerebral hemorrhage in 1945, but she left before Eleanor arrived. At the time, rumors circulated that the president had also had a liaison with another woman. In the 1970s, Elliot Roosevelt, one of the Roosevelt sons, wrote a book claiming that his father had had an

affair with presidential secretary Missy LeHand. However, the president's other children insisted that the book presented an inaccurate account of their parents' private lives.[9]

More recently, the public has learned that before he became president, Dwight D. Eisenhower had a brief wartime romance with his driver, Kay Summersby, and that President Lyndon Johnson had a thirty-year relationship with Alice Glass, a free-spirited, idealistic Texan. But neither of these revelations attracted as much attention as the news that President John F. Kennedy had been linked with a great number of women, among them movie stars Marilyn Monroe and Angie Dickinson. Most Americans could recall images of the handsome former senator from Massachusetts with his beautiful wife, Jackie, and their children, at home in the White House in the early 1960s. They found it hard to believe that there were other women in his life.

To make matters worse, one of these women, Judith Campbell Exner, had ties to the notorious Chicago mobster Sam Giancana. In 1963, just nine months before he was assassinated, President Kennedy learned of Exner's ties to the underworld. A memo from FBI director J. Edgar Hoover provided him with details about her shady background. That memo was dynamite. If it leaked to the media, Kennedy was in trouble. If Hoover tried to blackmail him with it, Kennedy would have to abandon his attempts to clip the all-too powerful FBI director's wings. To protect himself, Kennedy stopped seeing Exner. The press did not get wind of the story until 1975, when the Senate Committee on Intelligence Operations uncovered the Kennedy-Exner relationship. In 1977, Judith Campbell Exner wrote a book, *My Story*, describing her affair with the late president.

Twentieth-century presidents' extramarital ro-

mances did not become common knowledge until years after their deaths. Neither their opponents nor the media felt that a government official's private life should be open to public discussion. What was obvious to most Washington insiders was hidden from the outside world. This self-imposed censorship may have served the public interest. Roosevelt and Kennedy might not have been able to accomplish as much as they did if they had been called upon to defend their personal conduct to the public.

Today society seems more open and permissive about premarital and extramarital relationships. Yet Americans are holding their public servants to higher standards of personal conduct than they did in the past. They are also demanding to know more about the private lives of those they elect to office. In 1988, Senator Gary Hart of Colorado lost his second bid for the Democratic presidential nomination when he challenged the press to confirm rumors that he was cheating on his wife. "Follow me around. I don't care. I'm serious. Put a tail on me, go ahead. They'd be very bored."[10]

Reporters from the *Miami Herald* already had put a tail on him. In May 1987, their surveillance of his Washington townhouse produced the front-page story that would-be model Donna Rice had spent the night with Hart. Soon other newspapers and magazines featured detailed accounts of Hart's cruise to Bimini, with Donna Rice and other guests, on board a yacht appropriately named *Monkey Business*. Unable to deny the story or the accompanying photographs, Hart dropped out of the presidential race. In December, he changed his mind and went out on the campaign trail. But by March 1988, he was convinced that he had lost the support of the voters and withdrew his bid for the nomination once again.

In the more permissive last decades of the century,

the private lives of candidates and government officials have once more been subjected to public scrutiny. While voters certainly have the right to demand information about the character of a candidate who campaigns for their support, politicians do not necessarily have to provide it. Of course, reporters may discover whatever the politicians are trying to conceal. What's more, the public does not have to vote for candidates who are less than open about their personal lives. Nevertheless, it is also important to remember that some of the nation's most outstanding leaders have not always led the most exemplary private lives.

The duel between Alexander Hamilton
and Aaron Burr in 1804 cost
Hamilton his life and
Burr his political career.

Above: During debates over slavery
during the 1850s, Representative
Preston S. Brooks of South Carolina
attacked and severely wounded
Senator Charles Sumner of Massachusetts.

Facing page: John Quincy Adams's (*top*)
participation in what was viewed as a
"Corrupt Bargain" with Speaker of the
House Henry Clay led to his defeat
of Andrew Jackson (*bottom*) in 1825.

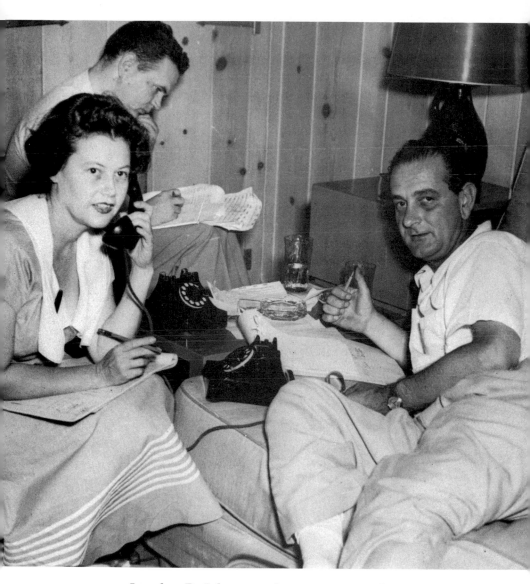

Lyndon B. Johnson, shown awaiting the
results of the Democratic primary for
the U.S. Senate, was accused by his
opponent, Coke Stevenson, of having
bought votes in the 1948 race.

Richard M. Nixon (*right*) decided not
to contest the close election results
of 1960. Both he and his opponent,
John F. Kennedy (*far left*), had been
accused of election irregularities.

Andrew Jackson's wife,
Rachel Donelson Jackson,
was accused of adultery
and bigamy because of
a previous marriage.

Margaret (Peggy) O'Neale Timberlake Eaton,
wife of a cabinet member, had
Andrew Jackson's cabinet officials
in turmoil, and was responsible
for cabinet resignations.

Above: A popular cartoon in 1884 shows
Democratic presidential candidate
Grover Cleveland tormented by the
illegitimate child he
acknowledged and supported.

Below: Franklin D. Roosevelt, shown here with
his mother and his wife, Eleanor, was protected
by the press during his affair with Lucy Mercer.

Senator Gary Hart of Colorado lost his
bid for the Democratic presidential
nomination in 1988 when he challenged
the press to confirm rumors that
he was unfaithful to his wife.

President Ulysses S. Grant's administration faced more accusations of financial misconduct than did any administration prior to his.

A popular cartoon in 1875 illustrates the defrauding of the government by whiskey distillers and Internal Revenue agents.

President Richard M. Nixon became an instant hero with his "Checkers Speech," in which he refuted charges that he had misused private contributions.

Senator Lyndon B. Johnson's secretary, Robert G. "Bobby" Baker, was found guilty of income tax evasion, larceny, and fraud.

New York representative Adam Clayton Powell, Jr., was expelled by Congress because of his financial transactions.

Vice-president Spiro T. Agnew resigned
from office to avoid impeachment proceedings
and pleaded guilty to income tax evasion.

Representative Mario Biaggi was convicted of racketeering during the Wedtech scandal.

Neil Bush, third son of President George Bush, was accused of a conflict of interest during the Savings and Loan scandals.

Senator Ted Kennedy arrives for
the inquest into the death
of Mary Jo Kopechne, killed in
an automobile accident when
the senator was driving.

Thomas Eagleton (*right*), after
charges of mental instability,
was the first vice-presidential
candidate to be replaced by a
presidential candidate.

President Richard M. Nixon
resigned from office in 1974
to avoid impeachment
because of his involvement
in the Watergate scandal.

U.S. Marine Lieutenant Oliver North
testifies before joint congressional
hearings about his role in
the Iran-Contra affair.

5
POLITICAL OFFICE FOR PERSONAL PROFIT: SOME CLASSIC EXAMPLES

Fame and fortune had favored him. Trained as a lawyer, he became the owner of a local newspaper by the time he was twenty-two years old. A pleasant man with a perpetual smile on his face, he began to work his way up the political ladder. In the 1850s, he helped to organize the newly formed Republican party in his home state of Indiana. By 1854, he was elected to the House of Representatives, where he remained for fifteen years, rising to the powerful post of Speaker after nine years. In recognition of his service, a tiny town in California even bore his name. Then he became vice president of the United States and let it be known that he had hopes of winning the highest office in the nation. However, the incumbent, President Grant, decided to seek another term and would not tolerate an ambitious second in command. Like so many other discarded vice presidents, he might have finished his term in political obscurity, but in September 1872, Schuyler Colfax learned that he would have to defend himself publicly against charges of corruption. A newspaper, the *New York Sun*, broke the sensational story of the Crédit Mobilier scandal, which involved Colfax and many influential members of Congress.

To take advantage of government programs funding the spread of railroads across the nation, the directors of the Union Pacific set up Crédit Mobilier,

ostensibly a railroad construction company. Actually, the company funneled federal monies directly into the pockets of its directors and shareholders. When Crédit Mobilier received construction contracts, it divided them among other firms the Union Pacific controlled, falsely inflated costs, and ended up making huge profits totaling more than $20 million. The profits were distributed to company shareholders in the form of enormous dividends. As a result, speculators were encouraged to raise bids on the price of company shares on the stock market, allowing stockholders to make even more money by selling the shares they owned.

To keep Congress from exposing this outrageous situation, Crédit Mobilier officers sold shares of company stock to congressional representatives at bargain prices. Schuyler Colfax, then Speaker of the House, bought twenty shares in the company, and other representatives, including James A. Garfield, also purchased the stock. Republican congressman Oakes Ames of Massachusetts, an officer of Crédit Mobilier, had boasted that he intended to distribute the shares, amounting to about $33 million, "where they will do the most good for us."[1] In effect, Ames encouraged members of Congress to represent the railroad construction company, not the public, and left them vulnerable to charges of conflict of interest. (Conflicts of interest arise when officeholders' private and personal concerns unduly influence their official decisions and cause them to neglect the public interest.)

Belatedly reacting to newspaper exposés of the scandal, the House of Representatives finally decided in 1873 to hold hearings on Crédit Mobilier's shady dealings. Many congressmen swore that they had innocently invested in the company, and the gullible public accepted their testimony. During this period of industrial growth and construction, most Americans believed that what was good for business was good for the coun-

try. Unlike his former colleagues, Vice President Colfax denied having any involvement in Crédit Mobilier. Under questioning, he claimed to have severed his business connection with Oakes Ames some years earlier. However, Ames's carefully kept notes revealed that the vice president had held onto the company's stock and continued to receive substantial dividends from it. Fortunately, for Colfax, he was not penalized for perjury (lying under oath). Moreover, Congress decided not to impeach him (remove him from office) because his term was about to expire anyhow.

Colfax spent the rest of his life as a popular lecturer touring the country. In 1885, he collapsed and died of a heart attack on his way to a speaking engagement. The House censured Ames for his role in the scandal. Ironically, President Grant's new vice president, Henry Wilson, admitted that his wife had paid $2,000 for Crédit Mobilier stock, but when he learned that the company expected preferential treatment, he made her return the shares. Despite the fact that Congressman James Garfield had accepted the stock, he was elected president in 1880.

Crédit Mobilier was one of the most notorious scandals of the era, but there were many others. In fact, the Grant administration faced more accusations of financial misconduct than had any previous administration—even though Grant did not derive any personal benefit from the corruption around him. A military hero, Grant had had no previous experience in politics. Trusting his subordinates and lax at the helm of government, he had left his officials to their own devices. During his two terms as president, no cabinet department escaped congressional scrutiny, but it was Grant's own secretary of the treasury, Benjamin Helm Bristow, who discovered a scandal that was closest to home, the Whiskey Ring.

The Whiskey Ring was a nationwide network of

whiskey distillers and Internal Revenue agents who had defrauded the government of millions of dollars of taxes levied on whiskey by having falsified distillery production reports ever since Lincoln's day. In April 1875, a newspaper publisher tipped off Treasury Secretary Bristow about the existence of the ring, and the secretary got funds from Congress to launch an investigation. Heading the ring during the Grant era was General John McDonald, a supervisor for the Internal Revenue Service who was based in St. Louis. The president had named McDonald to the post on the recommendation of his personal secretary, General Orville E. Babcock. When Secretary Bristow briefed the president about the scandal in general terms, Grant replied, "Well, Mr. Bristow, there is at least one honest man in St. Louis on whom we can rely—John McDonald. I know that because he is an intimate acquaintance and confidential friend of Babcock's."[2] Bristow had to disillusion the naive president. Confronted with evidence of his guilt, McDonald made a full confession to Bristow.

In May 1875, 350 men were arrested as members of the ring. Unsubstantiated rumors implicated the president's oldest son, Frederick Dent Grant, and the president's brother, Orvil Grant, but no evidence of their involvement was ever found. In July, when Grant learned that Babcock was also tied to the Whiskey Ring, he insisted that his secretary was being made a scapegoat for others. The president came to Babcock's defense and gave a written deposition (sworn statement) at his secretary's trial, which helped him win an acquittal in 1876. Nevertheless, Grant fired him. Babcock then got a job as an inspector of lighthouses. He drowned in 1884. McDonald eventually went to jail, where he wrote a book about the Whiskey Ring, claiming that Babcock was certainly involved in the illegal operation.

A third major scandal of the Grant era focused national attention on Secretary of War William W. Belknap and the beautiful Tomlinson sisters, Carita (Carrie) and Amanda. Amanda Tomlinson introduced Caleb P. Marsh, a New York contractor, and his wife to William Belknap and his wife, her sister Carrie. During a visit to the Marshes, Carrie, then pregnant, became ill, and it was Mrs. Marsh who nursed her back to health. In gratitude, Carrie offered to help Mr. Marsh obtain a War Department post, a tradership at Fort Sill, in August 1870. These positions were very profitable, allowing traders to sell cheap, shoddy goods to Native Americans at high prices. Marsh claimed that Carrie warned him, "If I can prevail upon the Secretary of War to award you a post, you must be careful to say nothing to him about presents, for a man once offered him $10,000 for a tradership of this kind and he told him that if he did not leave the office he would kick him down stairs."[3]

The only problem with Carrie's offer was that John S. Evans already held the lucrative position and did not want to give it up. As a compromise, Marsh and Evans agreed to a partnership, requiring Evans to pay Marsh $12,000 a year. Marsh paid half of that sum to Carrie in annual kickbacks (illegal payments from profits derived from government favors or posts). Marsh faithfully gave Carrie her share of the money until she died suddenly in December. Then he turned the funds over to her sister Amanda for the benefit of Carrie's child, but the child died in June 1871. However, Marsh continued to make the payments to Amanda. These helped her indulge in her luxurious life-style.

In 1874, when Belknap married Amanda, sums from Marsh defrayed the costs of her lavish wardrobe and elegant home. Amanda loved expensive clothes and set fashion trends for the ladies of Washington. This was much like first lady Mary Lincoln, whose

shopping sprees had run up a debt of $27,000 a decade earlier. In addition, Amanda spent exorbitant sums of money refurnishing her home. Her extravagant purchases also reminded Washingtonians of Mary Lincoln, who could not stay within the budget Congress set for redecorating the White House. Both ladies' excessive spending eventually came under congressional scrutiny. President Lincoln had paid his wife's debts out of his own pocket, but evidence surfaced to suggest that Secretary Belknap did not follow the late president's example.

Whether or not Belknap knew about his wife's arrangement with Marsh became the subject of considerable controversy. In 1876, after a congressional investigating committee uncovered the Marsh kickback scheme, the contractor implicated the secretary of war in the scandal. Yet Belknap professed to be innocent and unaware of any wrongdoing. Then the House Committee on Expenditures in the War Department heard Marsh testify that Belknap sent him instructions as to how and where the payments for his wife were to be made. The committee felt there were sufficient grounds to recommend that the secretary of war be impeached.

Learning of the congressional findings, both Secretary of the Treasury Bristow and Secretary Belknap rushed to Grant's side. Bristow urged the president to support impeachment. Belknap arrived at the White House just after Bristow departed and offered Grant his resignation. It was promptly accepted. Congress and the press publicly criticized Grant's decision. Members of the House went ahead and voted unanimously to impeach the secretary of war. However, the Senate acquitted him of the charges by a vote of 37–24, on the grounds that the legislature lacked jurisdiction over a cabinet member who had previously resigned. Belknap spent the remainder of his life in

private law practice, doing his best to keep Amanda in the style to which she had grown accustomed.

The public tired of the constant scandals that plagued Grant's administration. A poor judge of character, Grant just could not believe that the men he liked and appointed to office were dishonest. He admired rich men and did not stop to question how they had made their fortunes. This was an era when people who had wealth enjoyed flaunting it—especially those with new wealth from railroad construction and financial speculation in the stock market. A product of his times, Grant enjoyed flaunting it, too. He certainly did not object when his wife accepted expensive gifts of clothing and jewelry from people who did business with the government. Yet he was personally honest and, in 1876, did not leave office a rich man. He invested what capital he had and lost it, the victim of a swindle. Stricken with throat cancer, Grant spent his last days feverishly trying to complete his memoirs so that his family would have a comfortable and secure future. He died in July 1885, leaving a legacy of scandals on a scale that would not be matched or exceeded until the election of Warren G. Harding in 1920.

Like Grant, Harding was personally honest. He was described as "the best of the second raters."[4] Never having graduated from college, he was a friendly, pleasant man with no intellectual pretensions. As a senator, he was absent from the Senate for more than half the time. He openly admitted his shortcomings and promised to recruit some of the "best minds" in the nation to run the government. Although he did appoint such distinguished men as Herbert Hoover to head the Department of Commerce and Charles Evans Hughes to direct the State Department, for the most part he named unscrupulous cronies from his home state of Ohio to government posts. These associates looted the government and lined their own

pockets with the proceeds. They used political office for personal profit. After Harding's death, the public learned just how corrupt his administration had been. Shady dealings involving the "Ohio Gang" and the Veterans Bureau made headlines, and the "Teapot Dome" scandal became a symbol of the entire era for generations to come.

The "Ohio Gang" operated an influence-peddling scheme. (Influence peddlers accept payoffs for using their connections in government to help people get favors.) They made profits by helping people get around the Prohibition law. Beginning in 1919, Prohibition had made it illegal to sell or transport alcoholic beverages nationwide. In defiance of the government ban, bootleggers, who illegally sold alcoholic beverages to the public in violation of Prohibition laws, did a brisk business. The "Ohio Gang" made it possible for them to get permits to withdraw liquor from government warehouses and arranged for them to receive immunity from prosecution. (If they were caught selling or transporting alcoholic beverages, they would not be tried.) One bootlegger, George Remus, later claimed to have paid over $250,000 for these political favors.[5]

Members of the gang were united by a network of friendships, mixing political and personal relationships. Ringleader Jesse W. Smith regularly played poker with the president. He never held a government post but operated out of an office in the Justice Department, right near his pal Attorney General Harry M. Daugherty, whose apartment he also shared. Daugherty, Harding's longtime friend and sometime mentor, had served as the president's campaign manager before being rewarded with the position of attorney general. Other members of the Ohio Gang were hangers-on from the president's home state.

In late 1922, the House Judiciary Committee considered fourteen charges of misconduct against

Daugherty for his haphazard approach to law enforcement, including his failure to prosecute bootleggers. Since his accusers did not submit sufficient evidence against him to support their charges, Daugherty was cleared in January 1923. Harding had stood by him throughout the investigation. Then, in May 1923, Jesse Smith committed suicide in the wake of rumors about the Ohio Gang's illegal activities. On Harding's instructions, the attorney general had told Smith that he could not accompany the president on a trip to the West because his conduct was under suspicion. Daugherty suggested that his friend return to Ohio instead. In 1924, after a Senate investigation into the Ohio Gang's shady dealings, the attorney general resigned under fire. He was indicted—formally accused of defrauding the government as well as engaging in a number of financial irregularities. Daugherty managed to burn records of his own wrongdoing, and after two juries were unable to reach a verdict in his case, all charges against him were dropped.

Director of the Veterans' Bureau Charles R. Forbes made a fortune in kickbacks by selling off hospital supplies and narcotics as surplus goods and receiving a percentage of the sales as an illegal commission. In 1922, when Harding called him to account for his activities, he insisted that he had merely unloaded damaged merchandise. Although the president believed him, Congress did not. As complaints against him mounted, he submitted his resignation. In 1923, the Senate probed into his dealings and turned the findings over to the Department of Justice. Forbes was indicted for conspiracy to defraud the government, and in 1924 he was found guilty, sentenced to a two-year prison term, and fined $10,000.

The most notorious scandal of Harding's day, perhaps of any day, is known to most Americans as "Teapot Dome." It is a classic example of bribery (taking money

in exchange for a political favor). Teapot Dome was actually an underground navy oil reserve in Wyoming that had been set aside during President Woodrow Wilson's administration to prevent future shortages of petroleum. Harding's secretary of the interior, Albert B. Fall, persuaded Navy Secretary Edwin L. Denby to transfer the oil reserves to his department for private development. Congress had authorized such development in 1920.

Fall was a swaggering, self-confident New Mexico rancher who had come to Harding's attention when the two men served in the Senate. As president, Harding offered to make this poker-playing colleague secretary of state, but Fall wanted to be placed in charge of the Department of the Interior. Harding obliged him. Fall was to give the words "private development" an entirely new meaning—personal enrichment. In 1921, Fall quietly leased one of the reserves, at Elk Hills, California, to his friend of some thirty years, Edward Doheny, head of the Pan American Petroleum and Transport Company. Doheny "loaned" Fall the sum of $100,000, delivered in a little black bag. In 1922, the interior secretary discreetly arranged for Harry F. Sinclair of the Mammoth Oil Company to drill oil at the Teapot Dome reserve in Wyoming. Sinclair gave him $308,000 and a herd of cattle.

In April 1922, Wyoming senator John B. Kendrick heard rumors that Teapot Dome had been secretly leased to private interests. The Interior Department issued a denial. Then the *Wall Street Journal* reported the story. Only after Kendrick prompted the Senate to demand information on oil leasing did the department concede that it had made deals with commercial developers. Conservationists then prodded the Senate Committee on Public Lands to look into the navy oil reserve projects. A now cooperative Secretary Fall sent loads of documents to Capitol Hill with a cover letter from Pres-

ident Harding stating that Fall and Denby's proposal for private leasing "was submitted to me prior to the adoption thereof, and the policy decided upon and the subsequent acts have at all times had my entire approval."[6] Then, as now, leasing government property to private developers was an acceptable, if debatable, policy.

On August 2, 1923, Harding died unexpectedly while on a trip out West. Some said his death was timely, for just two months later, the Senate Committee on Public Lands began public hearings on Teapot Dome that exposed the sensational scandal. Montana senator Thomas J. Walsh heard stories that Fall had suddenly started spending large sums of money improving his New Mexico ranch just around the time he leased Teapot Dome to Harry Sinclair. Fall's literal interpretation of "private development" was certainly not what Congress had in mind. So Walsh asked the Senate to look into the secretary of the interior's newfound wealth. After a lengthy investigation, the Senate Committee on Public Lands finally turned up evidence of bribes Fall had taken from Sinclair and Doheny.

Normally, the attorney general would have prosecuted Fall and his associates. However, Attorney General Daugherty was a longtime friend of the interior secretary and could not be trusted to pursue the case impartially. Therefore, Senator Walsh proposed that President Calvin Coolidge, Harding's successor, appoint a special prosecutor to present the government's case against Fall. (Special prosecutors are independent lawyers who do not hold government positions. Because they are thought of as objective and uninvolved in administration concerns, they are brought in to try legal cases with political consequences.) Pressure was also building to impeach Navy Secretary Denby. Although innocent of any wrongdoing, Denby resigned to spare the new president embarrassment.

It took years to resolve the complicated legal issues raised in the lawsuits against Fall and the oil magnates. In 1927, the Supreme Court upheld lower-court decisions to cancel the leases given to Sinclair and Doheny on the grounds that these men, with the help of the secretary of the interior, had conspired to defraud the government. Fall was sentenced to a year in jail for taking a bribe. He became the first cabinet member to be sent to prison for a crime committed in office. Sinclair and Doheny were acquitted. One bright note in this otherwise grim story is that Edward Doheny built storage tanks at Pearl Harbor for the oil he had drilled and refined. These tanks were spared during the Japanese surprise attack in 1941 and helped the navy win the battle of the Pacific during World War II. [7]

Neither President Grant nor President Harding personally profited from the notorious scandals that occurred during their administrations. However, they were surrounded by greedy and unscrupulous associates. Both Grant and Harding were inexperienced and indifferent chief executives. They expected their subordinates to conduct the business of government with little presidential direction or control. The presidents' naive faith in their appointees, combined with their lack of political leadership, produced the nation's most incompetent and corrupt administrations.

6

POLITICAL OFFICE FOR PERSONAL PROFIT: HIGHLIGHTS FROM THE PAST FORTY YEARS

On September 23, 1952, a tense thirty-nine-year-old senator from California looked directly into the television camera and began to speak. If his unprecedented address to the nation did not succeed, he would be dumped from the Republican ticket in disgrace. No longer would he be Dwight D. Eisenhower's running mate in the upcoming presidential election. The senator was accused of having a slush fund (accepting unaccounted-for monies to be used for his personal expenses). Admittedly, he was far from wealthy. He had had to work his way through college and law school, and as a young congressman he was known to "count pennies" to make ends meet. Never a quitter, he was determined to clear his name and his reputation.

He explained to his unseen audience that the private contributions he received made it possible for him to continue his fight against corruption and communism and to get his message to the people. Referring to his wife, he stated, "Pat doesn't have a mink coat, but she does have a respectable Republican cloth coat; and I always tell her that she'd look good in anything."[1] With tears in his eyes, he went on to bare his soul and his expenses, mentioning that he did accept one gift, a cocker spaniel puppy named Checkers for his children. Public response to the speech, known forever as the "Checkers Speech," made Richard Nixon an instant

hero and guaranteed him the vice-presidential slot on the Republican ballot.

His remark about Pat Nixon's "respectable cloth coat" was a dig at the outgoing Democratic Truman administration and its supposedly lax attitude toward gifts. The Republicans were making political capital out of 1949 Senate hearings that had tried unsuccessfully to link Truman's longtime friend and military aide, Brigadier General Harry H. Vaughan, to an influence-peddling group known as the "five percenters." The committee did find that Vaughan had naively arranged to have a manufacturer friend ship deep-freeze units (freezers) to the president and other members of the government. Nixon's specific comment referred to a $9,540 mink coat Democrat E. Merl Young, a former federal loan examiner, accepted as a gift for his wife from a lawyer whose client had applied to borrow federal funds. The story had come to light in 1951 during Senate hearings on the activities of the Reconstruction Finance Corporation, the federal loan agency. That mink coat warmed the hearts of the Republican campaign staff. However, a few years later, another coat would embarrass the second Eisenhower administration.

In February 1958, the House Special Subcommittee on Legislative Oversight disclosed that Eisenhower's chief of staff, Sherman Adams, a man known for his honesty, had been involved in influence peddling. He had accepted a $700 vicuña* coat and other gifts from New England industrialist Bernard Goldfine in exchange for confidential information from the Federal Trade Commission. There were other irregularities as well. Eisenhower supported Adams, insisting that "a gift is not necessarily a bribe. One is evil, the other is a

* A vicuña is a member of the camel family, native to the Andes from Ecuador to Bolivia in South America.

—78—

tangible expression of friendship."[2] However, in September 1958, Eisenhower, praising Adams's six years of service, accepted his resignation for the good of the Republican party.

Eisenhower's own attitude toward gifts is revealing. Like Grant, another military hero turned president, this former World War II general did not see anything wrong with accepting presents from a grateful public or from friends. It is estimated that during the first three years of his eight-year tenure in office, he received about $40,000 worth of equipment and animals for his Gettysburg farm. The president did not think he was guilty of any conflict of interest because he refused gifts from corporations or businesses and put all donations on the record. However, lawyers of the New York City Bar Association created a Committee on the Federal Conflict of Interest Laws in 1958 and suggested that presidents should set an example for their administrations by passing along gifts to charities or museums.[3] In fact, chief executives of the United States may not accept personal presents from foreign governments, but they are free to accept them from private American citizens.

The problem of political gifts also plagued Senator Lyndon B. Johnson. In 1955, when he was Senate majority leader, Johnson had appointed Robert G. "Bobby" Baker as his secretary. For the next six years, he treated Baker as the son he had never had. However, by 1963 some of Baker's questionable business dealings came to the attention of the Senate Committee on Rules and Administration. Baker resigned his post to avoid answering charges, but the committee continued to look into his complicated transactions.

In 1964, during Johnson's presidential campaign, the committee revealed that Baker was vice president of an insurance company engaged in questionable dealings with the Johnson family. In 1957, Don B.

Reynolds, head of the company, had sold Johnson a $100,000 life insurance policy only after purchasing advertising time on the Johnson radio station in Texas. In 1959, Baker had urged Reynolds to purchase a stereo set that Mrs. Johnson had admired. The gift was duly sent. Two years later, as vice president, Johnson bought another $100,000 policy from Reynolds.

The election of 1964 vindicated Johnson, as did a 1965 Senate report that cleared him of any improprieties in the life insurance deals (this was despite objections from the Republican minority). As president, Johnson disassociated himself from his former aide, stating on television, "I haven't seen him . . . or haven't talked to him since he resigned from the Senate."[4] He also did his best to discredit Reynolds. In 1964, as a result of the prolonged Baker investigation, the Senate created a permanent ethics committee to set standards of professional conduct for its members and investigate breaches of its guidelines. In January 1967, Bobby Baker was convicted of conspiracy to defraud the government, evasion of income taxes, and other charges. He went to prison.

A gift received by a longtime Johnson friend, Supreme Court Justice Abe Fortas, raised serious questions about his personal and professional ethics. In 1969, a *Life* magazine article revealed that he had accepted $20,000 from a charitable foundation run by the Wolfson family. It was the first yearly installment of a series of payments that were to continue for the rest of Fortas's life. At the time, Louis Wolfson, a financier, was serving a one-year sentence in prison for stock manipulation. Eleven months later, Fortas returned the money.

The disclosure infuriated the public. They felt that Fortas's actions made a mockery of judicial impartiality and independence. Even though he had given the money back, Fortas had left himself open to charges of

conflict of interest, if not worse. Members of Congress proposed to investigate his conduct, and some even spoke of impeachment proceedings. Rather than prolong the controversy, Fortas chose to resign from the Court and return to private law practice. However, he denied any wrongdoing. He died in 1982.

During the Johnson years, the financial transactions of New York representative Adam Clayton Powell, Jr., also raised ethical questions. A black congressman, Powell was a popular Harlem pastor and noted civil rights advocate. On January 9, 1967, the House Democratic leadership voted to remove him from his chairmanship of the Education and Labor Committee, charging him with misusing approximately $46,000 in public funds. The next day, the full House barred him from the legislative body for five weeks while a special investigating committee examined his credentials. The committee found that in addition to taking private trips at public expense, Powell had put his wife on his office payroll, practices some other members of Congress indulged in as well. In February, the committee recommended that he be censured, fined $40,000 for misconduct, and stripped of his seniority (thereby losing credit for his many years of service and effectively denying him choice committee assignments or leadership positions). Instead, members of the Ninetieth Congress expelled him by a vote of 307 to 116. In the wake of the Powell investigation, the House set up a permanent ethics committee similar to the one the Senate established three years earlier.

Outraged by Powell's expulsion from Congress, the nation's black civil rights leaders rallied to his side. According to them, the House singled out Powell for punishment because of his determined stand on civil rights issues. They claimed that the members of Congress removed Powell from office because of his flamboyant personality and energetic leadership. In his six

years as chairman, he had dominated the House Committee on Education and Labor. Through his efforts, the House had passed more than sixty laws, including the "Powell amendment," which denied federal funds to racially segregated schools.

From his vacation retreat in Bimini, an island in the Bahamas, the defiant Powell filed suit in federal court. He agreed that the Constitution permits the legislature to judge the qualifications of its members and to discipline them. However, he claimed that his expulsion was illegal because he had met constitutional requirements for age, residency, and citizenship. He also charged that the House action discriminated against his black constituents by denying them representation. On April 7, the federal court dismissed his case on the grounds that separation of powers prevented the judiciary from telling Congress what to do. Powell's attorneys filed an appeal. In 1969, the Supreme Court vindicated him. Meanwhile, on April 11 a special election was held in Harlem to fill his vacant seat. Powell remained in Bimini to avoid arrest in another legal matter. Nevertheless, he got 74 percent of the vote and was returned to Congress. Defeated in a 1970 Democratic primary election, he retired from politics and died of cancer in 1972.

Among the many problems that beset the Nixon administration in the early 1970s* were charges of financial misconduct leveled against Vice President Spiro T. Agnew. The son of Greek immigrants, he had worked his way through college and law school in Baltimore, Maryland, rising quickly in local Republican circles to become governor of the state. When he was being considered for the vice-presidential nomination, Republican background checks failed to uncover his shady dealings. From 1967 to 1969, Governor Agnew

* See Chapter 8 for a discussion of the Watergate scandal.

had received $1,000 a week in kickbacks, totaling $250,000, from Maryland contractors for awarding them state construction projects. Moreover, after he became vice president, Agnew accepted $50,000 owed to him from his gubernatorial days. These facts did not come to light until after the Nixon-Agnew ticket had been reelected to a second term in office.

Accused of influence peddling, taking kickbacks, and accepting bribes, Agnew chose to take his case to the American people. In August 1973, he appeared on television and confessed to the nation that the Justice Department had been investigating his activities for some time. He professed his innocence, but his speech was not very convincing. In the past, he had made enemies in the news media by attacking reporters for their biased and inaccurate reporting of the Nixon administration. Now, they relentlessly covered all of the charges leveled against him. In October 1973, he resigned from office to avoid impeachment. To avoid indictment, he chose to plead guilty to a charge of income tax evasion. Judge Walter B. Hoffman sentenced him to a $10,000 fine and three years' unsupervised probation.

During the administrations of Gerald R. Ford and Jimmy Carter, bribery and corruption surfaced again in Congress, despite the existence of ethics committees. Under Republican president Ford, the Justice Department began looking into the activities of Tongsun Park, a South Korean rice broker. From 1967 to 1976, he had given gifts and cash totaling around $850,000 to thirty-one members of Congress, all Democrats. A grand jury indicted him on thirty-six counts, including bribery, but the charges were dropped when he agreed to testify against the members of Congress. As a result of his disclosures, the House officially reprimanded three representatives from California: John McFall and Edward Roybal for not reporting Park's

contributions and using them for personal expenses, and Charles Wilson for lying to the House Ethics Committee about the money he received. Edward Patten of New Jersey was also faulted for lying about a cash gift from Park. Eight other members of Congress, including Speaker Tip O'Neill, were cleared of charges. (Park had given two birthday parties for O'Neill, spending $7,500 on the celebrations.) Only one representative went to prison, Richard T. Hanna, also of California, who was released after serving twelve months of his thirty-month sentence for conspiracy to defraud the government.

Morality and honesty in government were major themes of Democrat Jimmy Carter's presidential campaign. The former governor of Georgia, intent on cleaning house—and the Senate—found a lot of dirt, some of it hurtful to his own party. In March 1978, his administration embarked on a twenty-three-month investigation of bribery and corruption in Congress, known as Abscam (Arab Scam). In a rented Washington, D.C., house and hotel suites in New York and New Jersey equipped with hidden video cameras, the FBI had a phony Arab sheik, actually a cooperative ex-convict, and their own agents, in disguise, offer bribes to a number of representatives. The dark-complexioned "sheik," duly garbed in Arab robes, communicated in a series of nods, smiles, and foreign-sounding grunts while his henchmen, in pinstripe suits, "translated" for him. At various times, members of Congress were asked to help the "sheik" get federal grants or gambling licenses or set up real estate deals. Incredibly, most of the congressmen fell for the ruse.

Republican senator Larry Pressler of South Dakota was recorded rejecting the offer: "Wait a minute, what you are suggesting may be illegal."[5] However, six representatives and one senator fell into the trap. Videotaped peddling their influence in exchange for bribes

were Democratic senator Harrison Williams of New Jersey, Democratic representatives Raymond Lederer and Michael "Ozzie" Myers of Pennsylvania, New Yorker John Murphy, John Jenrette of South Carolina, Frank Thompson, Jr., of New Jersey, and Republican representative Richard Kelly of Florida. The FBI shut down the operation on February 2, 1980, after it learned that the media were planning to report the Abscam story to the public.

As a result of Abscam, Harrison Williams became the fourth senator in history to be convicted of a crime while serving in office. He and representatives Lederer, Myers, Murphy, and Thompson each received three-year terms. Jenrette got two years; Kelly, eighteen months. Most of the congressmen were eventually paroled before completing their prison sentences. None returned to the legislature. Their trials raised interesting questions about entrapment (inducing people to commit crimes and then arresting them), which have yet to be resolved.

Not surprisingly, in 1977 and 1978 Congress tightened its codes of ethics. Members and their staffs were required to disclose personal financial information and were forbidden to accept major gifts from lobbyists (individuals seeking to influence government decisions on behalf of their clients).[6] New limits were placed on their outside incomes from speeches and books. The 1978 Ethics in Government Act also prohibited cabinet secretaries and administrators from accepting gifts in connection with their official acts. As a condition of appointment, they had to submit their financial records for government review.

In addition to Abscam, other scandals troubled the Carter administration. In 1977, the president had to accept the resignation of his friend, Budget Director Bert Lance, after a three-year government probe into the former Georgia bank officer's financial dealings.

The controversial activities of the president's brother Billy outraged the public and led to a Senate investigation in 1980. Although refusing to register as an agent of the Libyan government, Billy Carter had accepted a free trip to Libya in 1978, founded the Libyan-Arab-Georgia Friendship Society, and received $220,000 from the Libyan government. Once it was learned that Billy had never exerted influence on American foreign policy, the public uproar died down.

According to at least one observer, Ronald W. Reagan's presidency may have set a record for the number of scandals taking place within one administration—225 and still counting.[7] Among these was the Wedtech affair. As a small machine shop employing minorities, Wedtech had received certain federal benefits in 1980 and 1981. Its work was so shoddy that it had difficulty in securing military contracts or meeting the schedules of those it had obtained. Yet by 1984, the company had come to President Reagan's attention. He praised John Mariotta, one of Wedtech's founders, for "providing jobs and training for the hard-core unemployed of the South Bronx. . . . People like John Mariotta are heroes for the eighties."[8] However, Mariotta and his associates certainly were not heroes. The little machine shop siphoned off federal funds to enrich its directors and political allies, not to help minority workers.

Despite the company's lack of experience or qualifications, Wedtech's "street smart" directors hoodwinked the government into awarding them substantial military contracts. They became a multimillion-dollar defense contractor by developing a complex network of influential political contacts. For example, in 1982 they hired former White House aide Lyn Nofziger as a lobbyist. He wrote to James E. Jenkins, a deputy attorney general in the Department of Justice, to enlist his help in securing a $28 million army contract for Wedtech.

By law, Nofziger was not supposed to involve himself with lobbying for one year after leaving his White House post, but he wrote the letter only eight months after his resignation. At the same time, Attorney General Meese was asked to use his influence to help Wedtech get the contract.

When their efforts succeeded, these political contacts were suitably rewarded. Jenkins became a Wedtech consultant. Nofziger's lobbying firm received substantial shares in the Wedtech corporation. Meese invested funds in a company connected to Wedtech and made a 90 percent profit on his investment. Many other politicians received payoffs as well, including New York congressmen Mario Biaggi and Robert Garcia. Biaggi received $1.8 million worth of stock in Wedtech for his help. Garcia and his wife were given a $20,000 loan and $76,000 in various payments from the company. Soon Wedtech had to get military contracts just to be able to meet its mounting political debts and the rising costs of its inefficiently run operations. In December 1986 it went bankrupt.

Federal and state officials cooperated to expose the Wedtech scandal. As a result of their investigations, the company's founders went to prison, and a number of national and local politicians were publicly disgraced. Among them was Congressman Biaggi. In August 1988 he was convicted of racketeering. Sentenced to an eight-year prison sentence, he was released because of poor health in June 1991, six months before he would have been eligible for parole. Lyn Nofziger's 1988 indictment for violating the 1978 government ethics law was overturned on appeal. In July 1988 Attorney General Meese resigned from his post after a series of official inquiries into his more questionable activities, including Wedtech. In 1989, the Garcias appealed their conviction on charges of extortion but failed to clear themselves in a new trial held in 1991.

They launched another appeal while awaiting sentencing in 1992. Meanwhile Congress tightened its conflict-of-interest guidelines by passing the Ethics Reform Act of 1989. This federal law prevented government employees from accepting gifts or fees for public appearances or writings, even if they were non-job related, and further restricted the lobbying activities of former administrators.

In the 1980s, women received significant political recognition, but not all of it was positive. Ronald Reagan's appointment of Sandra Day O'Connor as the first woman to serve on the Supreme Court in 1981 was publicly acclaimed. However, some of the other women the president named to government posts were discredited when the public learned that they had used their offices for personal profit. In February 1983, Environmental Protection Agency (EPA) administrator Anne Burford, along with many of her senior aides, was accused of mismanagement and conflict of interest. It was claimed that they conveniently overlooked "friendly" chemical companies' violations of environmental laws. Burford resigned under fire.

Meanwhile, her associate, Rita Lavelle, head of the toxic waste cleanup program, faced conflict-of-interest charges because she had handled cases involving her former employer, Aerojet General Corporation, an unethical practice. Under her direction, the EPA showed favoritism to certain polluters and delayed cleaning up several toxic waste sites. She also accepted luncheon invitations from firms under fire from the EPA. In 1983 she was found guilty of lying to Congress and eventually served three months of a six-month prison term. In all, five House panels and one from the Senate looked into EPA activities.

In June 1989 a House subcommittee exposed mismanagement and corruption in the Department of Housing and Urban Development (HUD) during the

Reagan years. Committee members learned that HUD agents had failed to turn in monies they collected from the sale of foreclosed houses (houses whose owners could not meet their mortgage payments). Instead, they kept the money for themselves. One of these agents, Marilyn Louise Harrell, made headlines as "Robin HUD" when she claimed to have distributed much of her ill-gotten gains to the poor. Her boss, Secretary Samuel Pierce, also came under fire. He was accused of favoritism in selecting projects to receive HUD funds.

Republican women were not the only members of their sex to be involved in political scandals. When New York Democrat Geraldine Ferraro agreed to become Walter Mondale's running mate in the 1984 presidential campaign, she exposed herself to public scrutiny. As the first woman to become the vice-presidential nominee of a major political party, she was an especially tempting target. The nation soon learned that Ferraro had had to refund the $134,000 her family contributed to her 1978 congressional campaign under orders from the Federal Election Commission. By law, each person may donate only $1,000 to a candidate. Then the House Ethics Committee looked into conflict-of-interest charges against her because Representative Ferraro had claimed an exemption from the congressional requirement that she disclose her husband's (John Zaccaro's) income tax return for public scrutiny. At a two-hour press conference on August 2, 1984, she finally released her own and her husband's tax returns. She admitted underpaying her taxes by $53,459, claiming her accountant had made the error. Only a week earlier, she had paid the amount owed plus interest. During the 1980s, women had shown promise of becoming equal partners in political corruption.

During the Reagan years, even the judiciary was

not immune to charges of wrongdoing. In 1983 black federal judge Alcee Hastings of Miami was accused of accepting a $150,000 bribe. After he was acquitted by a jury, a committee of judges overturned the jury's decision. Then the House of Representatives impeached him, and in October 1989, the Senate removed him from office by a vote of 69–26. In the same year, they also ousted white federal judge Walter Nixon of Mississippi, who was convicted of perjury. He was serving a prison sentence at the time of his impeachment.

Most Americans looking back on the Reagan era will probably single out the collapse of the savings and loan industry as the most devastating scandal of the 1980s and 1990s. It began on October 15, 1982, when President Reagan signed a law deregulating savings and loans institutions (S&Ls), cutting them loose from restrictions that had limited the types of investments these thrift institutions could make with depositors' money. It was hoped that S&Ls would be better able to compete in the financial marketplace, but what happened was one of the biggest financial disasters in American history. Shady financial speculators and real estate operators got themselves appointed to boards of directors and otherwise gained control of the S&Ls. It did not take them long to demand large salaries or sizable fees for their services and turn deregulation to their personal advantage.

Charles Keating's Lincoln Savings and Loan of California became a symbol of much that was wrong with the S&L industry. The thrift attracted new depositors by offering high rates of interest on savings accounts. To pay these rates, Keating recklessly invested depositors' money in dubious real estate schemes. He also sold them junk bonds (high-interest, high-risk investments that have often been used to finance corporate takeovers). He misled his depositors by claiming that these bonds were covered by federal deposit insurance

when they were not. In 1989, Keating's Lincoln Savings and Loan failed after running up a debt of $2 billion. When the junk bond market collapsed and real estate sales went into a slump in the late 1980s and early 1990s, many other S&Ls also became insolvent (unable to pay off their debts or refund their depositors' money).

In response, on August 9, 1990, President Reagan's successor, George Bush, signed a law to bail out the bankrupt thrifts. The government took over 472 bankrupt thrifts and merged or closed 211 of them within a year's time. At least 500 more were in trouble. Estimates of what the bailout would actually cost the American taxpayer kept rising. In 1990, it was estimated that it would exceed $1 trillion, the equivalent of about $30 a month for every American family over the next forty years.[9] The Justice Department pressed charges against more than 300 other S&L executives and staff members and won 231 convictions. Over 75 percent of those accused of crimes were sent to prison, and the former bank directors paid back $56 million to their creditors, a small portion of the enormous sums they had squandered or stolen. At his state trial in 1991, Charles Keating was found guilty of seventeen counts of fraud. He also faced federal charges.

Not only had the bankers played fast and loose with depositors' money, they had also made large contributions to Republican and Democratic political campaigns in an effort to discourage new banking regulations and to stave off investigations into their shady transactions. For example, Charles Keating donated $1.3 million to five senators: Democrat Alan Cranston of California, Democrat John Glenn of Ohio, Republican John McCain of Arizona, Democrat Don Riegle of Michigan, and Democrat Dennis DeConcini of Arizona. Among the many politicians who received S&L contributions, the Senate Ethics Committee

singled out these five senators for a fourteen-month investigation starting in 1990. Known as the Keating Five, they faced charges that they had improperly intervened with federal regulators in 1987 to help the Lincoln Savings and Loan. Cranston, Riegle, and De-Concini were members of the Senate Banking Committee.

During twenty-six days of televised hearings, the public learned that DeConcini had championed the appointment of a Keating business associate to the Federal Home Loan Bank Board, the agency in charge of S&Ls. On Keating's behalf, the five senators had voiced their opposition to proposed federal rules limiting the thrifts from making speculative investments, for example, in junk bonds. They also demanded to know why federal examiners were conducting such a prolonged and intensive investigation of the Lincoln Savings and Loan. As soon as they learned that the examiners planned to turn over their findings to the Justice Department for use in a possible criminal prosecution, the senators backed off.

At the hearings, the senators claimed that they did nothing more for Keating than they would have done for other campaign contributors and constituents (the people whom they represent). As Cranston explained, "I had good reason to believe that a business which employed almost 1,000 of my constituents, in my state of California, and thus benefited their families and the communities where they live, was being dealt with improperly."[10] In the absence of rules clearly defining proper and improper services to supporters, the Ethics Committee recommended that the Senate establish such guidelines. In April 1991, a group of senators, headed by Kentucky Democrat Wendell H. Ford, began to study the problem. Because Cranston was most involved in helping Keating, he was reprimanded by the Senate. The other four senators received written

rebukes from the Ethics Committee. Cranston, recuperating from cancer surgery, did not plan to run for reelection.

Among the many others linked to the S&L scandals was Neil Bush, third son of the president. As a director of the failed Silverado Savings and Loan in Denver, he was accused of a conflict of interest because he voted to lend $900,000 to Kenneth Good, a real estate speculator who had invested in Bush's oil exploration company, JNB. In addition, Bush approved $100 million in loans to another JNB investor, Bill Walters, a Denver developer. Federal investigators claim that Bush did not inform the bank of his business connections with the two loan applicants. Bush defended himself by stating that "everybody has relationships, everybody knows everybody."[11]

In April 1991, after a fourteen-month inquiry, federal regulators accepted the findings of an administrative law judge, that Bush had been involved in a conflict of interest and ordered him to avoid such conduct in the future. This was the lightest penalty that could be imposed on him. In June, Bush and ten other Silverado officials agreed to pay $49.5 million to settle a civil lawsuit brought by the Federal Deposit Insurance Corporation, charging them with "gross negligence." Most of the payment would come from the S&L's liability insurance. Meanwhile, a family friend raised money to cover the costs of Neil Bush's legal defense.

As this historical survey has shown, political corruption is an equal-opportunity enterprise. It is nonpartisan, no longer sexist, nor limited to one branch of government. To make politicians immune to the "fast buck" and other forms of political corruption, some have suggested that a limit be placed on the length of time public officials may hold office, following the example of the Twenty-second Amendment, passed in 1951, which limited the president to two terms. (The

amendment restored a political tradition interrupted by Franklin Roosevelt's unprecedented four terms.) Among other objections to this proposal is the possibility that greedy politicians would simply have to make the "fast buck" in a shorter period. Besides, the public always has the option of rejecting incumbents up for reelection. It may be that politicians' actions merely reflect the values of society at large. As long as Americans respect individuals who "get rich quick" by any means, the temptation to accept "easy money" will persist.

7
PUBLIC DISPLAYS OF PERSONAL MISCONDUCT

On the evening of July 18, 1969, some time after 11 P.M., on Chappaquiddick Island off Martha's Vineyard, Massachusetts, a 1967 Oldsmobile plunged off Dike Bridge into Poucha Pond, where it turned over and sank. The driver managed to escape. His passenger, a young woman in her twenties, did not. The driver did not report the accident until the next morning, some ten hours later. Instead, after a vain attempt to free his companion, he returned to the cottage where he had been attending a party. Discreetly, he asked his cousin, Joe Gargan, and a friend, Paul Markham, both lawyers, for help. They drove him back to the pond and repeatedly dove underwater to see if they could rescue the passenger. When their efforts failed, they advised him to notify the police.

He sounded them out on the possibility of claiming that the passenger had been driving the car alone, but they advised him to tell the truth.[1] Impulsively, he left the car, dove into the water, and swam across the narrow channel to Edgartown, Massachusetts. He proceeded to his motel room, where he changed clothes. At about 2:30 in the morning, he left the room and casually engaged a bystander in conversation about the noise coming from the hotel next door. In doing so, he had established an alibi as to his whereabouts if needed. The driver was Senator Edward Moore "Ted"

Kennedy. His passenger was Mary Jo Kopechne, a campaign aide to his late brother Bobby.

Reared in a wealthy, highly competitive family, Ted Kennedy knew what was expected of him. He had recently become the focus of his family's ambitions, the standard-bearer for three older brothers who had fallen in service to their country. Joseph, Jr., was killed on an aerial mission during World War II; John was assassinated in a presidential motorcade in Texas in November 1963; Robert, a senator from New York, was shot to death campaigning for the presidency in California in June 1968. Everyone had looked to Ted to carry on the family tradition, but within a year their hopes were dashed. The automobile accident on Chappaquiddick Island not only killed Mary Jo Kopechne—it destroyed Ted Kennedy's presidential prospects as well.

On the morning of July 19, at about 9:45, after another conversation with Markham and Gargan, Senator Kennedy finally made his way to the Edgartown police station. He gave a brief statement to Chief Dominick J. Arena, identifying Mary Jo Kopechne and admitting that he was the driver of the submerged automobile. He gave the approximate time of the accident and explained that he had been in a state of shock for about ten hours. What Kennedy did not tell Chief Arena was that before the accident he and Mary Jo had both attended a party for some of Robert Kennedy's former campaign workers. The senator also failed to mention that he had had a lot to drink that evening and that the driver's license he failed to produce at the police station had actually expired. He omitted the fact that he and his friends had made a futile attempt to rescue Mary Jo themselves.[2]

Chief Arena regarded the matter as a routine motor vehicle fatality. He had no reason to doubt the senator's statement, especially since Kennedy had voluntarily

turned himself in. Massachusetts law did not specify how much time drivers could take between leaving the scene of an accident and reporting it. So the chief was willing to accept Kennedy's explanation of why he waited ten hours before contacting the authorities. Kennedy promised to make himself available for further questioning. Then he left for his family home in Hyannis Port, where he went into seclusion.

Having learned of the senator's involvement in a fatal accident, hordes of reporters rushed to the Edgartown police station and the Kennedy compound in Hyannis Port. Eager for news, they asked why the married senator had been driving with the pretty young campaign worker late at night. They tried to find out how much he had had to drink and how fast he had been driving. They even found a witness who contradicted Kennedy's version of the time the accident took place. Neither the senator nor his aides would respond to their questions. Until now, the media had refrained from reporting embarrassing stories about the Kennedys' private lives, but the way this accident was being handled led reporters to suspect that an elaborate cover-up was being staged.[3]

Once Kennedy had given his statement to the police, Gargan made sure that all evidence of the party was quietly removed from the cottage on Chappaquiddick Island. He broke the news of Mary Jo's death to those of her co-workers who had attended the party and arranged for them to be escorted from Cape Cod before they could be questioned. Earlier, when Mary Jo's body was recovered, the doctor, certain that she had drowned and unaware of the identity of the driver, saw no need to perform an autopsy. The body was flown to the Kopechne home in Pennsylvania at the senator's expense. Ted Kennedy remained at Hyannis Port, holed up with speech writers and advisers until July 22, when he and his wife attended Mary Jo's

funeral service, still avoiding the reporters who pursued them.

On July 25, the senator made a brief appearance in an Edgartown court, where he pleaded guilty to the charge of leaving the scene of an accident. He received a suspended sentence. That night he addressed a nationwide audience on television, denying rumors of sexual misconduct but failing to explain why he did not report the accident immediately. He asked the citizens of Massachusetts to let him know whether he should remain in office, concluding, "I pray that I can have the courage to make the right decision. Whatever is decided, whatever the future holds for me, I hope I shall be able to put this most recent tragedy behind me and make some future contribution to our state and mankind whether it be in public or private life."[4]

What the immediate future held for Ted Kennedy was a series of complicated but unsuccessful legal roadblocks to prevent an inquest (a judicial inquiry) into the nature and causes of the accident. However, it was finally held in January 1970. In his report on the court's findings, made public in April, Judge James A. Boyle wrote: "There is probable cause to believe that Edward M. Kennedy operated his motor vehicle negligently . . . and that such operation appears to have contributed to the death of Mary Jo Kopechne."[5] There were no further legal proceedings, nor was the senator penalized for his actions. In November 1970, Ted Kennedy was reelected to the Senate with a 469,434-vote margin of victory, far short of the 1,129,244-vote margin by which he had defeated his opponent in 1964. On November 27, 1970, the senator took a driving test, and his license was restored. Although his public life seemed to be returning to normal, his private life had already begun to fall apart. A month after Chappaquiddick, his wife Joan miscarried. She drifted into alcohol-

ism, for which she eventually sought treatment, but by the end of the decade the marriage had failed.

In the long run, the accident need not have cost Ted Kennedy the presidency. But the way he handled the tragedy raised questions about his character, questions that have haunted him to this day. Was he competent to function under pressure, a quality essential to presidents? Did he take advantage of his political connections? Had the senator concealed the facts in an elaborately staged cover-up? Did Ted Kennedy try to put himself above and beyond the law? Some Kennedy supporters brought up other questions. Was he treated fairly by the press and law enforcement officials? Was the senator denied rights granted to most private citizens because of his well-publicized name? No matter how these questions were answered, Chappaquiddick became a symbol of Ted Kennedy's inability to live up to his brothers' legacy. It did not prevent the senator from becoming one of the nation's foremost spokesmen for the nation's poor and unfortunate, but it did put the presidency just beyond his reach.

The issue of concealing personal information from the public surfaced again during the 1972 presidential campaign. Shortly before sunrise on the morning of July 14, 1972, the Democratic National Convention, meeting in Miami Beach, Florida, nominated Missouri senator Thomas F. Eagleton as the party's candidate for vice president in the upcoming election. Senator George S. McGovern of South Dakota was the party's presidential nominee. McGovern admitted that he would have preferred Ted Kennedy as his running mate. However, Kennedy would have drawn too much fire from the opposition. Earlier, when Kennedy had considered running for president himself, a survey had shown that he was unlikely to win. Sixty percent of those polled indicated that they trusted incumbent

President Richard Nixon more than they trusted Kennedy. Seventy percent felt that he had withheld information about the accident at Chappaquiddick.[6]

Thomas Eagleton, McGovern's second choice, would strengthen the Democratic ticket. A liberal Catholic from Missouri, he had never lost a race in his home state. What's more, he had the support of organized labor. No background check on Eagleton was done. McGovern staffers had asked him a few superficial questions and had taken his word that he had nothing to hide.

On July 25, just two weeks after he was nominated, Senator Eagleton revealed some disturbing facts about himself at a news conference in Custer, South Dakota. With George McGovern at his side, he told reporters that from 1960 to 1966 he had been hospitalized three times for nervous exhaustion, fatigue, and depression and had twice undergone electric shock treatments. The story created quite a sensation, even though the public no longer regarded mental illness as a sign of immorality or lunacy. Reporters went to great lengths to dig up more "dirt" about the senator's condition. Columnist Jack Anderson even wrote that Eagleton had been arrested for drunk driving, a story based on rumors, not facts. Within a short time, Anderson had to issue a retraction and an apology.

Although Eagleton knew his disclosure would hurt the Democratic ticket, he was compelled to call the July 25 press conference. He had been tipped off that reporters from the Knight newspaper chain were about to print an article exposing his earlier emotional problems, and he decided to get to the public first. How the Knight reporters learned about Eagleton's illness is not known, but some interesting clues have turned up. Bob Woodward and Carl Bernstein, investigative reporters for the *Washington Post*, discovered that the Secret Service had forwarded information about the Demo-

cratic candidates to the White House. John D. Ehrlichman, President Nixon's assistant for domestic affairs, had received copies of Eagleton's health records. These were turned over to the Plumbers Unit, an undercover group of White House aides who, among other assignments, collected unsavory items about the president's political opponents and planted them with the media.[7] Could it have been that in the wake of his 1960 narrow loss to John F. Kennedy, President Nixon and his associates were determined to win the 1972 election at any cost, even at Senator Eagleton's expense?

At first, George McGovern supported his controversial running mate, stating that he stood by Eagleton "1,000 percent."[8] However, McGovern was under enormous pressure to drop the Missouri senator from the ticket. Some Democrats argued that a discussion of Eagleton's health would distract the public from the more serious issues of the campaign, such as America's role in the increasingly unpopular Vietnam War. They also claimed that Eagleton's lack of candor at the time of his nomination would make it hard for him to win support now. McGovern stalled for time, telling the public that both he and Eagleton would evaluate the difficult situation confronting them.

Finally, on July 31, the two men called a joint press conference in which McGovern announced Eagleton's withdrawal from the campaign. McGovern explained that he wanted to put an end to the debate over the vice-presidential candidate because it threatened to divide the party. On August 8, the Democratic National Committee confirmed the nomination of Kennedy brother-in-law R. Sargent Shriver as a substitute for Eagleton. In November, the new Democratic team was overwhelmingly defeated by Republicans Richard M. Nixon and Spiro T. Agnew. However, in the 1980 senatorial elections, Thomas Eagleton beat his opponent by a margin of 89,460 votes.

Eagleton was the first vice-presidential nominee in American history to be replaced. For some Americans, his departure raised questions about the need for thorough background checks to uncover a candidate's past indiscretions and misfortunes and about the desirability of having the party's presidential nominee choose the vice-presidential candidate. Others were more concerned about having someone with a history of mental instability serve in the second-highest office in the land. Evidently, the public had forgotten that while holding office, one of the nation's most outstanding presidents, Abraham Lincoln, had suffered bouts of depression (called melancholia in those days). Moreover, Warren G. Harding had been elected to the chief executive's post even though he had suffered a mental breakdown in his mid-twenties. Of course, Harding's record as president is not much of a recommendation to those who would vote for leaders who once had emotional problems.

In both the Kennedy and Eagleton episodes, prominent senators were discredited, not so much for what they did as for what they failed to do. Once they had covered up or concealed their personal problems from the public, they no longer seemed trustworthy. Their characters as well as their abilities were now suspect. They could no longer seek higher office, but at least they were not permanently barred from public life. As Senators Ted Kennedy and Tom Eagleton belatedly discovered, being a politician does not automatically guarantee immunity from personal problems or from having those problems aired in public.

The pressures of political office may indeed create or aggravate personal problems. To relieve stress, some officials have become dependent on alcohol and/or drugs. Substance abuse is nothing new. About a hundred years ago, so the story goes, President Abraham

Lincoln was questioned about the drinking habits of one of his generals, Ulysses S. Grant. He supposedly said that since Grant was so successful on the battlefield, he'd like to know what brand of liquor Grant was drinking so he could send some to his other generals. In another version of the tale, he is said to have replied, "But he fights,"[9] a reference to the fact that Grant, unlike most of Lincoln's generals, was willing to attack the Confederate armies. A West Point graduate, Grant had left the military in 1854 when his excessive drinking came to the attention of his commanding officer at Fort Vancouver, a lonely western outpost. He returned to army life only at the outbreak of the Civil War, but what a difference his presence made to the outcome of that conflict. By the time he became president, Grant no longer had a drinking problem.

In more recent times, charges of alcoholism brought about the downfall of well-known Washington figures, including the once dominant chairman of the House Ways and Means Committee, Democrat Wilbur Mills of Arkansas, and the former chairman of the Senate Armed Services Committee, Republican John Tower of Texas. In 1974, Congress ousted Mills from the chairmanship after his drinking bouts created a public scandal. For years, reporters and his colleagues on Capitol Hill knew that Mills was often drunk when he presided over his revenue-raising committee and shaped the nation's tax policies. The public learned about his drinking problem only when the married congressman became involved with stripper Fanne Foxe in a series of bizarre incidents, climaxed by his appearance on stage at her burlesque show. Journalists could not ignore this blatant display of misconduct. Then Mills finally admitted that he was an alcoholic and sought help. It took several well-publicized stays in treatment centers before he recovered. Having lost the

chairmanship of his committee, he chose to retire at the end of his term. After forty-odd years in Congress, he became a tax consultant.

Were reporters and politicians negligent in not sharing what they knew about Mills with the rest of the nation? Perhaps they were not only tolerating misconduct but at the same time were protecting themselves, reasoning, "If I don't tell on you, then you won't be able to tell on me if I stray from the straight and narrow." Possibly, their "inside knowledge" gave these members of the Washington community a sense of superiority over the rest of the nation. Of course, the game was up once Mills made a public spectacle of himself. Indiscretions are far more difficult to conceal or explain away when they are displayed out in the open.

The American people have not always had to wait until politicians embarrassed themselves and their supporters in public to learn about their drinking problems, not when matters of national security were at stake. In December 1988, President George Bush nominated John Tower to become secretary of defense. In 1987, under President Reagan, the former senator had chaired an important government investigatory commission. He had also served the nation as an arms negotiator before leaving the government to work as a consultant for defense contractors. Despite Tower's impressive qualifications, his former colleagues on the Senate Armed Services Committee had doubts about his fitness to serve as defense secretary. They were unsettled by repeated accusations that he had been seen in the company of women other than his wife and that he drank too much.

When the FBI reopened its background checks on him, they discovered that he had indeed been a heavy drinker during the 1970s, but they found no evidence that he still had a problem with alcohol. Nevertheless, the committee decided to reject him. The nomination

went to the full Senate for a vote. Tower pledged that if confirmed, he would give up drinking altogether, but for the first time in thirty years, the Senate rejected a presidential cabinet appointee. In view of Tower's past, the position of secretary of defense was seen as too sensitive a post to entrust to him. However, President Bush did not need Senate approval to make him the chairman of the Foreign Intelligence Advisory Board, a post Tower held until his death in a plane crash in 1991.

Drug abuse also took its toll in the nation's capital. In the first official government investigation into drugs and politics, two of President Carter's aides were accused of using cocaine. There was not enough evidence to indict either man. Then, in 1982, the House Ethics Committee issued a report revealing that three members of Congress, twenty Senate employees, and twenty-two House employees had been involved with drugs since 1978. Representatives John L. Burton of California and Frederick W. Richmond of New York had already retired from government. Burton entered a treatment center and resumed his law practice while Richmond spent several months in prison. The third congressman was eventually cleared of all charges.[10]

The drug problem became such a politically charged issue that even brief recreational use of a forbidden substance sometime in the past could jeopardize a promising career. On November 7, 1987, just nine days after President Ronald W. Reagan proposed him for the Supreme Court, Judge Douglas Ginsburg had to withdraw his nomination. A furor had developed once it was revealed that he had smoked marijuana on several occasions during the 1970s while teaching law at Harvard. He had not used it since then. However, President and Mrs. Reagan were leading a national campaign against drugs. Ginsburg proved to be a political embarrassment to them, so he was asked to bow out.

The public is far less tolerant of concealed alcohol and drug dependencies today than it was in the past. The American people are beginning to demand certain rigorous standards of personal conduct from their leaders. The government requires random drug testing for transit workers whose jobs affect the public safety; alcohol testing may soon be added. Some would extend these tests to people in sensitive government jobs. Others are concerned that the tests are not reliable and might violate the constitutional protection against self-incrimination. Yet when individuals step forward and admit their problems, the American people can be forgiving and understanding. Betty Ford, wife of former president Gerald R. Ford, and Kitty Dukakis, wife of the 1988 Democratic presidential candidate, Michael S. Dukakis, earned the nation's respect when they spoke out about their battles with addiction. However, they were married to public officials—they were not officeholders themselves.

Less dangerous than substance abuse, but just as damaging to reputations, is "foot-in-mouth" disease, a common political affliction. Ethnic and racial slurs have caused considerable embarrassment and have occasionally ruined careers. President Jimmy Carter's brother Billy, an uninhibited character with a well-known fondness for beer, made a number of spontaneous and irresponsible public statements. He managed to offend many of the groups who had supported his brother in the 1976 election with his thoughtless remarks. For example, he told Atlanta Braves pitcher Phil Niekro, "I didn't know you were a Polack. I thought you were a bastardized Jew."[11] While much-publicized comments such as these did not cause Jimmy Carter to lose his 1980 reelection bid, they certainly did not help his campaign. On the other hand, in 1983, President Reagan's secretary of the interior, James Watt, did lose his job after he referred

to members of a new commission as "Three Democrats, two Republicans, every kind of mix you can have. I have a black, a woman, two Jews, and a cripple."[12]

Most officeholders and office-seekers employ speechwriters to help them come up with memorable phrases to make headlines, impress audiences, and even earn a place in history books. This is a time-honored practice long accepted by a knowing public. However, when politicians mouth other politicians' words, claiming them as their own, they are asking for trouble. On September 23, 1987, Democratic presidential hopeful Senator Joseph R. Biden, Jr., of Delaware had to drop out of the race for the Democratic nomination after being charged with plagiarism and falsification of his academic credentials. (The latter problem was also to plague George Bush's 1988 running mate, Dan Quayle.)

Biden, the respected chairman of the Senate Judiciary Committee, had developed a reputation as an orator on the campaign trail. However, John Sasso, campaign manager for Democratic contender Governor Michael Dukakis of Massachusetts, secretly tipped off reporters that many of Biden's most inspiring utterances had, in fact, been lifted from a speech given by British Labour Party leader Neil Kinnock. Biden made the doubtful claim of having coal-mining ancestors "who read poetry and taught me how to sing verse."[13] The actual author of those words did indeed come from a coal-mining family. In the past, Biden had given him credit for the lines he borrowed, but in the Iowa campaign he forgot to do so and passed Kinnock's oratory off as his own. He also failed to acknowledge the material he took from the late senators Robert Kennedy and Hubert Humphrey. After publishing line-by-line comparisons of Biden's and Kinnock's speeches, journalists also revealed that Biden had inflated his achievements as an undergraduate at the

University of Delaware and at Syracuse University, where he was a law student. He had even been disciplined for plagiarism at Syracuse University.

This incident had two interesting consequences. The scandal ultimately backfired on the Dukakis campaign. When John Sasso was revealed to be the source who exposed Biden's plagiarized speeches, he was forced to resign so as not to tarnish Dukakis's image as an "up-front," "play-by-the-rules" candidate. More important, the scandal probably saved Joseph Biden's life. Shortly after he withdrew his bid for the Democratic nomination, Biden was diagnosed as having an aneurysm, a weakened artery wall, right near his brain. The stress of the campaign might have caused the aneurysm to burst, which could have killed him. On February 12, 1988, Biden checked into Walter Reed Army Medical Center to have it repaired. A month later, he developed a blood clot in the same area; this required immediate medical attention. Then he was hospitalized again for further surgery. Once he returned to good health, Biden resumed his duties as chairman of the Judiciary Committee. In 1990, he was reelected to the Senate by a margin of 47,446 votes.

To err is human. However, many American politicians have shown their humanity in ways that raised not just eyebrows, but serious questions about their competence. Concealing information about accidents, emotional problems, substance abuse, or use of others' work cast doubts on politicians' characters and leadership abilities. The American people today are more forgiving and understanding of all-too-human shortcomings. However, they are unlikely to forgive or forget lies, misstatements, and denials that cover up personal misconduct.

8
ABUSE OF POWER

An hour or so after midnight, on June 17, 1972, five men carrying listening devices, cameras, and burglary tools broke into Democratic National Committee headquarters in Washington, D.C. Each of the five had previous ties to the Central Intelligence Agency (CIA), the agency that collects secret information on foreign nations. However, their present undercover job had no connection with international data gathering or espionage. Instead, they were repairing defective electronic eavesdropping equipment, previously installed to spy on the Democrats and find out what they were planning for the upcoming presidential election in November. As a precaution, the burglars had put on surgical rubber gloves so that they would leave no fingerprints behind. However, they had taped the door locks, and this attracted the attention of security guard Frank Wills. He phoned the police, and in a short time the five men were arrested at the Watergate complex.

Theirs was a minor crime that was relegated to the back pages of the newspapers. The press and the public did not realize that the Watergate burglars were working for the Committee to Reelect the President (CREEP). CREEP was a political organization set up to help incumbent president Richard M. Nixon win a second term of office. Personally loyal to him, some CREEP members adopted a "no-holds-barred"

approach to campaigning. Without informing the president, they had planned the bugging of the Democratic headquarters. However, the break-in was bungled, and now they risked exposure. Hastily, they sought to cover their tracks by destroying evidence linking them to the burglars.

To make matters worse, many members of CREEP had ties to the White House. CREEP director John Mitchell, who allowed eavesdropping equipment to be secretly installed at Democratic national headquarters, had served in the cabinet as attorney general. He was also Nixon's former law partner. White House chief of staff H. R. "Bob" Haldeman, and Presidential Assistant for Domestic Affairs John Ehrlichman, two of the president's closest advisers, as well as Presidential Counsel John Dean were also involved in the seamier side of CREEP activities. Compromising the president even more, Watergate break-in ringleaders G. Gordon Liddy, a former FBI agent, and E. Howard Hunt, a mystery novelist, had previously worked in the Plumbers Unit. Located in a White House basement office, this undercover group of political operatives, supervised by Ehrlichman, resorted to a wide range of illegal activities, such as burglaries, to track down information potentially harmful to the president's opponents.

At the time of the arrest, Liddy and Hunt were in another part of the Watergate complex, but their role in the break-in was soon discovered. One of the burglars had even carried a notebook with the name "E. Hunt W. H." scrawled inside. Another burglar, James McCord, Jr., was soon identified as a CREEP employee. Intrigued by these developments, reporters decided to look into links between the burglars and the Nixon campaign organization. It was only a matter of time before they found what they were seeking.

Nixon could have taken immediate steps to prevent the Watergate affair from becoming a major scandal.

All he had to do was let his associates take the blame for their actions. However, his administration might have been discredited just before the election. Moreover, the president was loyal to his White House subordinates. He relied on them to see people and handle matters distasteful to him. Now he felt they needed his protection. He decided to take charge of the cover-up to conceal their role in the illegal proceedings. As he recently admitted, "In retrospect, while I was not involved in the decision to conduct the break-in, I should have set a higher standard for the conduct of the people who participated in my campaign and Administration. I should have established a moral tone that would have made such actions unthinkable."[1]

The president of the United States was ready to abuse the powers of his office to block any inquiry into the break-in. His decision turned a minor crime into a major one. As early as June 23, 1972, he urged Haldeman to use the CIA to halt the FBI's investigation of the case. The FBI was already tracing the serial numbers of the brand-new $100 bills found in the pockets of the arrested men. These would eventually lead them to the CREEP slush fund managed by Maurice Stans, former secretary of commerce. The president was worried: "Of course, this Hunt, that will uncover a lot of things. You open that scab there's a hell of a lot of things and we just feel that it would be very detrimental to have this thing go any further."[2]

The president and his men devised cover story after cover story, distancing themselves from the break-in. At a June 22 press conference, Nixon denied that the White House had any involvement in the affair. John Mitchell quietly resigned from CREEP. Then the White House decided to make Liddy the scapegoat for the bungled burglary by having witnesses testify that he had misguidedly gone off on his own and masterminded the deed. In August, the president issued a

statement that John Dean had questioned members of the White House staff and had found no ties to the Watergate defendants. This was an outright lie—Dean had never conducted any investigation.

A gullible public was willing to believe the president. They reelected him by a wide margin, giving his Democratic opponent, George S. McGovern, only 17 electoral votes to Nixon's 520. However, despite John Dean's efforts to coach members of the CREEP staff questioned by FBI agents, ties among the Watergate defendants, CREEP officials, and members of the White House staff were emerging. In desperation, the president and his men prepared to lie, withhold evidence, and even to pay hush money to keep the Watergate defendants from admitting what they knew. That is why, in January 1973, five of the Watergate burglars pleaded guilty to the break-in.

In February, the Senate voted to set up a Select Committee on Presidential Campaign Activities to investigate the growing scandal. Democratic senator Sam J. Ervin of South Carolina, an expert on constitutional law, chaired the group of seven senators. The president and his men held numerous strategy meetings, frantically trying to anticipate what Ervin's Watergate Committee might uncover. Initially, the president took a defensive position: "All this information, we have nothing to hide. We have to handle it. You see, I can't be in the position of basically hunkering down because you have a lot of tough questions on Watergate, and not go out and talk on their issues because it is not going to get better. It is going to get worse."[3] Handling it meant withholding facts and making partial admissions only when necessary. As the president predicted, matters grew worse.

In late March, burglar James McCord publicly admitted that he had lied under oath and confessed that

politicians had planned the break-in. To placate an irate nation, the president decided to let loyal John Mitchell take responsibility for the whole Watergate affair. Skeptical reporters still searched for higher-ups. At the end of April, in order to protect himself, Nixon reluctantly accepted the resignations of Bob Haldeman and John Ehrlichman, along with his attorney general, and appointed their replacements. At the same time, he fired John Dean for failing to write up an account of his August "investigation." He quickly appointed replacements. Some of the president's men, including Dean, defected and offered to tell all to the Watergate Committee. On May 22, 1973, the president finally had to admit that he had limited the scope of the FBI's Watergate investigation, but he claimed he had done so in the interests of national security.

From May to late September, fascinated Americans abandoned their soap operas and quiz shows to watch the televised Watergate Committee hearings. John Dean shocked them with his testimony about the cover-up. They also learned that the president had kept an "Enemies List" of people who had opposed him. Included on this list were actors Bill Cosby and Paul Newman and CBS reporter Daniel Schorr. The administration planned to get even with them by having the Internal Revenue Service review their tax returns and having the FBI question their associates about their personal lives. These government agencies were not meant to be used for political revenge. In fact, the Constitution had been written to prevent such abuses of power. The public also learned about the dirty tricks Republicans had played on their opponents during the campaign, such as sending forged letters to discredit primary candidates, cutting telephone lines to Democrats, and sending unordered meals to candidates' headquarters. Americans found out that important

business executives were promised favors or threatened with tax audits in order to get them to contribute to the Nixon campaign.

The most sensational disclosure came from witness Alexander Butterfield, a deputy assistant to the president. He revealed that Nixon had secretly taped conversations with his staff. Other presidents had also recorded some private discussions, but this was the first time the public learned about the practice. The tapes proved to be a turning point in the Watergate investigations. Both the Senate committee and the new special prosecutor, Archibald Cox, surmised that the information they contained could convict the president's men. Both wanted copies of the tapes. However, Nixon refused to cooperate with them, so the issue went to the federal courts. District and appeals judges ruled against the president.

Nixon offered Cox summaries of the tapes instead. The special prosecutor needed complete copies of the original conversations as evidence for the criminal cases he was preparing; because of this, he rejected the proposal. The irate president ordered his dismissal. He could not fire Cox directly because he had not appointed him, but he could and did accept the resignations of his attorney general and deputy attorney general on Saturday, October 20, when they refused to fire Cox. He also found an official who would carry out his order. As a result of this "Saturday Night Massacre," the deans of seventeen law schools joined an outraged public in calling for Nixon's impeachment. Just three days later, the president turned over some tapes to the court. However, the public soon learned that there was an 18½-minute gap in a crucial tape, the result of deliberate erasures. To restore confidence in his administration, Nixon announced the appointment of a new special prosecutor, Leon Jaworski, on November 1.

In the opening months of 1974, the House of Representatives voted to start impeachment proceedings against the president. Meanwhile, a grand jury charged his former aides with conspiracy. In order to prepare airtight cases against the president and his men, the House Judiciary Committee and Special Prosecutor Jaworski requested more tapes. On April 29, Nixon reluctantly agreed to release 1,200 pages of heavily edited transcripts. Their crude, unpresidential language shocked the public. Dissatisfied with Nixon's response, Jaworski appealed directly to the Supreme Court for possession of the actual tapes.

By the end of July, Nixon's grip on the presidency was faltering. On the 24th, in *United States* v. *Nixon*, a unanimous Supreme Court directed the president to hand over the tapes to the special prosecutor's office. The justices denied Nixon's claim to executive privilege (the right to withhold confidential information from another branch of government). Between July 27 and July 30, the House Judiciary Committee voted three articles of impeachment against the president. On July 29, Nixon's support in Congress further eroded when another tape was released. It revealed that as early as June 23, 1972, the president had indeed tried to use the CIA to block the FBI's investigation of the break-in.

On August 9, 1974, Nixon resigned before the impeachment process could proceed. Never before in American history had a president chosen to leave office before his term expired. Had he fought the charges against him, the business of government might have ground to a standstill, leaving the United States vulnerable to its enemies. Instead, the nation's first unelected vice president, Gerald R. Ford, was sworn in as chief executive. Under the provisions of the Twenty-fifth Amendment, the president and

Congress had appointed Ford to be second in command, replacing Spiro Agnew, who had stepped down.*

On September 8, Ford pardoned Nixon, setting off another round of controversy. While the public questioned the wisdom of his decision, experts argued over constitutional issues. They debated whether Nixon could have received a fair and speedy trial in view of all of the publicity surrounding the Watergate cover-up. They also disagreed about the tapes. Some insisted that they could have been used in his trial, while others claimed that such evidence violated the Fifth Amendment guarantee against self-incrimination. Eventually, Ford's decision gained acceptance.

Nixon was granted a pension and other benefits of a retired chief executive. In later years, the former president was treated as an elder statesman and was often consulted on foreign policy matters. In an April 2, 1990, interview, however, Nixon explained that he was still paying a price for Watergate. "By paying a price, I mean in terms of being able to influence the course of events. I mean, every time I make a speech, or every time I write a book, inevitably the reviewers refer to the 'disgraced former President.' "[4] Other participants in the Watergate scandal were less fortunate than Nixon. Two former cabinet officers and twenty-six other members of his administration went to prison. Liddy served the longest sentence, $4\frac{1}{2}$ years.[5]

As a case study in the abuse of power, the Watergate affair was unique. Unlike other political scandals in American history, the president and his men had not lied to conceal illegally gained personal wealth nor misconduct in their personal lives. They were motivated by political power. In violation of the Constitution and the laws of the United States, they used government agen-

* See Chapter 6, pp. 82–83.

cies to neutralize opponents, block investigations, and deceive the public so that they could remain in office for another four years. In a wave of reforming zeal, Congress tightened campaign finance laws, investigated the FBI and the CIA, and broadened the Freedom of Information Act to make it easier for citizens to find out what the government was doing. The reforms fell short of their goal; ten years later, government officials found other ways to abuse the powers of their office and set off the Iran-Contra scandal.

In 1984, some of President Ronald W. Reagan's advisers illegally undertook secret operations that defied stated American foreign policy positions and congressional directives. They were members of the National Security Council (NSC), the presidential group responsible for assessing international conditions affecting the United States. The NSC administrators acted in what they thought were the best interests of the United States. However, they broke laws, they lied, and they concealed information from their superiors and from Congress. They felt that the ends they served justified the means they used. Many Americans thought otherwise. Pieces of the puzzling story are still coming to light.

The Iran-Contra scandal may be said to have started as a result of an unpublicized NSC review of American policy toward Iran. Lebanese Shiite Muslims, acting as agents for fanatical leader Ayatollah Khomeini and his fundamentalist government in Iran, had taken five Americans hostage, including William Buckley, a Middle East CIA station chief. The review was prompted by reports filtering back to Washington that Buckley was being tortured so that he would reveal secret government information to his captors. The announced policy of the United States, stated in law, was to refuse to negotiate with these terrorists to

secure the captives' release. The American government had already branded Iran a terrorist nation and joined other nations in refusing to ship arms to Iran. However, the NSC concluded that the policy of isolating Iran was not producing results. Support for a new approach to the hostage situation gained momentum in 1985, when four more Americans were seized and it was learned that Buckley had died.

Briefed by NSC advisers, President Reagan held a meeting on August 6 to discuss possible negotiations with supposed Iranian moderates to exchange arms for hostages. Secretary of State George Shultz and Secretary of Defense Caspar Weinberger opposed the plan. Although Iran had been waging a war with Iraq since 1980 and needed arms, the two secretaries did not think that trading with the hostile and fanatical regime would be beneficial to American interests. They doubted there were any moderates left in Iran. On the other hand, Vice President George Bush later explained why he, and some others, accepted the idea. "I went along with it—because you know why, . . . when I saw Mr. Buckley, when I heard about Mr. Buckley being tortured to death, later admitted as a CIA Chief. So if I erred, I erred on the side of trying to get those hostages out of there."[6] Although the law required that Congress be told of secret operations and arms shipments to Iran, no one in the administration informed them of the new policy.

The United States used the Israelis, already selling arms to Iran, to open a back-channel, or unofficial, dialogue with the fundamentalist regime. After Iran received two shipments of American missiles from Israel, one hostage was set free. Then the Iranians began to demand more up-to-date, sophisticated offensive missiles. Meanwhile, in December 1985, National Security Adviser Robert C. McFarlane chose to resign, and Vice Admiral John Poindexter succeeded him.

On January 17, 1986, President Reagan signed a one-page document permitting direct U.S. arms sales to Iran, despite Shultz's and Weinberger's continued opposition. In February, the first of four shipments was made, but no further hostages were released. Then McFarlane and the deputy director for political-military affairs, U.S. Marine Lieutenant Colonel Oliver North, flew directly to Iran on May 25 on a foolhardy clandestine mission. They took the remaining arms shipments with them in the hope of freeing the hostages. The two men risked being taken captive by the Iranians and being forced to reveal American foreign policy secrets. After several days of frustrating talks with the so-called moderates, a disgusted McFarlane broke off the meetings and returned to the United States with North. After a year of trading arms for hostages, three captives were released, but three more were taken. The policy of secret deals with Iran was a failure.

Meanwhile, NSC staffers also faced the problem of funding the Contras, a rebel force sponsored by the CIA to overthrow the left-wing, Marxist Sandinista government in Nicaragua. Opposed to such ventures, in 1983 Congress had passed a series of amendments to defense-spending bills, proposed by Massachusetts Democrat Edward P. Boland. These placed a cap of $24 million on aid to the Contras and limited the aid to food and medical supplies. In April 1984, after members of Congress learned that the CIA had secretly mined Nicaraguan harbors, the outraged representatives voted for another Boland amendment, which prohibited the Reagan administration from financing Contra operations. It became law on October 12, 1984.

As early as July 1984, working with the approval of McFarlane and CIA director William Casey, Oliver North made arrangements to defy the Boland amendments. At Casey's suggestion, he contacted Richard Secord, a retired Air Force general, and Secord's part-

ner, Albert A. Hakim, a naturalized American citizen born in Iran. North solicited funds from private citizens and other countries. Secord and Hakim used these funds to buy arms for the Contras, opening confidential Swiss bank accounts to hide their transactions. A secret air base was set up for resupplying the rebels. The first of four arms shipments was delivered to the Contras in November.

Apparently there was no connection between the Iranian operation and the war in Nicaragua. However, once the United States began to sell arms directly to the Iranians, proceeds from these sales were used to fund the Contras. This illegal arrangement was concealed from Congress and most members of the Reagan administration, including the two chief architects of American foreign policy, the secretaries of state and defense. In April 1986, Oliver North drafted a "Diversion Memo" for his boss, Admiral Poindexter, stating that funds from the Iranian arms sales would be used to supply the Contras. Of the $30 million collected from Iran, only $4 million actually ended up in the hands of the Central American rebels. Shipments to the Contras continued throughout the year in defiance of congressional laws. However, it was not long before the whole Iran-Contra scandal made headlines.

As early as December 1985, reporters had learned about the secret arms sales to Iran, but the White House asked that the story be suppressed to protect the hostages. The press cooperated. Then, on November 3, 1986, a Middle Eastern newspaper broke the story of McFarlane's and North's covert arms-for-hostages flight to Iran. The next day, the Iranians confirmed this account. Although the president's press secretary, McFarlane, and State Department spokespersons issued denials, major American newspapers continued to raise questions about the mission. An irate public demanded answers.

In the hope that other hostages would be released, President Reagan at first refused to comment on the disclosure. When he did discuss the matter in public, his confused and misinformed statements soon led to the conclusion that although he had probably endorsed his advisers' decisions, he had little detailed knowledge of what they were doing. For example, on November 13 he addressed a nationwide television audience, insisting, "We did not—repeat—did not trade weapons or anything else for hostages—nor will we."[7] Six days later, at a press conference, the president conceded that Iran had been given some defensive weapons and spare parts. Evidently, he did not realize that offensive missiles had been sent to Iran. When corrected, he admitted, "If I have been misinformed, then I will yield on that."[8]

To refresh his memory and calm the public, he asked Attorney General Edwin Meese to look into the Iranian arms sales. On November 25, the attorney general set off shock waves throughout the government and the nation when he made public his discovery of North's "Diversion Memo." Meese prepared to launch a criminal investigation into the Iran-Contra affair, but his leisurely methods gave North and Poindexter time to destroy many vital documents. Before the year was out, Special Prosecutor Lawrence Walsh had taken charge of the inquiry.

After the "Diversion Memo" came to light, Ronald Reagan accepted Admiral Poindexter's resignation and fired Oliver North. The next day, November 26, 1986, the president appointed a commission under the leadership of former Republican senator John Tower of Texas* to study the operations and functions of the NSC and its role in the scandal. Its report, released on February 27, 1987, faulted the president's sloppy

* See Chapter 7, pp. 104–105.

management style. Reagan was criticized for allowing advisers to carry out broad presidential directives without supervision. The commission also condemned the NSC for its lack of control over subordinates, flawed review procedures, and failure to consult with cabinet officials.

On March 4, 1987, Reagan admitted, "I told the American people I did not trade arms for hostages. My heart and my best intentions still tell me that's true. But the facts and the evidence tell me it is not."9 Unlike President Nixon, Ronald Reagan had not invented elaborate cover stories to protect himself or his men. He simply denied that he knew anything or claimed that he forgot whatever it was he did know. Whether he deceived the public by not letting on to what he knew or whether he had really failed to take charge of his administration, his denials certainly did not inspire confidence in his presidency.

As 1986 drew to a close, Congress took matters into its own hands, starting with a preliminary inquiry by the Senate Intelligence Committee. Then, in January 1987, both the House and the Senate created select committees to investigate the scandal. By March, the two committees decided to combine their efforts under the leadership of Senator Daniel K. Inouye of Hawaii and Representative Lee H. Hamilton of Indiana, both Democrats. From May to August, they held public hearings that received nationwide television coverage.

At the joint congressional hearings, television audiences were attracted to and repelled by the uniformed, bemedaled, all-American Oliver North. North eloquently defended the illegal transactions he had arranged. He admitted to shredding vital documents, altering chronologies of events, and lying to Congress to conceal what had been done. The public learned that North had accepted a $13,000 gift from Secord and Hakim to protect his home. The two men had

made millions in profit from the arms deals, millions that never reached the Contras. In her testimony, North's loyal secretary, Fawn Hall, described how she altered some classified documents, shredded others, and smuggled the rest out of North's office after he had been dismissed. She justified her behavior by stating, "I believed in Colonel North and there was a very solid and very valid reason he must have been doing this for and sometimes you have to go above the written law, I believe."[10] However, the Constitution makes the activities of public officials and citizens alike subject to the nation's written laws.

Having already erased incriminating documents stored in his computer, calm, pipe-smoking John Poindexter was the least credible witness. His testimony was punctuated with statements such as "I don't recall" and "I don't remember that." He did admit that he tore up a presidential directive permitting arms sales to Iran, explaining: "I thought it was a significant political embarrassment to the President, and I wanted to protect him from possible disclosure of this."[11] CIA director William Casey did not appear before the committee. He had resigned in February after it was learned that he had a brain tumor. He died on May 6, just as the public hearings were getting underway.

After examining over three thousand documents and taking testimony from more than five hundred witnesses, the committee issued its final report. Echoing the Tower Commission report, it found that President Reagan had not carried out his constitutional responsibilities. He had failed to control his subordinates and remain informed of their activities. However, the committee did not recommend his impeachment. It characterized the arms sales to Iran and the diversion of funds to the Contras as errors in judgment, not criminal actions.

Members of Congress reasoned that unlike sullen

Richard Nixon, Ronald Reagan was open with them. He did not claim executive privilege and even made parts of his personal diary available to the investigators. He had encouraged his subordinates to cooperate with Congress. Moreover, it was and is still unclear how much the president actually knew about what was going on in his administration. (It is also uncertain how involved Vice President George Bush was in the whole operation.)[12] When President Reagan retired from office in January 1989, his popularity ratings remained high.

While a majority of the committee regarded the Iran-Contra affair as a policy dispute between the president and Congress, not everyone in government agreed. Special Prosecutor Walsh asked a grand jury to bring charges against the admitted Iran-Contra conspirators. In order to gain their cooperation, the joint congressional committee had had to grant them immunity, protecting them from prosecution for the statements they made under oath. Those statements could not be used against them in criminal proceedings. So there were limits to what Walsh and the grand jury could do.

Nevertheless, in 1988, Oliver North, Richard Secord, Albert Hakim, and John Poindexter, among others, were indicted. They were accused of lying to Congress, destroying government property, conspiring to defraud the government, and other crimes. In 1990, Poindexter's trial created a minor sensation when former president Ronald Reagan agreed to give videotaped testimony. With his poor memory, he contributed much publicity but little information. The admiral was the first Iran-Contra defendant to be sentenced to prison, receiving a six-month term, which was soon appealed. The other major defendants had already received suspended sentences and were placed on two years' probation. (Earlier, McFarlane had pleaded

guilty to the less serious charge of withholding information from Congress and had received a suspended sentence.) Only North was required to do community service.[13] On appeal, both North and Poindexter's convictions were overturned because immunized testimony had been used at their trials.

In 1990, a popularly elected government replaced the Sandinistas in Nicaragua, and two American hostages still held in Lebanon were released. To improve relations with the West in 1991, Shiite Moslems in Iran and Lebanon released the six remaining American captives as part of a Middle East hostage exchange arranged with the help of the United Nations secretary-general Javier Perez de Cuellar. Meanwhile, Special Prosecutor Walsh continued his investigation into the scandal. He learned that the CIA had been more deeply involved in the Iran-Contra operation than had previously been thought. In 1991, the former head of the CIA's Central American task force, Alan D. Fiers, Jr., and the former CIA director of European operations, Duane R. Clarridge, pleaded guilty to withholding information from Congress, as did Elliott Abrams, Reagan's assistant secretary of state for inter-American affairs. Then the Senate reluctantly approved the nomination of Reagan's former CIA deputy director, Robert M. Gates, to head the agency despite claims that he had known about the Iran-Contra affair earlier than he had previously admitted. In the same year, George Bush signed into law a reform measure requiring the president to give Congress written approval in advance of any covert operations conducted by the federal government.

The motives of the Iran-Contra conspirators may have been more patriotic and noble than those of their Watergate counterparts, but in both cases, officials used the institutions of government for unlawful purposes. What's more, they lied to investigators, Con-

gress, and the public in an attempt to conceal their illegal activities. Unlike previous scandals, the Watergate and Iran-Contra affairs posed a serious threat to constitutional government because officials placed themselves above the laws they were sworn to obey. Americans learned an important lesson from these two episodes. Instead of passively assuming that the Constitution and the laws will be automatically obeyed, the public and its representatives would have to be ever vigilant to guard against abuses of power.

9
SOME MORE THOUGHTS ABOUT SCANDALS

Political scandals involving the public and private lives of government officials have certainly enlivened American history. Every generation has had its dishonest or indiscreet politicians, but the Grant, Harding, Nixon, and Reagan eras are infamous for their political corruption and abuses of power. Why have these four administrations achieved such notoriety? The "presidential laziness factor" is one popular explanation. During the nation's four most scandal-ridden periods, the chief executives took a "hands-off" approach to government. They preferred to outline general policies and leave the details to others. Their willingness to let subordinates manage day-to-day matters, with little if any supervision, certainly made their appointees more vulnerable to temptation. However, this line of reasoning falls short of the mark. After all, passive presidents like Calvin Coolidge and Dwight Eisenhower were also known to delegate authority, but their administrations were marked by fewer scandals than the other four. What's more, even activist presidents like Harry Truman, who enjoyed running the government and making his own decisions, could not always keep their aides from getting into trouble.

The "desire to make up for lost time" may cause some eras to be more susceptible to scandals than others. During wartime, American civilians are often

asked to sacrifice their comforts and deprive themselves of pleasures for the sake of the war effort. Historian Thomas A. Bailey suggests that once peace is declared, people become greedy and selfish.[1] They are too occupied in making up for lost time to care when government officials scheme to "get rich quick" by fair means or foul. Grant took office in the wake of the Civil War, Harding was sworn in after World War I, and Nixon presided over the winding down of the Vietnam War. However, Bailey's approach fails to account for the scandal-ridden Reagan presidency, which was not preceded by any major war.

"Cycles of selfishness" offers a more promising explanation. According to historian Arthur Schlesinger, Jr., politics alternate between periods of public purpose and periods of private interest.[2] In public-purpose eras, politicians tend to be idealists, people who devote their energies to reforming and rebuilding society. Eventually, they become exhausted, if not disillusioned, when they discover that they are unable to solve all of the nation's problems. After these idealists experience an inevitable burnout, politics shifts to narrower, more attainable goals.

During private-interest eras, individual needs replace loftier aims. At this time, attention focuses away from government and onto people's more selfish concerns. Government regulations are seen as ineffective, meddlesome, and injurious to the private sector of the economy. It is felt that the private sector should be left alone to expand and prosper. In such an atmosphere, politicians become preoccupied with their own self-enrichment, the ultimate private interest. It is no wonder that major scandals result.

If you apply Schlesinger's approach to the four most corrupt administrations in American history, you will discover that each came to power after a previous period of reforming zeal. Radical reconstruction of the

South was followed by the Grant administration. Progressive era reforms had run out of steam by the time Harding took office. Civil rights and antipoverty programs had already reached their peak before Nixon was elected. Carter's moral crusade faded just prior to Reagan's presidency. Of course, if you are not satisfied with any of these explanations, you might formulate one of your own.

From all of this, it would seem as though Americans are doomed to be governed by "crooked politicians." However, over the years, the people and their leaders have been making the government more corruption-proof. Scattered throughout the chapters of this book are references to some of the remedies they have used. After Burr's earlier attempt to steal the presidency, Congress and the states passed the Twelfth Amendment in 1804, separating the election of the president and vice president. At the turn of the century, the introduction of the direct primary gave voters a new weapon to use in their battle with political machines over control of party nominations.

More recently, as a result of scandals, during the 1960s, the Senate and the House set up ethics committees to monitor members' behavior. In the 1970s, after Watergate, came another spate of reforms to curb the FBI and the CIA, to change the way campaigns are financed, and to make knowledge of government activities more accessible to the public. In reaction to Abscam, ethics laws placed further limits on lawmakers' outside income and forbade them to accept major gifts from lobbyists. Along with cabinet secretaries and administrators, they had to submit their financial records for government review. In the 1980s, after Wedtech and other scandals, politicians were asked to make additional financial disclosures about themselves to satisfy the public that they were honest. For a long time now, many officials, including the president, have been

required to put their personal holdings in blind trusts, to turn them over to professional business managers to handle without being consulted.

In 1991, after additional facts about Iran-Contra came to light, President Bush signed a law that requires a president to give Congress his written approval of any secret operations conducted by the federal government before these take place. In the same year, a Senate committee responded to the Keating Five inquiry by preparing to draw up guidelines that senators could use when they were asked to perform services for their constituents and supporters. Currently, several states are considering legislation to place a limit on the number of terms their elected representatives may serve in office. The battle against political corruption and abuses of power is an ongoing process.

Americans may also seem doomed to be governed by politicians whose private misconduct and misfortunes resemble the twists and turns of a soap opera plot. In their day, Peggy Eaton's impact on Jackson's cabinet, Harding's romantic entanglements, Mills's impromptu appearance on a burlesque stage, Ted Kennedy's accident at Chappaquiddick, and Thomas Eagleton's mental health fed the nation's passion for melodrama. However, there are even more politicians who lead ordinary, quiet lives. The impression that politicians are cheats, liars, philanderers, or addicts has arisen because the few who have erred receive a great amount of attention. What is lost in all of the ballyhoo is the fact that these few have deceived the nation. Their omissions and cover-ups are perhaps even more harmful to the government and the people they serve than their much publicized mistakes and misfortunes.

Americans have to make judgments about the

characters of the politicians they elect to office. However, it is not easy for them to get the information they need. In the nineteenth century, officials' romantic liaisons were common knowledge. Yet in the twentieth century, the extramarital affairs of Warren Harding, Franklin Roosevelt, John Kennedy, and Lyndon Johnson were kept from the public. Now, with the exposure of Gary Hart's infidelity, candidates can no longer be assured of privacy.

The public certainly has a right to know about politicians' private lives when their personal conduct may affect their job performance. Look at the damage dependence on addictive substances can cause. Not only does it impair politicians' judgment, it can leave them vulnerable to blackmail. Of course, legislative confirmation hearings can sometimes expose this problem, as they did with John Tower in 1989, and ethics committees can issue reports on drug use in Congress and recommend disciplinary proceedings, as was done in 1982. However, some Americans want additional safeguards enacted into law.

No one would dream of asking all candidates and appointees to submit to lie detector tests before taking government posts, but some have suggested that public servants in sensitive jobs be required to undergo drug tests because so many people depend on their judgment and skills. However, drug testing raises questions about the reliability of the tests and the protection of officeholders' constitutional rights. Yet few object when automobile drivers are stopped and given sobriety tests. The issue is still being debated. Perhaps potential candidates should receive more thorough background checks, and the choice of a vice-presidential candidate should not be left to the presidential nominee. In the absence of such measures, politicians will continue to find journalists constantly

snooping into their private lives. Many have nothing to hide. As for the others, perhaps they may be induced to "clean up their acts."

Scandals should not be dismissed as mere political pranks or typical human weaknesses. They can be alarming signs of governmental or personal breakdowns. For this reason, it would be nice to have a series of tidy formulas for determining which officeholders are corrupt or indiscreet. Pinocchio's nose grew longer every time he told a lie. It would be beneficial if politicians experienced the same phenomenon. Then you would know who was telling the truth and who wasn't. Alas, Pinocchio was only a fairy tale character. Yet the American constitutional system does provide ways to detect deceptions and cure them through checks and balances and elections. Although the government is not scandal-proof, it is not permanently scandal-ridden.

Remember how Congress questioned public officials involved in the Belknap scandal, Teapot Dome, Watergate, Iran-Contra, "Robin HUD," and the Keating Five, among others. Think back to how Congress disciplined its own members, including Brooks, Rousseau, and Tillman, and exercised its constitutional powers to impeach Judges Hastings and Nixon. Recall how the Department of Justice, special prosecutors in the executive branch, and judges in the federal judiciary dealt with participants in such scandals as the Whiskey Ring, Abscam, and Wedtech. Reporters, collectively known as the "fourth branch of government," have also brought many scandals to the attention of the public and the government. They broke stories ranging from Crédit Mobilier to Watergate, from Cleveland's bachelor fatherhood to Hart's affair. Although for years they did not disclose what they knew about many twentieth-century presidents' marital infidelities, in an

open democratic society like ours nothing stays hidden too long.

The constitutional system also provides for free and frequent elections. However, they are an imperfect mechanism for "cleaning house." Although voters have the means to "throw the rascals out," they do not always succeed. In 1876, Hayes was permitted to "steal" the presidential election from Tilden, and in 1948, despite charges of electoral fraud, Lyndon Johnson still became a senator. Loyal voters have also re-elected politicians like Adam Clayton Powell, Ted Kennedy, and Joseph Biden, whose reputations were tarnished by scandal.

In case you're wondering, there is an explanation for why Americans reject "Mr. or Ms. Clean" and vote for "Mr. or Ms. Dirty Politician" instead. (Remember that Grant, Nixon, and Reagan each served two terms in office.) The media have popularized the term "Teflon Effect" to describe the way in which the image of a popular president remains clean and shiny despite the scandals that have taken place during his administration. The same holds true for other elected public officials. (For those of you who do not cook or wash dishes, Teflon pans require little or no effort to remove grime. Like affable presidents and other congenial politicians, these nonstick products shed dirt easily.) When a chief executive grins broadly, sounds reassuring, or looks presidential, the public will tend to shrug off any charges against him. That is why the misdeeds of their subordinates did not rub off on Harding, Eisenhower, or Reagan during their lifetimes. According to the same line of reasoning, the public is less likely to forgive presidents whose public image is less than open and friendly. A brooding, scowling, intense president like Richard Nixon did commit the unforgivable act of conspiring with his staff to deceive the public. Yet it is

tempting to ask whether the public would have forgiven him if he had had, for example, Harding's looks, Eisenhower's smile, or Reagan's skills as the "Great Communicator."

Americans can no longer afford to "judge a book by its cover"; they should look at its content instead. The public has to take the time to be informed and use that information in the voting booth. Despite the Teflon Effect, the greatest asset the American republic has is the common sense of its people. As Abraham Lincoln put it in an 1858 speech, "You can fool all the people some of the time, and some of the people all the time, but you cannot fool all the people all of the time." For the most part, history has proved him right.

SOURCE NOTES

—————CHAPTER TWO—————

1. Quoted in Roger Butterfield, *The American Past* (New York: Simon & Schuster, 1947), p. 42.

2. Quoted in Sol Barzman, *Madmen and Geniuses: The Vice-Presidents of the United States* (Chicago: Follett, 1974), p. 28.

3. Quoted in Butterfield, *The American Past*, p. 33.

4. Ibid., p. 42.

5. Ibid.

6. *Congressional Globe*, 34th Cong., 1st sess., Appendix, p. 530.

7. Robert C. Byrd, *The Senate 1789–1989: Addresses on the History of the United States Senate* (Washington, D.C.: U.S. Government Printing Office, 1988), p. 210.

8. *Congressional Globe*, 39th Cong., 1st sess., p. 3852.

9. Ibid., p. 3851.

10. Francis Butler Simpkins, *Pitchfork Ben Tillman* (Baton Rouge: Louisiana State University Press, 1944), p. 386.

11. Quoted in U.S. Congress, Senate Committee on Rules and Administration, *Senate Election, Expulsion and Censure Cases from 1793 to 1972*, 92d Cong., 1st sess. (Washington, D.C.: U.S. Government Printing Office, 1972), p. 96.

CHAPTER THREE

1. John Blum, Edmund S. Morgan. Willie Lee Rose, Arthur M. Schlesinger, Jr., Kenneth M. Stampp, and C. Vann Woodward, *The National Experience*, 5th ed. (New York: Harcourt Brace Jovanovich, 1981), p. 224. General reference: Paul C. Nagel, *Descent from Glory: Four Generations of the John Adams Family* (New York: Oxford University Press, 1983), esp. pp. 144–145.
2. Quoted in Irving Stone. *They Also Ran* (New York: Pyramid Books, 1964), p. 237.
3. Ibid., p. 234.
4. This account of Johnson's senatorial primary race summarizes information found in Robert A. Caro, "Annals of Politics: Lyndon Johnson's 1948 Senate Race: Part 4," *The New Yorker*, February 5, 1990, pp. 47–108.

CHAPTER FOUR

1. Quoted in Paul J. Boller, Jr., *Presidential Wives* (New York: Oxford University Press, 1988), p. 66.
2. Quoted in Brian Farrell, "Bellona and the General: Andrew Jackson and the Affair of Mrs. Eaton," *History Today*, 8 (July 1958): 475.
3. Quoted in Shelley Ross, *Fall from Grace* (New York: Ballantine Books, 1988), p. 60.
4. Sol Barzman, *Madmen and Geniuses: The Vice-Presidents of the United States* (Chicago: Follett, 1974), p. 71.
5. Irving Stone, *They Also Ran* (New York: Pyramid Books, 1964), p. 279.
6. Quoted in Roger Butterfield, *The American Past* (New York: Simon & Schuster, 1947), p. 239.
7. Samuel Hopkins Adams, "The Timely Death of President Harding," *The Aspirin Age, 1919–1941*, ed. Isabel Leighton (New York: Simon & Schuster, 1949), p. 87.

8. Joseph P. Lash, *Eleanor and Franklin* (New York: W. W. Norton, 1971), p. 220.

9. Dennis Hevesi, "Elliott Roosevelt, Mystery Writer and Kin to Presidents Dies at 80," *New York Times*, October 28, 1990, p. 38; Ross, *Fall from Grace*, pp. 173–174.

10. Quoted in Tom Morganthau, Margarey Garrard Warner, Howard Fineman, and Eric Calonius, "The Sudden Fall of Gary Hart," *Newsweek*, May 18, 1987, p. 22.

─────────CHAPTER FIVE─────────

1. Sol Barzman, *Madmen and Geniuses: The Vice-Presidents of the United States* (Chicago: Follett, 1974), p. 119.

2. Quoted in C. Vann Woodward, ed., *Responses of the Presidents to Charges of Misconduct* (New York: Delacorte Press, 1974), p. 156; also quoted in Shelley Ross, *Fall from Grace* (New York: Ballantine Books, 1988), p. 104.

3. Woodward, *Responses*, p. 151.

4. Samuel Hopkins Adams, "The Timely Death of President Harding," in *The Aspirin Age: 1919–1941*, ed. Isabel Leighton (New York: Simon & Schuster, 1949), p. 87.

5. Woodward, *Responses*, p. 266.

6. Quoted in Woodward, *Responses*, p. 271.

7. Thomas A. Bailey, *Presidential Saints and Sinners* (New York: The Free Press, 1981), p. 190.

─────────CHAPTER SIX─────────

1. Quoted in Sol Barzman, *Madmen and Geniuses: The Vice-Presidents of the United States* (Chicago: Follett, 1974), p. 258.

2. C. Vann Woodward, ed., *Responses of the Presidents to Charges of Misconduct* (New York: Delacorte Press, 1974), p. 365.

3. Ibid., pp. 370–371.

4. Ibid., p. 390.

5. Quoted in "The F.B.I. Stings Congress," *Time*, February 18, 1980, p. 19.

6. For further details and a comparison of the House and Senate ethics laws, see "Ethics Codes," *Congress and the Nation* (Washington, D.C.: Congressional Quarterly, 1981), vol. 5, *1977–1980*, pp. 891–915.

7. Shelley Ross, *Fall from Grace* (New York: Ballantine Books, 1988), p. 269.

8. James Traub, *Too Good to Be True: The Outlandish Story of Wedtech* (New York: Doubleday, 1990), p. 181.

9. John Greenwald, "S&L Hot Seat," *Time*, October 1, 1990, p. 34.

10. "Excerpts from Ethics Committee's Session on Five Senators," *New York Times*, November 17, 1990, p. 10.

11. Margaret Carlson, "It's a Family Affair," *Time*, July 23, 1990, p. 24.

————————CHAPTER SEVEN————————

1. Leo Damore, *Senatorial Privilege: The Chappaquiddick Cover-Up* (New York: Dell, 1988), p. 80.

2. Ibid, p. 22.

3. Peter Collier and David Horowitz, *The Kennedys: An American Drama* (New York: Warner Books, 1984), pp. 468–470.

4. Damore, *Senatorial Privilege*, p. 207.

5. Ibid., p. 392.

6. Ibid., p. 413.

7. Carl Bernstein and Bob Woodward, *All the President's Men* (New York: Warner Books, 1975), pp. 139–140, 347.

8. Sol Barzman, *Madmen and Geniuses: The Vice-Presidents of the United States* (Chicago: Follett, 1974), p. 303.

9. Roger Butterfield, *The American Past* (New York: Simon & Schuster, 1947), p. 178.

10. Summarized from Shelley Ross, *Fall from Grace* (New York: Ballantine Books, 1988), pp. 255–257.

11. Ed Magnuson, "The Burden of Billy," *Time*, August 4, 1980, p. 16.

12. Ross, *Fall from Grace*, p. 271.

13. Walter Shapiro, "Biden's Familiar Quotations," *Time*, September 26, 1987, p. 17.

———CHAPTER EIGHT———

1. Richard Nixon, *In the Arena: A Memoir of Victory, Defeat, and Renewal* (New York: Simon & Schuster, 1990), p. 41.

2. "The Complete Transcript of the New Tapes [June 23, 1972]," *The Fall of a President* (New York: Dell Books, 1974), p. 209.

3. "Meeting: The President and Dean, Oval Office, March 13, 1973," *The Presidential Transcripts* (New York: Dell Books, 1974), p. 69.

4. John Stacks and Strobe Talbott, "Paying the Price," *Time*, April 2, 1990, p. 46.

5. For a more detailed description of the penalties and what became of the men convicted in the Watergate scandal, see Barbara Feinberg, *Watergate: Scandal in the White House* (New York: Franklin Watts, 1990), pp. 114–115.

6. Quoted in William S. Cohen and George J. Mitchell, *Men of Zeal: A Candid Story of the Iran-Contra Hearings* (New York: Penguin Books, 1988), p. 272. In 1991, former hostage David P. Jacobsen claimed that William Buckley had not been executed as his captors had reported but had died of illness and neglect.

However, he agreed with the prevailing opinion that Buckley had probably been tortured prior to his death. "Ex-Hostage Casts Doubt on Report of Execution," *New York Times*, December 9, 1991, p. 14.

7. "The President's Address to the Nation," *The Tower Commission Report* (New York: Bantam and Times Books, 1987), p. 503.

8. "The President's News Conference," *The Tower Commission Report*, p. 507.

9. "Transcript of Reagan's Speech: 'I Take Full Responsibility for My Actions,'" *New York Times*, March 5, 1987, p. 18.

10. Quoted in Cohen and Mitchell, *Men of Zeal*, p. 136.

11. Quoted in Cohen and Mitchell, *Men of Zeal*, p. 199.

12. For Oliver North's 1991 statement of his belief that both the president and vice president knew everything that was going on see, Oliver North, "Reagan Knew Everything," *Time*, October 28, 1991, pp. 36–66; David Johnston, "North Says Bush Knew Shape of His Efforts to Aid Contras," *New York Times*, October 23, 1991, p. 16.

13. For a fuller account of the trials and penalties, see Don Lawson, *America Held Hostage: The Iran Hostage Crisis and the Iran-Contra Affair* (New York: Franklin Watts, 1991), chaps. 7, 8, and Epilogue.

------CHAPTER NINE------

1. Thomas A. Bailey, *Presidential Saints and Sinners* (New York: The Free Press, 1981), p. 186.

2. Arthur Schlesinger, Jr., *The Cycles of American History* (Boston: Houghton Mifflin, 1986), pp. 23–48.

GLOSSARY

Back-channel. Unofficial, informal, behind-the-scenes communications between officials of different, often hostile, governments.

Bill. A proposed law.

Bootleggers. Individuals who illegally sold alcoholic beverages to the public in violation of Prohibition laws.

Blind trusts. Financial holdings managed by business professionals who do not consult the owners of the holdings about the financial decisions they make.

Bribery. Taking money in exchange for political favors.

Cabinet. A group of officials chosen by the president to be in charge of government departments and advise him.

Central Intelligence Agency (CIA). An organization that collects secret information on foreign nations and their governments.

Censure. A formal punishment for misbehavior voted on by the House or the Senate requiring disgraced lawmakers to stand before their assembled colleagues and listen as an account of their misdeeds is read aloud.

Certifying boards. Officials who tabulate and confirm the results of elections.

Checks and balances. The constitutional doctrine that each of the three branches of the federal government shares certain responsibilities for making, carrying out, or interpreting laws, and each may properly examine and question the operations of the others.

Conflict of interest. A situation in which officeholders' private and personal concerns unduly influence their official decisions and cause them to neglect the public interest.

Congressional caucus. In the early days of the American republic, a group of lawmakers who belonged to the same political party and met to nominate a presidential candidate.

Constituents. The people lawmakers represent.

Democrat. The more liberal of the two major political parties, Democrats tend to believe in the active involvement of government and less defense spending.

Deposition. A sworn statement given to a court or legislative committee.

Deregulating. Cutting industries loose from government restrictions and limitations on the way they can do business.

Dirty tricks. Underhanded schemes to embarrass or discredit political opponents during election campaigns.

Dove. A supporter of negotiation rather than military intervention to resolve global conflicts; opponents of the Vietnam War were called doves.

Electoral college. A body set up by the Constitution to formally elect the president and vice president of the United States.

Electoral votes. Ballots, since 1804, cast separately for presidential and vice-presidential candidates. Within each state, the candidate with the highest popular vote receives all of the state's electoral votes. The number of electoral votes at a state's disposal is determined by the number of senators and representatives in the state's congressional delegation, based on the state's population. The candidate receiving a majority of electoral votes is declared the winner.

Entrapment. Inducing people to commit crimes and then arresting them.

Executive privilege. The president's claim to withhold confidential information from another branch of government.

Filibuster. A nonstop speech-making marathon in Congress that holds up government business.

Gerrymander. Drawing the boundaries for election districts to give one party a distinct advantage over the other. The word is a combination of the name of the Massachusetts governor Elbridge Gerry, who devised the system, and the salamander, whose shape a gerrymandered district resembles.

Ghosts. People paid to vote using the identities of deceased citizens whose names were kept on voting registration lists.

Grand jury. A group of individuals empowered to question witnesses and formally charge a person with a crime if there is sufficient evidence to support the charge.

Hawk. A supporter of strong military intervention to resolve global conflicts. Supporters of the Vietnam War were called hawks.

Hush money. Funds used as bribes to keep people from talking to the authorities.

Immunity. Protection from prosecution granted to witnesses for statements they make under oath before government committees and the courts. The statements cannot be used as evidence against them in criminal proceedings.

Impeachment. Removal from office through legislative proceedings. The House of Representatives hears evidence and decides whether to formally accuse an official of wrongdoing. If such charges are made, the Senate holds a trial to determine the official's innocence or guilt.

Incumbent. A person who presently holds a political office.

Indict. To formally charge with a crime.

official refers legislation to committees, appoints members of some committees, rules on questions of procedures, and recognizes members who wish to speak.

Special prosecutors. Independent lawyers who do not hold government positions, brought in to try legal cases with political consequences because they are thought of as objective and uninvolved in administration concerns.

Veto. Formal rejection by the president of a bill, which can be overriden by a two-thirds vote in both the Senate and the House of Representatives.

BIBLIOGRAPHY

—————PRIMARY SOURCES—————

Byrd, Robert C. *The Senate 1789–1989: Addresses on the History of the United States Senate*. Washington, D.C.: U.S. Government Printing Office, 1988.

Cohen, William S., and George J. Mitchell. *Men of Zeal: A Candid Story of the Iran-Contra Hearings*. New York: Penguin Books, 1988.

Congressional Globe. 34th Cong., 1st sess., 1856. Vol. 25, pt. 2, pp. 1289–1291, 1348–1352, pt. 3, pp. 1638–1643, Appendix.

Congressional Globe. 39th Cong., 1st sess., 1866. Vol. 37, pt. 5, pp. 3851–3854.

Congressional Record. 57th Cong., 1st sess., 1902. Vol. 35, pp. 1063, 2015–2043, 2087–2090, 3329, 3819.

Nixon, Richard. *In the Arena: A Memoir of Victory, Defeat, and Renewal*. New York: Simon & Schuster, 1990.

North, Oliver. "Reagan Knew Everything," *Time*, October 28, 1991, pp. 36–66.

The Presidential Transcripts. New York: Dell Books, 1974.

The Staff of the *Washington Post*. *The Fall of a President*. New York: Dell Books, 1974.

* Books especially recommended for students.

The Tower Commission Report. New York: Bantam and Times Books, 1987.

U.S. Congress. Senate. Committee on Rules and Administration. *Senate Election, Expulsion and Censure Cases from 1793 to 1972.* 92d Cong., 1st sess. Washington, D.C.: U.S. Government Printing Office, 1972.

SECONDARY SOURCES: BOOKS

Adams, Samuel Hopkins. "The Timely Death of President Harding." In *The Aspirin Age, 1919–1941*, edited by Isabel Leighton. New York: Simon & Schuster, 1949.

*Bailey, Thomas A. *Presidential Saints and Sinners.* New York: Free Press, 1981.

Barzman, Sol. *Madmen and Geniuses: The Vice-Presidents of the United States.* Chicago: Follett, 1974.

Bernstein, Carl, and Bob Woodward, *All the President's Men.* New York: Warner Books, 1975.

*Blum, John, Edmund S. Morgan, Willie Lee Rose, Arthur M. Schlesinger, Jr., Kenneth M. Stampp, and C. Vann Woodward. *The National Experience*, 5th ed. New York: Harcourt Brace Jovanovich, 1981.

*Boller, Paul J., Jr. *Presidential Wives.* New York: Oxford University Press, 1988.

Butterfield, Roger. *The American Past.* New York: Simon & Schuster, 1947.

Collier, Peter, and David Horowitz. *The Kennedys: An American Drama.* New York: Warner Books, 1984.

Damore, Leo. *Senatorial Privilege: The Chappaquiddick Cover-Up.* New York: Dell, 1988.

*Feinberg, Barbara. *Watergate: Scandal in the White House.* New York: Franklin Watts, 1990.

Garment, Susan. *Scandal: The Crisis of Mistrust in*

American Politics. New York: Times Books/ Random House, 1991.

Hamilton, Charles V. *Adam Clayton Powell, Jr.: The Political Biography of an American Dilemma.* New York: Atheneum, 1991.

*Kronenwetter, Michael. *The Threat from Within.* New York: Franklin Watts, 1986.

Lash, Joseph P. *Eleanor and Franklin.* New York: W. W. Norton, 1971.

*Lawson, Don. *America Held Hostage: The Iran Hostage Crisis and the Iran-Contra Affair.* New York: Franklin Watts, 1991.

Mayer, Martin. *The Greatest-Ever Bank Robbery: The Collapse of the Savings and Loan Industry.* New York: Charles Scribner's Sons, 1990.

Nagel, Paul C. *Descent from Glory: Four Generations of the John Adams Family.* New York: Oxford University Press, 1983.

Pizzo, Stephen, Mary Fricker, and Paul Muolo. *Inside Job: The Looting of America's Savings and Loans.* New York: McGraw-Hill, 1989.

*Ross, Shelley. *Fall from Grace.* New York: Ballantine Books, 1988.

Schlesinger, Arthur, Jr. *The Cycles of American History.* Boston: Houghton Mifflin, 1986.

Simkins, Francis. *Pitchfork Ben Tillman.* Baton Rouge: Louisiana State University Press, 1944.

*Stone, Irving. *They Also Ran.* New York: Pyramid Books, 1964, pp. 43–68, 219–239, 262–281.

Traub, James. *Too Good to Be True: The Outlandish Story of Wedtech.* New York: Doubleday, 1990.

White, Theodore H. *Breach of Faith: The Fall of Richard Nixon.* New York: Atheneum, 1975.

Wilmsen, Steven K. *Silverado: Neil Bush and the Savings & Loan Scandal.* Washington, D.C.: National Press Books, 1991.

Woodward, C. Vann, ed. *Responses of the Presidents to*

Charges of Misconduct. New York: Delacorte Press, 1974.

————SECONDARY SOURCES: PERIODICALS———— AND TELEVISION TRANSCRIPTS

"Abscam Investigation." *Congressional Quarterly's Guide to Congress*, 3rd ed. Washington, D.C.: Congressional Quarterly, 1982, pp. 857–861.

" 'Abscam 3 Scandal Clouded Congress' Image." *Congressional Quarterly Almanac*. Washington, D.C.: Congressional Quarterly, 1981, pp. 513–521.

"Billy Carter Tells His Side of the Story." *U.S. News & World Report*, September 1, 1980, p. 21.

Carlson, Margaret. "It's a Family Affair." *Time*, July 23, 1990, pp. 22–24.

Caro, Robert A. "Annals of Politics: Lyndon Johnson's 1948 Senate Race: Part 4." *The New Yorker*, February 5, 1990, pp. 47–108.

"Ethics Codes." In *Congress and the Nation*, vol. 5, *1977–1980*. Washington, D.C.: Congressional Quarterly, 1981, pp. 891–915.

Farrell, Brian. "Bellona and the General: Andrew Jackson and the Affair of Mrs. Eaton." *History Today*, 8 (July 1958): 474–484.

"Final Reckoning: A House Probe's Meager Results." *Time*, July 24, 1978, p. 14.

Greenwald, John. "S&L Hot Seat." *Time*, October 1, 1990, pp. 34–35.

"High Crimes and Misdemeanors." Transcript of a videotape produced by Sherry Jones for "Frontline," PBS. New York: Journal Graphics, 1990.

Magnuson, Ed. "The Burden of Billy." *Time*, August 4, 1980, pp. 12–21.

"More Surgery for Joe Biden." *Time*, May 16, 1988, p. 47.

Morganthau, Tom, Margarey Garrard Warner, Howard

Fineman, and Eric Calonius. "The Sudden Fall of Gary Hart." *Newsweek*, May 18, 1987, pp. 22–28.

New York Times.

"Nixon." Transcript of a videotape produced by Elizabeth Deane for "The American Experience," PBS. New York: Journal Graphics, 1990.

Shapiro, Walte. "Biden's Familiar Quotations." *Time*, September 26, 1987, p. 17.

———. "The Ghost of Gary Past." *Time*, December 28, 1987, pp. 14–20.

Stacks, John, and Strobe Talbott. "Paying the Price." *Time*, April 2, 1990, p. 46.

"The F.B.I. Stings Congress." *Time*, February 18, 1980, pp. 10–20.

"White House Struggles to Clean Up a Mess." *U.S. News & World Report*, August 11, 1980, pp. 19–22.

INDEX

ABOUT THE AUTHOR

Barbara Silberdick Feinberg is a Watts author (*Watergate: Scandal in the White House, Marx and Marxism*) with a doctorate in political science. She is a full-time writer who lives in New York City.